RUNTIME ERROR

by Bill Barnes
and Paul Southworth

OVERDUE MEDIA
Seattle

Also by Bill Barnes (with Gene Ambaum):

UNSHELVED
BILL BARNES & GENE AMBAUM
What Would Dewey Do ?
an UNSHELVED collection by Bill Barnes and Gene Ambaum
Library Mascot Cage Match
"...Barnes and Ambaum are in a league of their own."
BOOK CLUB
Read Responsibly
an UNSHELVED collection by Bill Barnes & Gene Ambaum
FREQUENTLY ASKED QUESTIONS
READER'S ADVISORY
TEEN ANGST
COOK BOOKS
LARGE PRINT
DON'T YOU HAVE ANYTHING LARGER?
an UNSHELVED collection by Gene Ambaum & Bill Barnes

Reprints *Not Invented Here* comic strips originally published on the *Not Invented Here* website from September 21, 2009 to March 31, 2011.

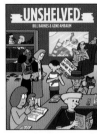

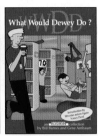

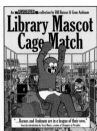

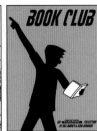

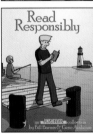

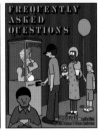

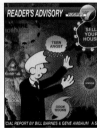

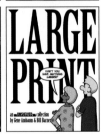

ISBN-13: 978-0-9740353-8-3

First printing: July 2011

Printed in China.

Foreword

Bill and I have been working together for over nine years now. We often tell people it's like we're married, and *Unshelved* is our child. It's an unexpected thing to tell a group of people over drinks, so it usually gets a laugh, but there's a lot of truth in it, too.

So I was a little surprised a couple of years ago when Bill took me out for a nice dinner. It's not that the romance is gone, but our relationship has become more practical (we usually edit scripts over burgers or teriyaki). This time he made reservations. The waiter had a napkin over his forearm. My shoes didn't squeak on the floor.

After we were seated, Bill gave me a box of chocolates and a French graphic novel. I was suspicious. It was nearly my birthday, but he's notoriously late with my presents.

He dropped the bomb. "I want an open relationship."

I knew he'd been thinking about starting a second comic, set in the tech industry. He'd even done some writing and drawing. But now he told me he had a plan. And more than that, he'd already hooked up with an artist, *Ugly Hill*'s Paul Southworth.

I won't lie. It wasn't easy hearing I couldn't be Bill's everything. But it's clear to anyone who's ever asked me for a sketch that I'm no Picasso. Paul could give Bill something I never could: beautiful drawings.

As Bill talked about the new comic, I could see that he needed to do it. I gave him my support. Then he showed me the progression of Paul's fabulous character designs. I couldn't wait to read it. That man really knows how to draw a hamster.

Now you're holding their eighteen month-old child in your hands. Everything has settled down, and I find that I'm not jealous of their relationship. Actually it's brought Bill and me closer together than ever. It's nice to have another baby in the house but, even better, it's great to have Paul as a sister-wife. We can kvetch about working with Bill, talk about our action figure collections, and bake buttery scones together most mornings. And Paul is far, far hairier than I am, so I get to blame him for clogging the shower drain.

So for us, the romance is far from dead. And for you, if you've never read *Not Invented Here*, it's just about to begin.

Gene Ambaum
March 2010, Seattle

"Gene Ambaum" is the pen name of the librarian who writes Unshelved, *a comic strip about a library. It's funnier than you'd think.*

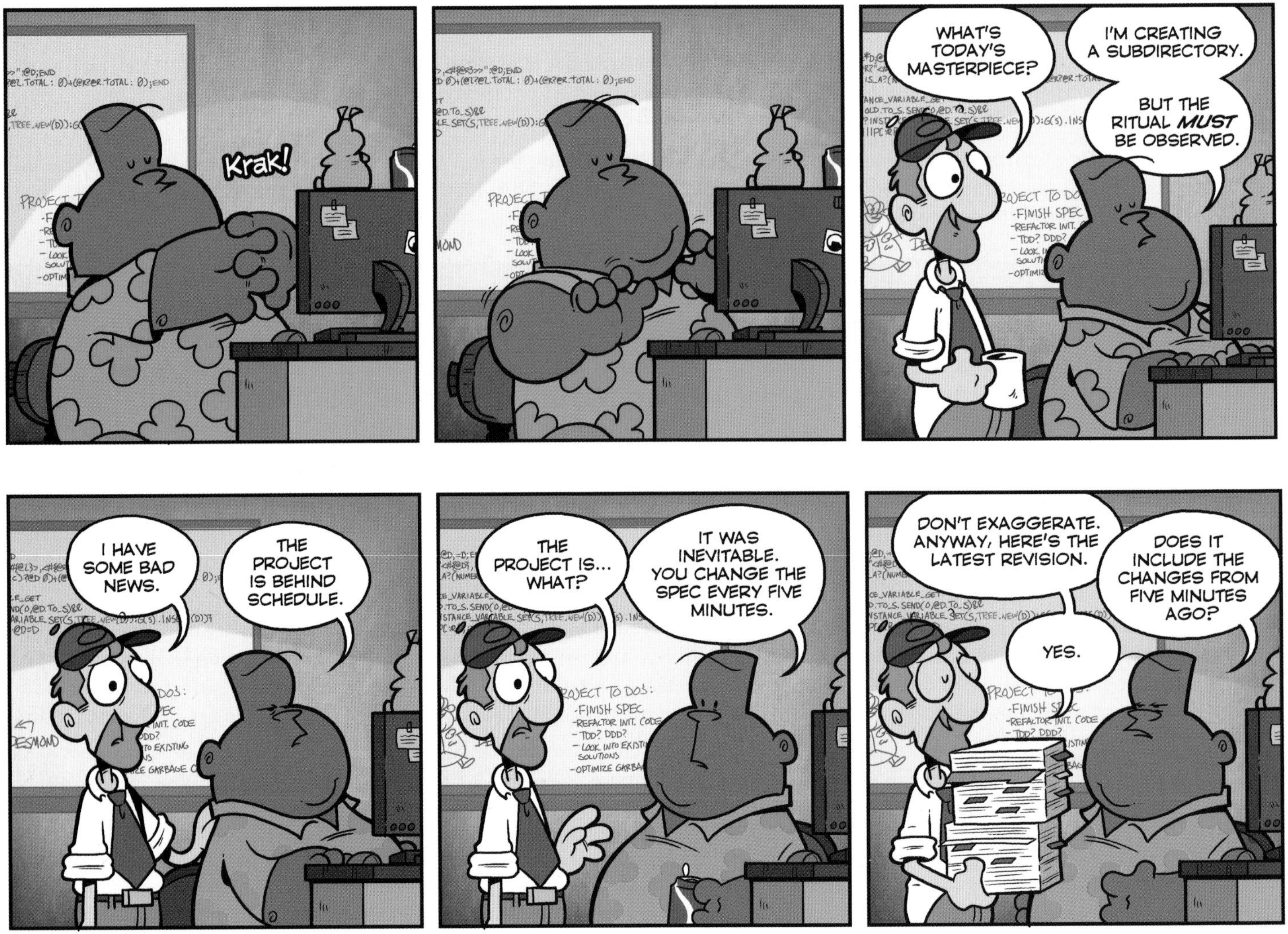
Krak!
WHAT'S TODAY'S MASTERPIECE?
I'M CREATING A SUBDIRECTORY.
BUT THE RITUAL *MUST* BE OBSERVED.
I HAVE SOME BAD NEWS.
THE PROJECT IS BEHIND SCHEDULE.
THE PROJECT IS... WHAT?
IT WAS INEVITABLE. YOU CHANGE THE SPEC EVERY FIVE MINUTES.
DON'T EXAGGERATE. ANYWAY, HERE'S THE LATEST REVISION.
DOES IT INCLUDE THE CHANGES FROM FIVE MINUTES AGO?
YES.

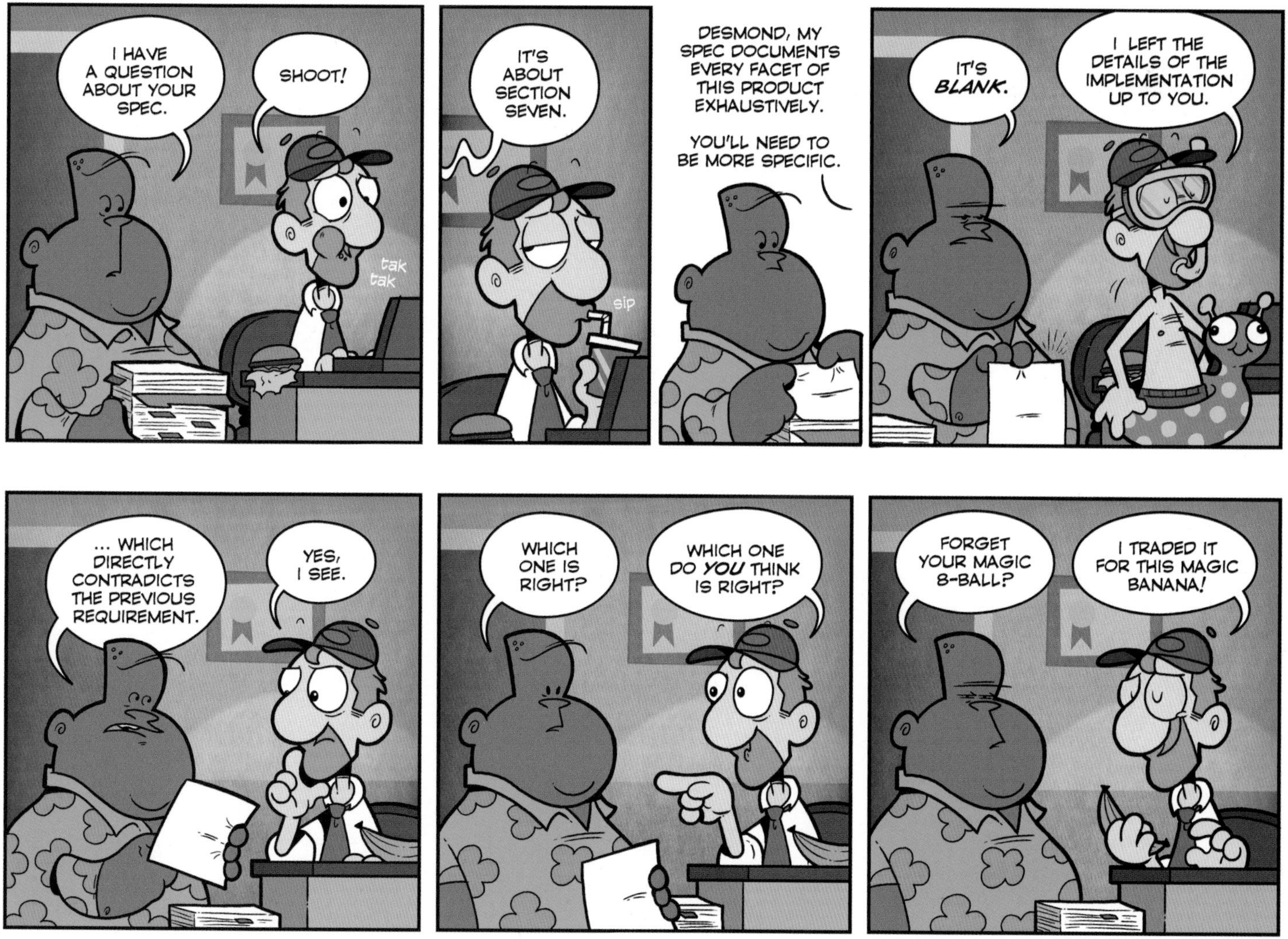
I HAVE A QUESTION ABOUT YOUR SPEC.
SHOOT!
tak tak
IT'S ABOUT SECTION SEVEN.
sip
DESMOND, MY SPEC DOCUMENTS EVERY FACET OF THIS PRODUCT EXHAUSTIVELY.
YOU'LL NEED TO BE MORE SPECIFIC.
IT'S *BLANK.*
I LEFT THE DETAILS OF THE IMPLEMENTATION UP TO YOU.
... WHICH DIRECTLY CONTRADICTS THE PREVIOUS REQUIREMENT.
YES, I SEE.
WHICH ONE IS RIGHT?
WHICH ONE DO *YOU* THINK IS RIGHT?
FORGET YOUR MAGIC 8-BALL?
I TRADED IT FOR THIS MAGIC BANANA!

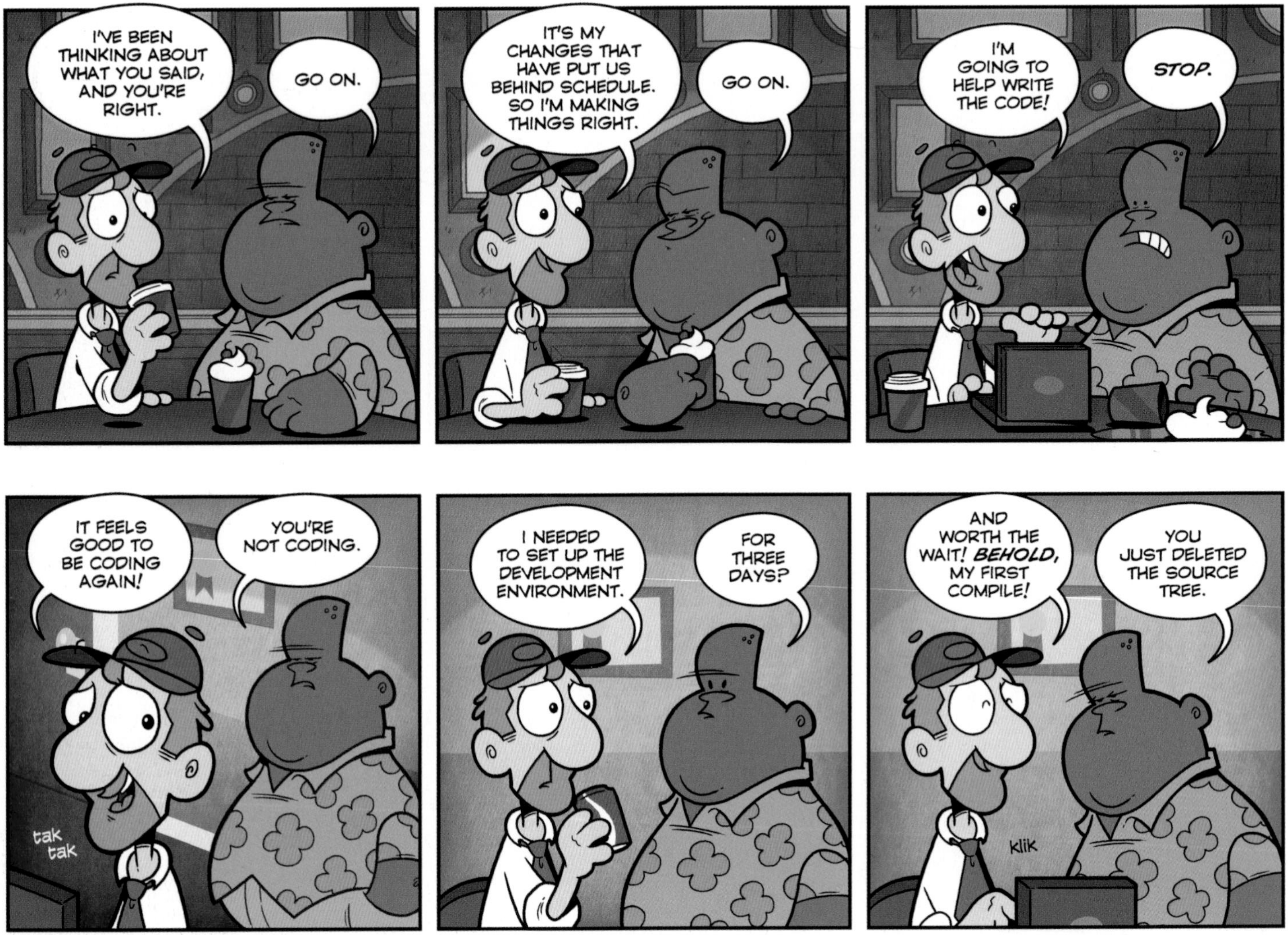
I'VE BEEN THINKING ABOUT WHAT YOU SAID, AND YOU'RE RIGHT.
GO ON.
IT'S MY CHANGES THAT HAVE PUT US BEHIND SCHEDULE. SO I'M MAKING THINGS RIGHT.
GO ON.
I'M GOING TO HELP WRITE THE CODE!
STOP.
IT FEELS GOOD TO BE CODING AGAIN!
YOU'RE NOT CODING.
tak tak
I NEEDED TO SET UP THE DEVELOPMENT ENVIRONMENT.
FOR THREE DAYS?
AND WORTH THE WAIT! BEHOLD, MY FIRST COMPILE!
YOU JUST DELETED THE SOURCE TREE.
klik

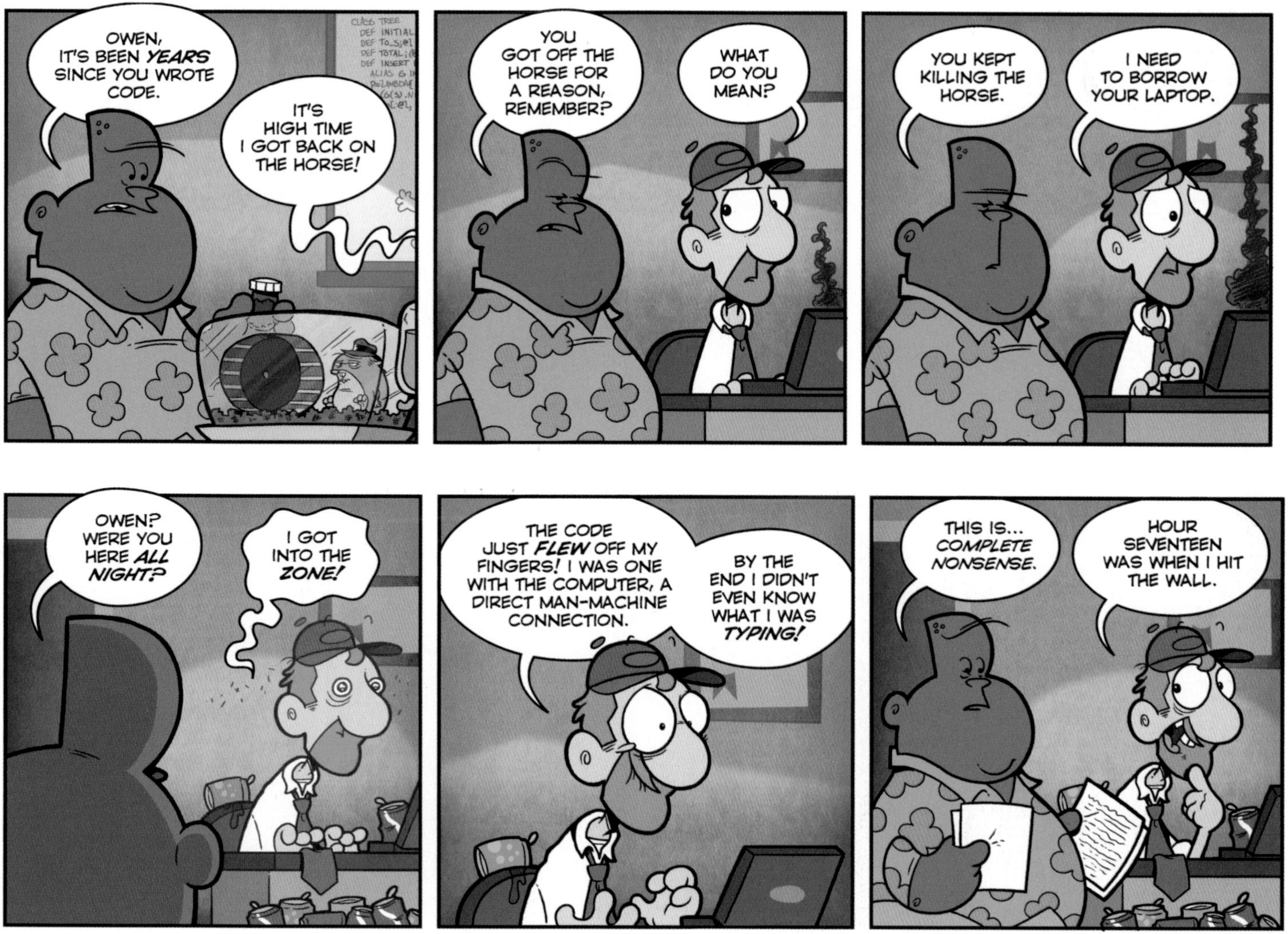
OWEN, IT'S BEEN *YEARS* SINCE YOU WROTE CODE.
IT'S HIGH TIME I GOT BACK ON THE HORSE!
YOU GOT OFF THE HORSE FOR A REASON, REMEMBER?
WHAT DO YOU MEAN?
YOU KEPT KILLING THE HORSE.
I NEED TO BORROW YOUR LAPTOP.
OWEN? WERE YOU HERE *ALL NIGHT?*
I GOT INTO THE *ZONE!*
THE CODE JUST *FLEW* OFF MY FINGERS! I WAS ONE WITH THE COMPUTER, A DIRECT MAN-MACHINE CONNECTION.
BY THE END I DIDN'T EVEN KNOW WHAT I WAS *TYPING!*
THIS IS... *COMPLETE NONSENSE.*
HOUR SEVENTEEN WAS WHEN I HIT THE WALL.

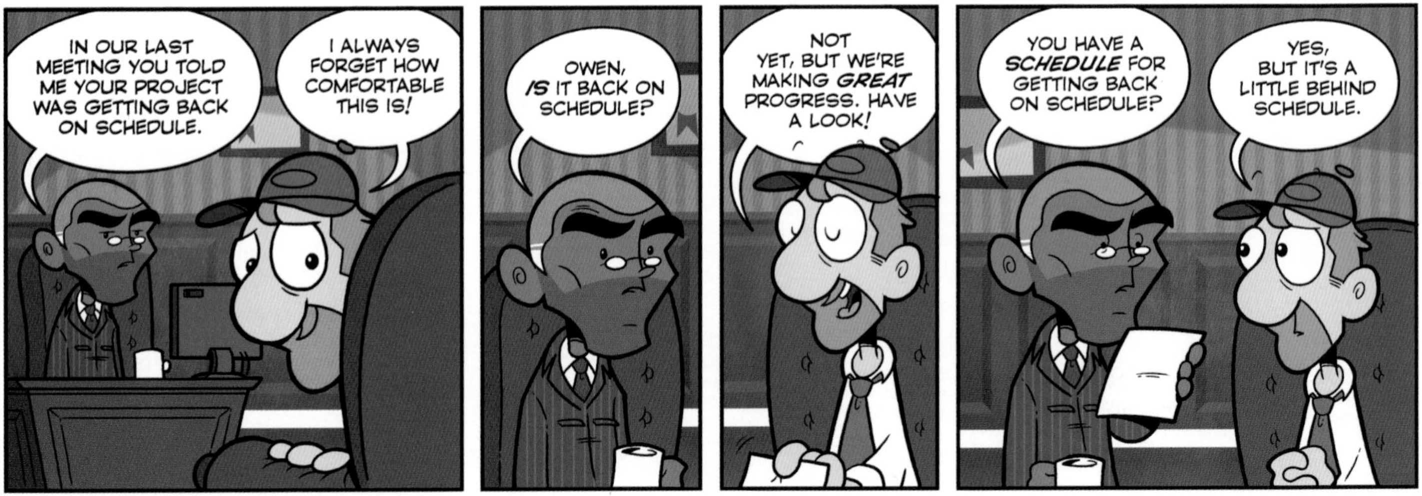
IN OUR LAST MEETING YOU TOLD ME YOUR PROJECT WAS GETTING BACK ON SCHEDULE.
I ALWAYS FORGET HOW COMFORTABLE THIS IS!
OWEN, *IS* IT BACK ON SCHEDULE?
NOT YET, BUT WE'RE MAKING *GREAT* PROGRESS. HAVE A LOOK!
YOU HAVE A *SCHEDULE* FOR GETTING BACK ON SCHEDULE?
YES, BUT IT'S A LITTLE BEHIND SCHEDULE.

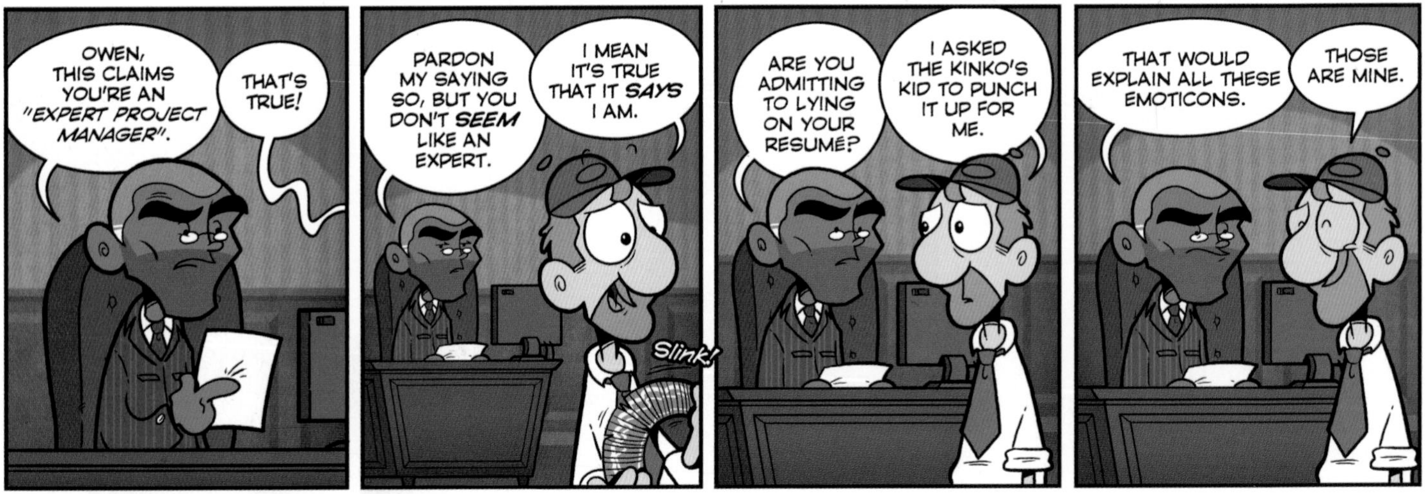
OWEN, THIS CLAIMS YOU'RE AN *"EXPERT PROJECT MANAGER"*.
THAT'S TRUE!
PARDON MY SAYING SO, BUT YOU DON'T *SEEM* LIKE AN EXPERT.
I MEAN IT'S TRUE THAT IT *SAYS* I AM.
Slink!
ARE YOU ADMITTING TO LYING ON YOUR RESUMÉ?
I ASKED THE KINKO'S KID TO PUNCH IT UP FOR ME.
THAT WOULD EXPLAIN ALL THESE EMOTICONS.
THOSE ARE MINE.

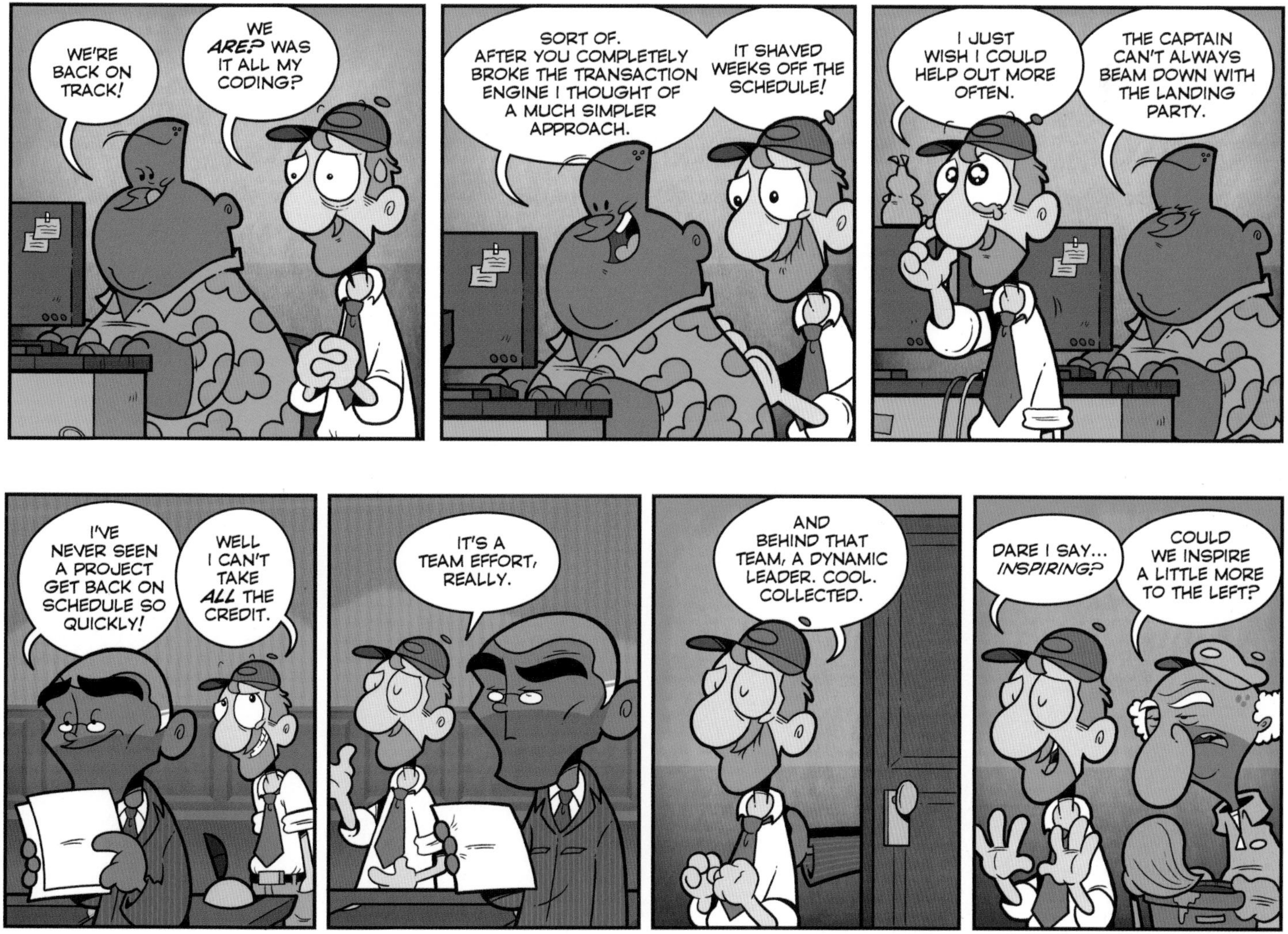
WE'RE BACK ON TRACK!
WE *ARE?* WAS IT ALL MY CODING?
SORT OF. AFTER YOU COMPLETELY BROKE THE TRANSACTION ENGINE I THOUGHT OF A MUCH SIMPLER APPROACH.
IT SHAVED WEEKS OFF THE SCHEDULE!
I JUST WISH I COULD HELP OUT MORE OFTEN.
THE CAPTAIN CAN'T ALWAYS BEAM DOWN WITH THE LANDING PARTY.
I'VE NEVER SEEN A PROJECT GET BACK ON SCHEDULE SO QUICKLY!
WELL I CAN'T TAKE *ALL* THE CREDIT.
IT'S A TEAM EFFORT, REALLY.
AND BEHIND THAT TEAM, A DYNAMIC LEADER. COOL. COLLECTED.
DARE I SAY... *INSPIRING?*
COULD WE INSPIRE A LITTLE MORE TO THE LEFT?

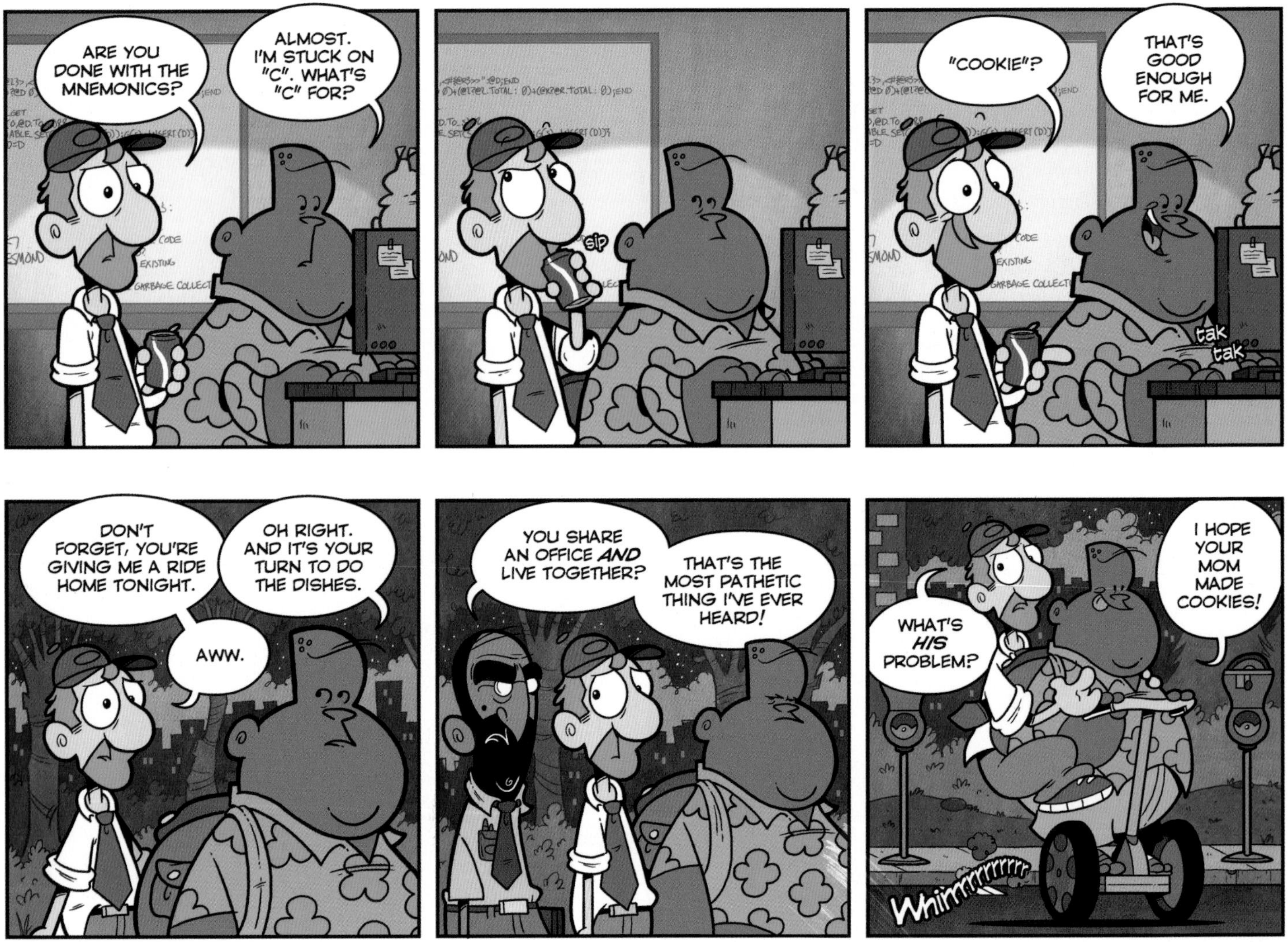
ARE YOU DONE WITH THE MNEMONICS?
ALMOST. I'M STUCK ON "C". WHAT'S "C" FOR?
sip
"COOKIE"?
THAT'S GOOD ENOUGH FOR ME.
tak tak
DON'T FORGET, YOU'RE GIVING ME A RIDE HOME TONIGHT.
OH RIGHT. AND IT'S YOUR TURN TO DO THE DISHES.
AWW.
YOU SHARE AN OFFICE *AND* LIVE TOGETHER?
THAT'S THE MOST PATHETIC THING I'VE EVER HEARD!
WHAT'S *HIS* PROBLEM?
I HOPE YOUR MOM MADE COOKIES!
Whirrrrrrrrrr

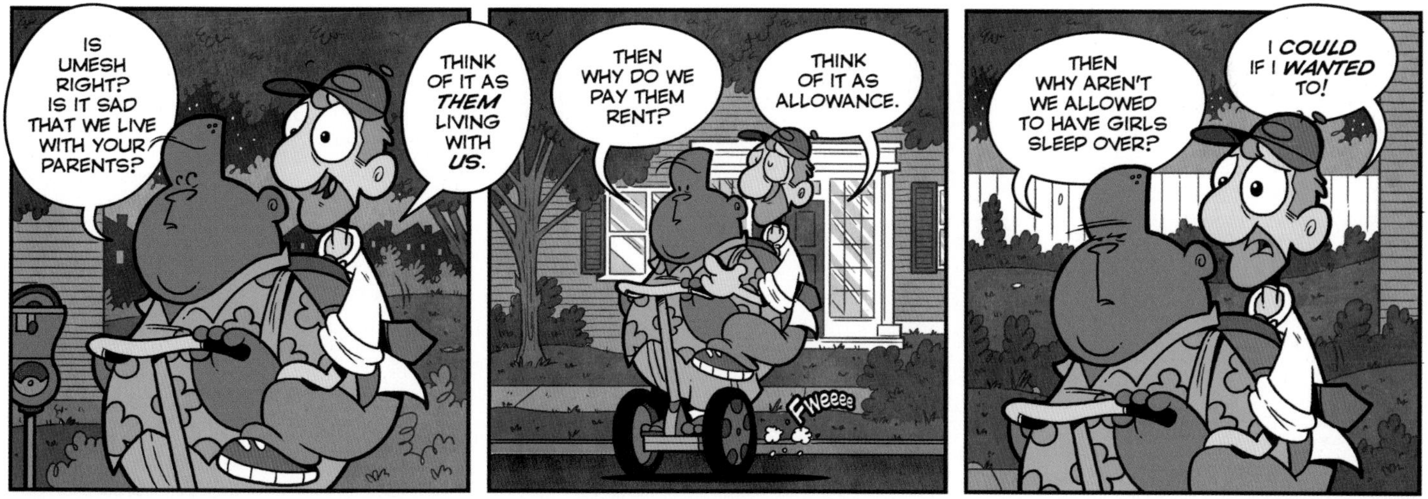
IS UMESH RIGHT? IS IT SAD THAT WE LIVE WITH YOUR PARENTS?
THINK OF IT AS THEM LIVING WITH US.
THEN WHY DO WE PAY THEM RENT?
THINK OF IT AS ALLOWANCE.
FWEEEE
THEN WHY AREN'T WE ALLOWED TO HAVE GIRLS SLEEP OVER?
I COULD IF I WANTED TO!

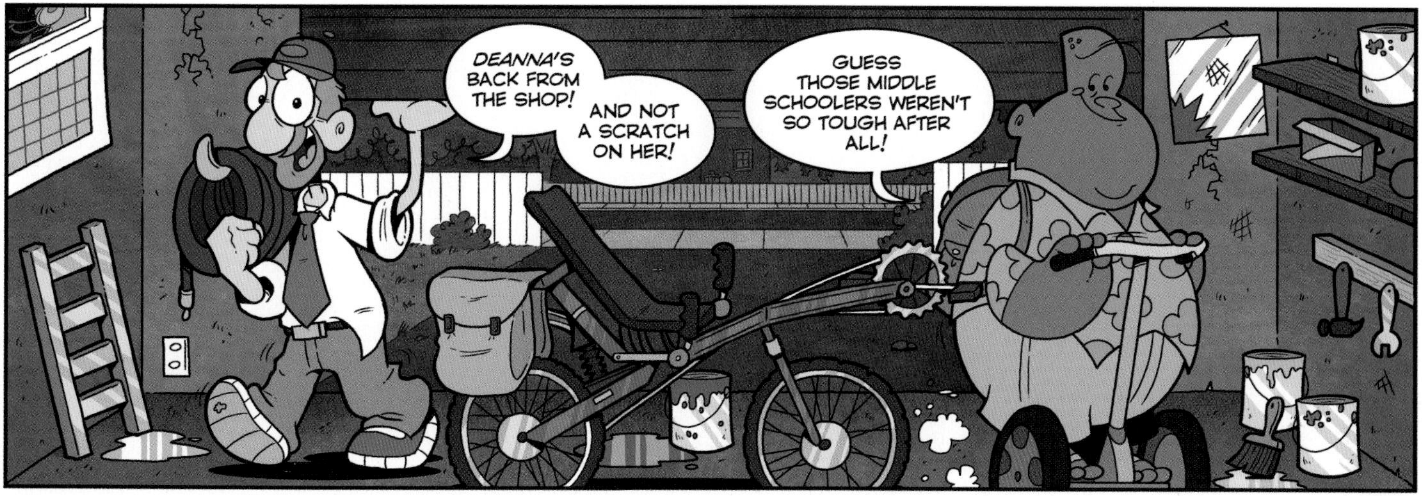
DEANNA'S BACK FROM THE SHOP!
AND NOT A SCRATCH ON HER!
GUESS THOSE MIDDLE SCHOOLERS WEREN'T SO TOUGH AFTER ALL!

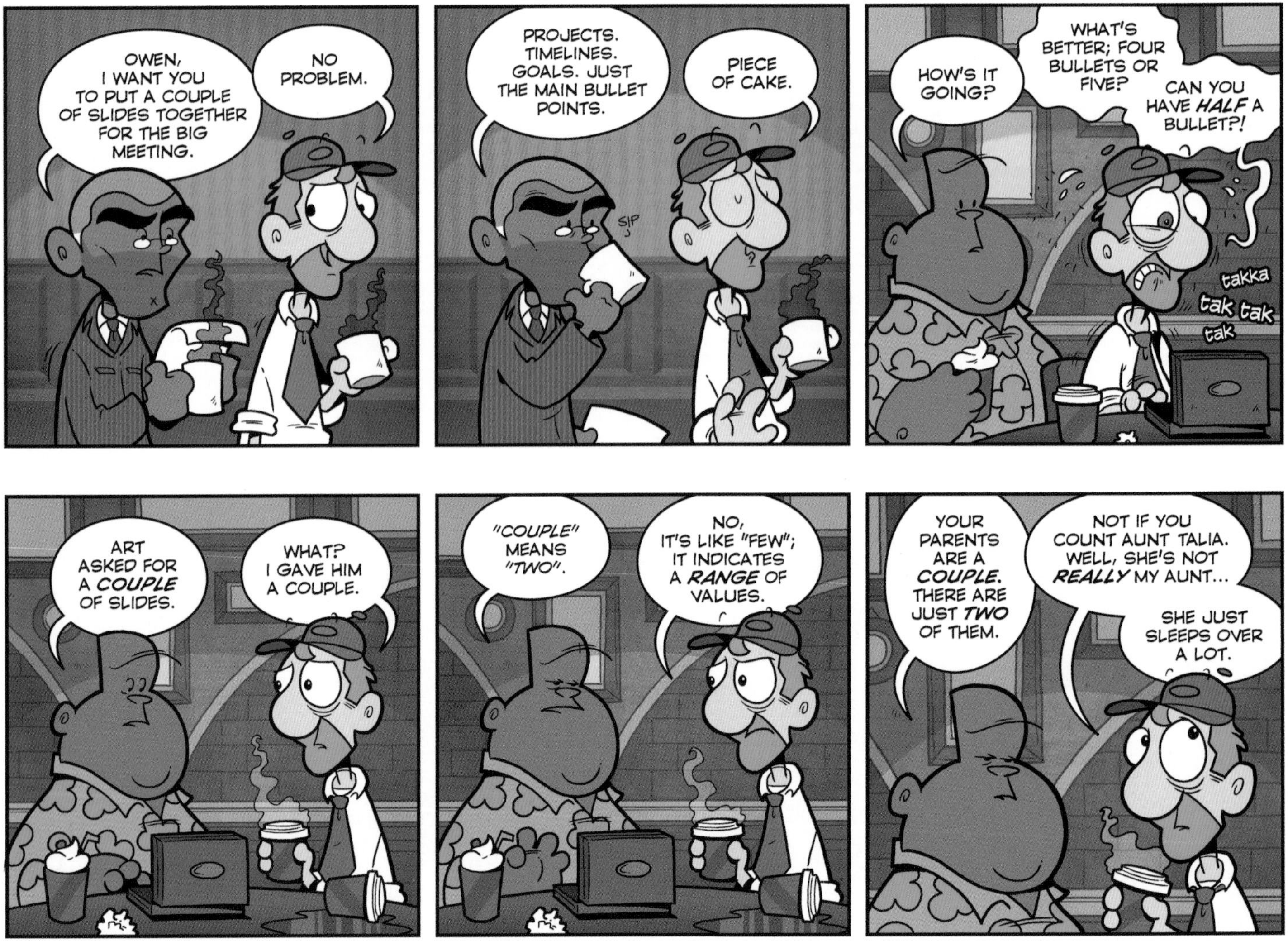
OWEN, I WANT YOU TO PUT A COUPLE OF SLIDES TOGETHER FOR THE BIG MEETING.
NO PROBLEM.
PROJECTS. TIMELINES. GOALS. JUST THE MAIN BULLET POINTS.
SIP
PIECE OF CAKE.
HOW'S IT GOING?
WHAT'S BETTER; FOUR BULLETS OR FIVE?
CAN YOU HAVE *HALF* A BULLET?!
takka
tak tak
tak
ART ASKED FOR A *COUPLE* OF SLIDES.
WHAT? I GAVE HIM A COUPLE.
"COUPLE" MEANS "TWO".
NO, IT'S LIKE "FEW"; IT INDICATES A *RANGE* OF VALUES.
YOUR PARENTS ARE A *COUPLE*. THERE ARE JUST *TWO* OF THEM.
NOT IF YOU COUNT AUNT TALIA. WELL, SHE'S NOT *REALLY* MY AUNT...
SHE JUST SLEEPS OVER A LOT.

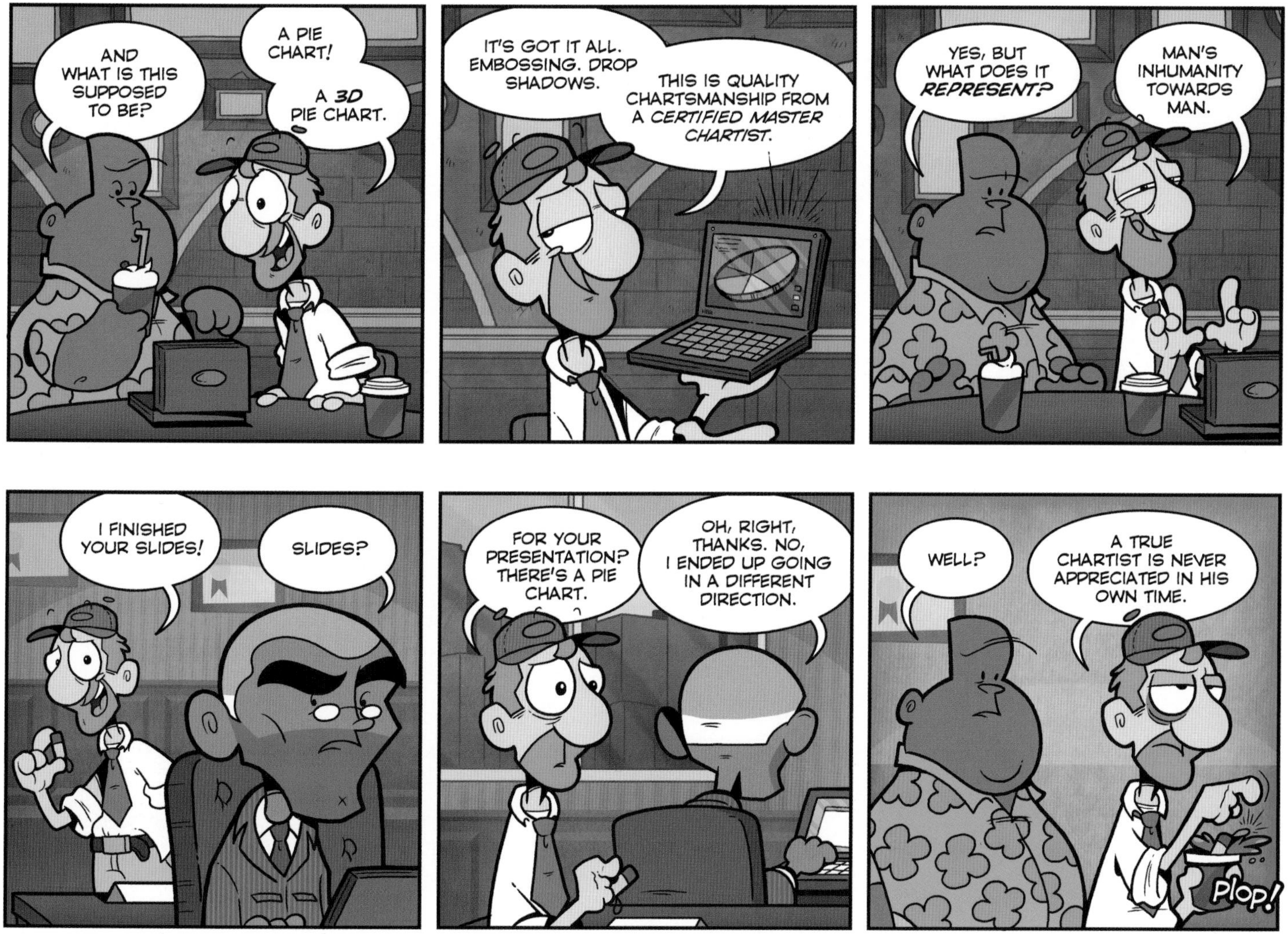
AND WHAT IS THIS SUPPOSED TO BE?
A PIE CHART!
A *3D* PIE CHART.
IT'S GOT IT ALL. EMBOSSING. DROP SHADOWS.
THIS IS QUALITY CHARTSMANSHIP FROM A *CERTIFIED MASTER CHARTIST*.
YES, BUT WHAT DOES IT ***REPRESENT?***
MAN'S INHUMANITY TOWARDS MAN.
I FINISHED YOUR SLIDES!
SLIDES?
FOR YOUR PRESENTATION? THERE'S A PIE CHART.
OH, RIGHT, THANKS. NO, I ENDED UP GOING IN A DIFFERENT DIRECTION.
WELL?
A TRUE CHARTIST IS NEVER APPRECIATED IN HIS OWN TIME.
PLOP!

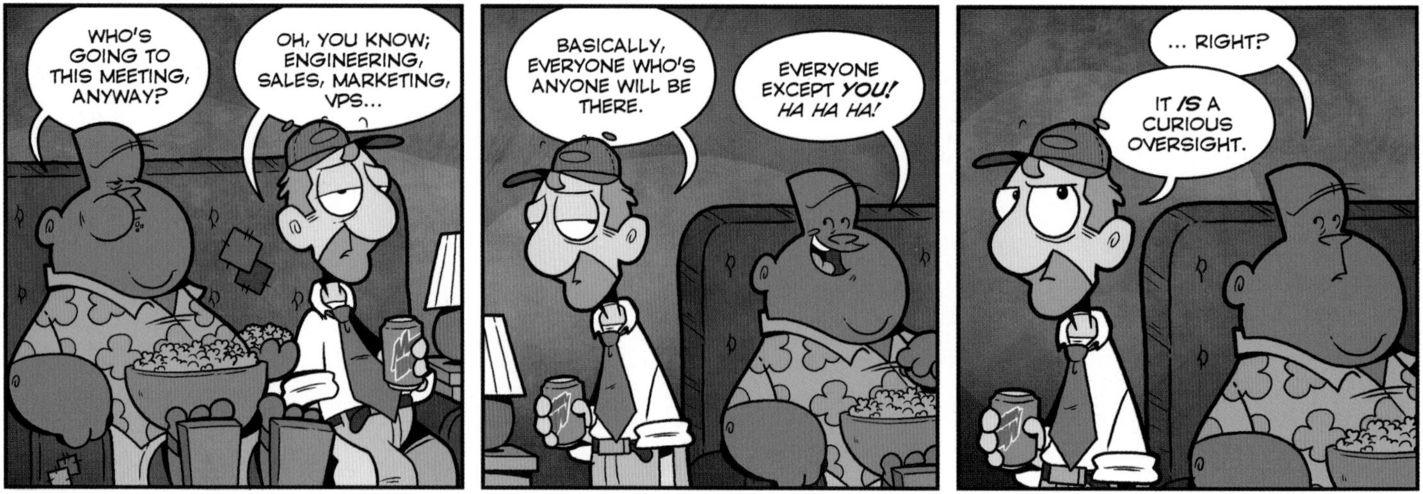
WHO'S GOING TO THIS MEETING, ANYWAY?
OH, YOU KNOW; ENGINEERING, SALES, MARKETING, VPS...
BASICALLY, EVERYONE WHO'S ANYONE WILL BE THERE.
EVERYONE EXCEPT *YOU! HA HA HA!*
IT *IS* A CURIOUS OVERSIGHT.
... RIGHT?

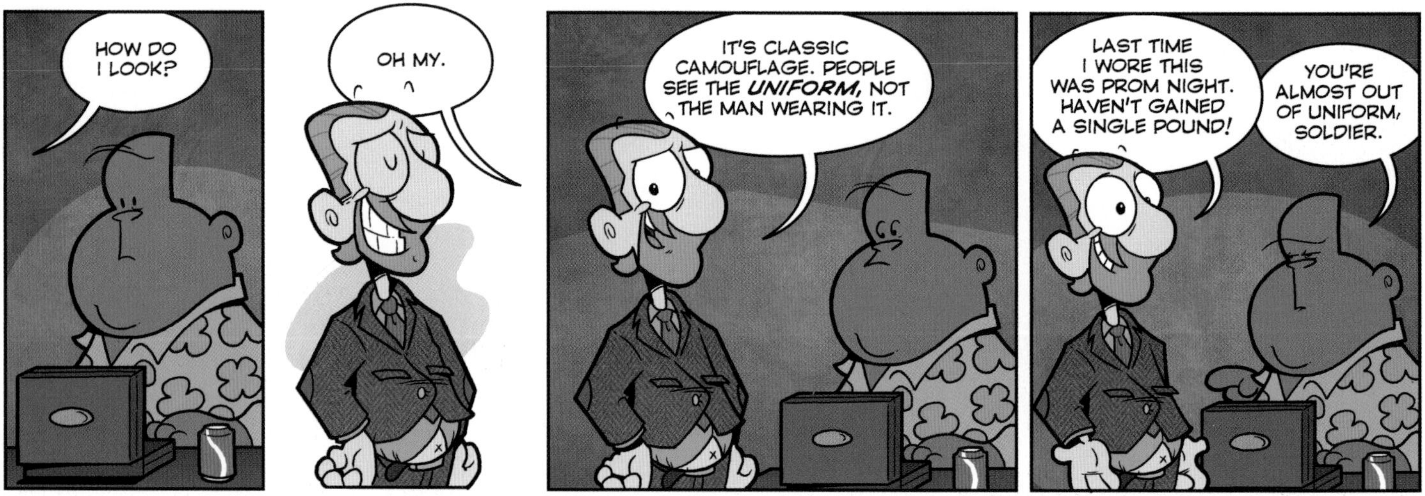
HOW DO I LOOK?
OH MY.
IT'S CLASSIC CAMOUFLAGE. PEOPLE SEE THE *UNIFORM,* NOT THE MAN WEARING IT.
LAST TIME I WORE THIS WAS PROM NIGHT. HAVEN'T GAINED A SINGLE POUND!
YOU'RE ALMOST OUT OF UNIFORM, SOLDIER.

RUNTIME ERROR

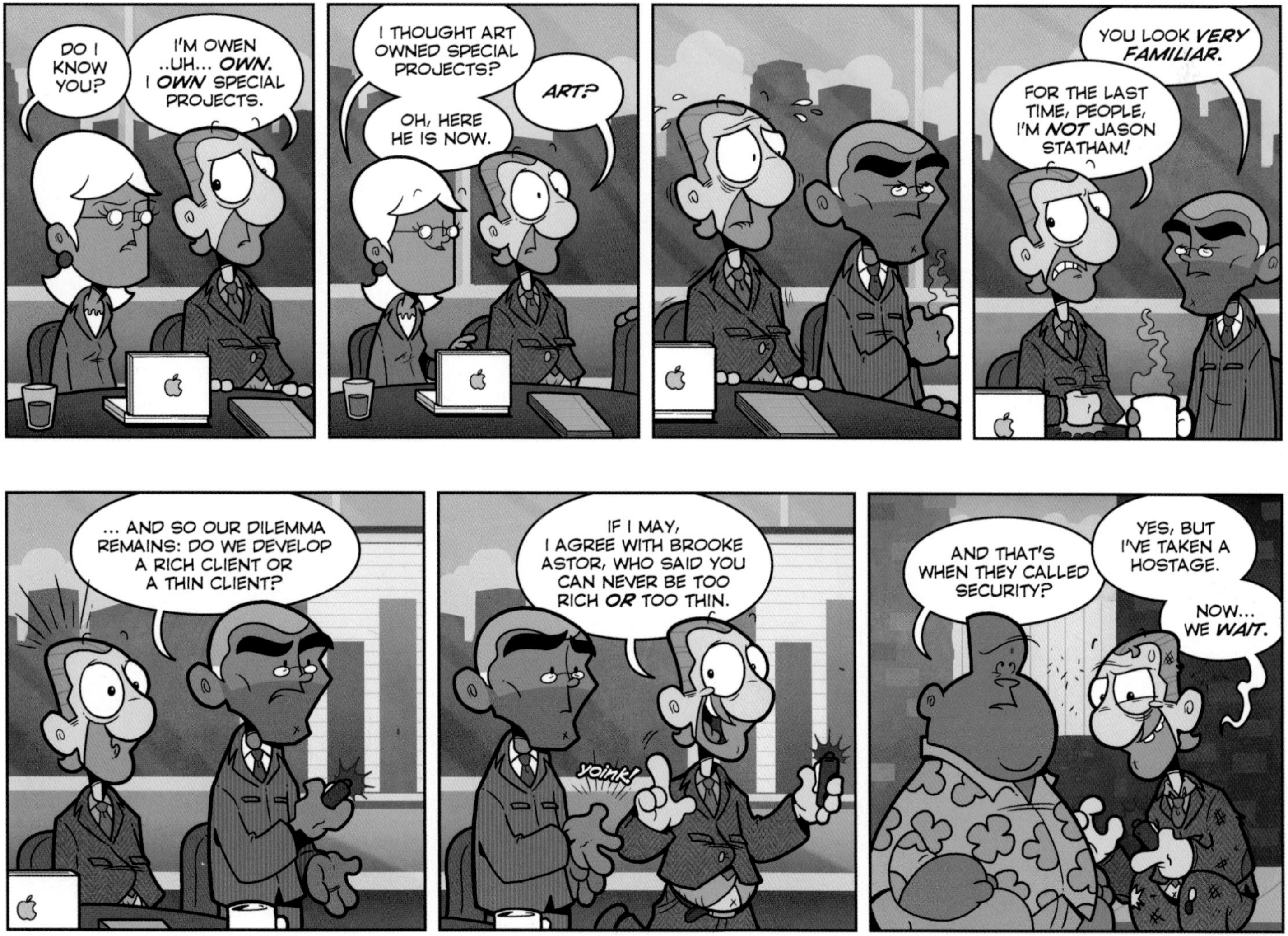
DO I KNOW YOU?
I'M OWEN ..UH... OWN. I OWN SPECIAL PROJECTS.
I THOUGHT ART OWNED SPECIAL PROJECTS?
OH, HERE HE IS NOW.
ART?
YOU LOOK VERY FAMILIAR.
FOR THE LAST TIME, PEOPLE, I'M NOT JASON STATHAM!
... AND SO OUR DILEMMA REMAINS: DO WE DEVELOP A RICH CLIENT OR A THIN CLIENT?
IF I MAY, I AGREE WITH BROOKE ASTOR, WHO SAID YOU CAN NEVER BE TOO RICH OR TOO THIN.
yoink!
AND THAT'S WHEN THEY CALLED SECURITY?
YES, BUT I'VE TAKEN A HOSTAGE.
NOW... WE WAIT.

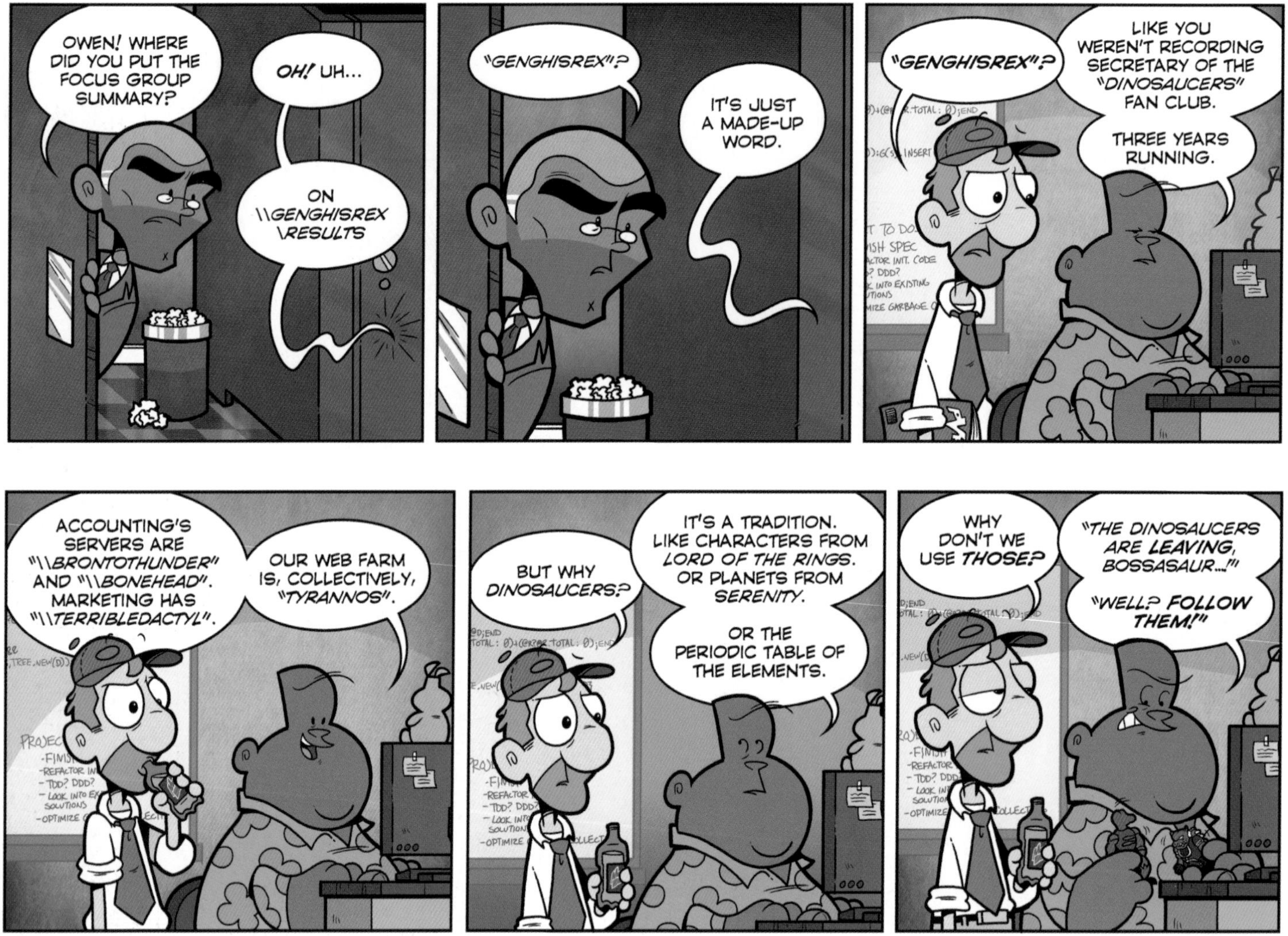
OWEN! WHERE DID YOU PUT THE FOCUS GROUP SUMMARY?
OH! UH...
ON \\GENGHISREX \RESULTS
"GENGHISREX"?
IT'S JUST A MADE-UP WORD.
"GENGHISREX"?
LIKE YOU WEREN'T RECORDING SECRETARY OF THE "DINOSAUCERS" FAN CLUB.
THREE YEARS RUNNING.
ACCOUNTING'S SERVERS ARE "\\BRONTOTHUNDER" AND "\\BONEHEAD". MARKETING HAS "\\TERRIBLEDACTYL".
OUR WEB FARM IS, COLLECTIVELY, "TYRANNOS".
BUT WHY DINOSAUCERS?
IT'S A TRADITION. LIKE CHARACTERS FROM LORD OF THE RINGS. OR PLANETS FROM SERENITY.
OR THE PERIODIC TABLE OF THE ELEMENTS.
WHY DON'T WE USE THOSE?
"THE DINOSAUCERS ARE LEAVING, BOSSASAUR..."
"WELL? FOLLOW THEM!"

RUNTIME ERROR

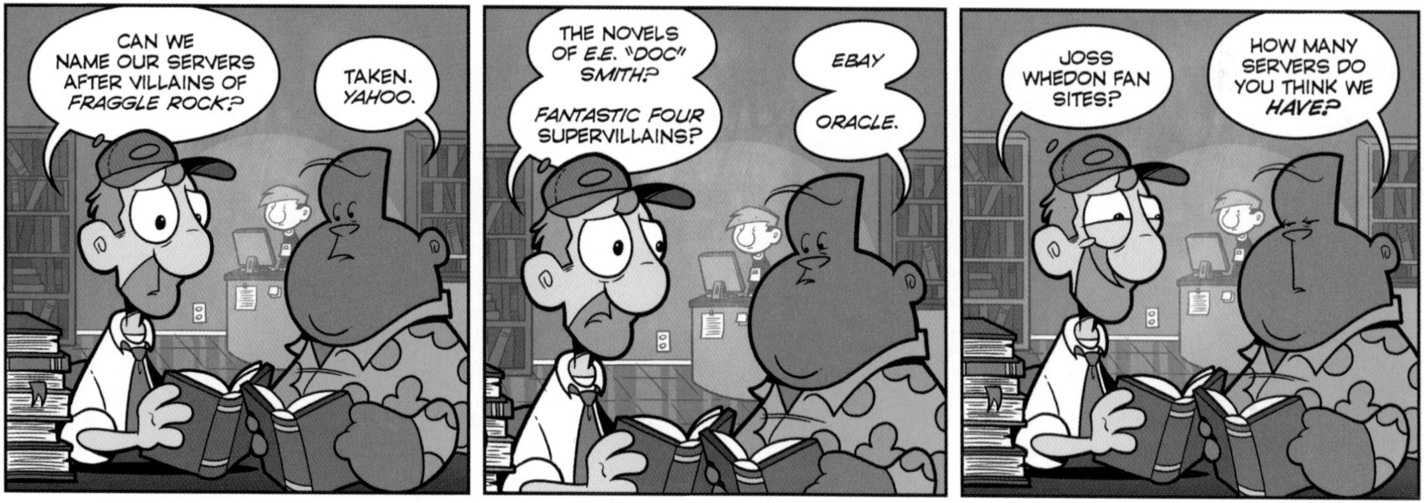
CAN WE NAME OUR SERVERS AFTER VILLAINS OF *FRAGGLE ROCK?*
TAKEN. *YAHOO.*
THE NOVELS OF *E.E. "DOC" SMITH?*
FANTASTIC FOUR SUPERVILLAINS?
EBAY
ORACLE.
JOSS WHEDON FAN SITES?
HOW MANY SERVERS DO YOU THINK WE ***HAVE?***

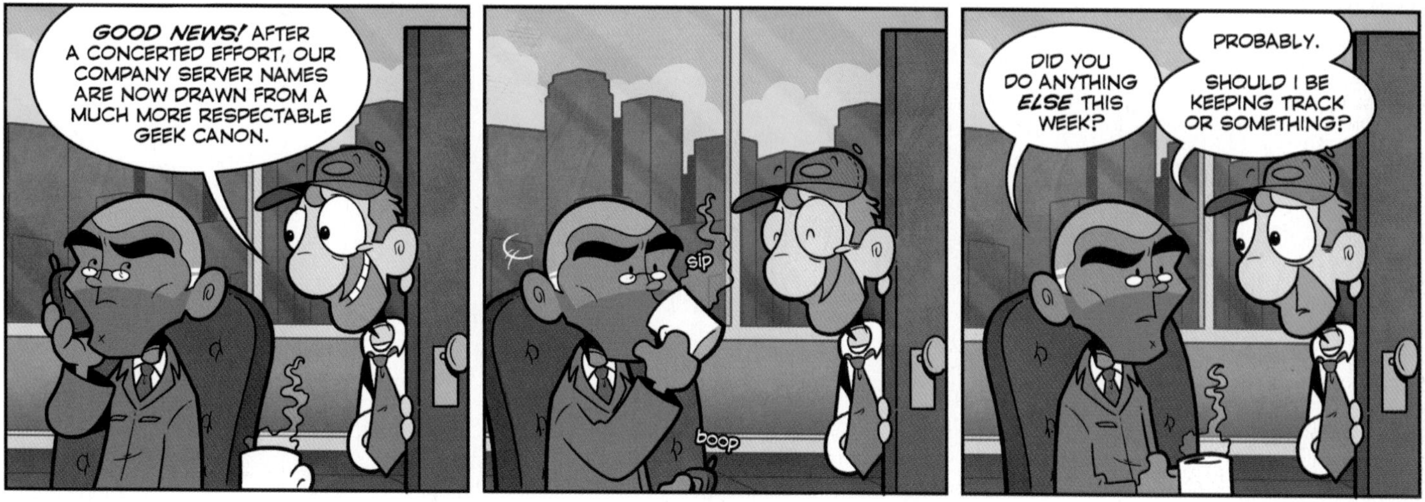
GOOD NEWS! AFTER A CONCERTED EFFORT, OUR COMPANY SERVER NAMES ARE NOW DRAWN FROM A MUCH MORE RESPECTABLE GEEK CANON.
sip
boop
DID YOU DO ANYTHING ***ELSE*** THIS WEEK?
PROBABLY.
SHOULD I BE KEEPING TRACK OR SOMETHING?

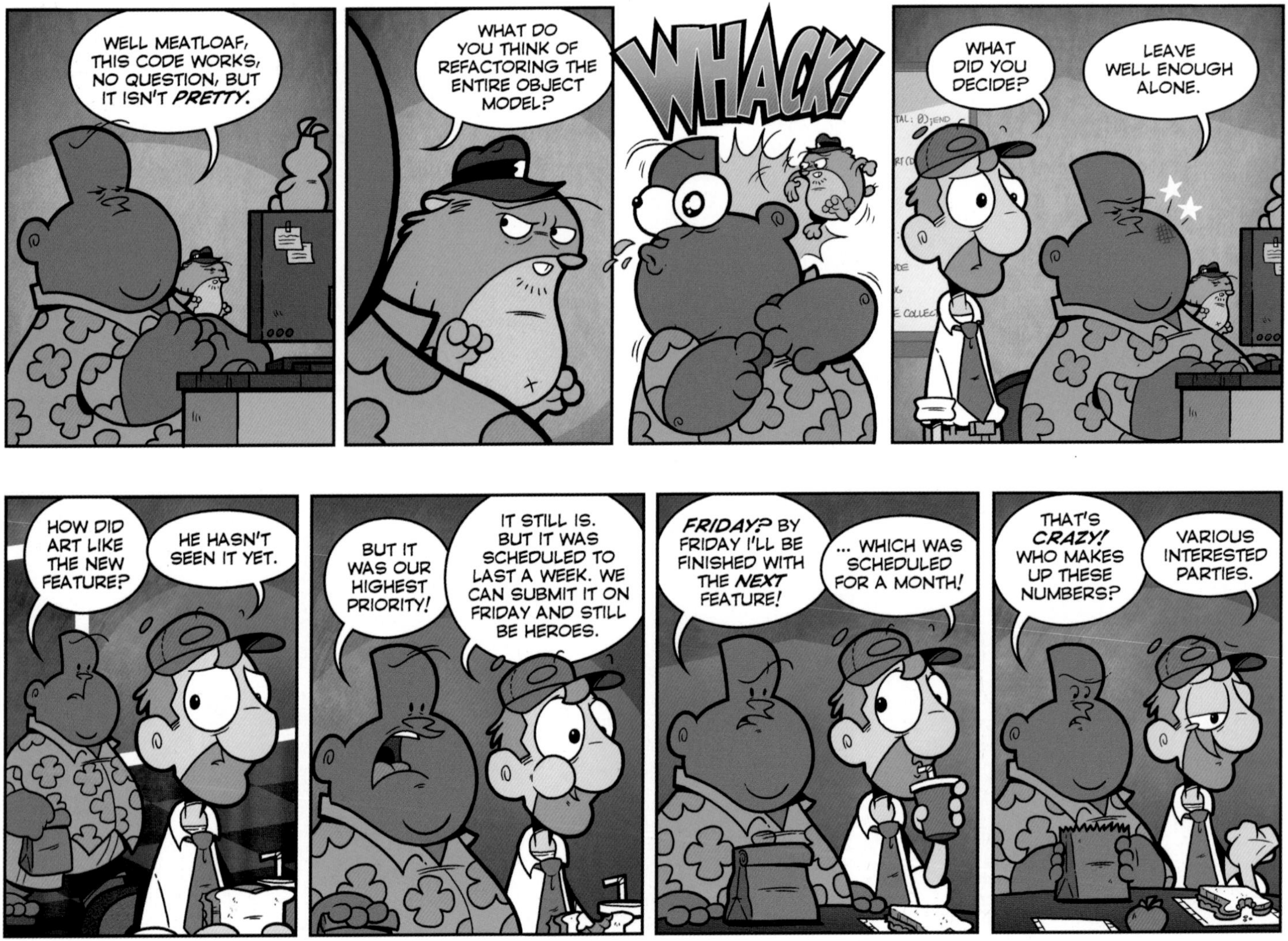
WELL MEATLOAF, THIS CODE WORKS, NO QUESTION, BUT IT ISN'T PRETTY.
WHAT DO YOU THINK OF REFACTORING THE ENTIRE OBJECT MODEL?
WHACK!
WHAT DID YOU DECIDE?
LEAVE WELL ENOUGH ALONE.
HOW DID ART LIKE THE NEW FEATURE?
HE HASN'T SEEN IT YET.
BUT IT WAS OUR HIGHEST PRIORITY!
IT STILL IS. BUT IT WAS SCHEDULED TO LAST A WEEK. WE CAN SUBMIT IT ON FRIDAY AND STILL BE HEROES.
FRIDAY? BY FRIDAY I'LL BE FINISHED WITH THE NEXT FEATURE!
... WHICH WAS SCHEDULED FOR A MONTH!
THAT'S CRAZY! WHO MAKES UP THESE NUMBERS?
VARIOUS INTERESTED PARTIES.

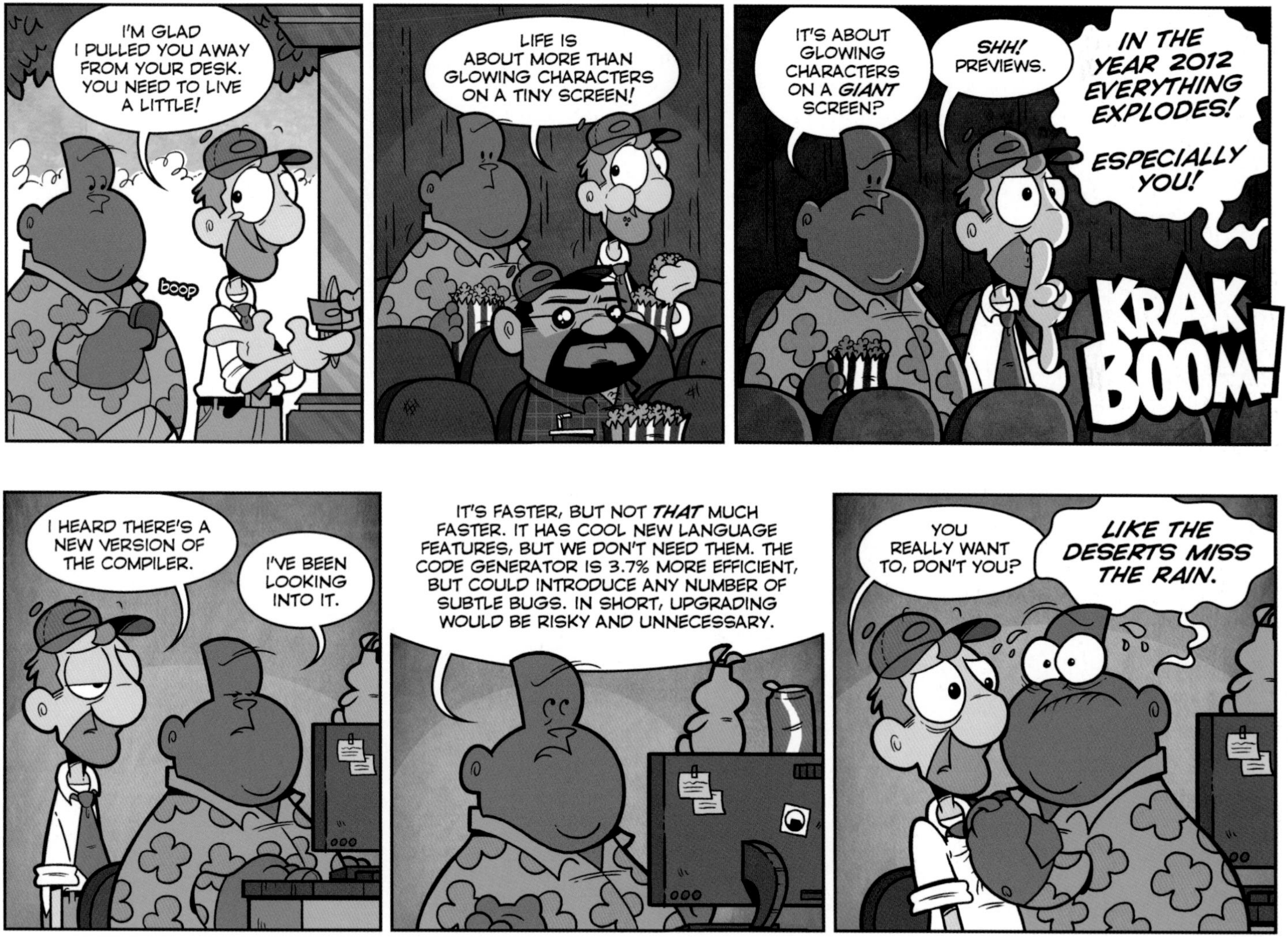
I'M GLAD I PULLED YOU AWAY FROM YOUR DESK. YOU NEED TO LIVE A LITTLE!
boop
LIFE IS ABOUT MORE THAN GLOWING CHARACTERS ON A TINY SCREEN!
IT'S ABOUT GLOWING CHARACTERS ON A *GIANT* SCREEN?
SHH! PREVIEWS.
IN THE YEAR 2012 EVERYTHING EXPLODES!
ESPECIALLY YOU!
KRAK BOOM!
I HEARD THERE'S A NEW VERSION OF THE COMPILER.
I'VE BEEN LOOKING INTO IT.
IT'S FASTER, BUT NOT *THAT* MUCH FASTER. IT HAS COOL NEW LANGUAGE FEATURES, BUT WE DON'T NEED THEM. THE CODE GENERATOR IS 3.7% MORE EFFICIENT, BUT COULD INTRODUCE ANY NUMBER OF SUBTLE BUGS. IN SHORT, UPGRADING WOULD BE RISKY AND UNNECESSARY.
YOU REALLY WANT TO, DON'T YOU?
LIKE THE DESERTS MISS THE RAIN.

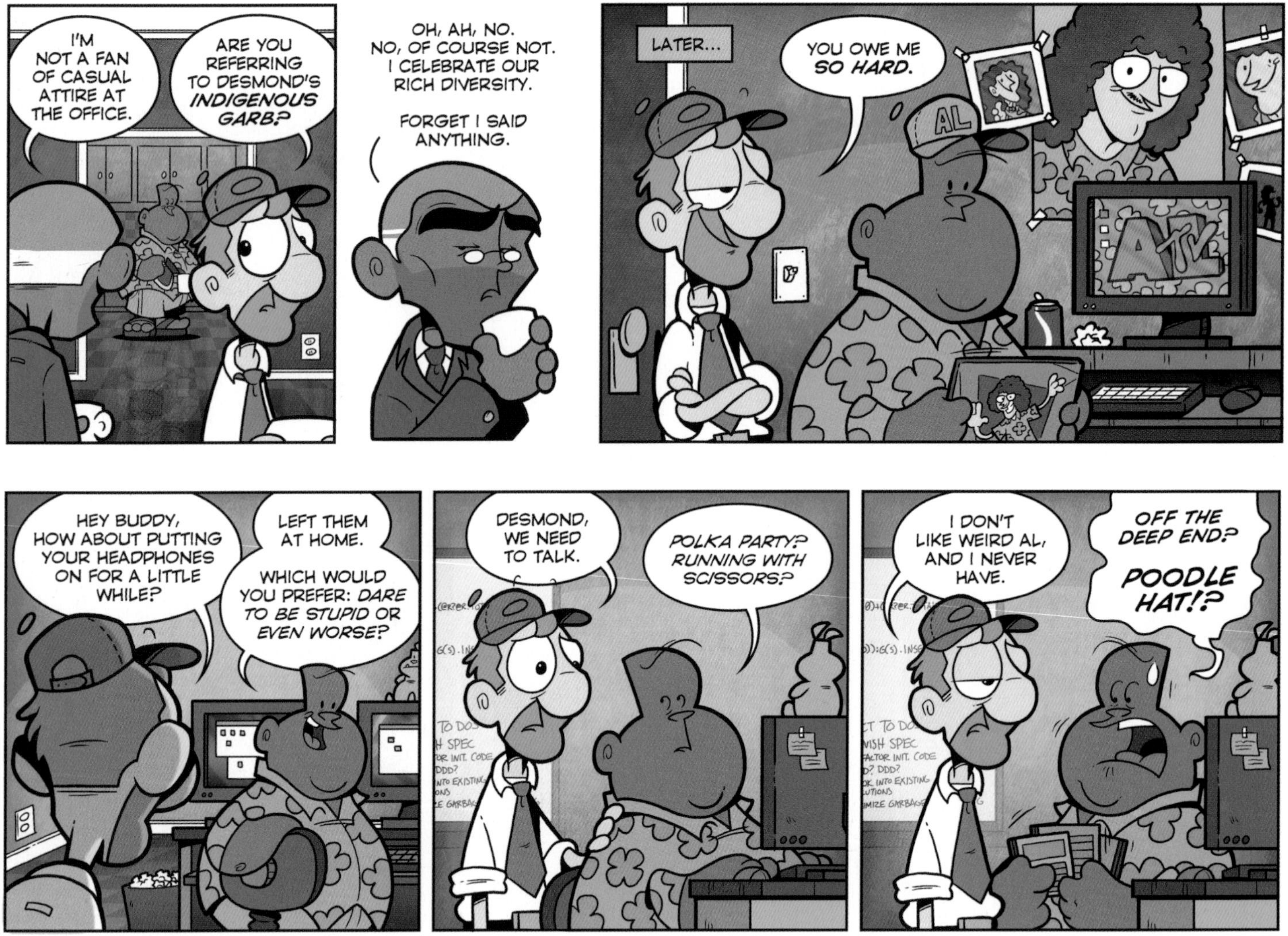
I'M NOT A FAN OF CASUAL ATTIRE AT THE OFFICE.
ARE YOU REFERRING TO DESMOND'S *INDIGENOUS GARB?*
OH, AH, NO. NO, OF COURSE NOT. I CELEBRATE OUR RICH DIVERSITY.
FORGET I SAID ANYTHING.
LATER...
YOU OWE ME *SO HARD.*
AL
ATV
HEY BUDDY, HOW ABOUT PUTTING YOUR HEADPHONES ON FOR A LITTLE WHILE?
LEFT THEM AT HOME.
WHICH WOULD YOU PREFER: *DARE TO BE STUPID* OR *EVEN WORSE?*
DESMOND, WE NEED TO TALK.
POLKA PARTY? RUNNING WITH SCISSORS?
I DON'T LIKE WEIRD AL, AND I NEVER HAVE.
OFF THE DEEP END?
POODLE HAT!?

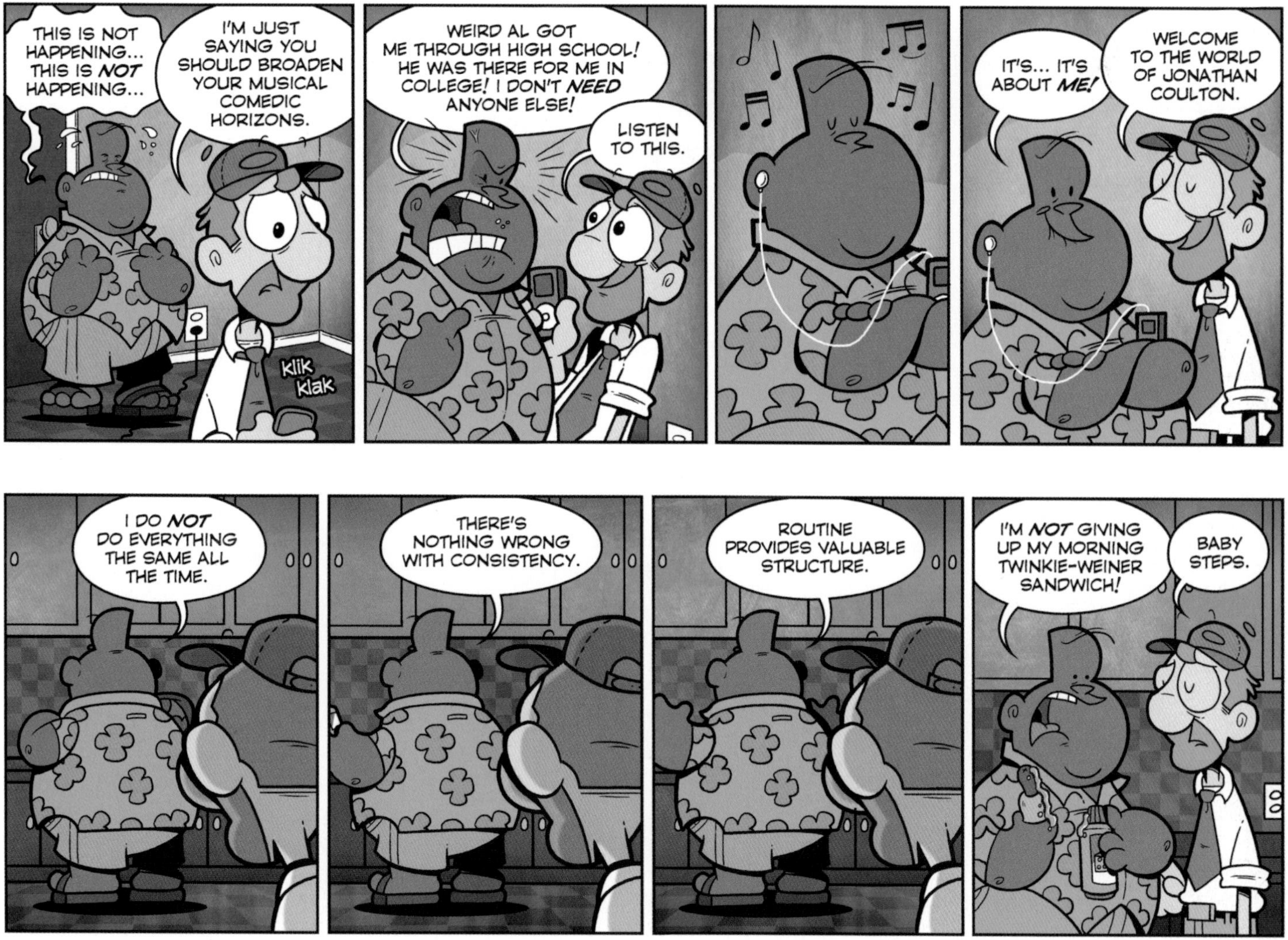
THIS IS NOT HAPPENING... THIS IS NOT HAPPENING...
I'M JUST SAYING YOU SHOULD BROADEN YOUR MUSICAL COMEDIC HORIZONS.
klik klak
WEIRD AL GOT ME THROUGH HIGH SCHOOL! HE WAS THERE FOR ME IN COLLEGE! I DON'T NEED ANYONE ELSE!
LISTEN TO THIS.
IT'S... IT'S ABOUT ME!
WELCOME TO THE WORLD OF JONATHAN COULTON.
I DO NOT DO EVERYTHING THE SAME ALL THE TIME.
THERE'S NOTHING WRONG WITH CONSISTENCY.
ROUTINE PROVIDES VALUABLE STRUCTURE.
I'M NOT GIVING UP MY MORNING TWINKIE-WEINER SANDWICH!
BABY STEPS.

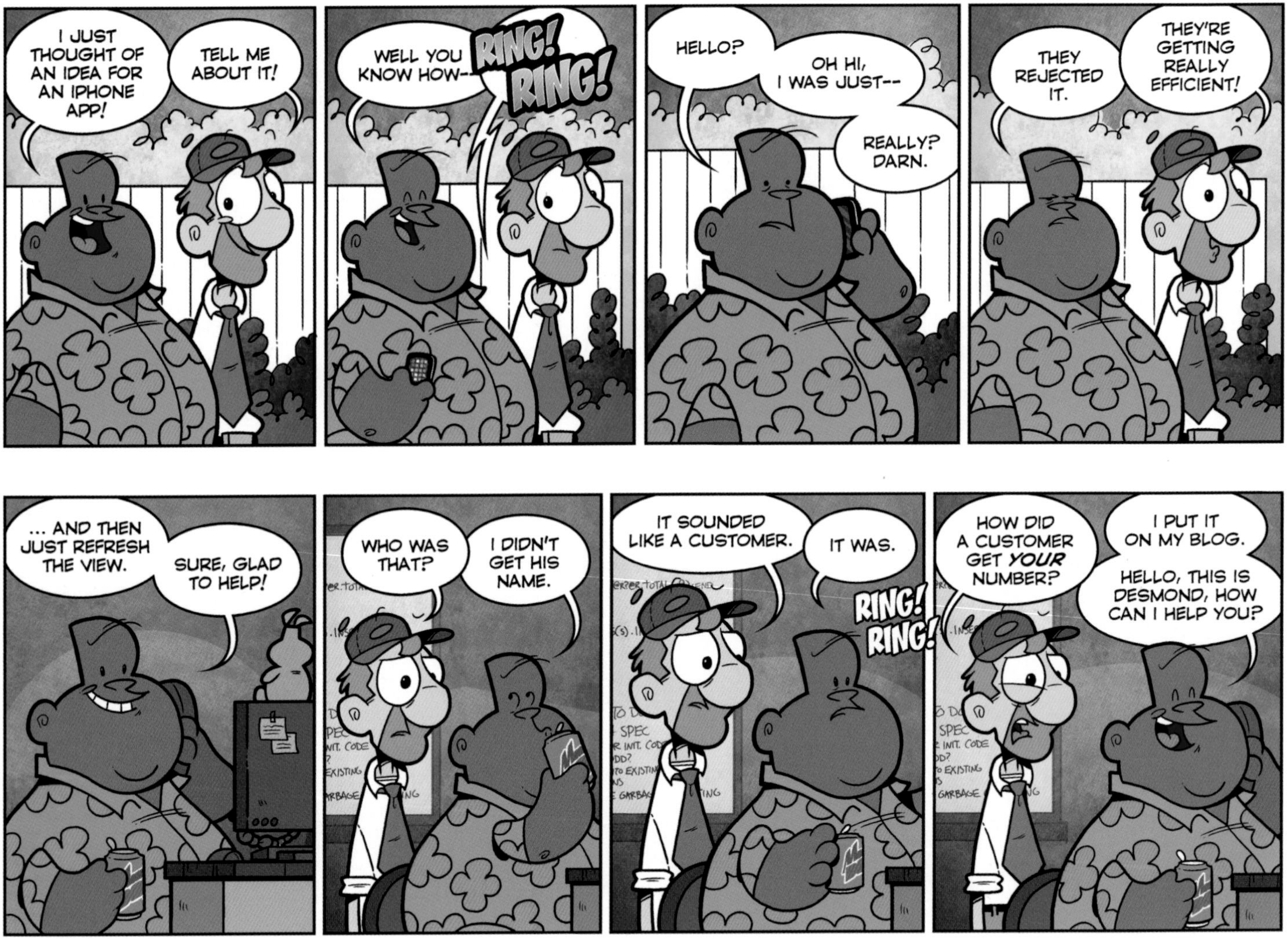
I JUST THOUGHT OF AN IDEA FOR AN IPHONE APP!
TELL ME ABOUT IT!
WELL YOU KNOW HOW--
RING! RING!
HELLO?
OH HI, I WAS JUST--
REALLY? DARN.
THEY REJECTED IT.
THEY'RE GETTING REALLY EFFICIENT!
... AND THEN JUST REFRESH THE VIEW.
SURE, GLAD TO HELP!
WHO WAS THAT?
I DIDN'T GET HIS NAME.
IT SOUNDED LIKE A CUSTOMER.
IT WAS.
RING! RING!
HOW DID A CUSTOMER GET *YOUR* NUMBER?
I PUT IT ON MY BLOG.
HELLO, THIS IS DESMOND, HOW CAN I HELP YOU?

RUNTIME ERROR

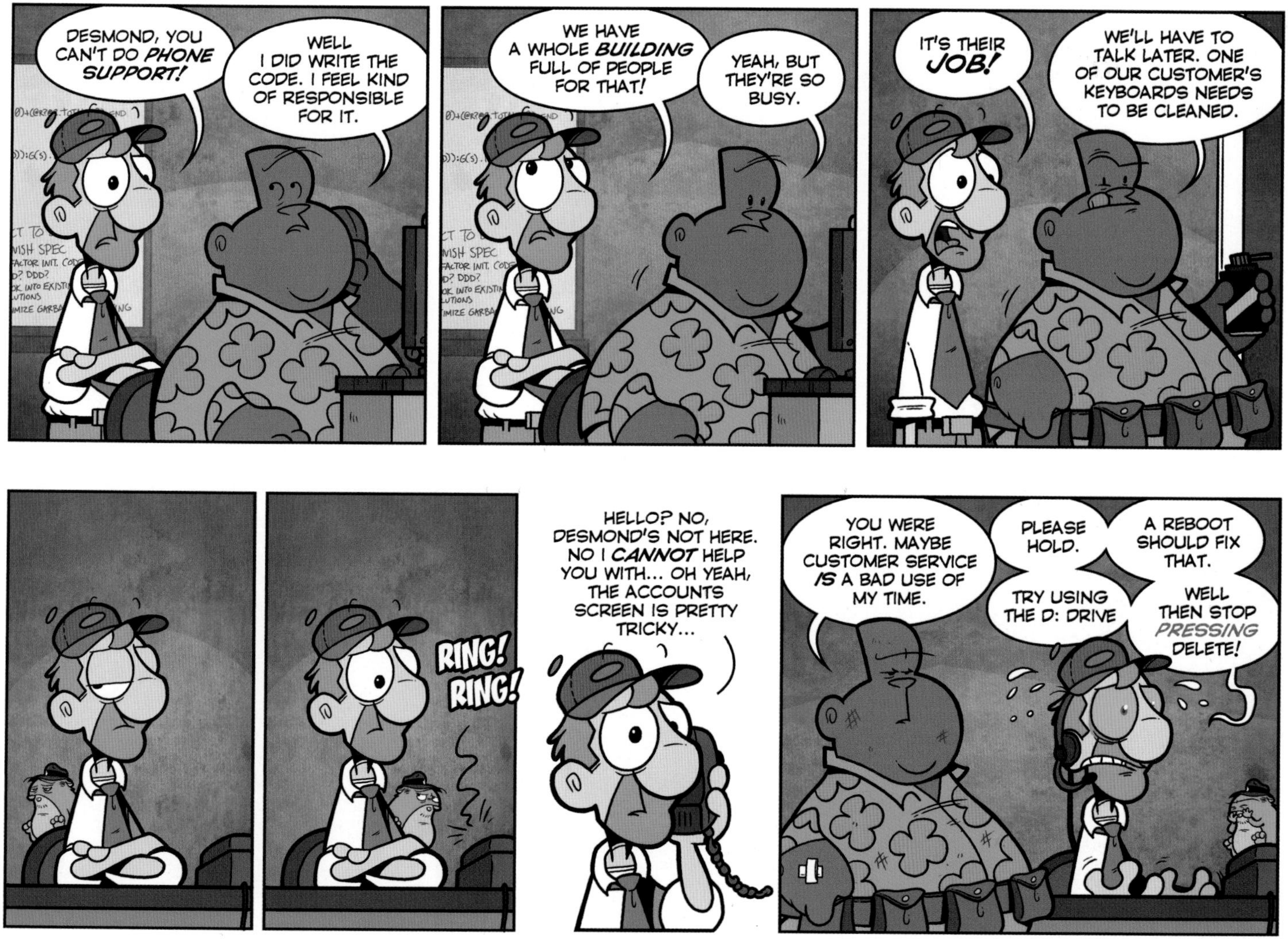

DESMOND, YOU CAN'T DO *PHONE SUPPORT!*
WELL I DID WRITE THE CODE. I FEEL KIND OF RESPONSIBLE FOR IT.
WE HAVE A WHOLE *BUILDING* FULL OF PEOPLE FOR THAT!
YEAH, BUT THEY'RE SO BUSY.
IT'S THEIR *JOB!*
WE'LL HAVE TO TALK LATER. ONE OF OUR CUSTOMER'S KEYBOARDS NEEDS TO BE CLEANED.
RING! RING!
HELLO? NO, DESMOND'S NOT HERE. NO I *CANNOT* HELP YOU WITH... OH YEAH, THE ACCOUNTS SCREEN IS PRETTY TRICKY...
YOU WERE RIGHT. MAYBE CUSTOMER SERVICE *IS* A BAD USE OF MY TIME.
PLEASE HOLD.
A REBOOT SHOULD FIX THAT.
TRY USING THE D: DRIVE
WELL THEN STOP *PRESSING* DELETE!

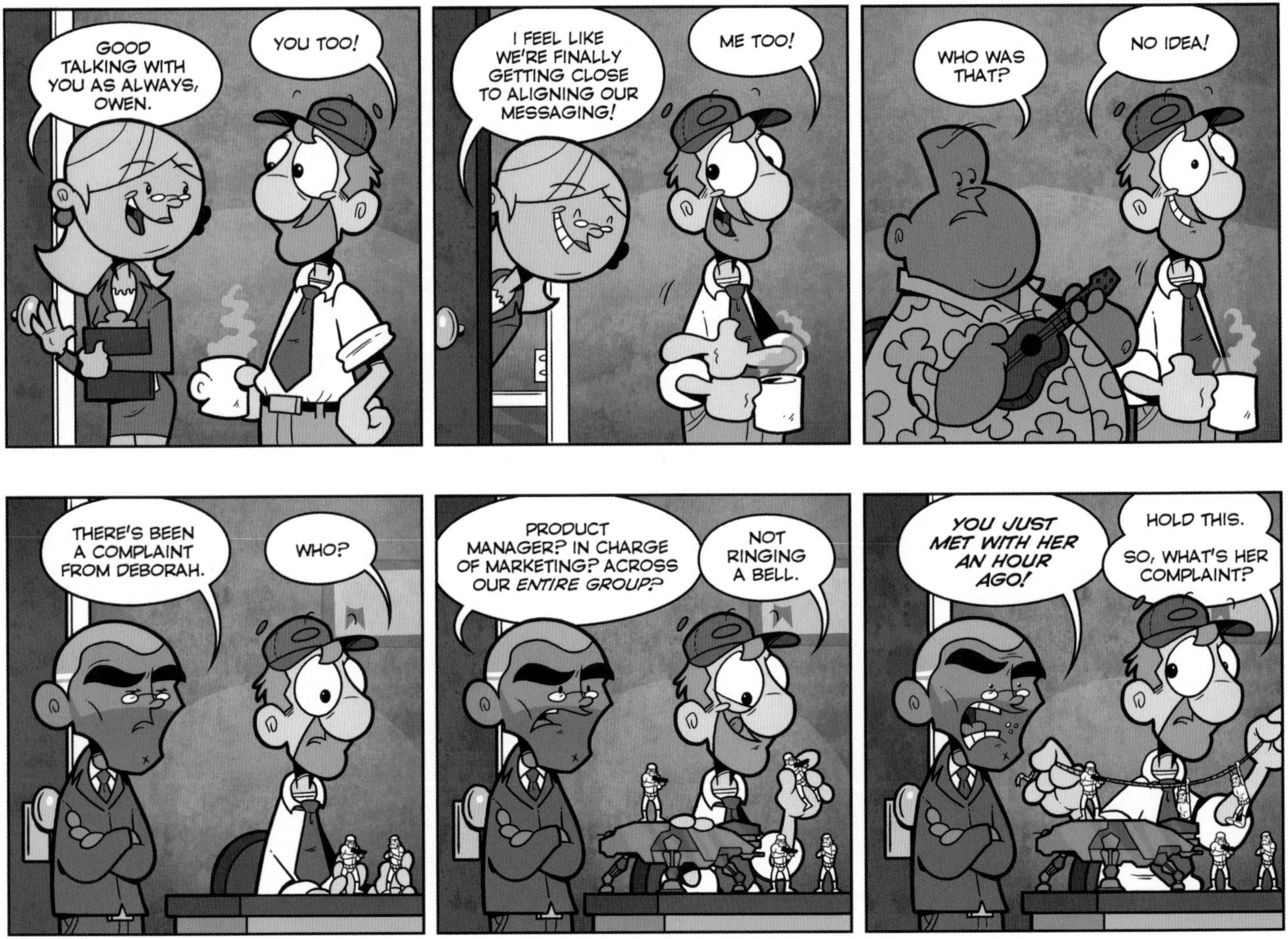
GOOD TALKING WITH YOU AS ALWAYS, OWEN.
YOU TOO!
I FEEL LIKE WE'RE FINALLY GETTING CLOSE TO ALIGNING OUR MESSAGING!
ME TOO!
WHO WAS THAT?
NO IDEA!
THERE'S BEEN A COMPLAINT FROM DEBORAH.
WHO?
PRODUCT MANAGER? IN CHARGE OF MARKETING? ACROSS OUR ENTIRE GROUP?
NOT RINGING A BELL.
YOU JUST MET WITH HER AN HOUR AGO!
HOLD THIS.
SO, WHAT'S HER COMPLAINT?

RUNTIME ERROR

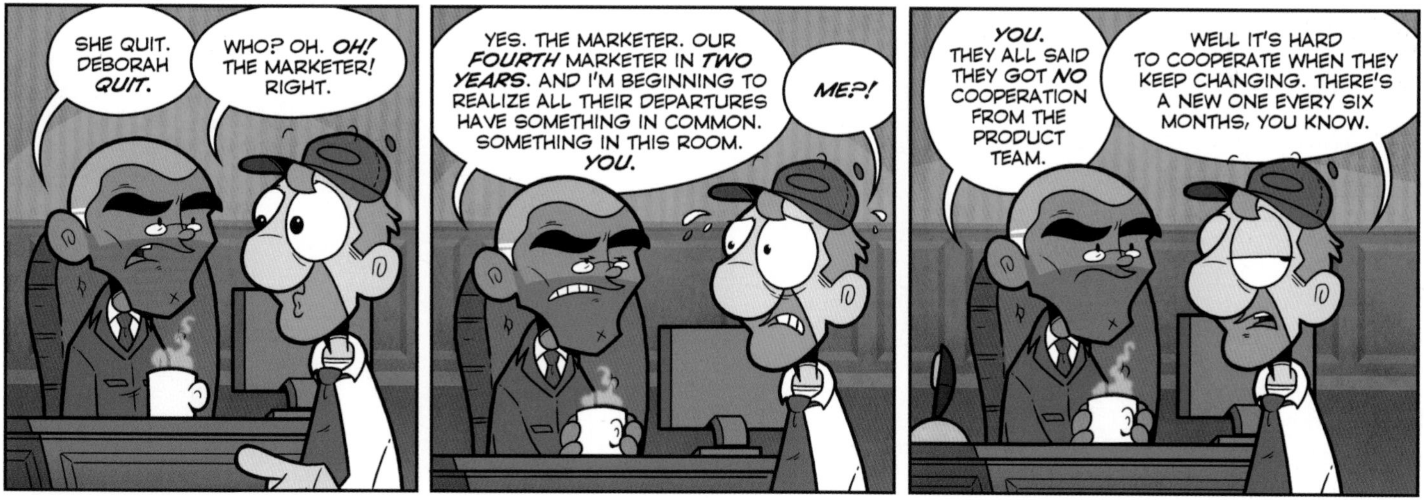

SHE QUIT. DEBORAH *QUIT.*
WHO? OH. *OH!* THE MARKETER! RIGHT.
YES. THE MARKETER. OUR *FOURTH* MARKETER IN *TWO YEARS*. AND I'M BEGINNING TO REALIZE ALL THEIR DEPARTURES HAVE SOMETHING IN COMMON. SOMETHING IN THIS ROOM. *YOU.*
ME?!
YOU. THEY ALL SAID THEY GOT *NO* COOPERATION FROM THE PRODUCT TEAM.
WELL IT'S HARD TO COOPERATE WHEN THEY KEEP CHANGING. THERE'S A NEW ONE EVERY SIX MONTHS, YOU KNOW.

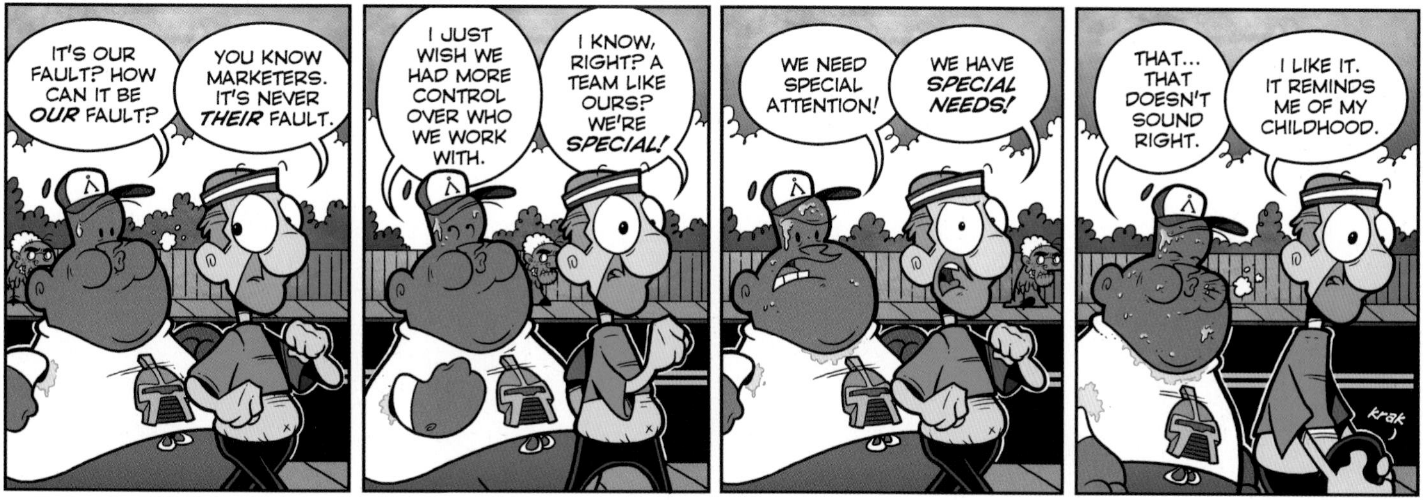

IT'S OUR FAULT? HOW CAN IT BE *OUR* FAULT?
YOU KNOW MARKETERS. IT'S NEVER *THEIR* FAULT.
I JUST WISH WE HAD MORE CONTROL OVER WHO WE WORK WITH.
I KNOW, RIGHT? A TEAM LIKE OURS? WE'RE *SPECIAL!*
WE NEED SPECIAL ATTENTION!
WE HAVE *SPECIAL NEEDS!*
THAT... THAT DOESN'T SOUND RIGHT.
I LIKE IT. IT REMINDS ME OF MY CHILDHOOD.
krak

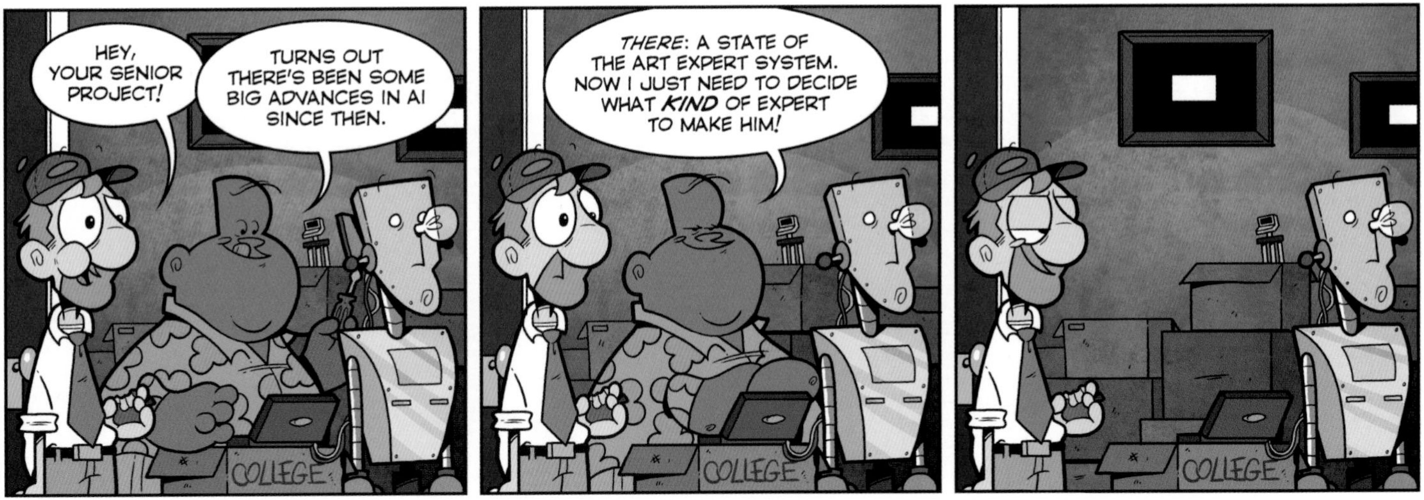
HEY, YOUR SENIOR PROJECT!
TURNS OUT THERE'S BEEN SOME BIG ADVANCES IN AI SINCE THEN.
COLLEGE
THERE: A STATE OF THE ART EXPERT SYSTEM. NOW I JUST NEED TO DECIDE WHAT KIND OF EXPERT TO MAKE HIM!
COLLEGE
COLLEGE

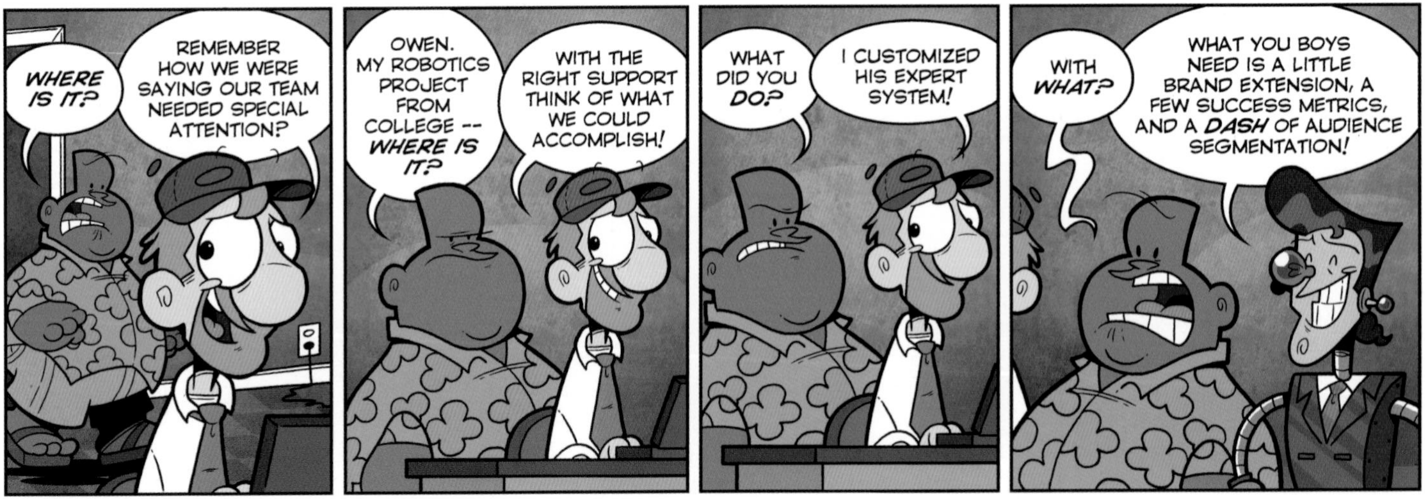
WHERE IS IT?
REMEMBER HOW WE WERE SAYING OUR TEAM NEEDED SPECIAL ATTENTION?
OWEN. MY ROBOTICS PROJECT FROM COLLEGE -- WHERE IS IT?
WITH THE RIGHT SUPPORT THINK OF WHAT WE COULD ACCOMPLISH!
WHAT DID YOU DO?
I CUSTOMIZED HIS EXPERT SYSTEM!
WITH WHAT?
WHAT YOU BOYS NEED IS A LITTLE BRAND EXTENSION, A FEW SUCCESS METRICS, AND A DASH OF AUDIENCE SEGMENTATION!

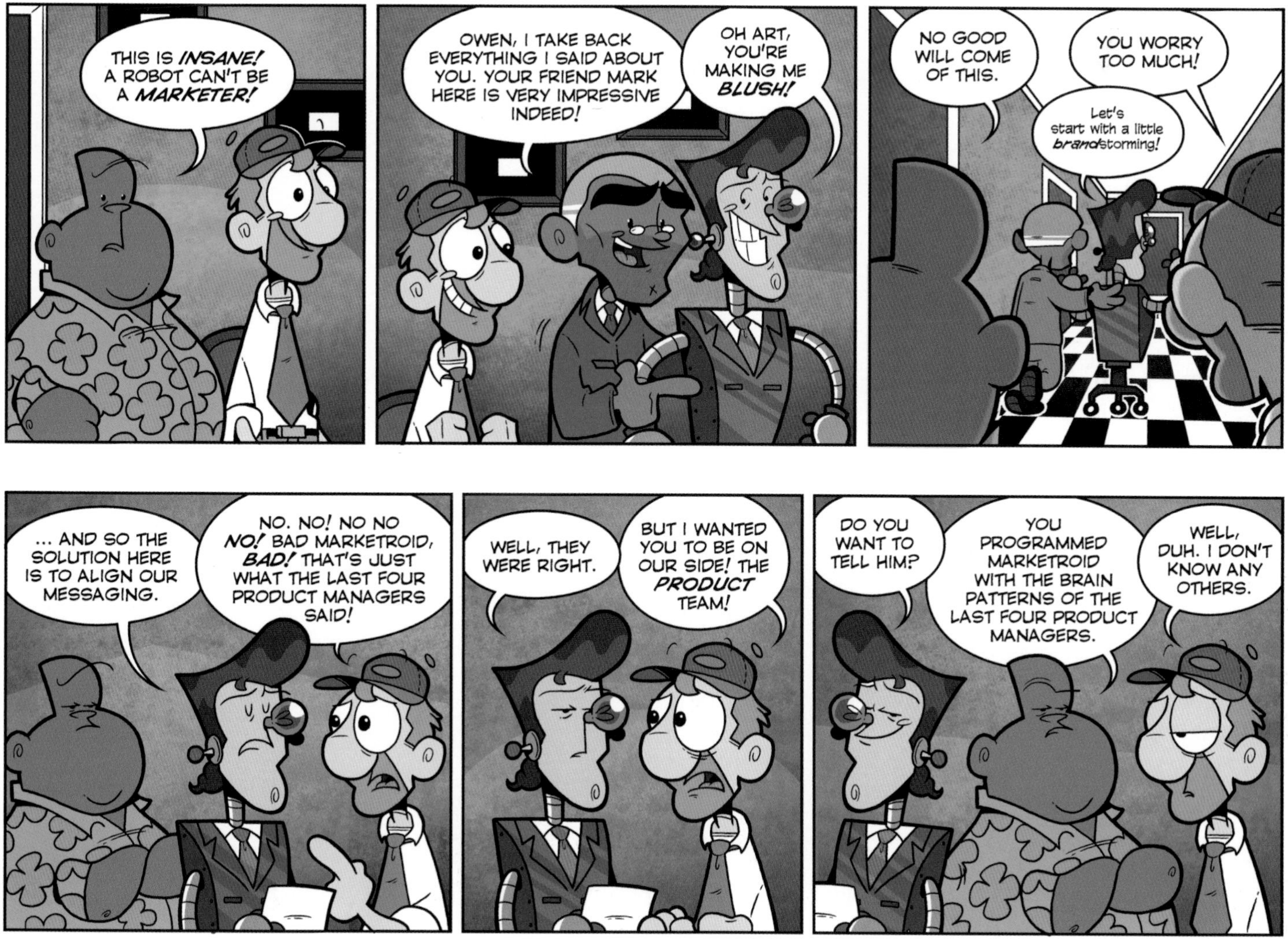
THIS IS *INSANE!* A ROBOT CAN'T BE A *MARKETER!*
OWEN, I TAKE BACK EVERYTHING I SAID ABOUT YOU. YOUR FRIEND MARK HERE IS VERY IMPRESSIVE INDEED!
OH ART, YOU'RE MAKING ME *BLUSH!*
NO GOOD WILL COME OF THIS.
YOU WORRY TOO MUCH!
Let's start with a little *brand*storming!
... AND SO THE SOLUTION HERE IS TO ALIGN OUR MESSAGING.
NO. NO! NO NO *NO!* BAD MARKETROID, *BAD!* THAT'S JUST WHAT THE LAST FOUR PRODUCT MANAGERS SAID!
WELL, THEY WERE RIGHT.
BUT I WANTED YOU TO BE ON OUR SIDE! THE *PRODUCT* TEAM!
DO YOU WANT TO TELL HIM?
YOU PROGRAMMED MARKETROID WITH THE BRAIN PATTERNS OF THE LAST FOUR PRODUCT MANAGERS.
WELL, DUH. I DON'T KNOW ANY OTHERS.

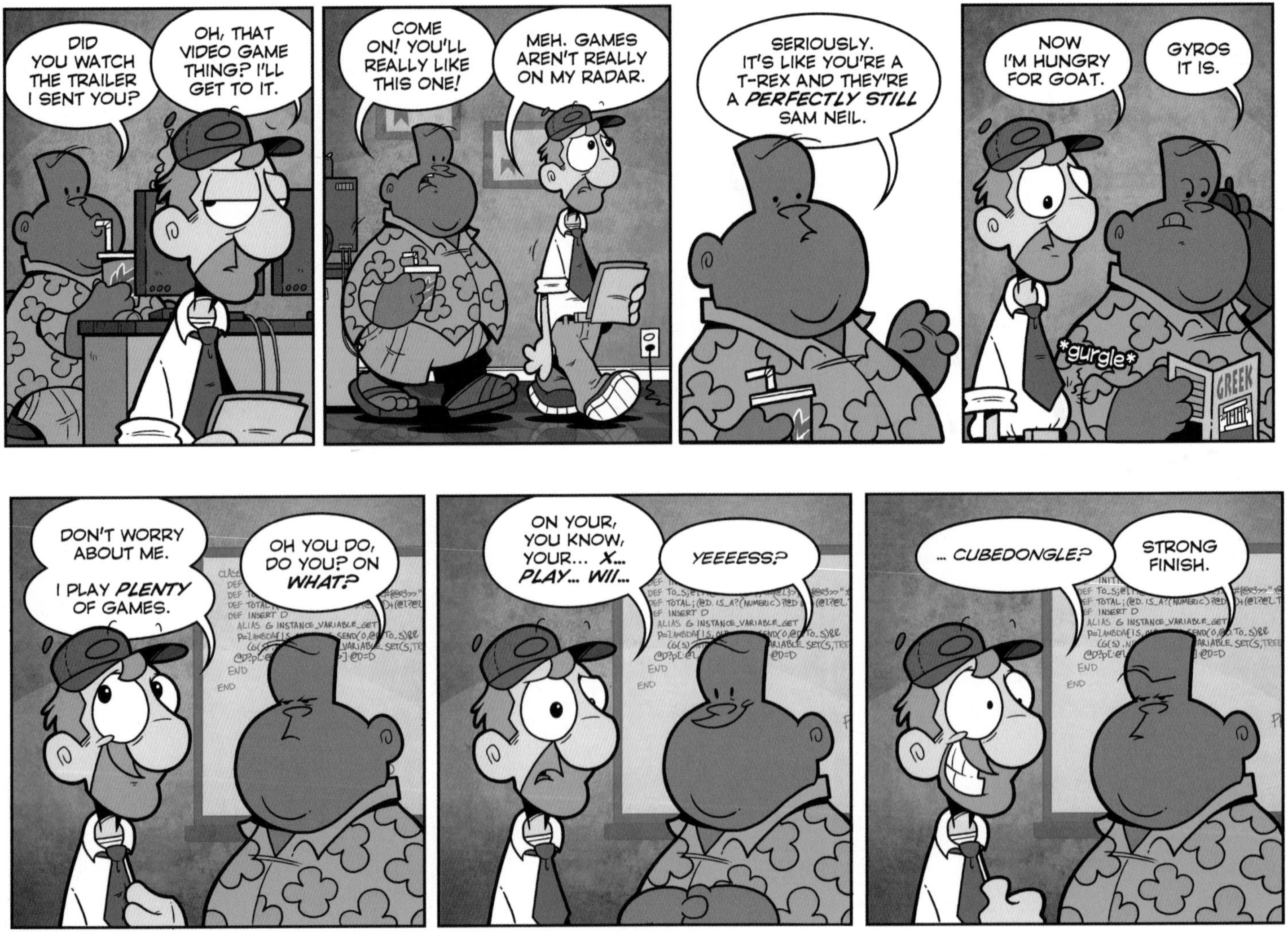
DID YOU WATCH THE TRAILER I SENT YOU?
OH, THAT VIDEO GAME THING? I'LL GET TO IT.
COME ON! YOU'LL REALLY LIKE THIS ONE!
MEH. GAMES AREN'T REALLY ON MY RADAR.
SERIOUSLY. IT'S LIKE YOU'RE A T-REX AND THEY'RE A *PERFECTLY STILL* SAM NEIL.
NOW I'M HUNGRY FOR GOAT.
GYROS IT IS.
gurgle
GREEK
DON'T WORRY ABOUT ME.
I PLAY *PLENTY* OF GAMES.
OH YOU DO, DO YOU? ON *WHAT?*
ON YOUR, YOU KNOW, YOUR... *X... PLAY... WII...*
YEEEESS?
... CUBEDONGLE?
STRONG FINISH.

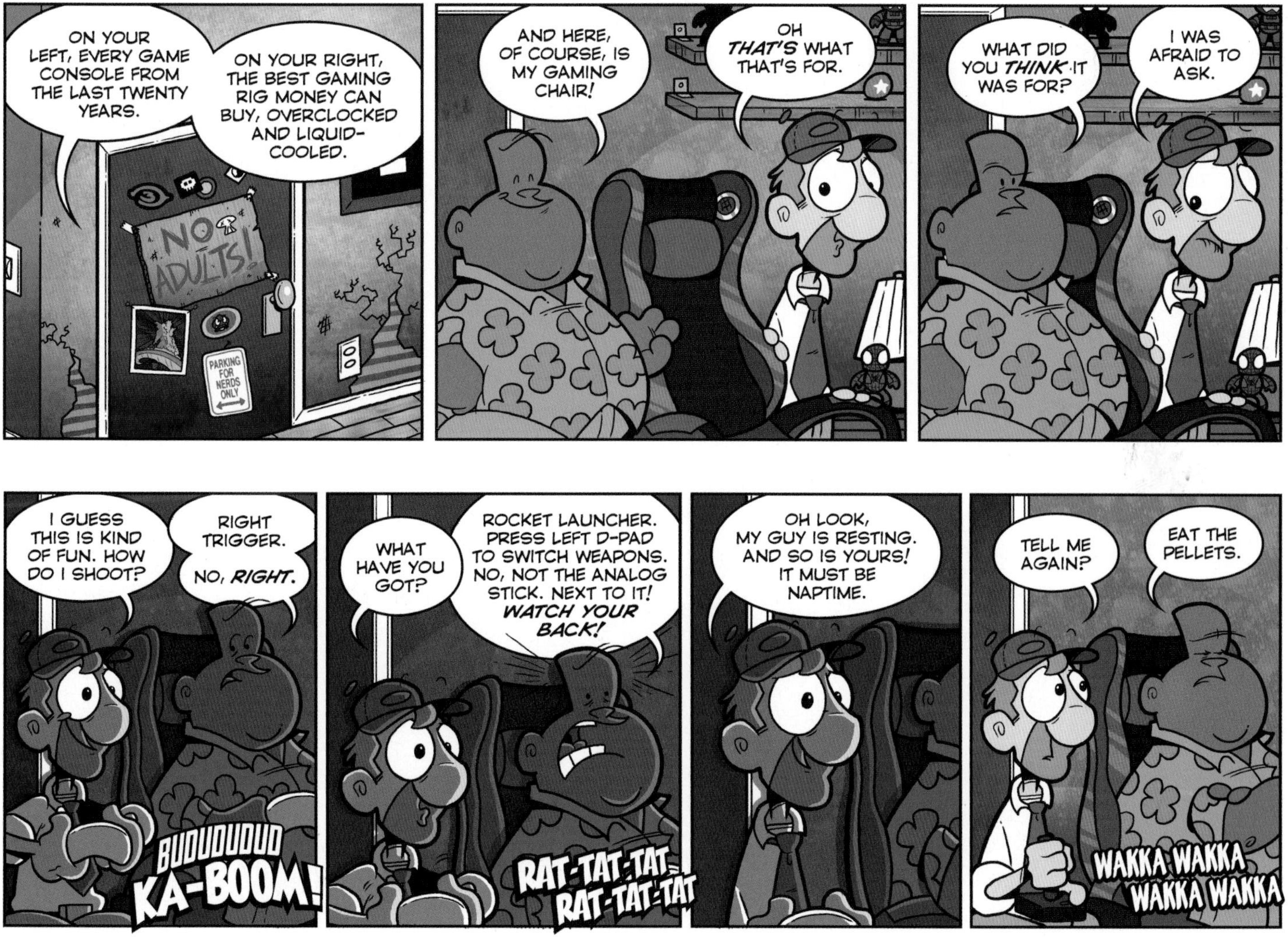
ON YOUR LEFT, EVERY GAME CONSOLE FROM THE LAST TWENTY YEARS.
ON YOUR RIGHT, THE BEST GAMING RIG MONEY CAN BUY, OVERCLOCKED AND LIQUID-COOLED.
NO ADULTS!
PARKING FOR NERDS ONLY
AND HERE, OF COURSE, IS MY GAMING CHAIR!
OH *THAT'S* WHAT THAT'S FOR.
WHAT DID YOU *THINK* IT WAS FOR?
I WAS AFRAID TO ASK.
I GUESS THIS IS KIND OF FUN. HOW DO I SHOOT?
RIGHT TRIGGER.
NO, *RIGHT*.
BUDUDUDUD
KA-BOOM!
WHAT HAVE YOU GOT?
ROCKET LAUNCHER. PRESS LEFT D-PAD TO SWITCH WEAPONS. NO, NOT THE ANALOG STICK. NEXT TO IT! *WATCH YOUR BACK!*
RAT-TAT-TAT
RAT-TAT-TAT
OH LOOK, MY GUY IS RESTING. AND SO IS YOURS! IT MUST BE NAPTIME.
TELL ME AGAIN?
EAT THE PELLETS.
WAKKA WAKKA
WAKKA WAKKA

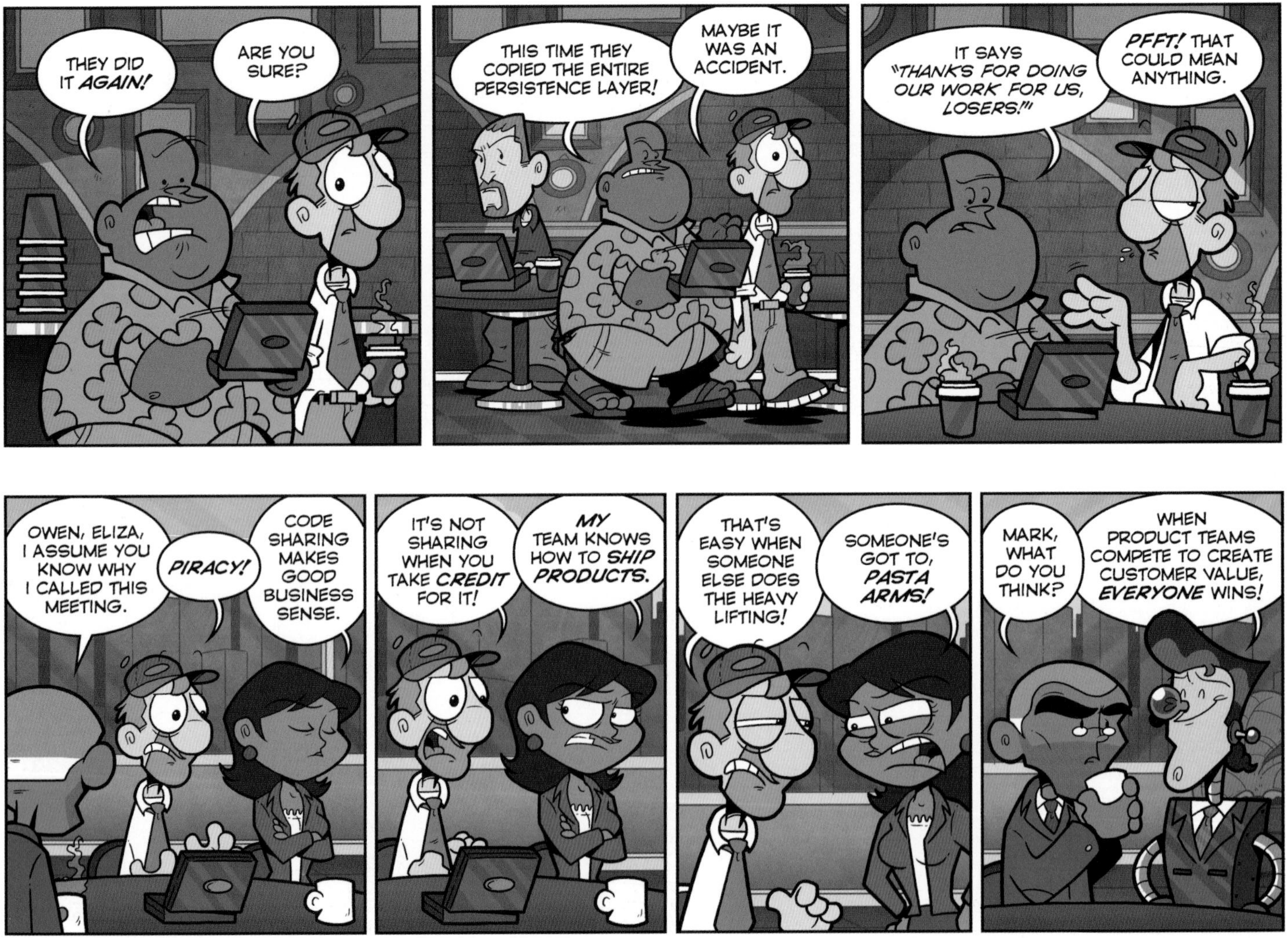
THEY DID IT AGAIN!
ARE YOU SURE?
THIS TIME THEY COPIED THE ENTIRE PERSISTENCE LAYER!
MAYBE IT WAS AN ACCIDENT.
IT SAYS "THANKS FOR DOING OUR WORK FOR US, LOSERS!"
PFFT! THAT COULD MEAN ANYTHING.
OWEN, ELIZA, I ASSUME YOU KNOW WHY I CALLED THIS MEETING.
PIRACY!
CODE SHARING MAKES GOOD BUSINESS SENSE.
IT'S NOT SHARING WHEN YOU TAKE CREDIT FOR IT!
MY TEAM KNOWS HOW TO SHIP PRODUCTS.
THAT'S EASY WHEN SOMEONE ELSE DOES THE HEAVY LIFTING!
SOMEONE'S GOT TO, PASTA ARMS!
MARK, WHAT DO YOU THINK?
WHEN PRODUCT TEAMS COMPETE TO CREATE CUSTOMER VALUE, EVERYONE WINS!

RUNTIME ERROR

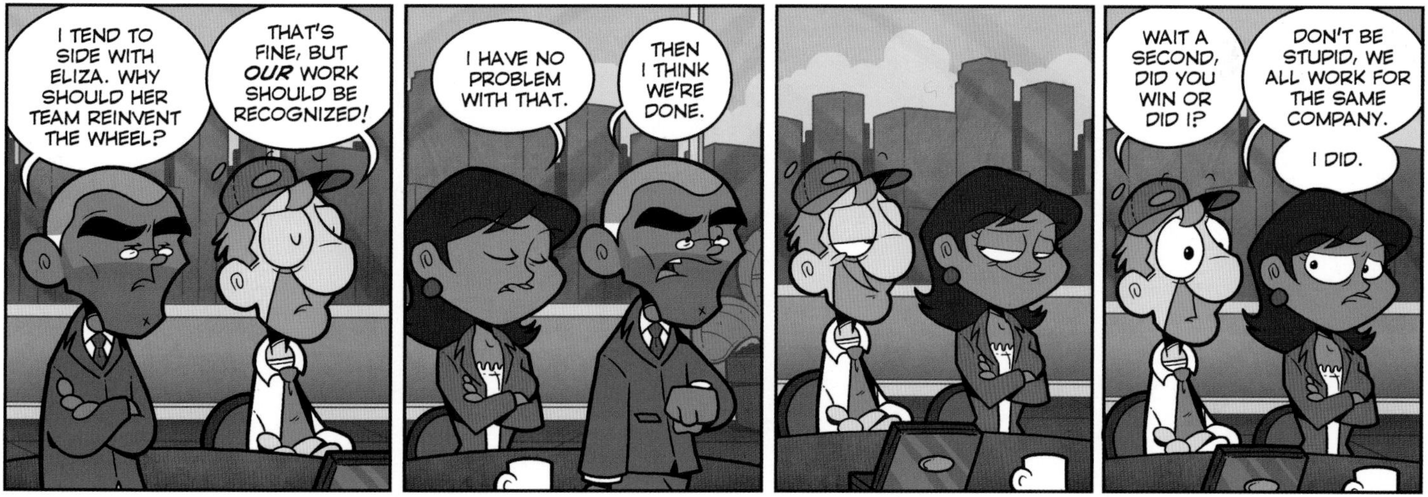
I TEND TO SIDE WITH ELIZA. WHY SHOULD HER TEAM REINVENT THE WHEEL?
THAT'S FINE, BUT *OUR* WORK SHOULD BE RECOGNIZED!
I HAVE NO PROBLEM WITH THAT.
THEN I THINK WE'RE DONE.
WAIT A SECOND, DID YOU WIN OR DID I?
DON'T BE STUPID, WE ALL WORK FOR THE SAME COMPANY.
I DID.

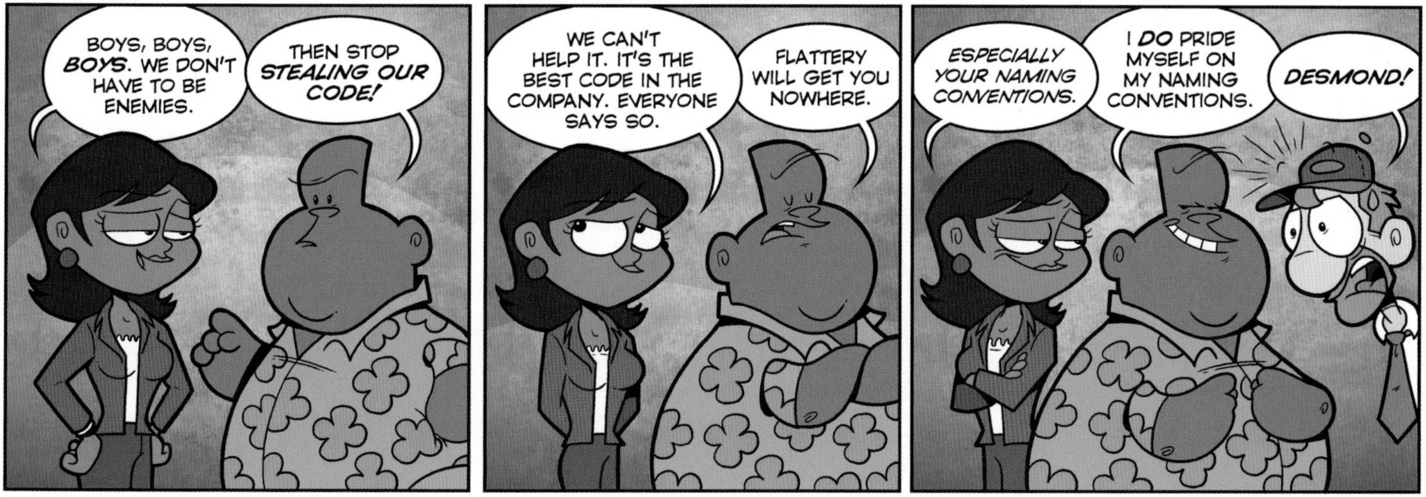
BOYS, BOYS, ***BOYS***. WE DON'T HAVE TO BE ENEMIES.
THEN STOP ***STEALING OUR CODE!***
WE CAN'T HELP IT. IT'S THE BEST CODE IN THE COMPANY. EVERYONE SAYS SO.
FLATTERY WILL GET YOU NOWHERE.
ESPECIALLY YOUR NAMING CONVENTIONS.
I ***DO*** PRIDE MYSELF ON MY NAMING CONVENTIONS.
DESMOND!

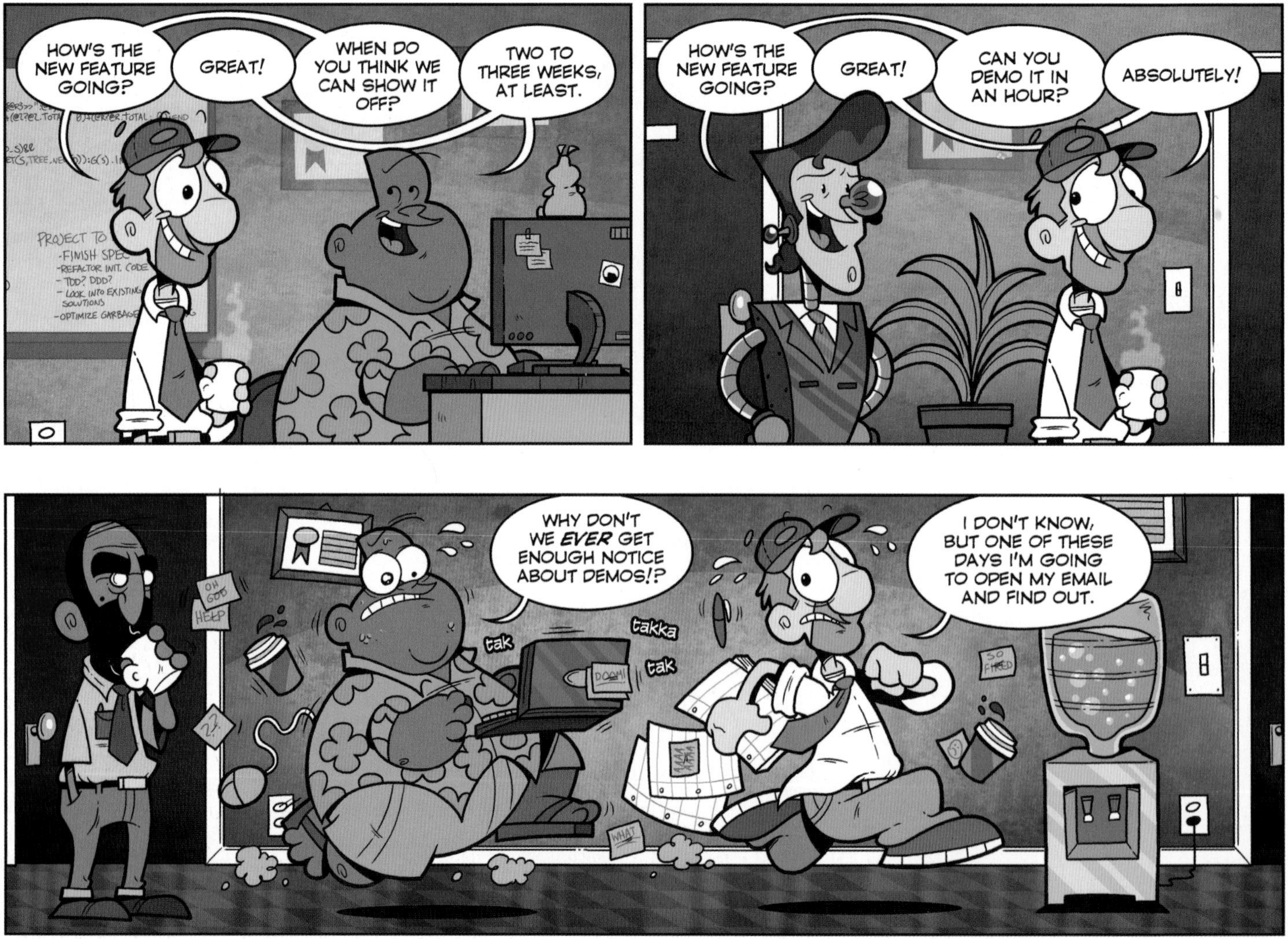
HOW'S THE NEW FEATURE GOING?
GREAT!
WHEN DO YOU THINK WE CAN SHOW IT OFF?
TWO TO THREE WEEKS, AT LEAST.
HOW'S THE NEW FEATURE GOING?
GREAT!
CAN YOU DEMO IT IN AN HOUR?
ABSOLUTELY!
WHY DON'T WE *EVER* GET ENOUGH NOTICE ABOUT DEMOS!?
tak
takka
tak
I DON'T KNOW, BUT ONE OF THESE DAYS I'M GOING TO OPEN MY EMAIL AND FIND OUT.

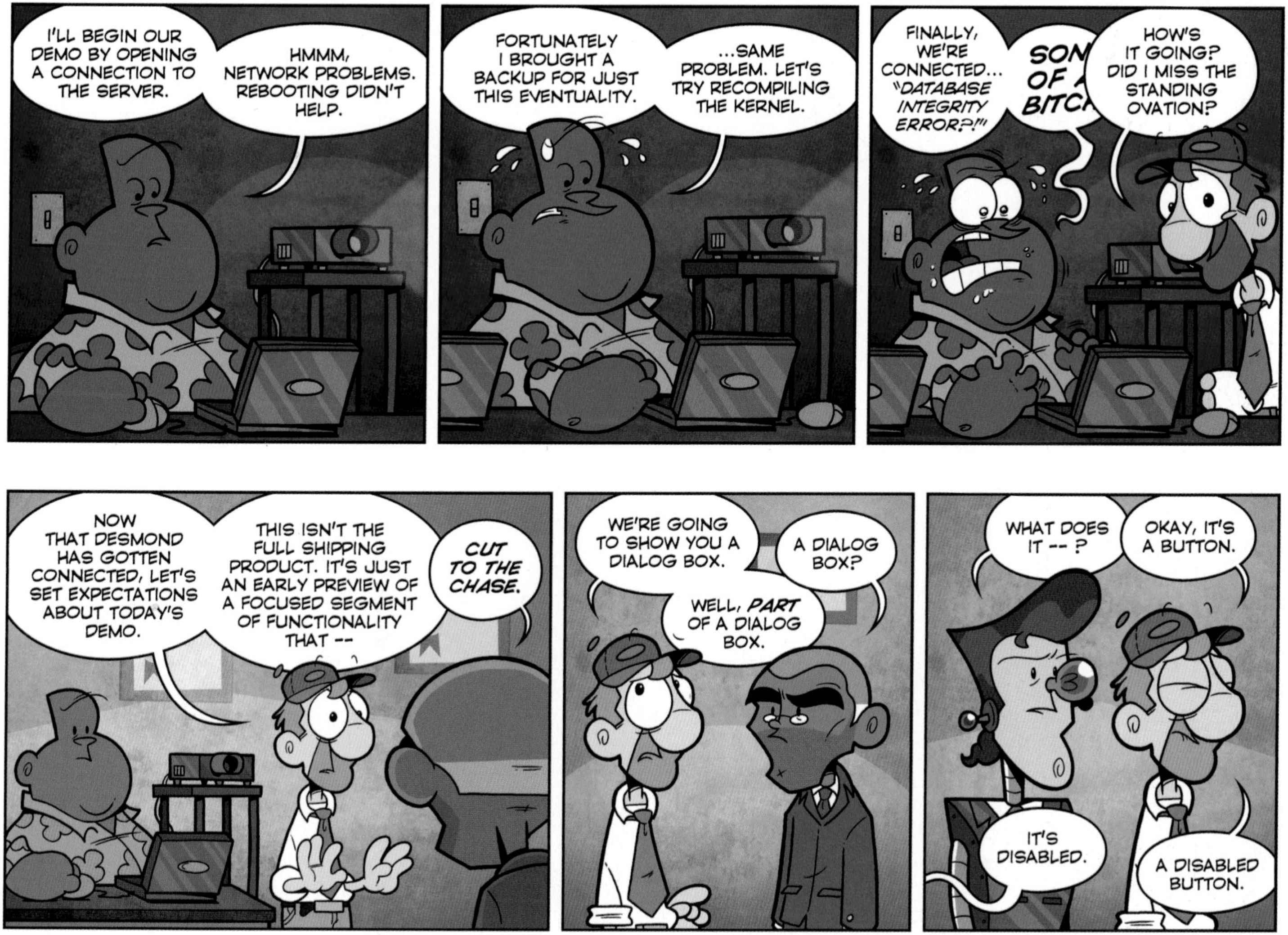
I'LL BEGIN OUR DEMO BY OPENING A CONNECTION TO THE SERVER.
HMMM, NETWORK PROBLEMS. REBOOTING DIDN'T HELP.
FORTUNATELY I BROUGHT A BACKUP FOR JUST THIS EVENTUALITY.
...SAME PROBLEM. LET'S TRY RECOMPILING THE KERNEL.
FINALLY, WE'RE CONNECTED... *"DATABASE INTEGRITY ERROR?!"*
SON OF A BITC
HOW'S IT GOING? DID I MISS THE STANDING OVATION?
NOW THAT DESMOND HAS GOTTEN CONNECTED, LET'S SET EXPECTATIONS ABOUT TODAY'S DEMO.
THIS ISN'T THE FULL SHIPPING PRODUCT. IT'S JUST AN EARLY PREVIEW OF A FOCUSED SEGMENT OF FUNCTIONALITY THAT --
CUT TO THE CHASE.
WE'RE GOING TO SHOW YOU A DIALOG BOX.
A DIALOG BOX?
WELL, *PART* OF A DIALOG BOX.
WHAT DOES IT -- ?
OKAY, IT'S A BUTTON.
IT'S DISABLED.
A DISABLED BUTTON.

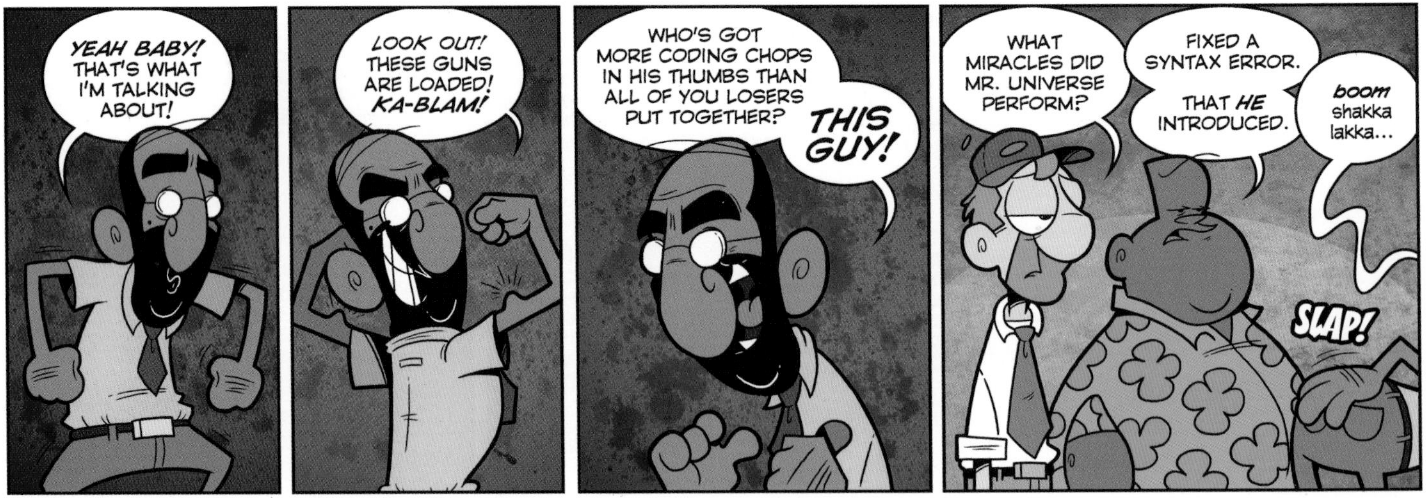
YEAH BABY! THAT'S WHAT I'M TALKING ABOUT!
LOOK OUT! THESE GUNS ARE LOADED! KA-BLAM!
WHO'S GOT MORE CODING CHOPS IN HIS THUMBS THAN ALL OF YOU LOSERS PUT TOGETHER?
THIS GUY!
WHAT MIRACLES DID MR. UNIVERSE PERFORM?
FIXED A SYNTAX ERROR.
THAT HE INTRODUCED.
boom shakka lakka...
SLAP!

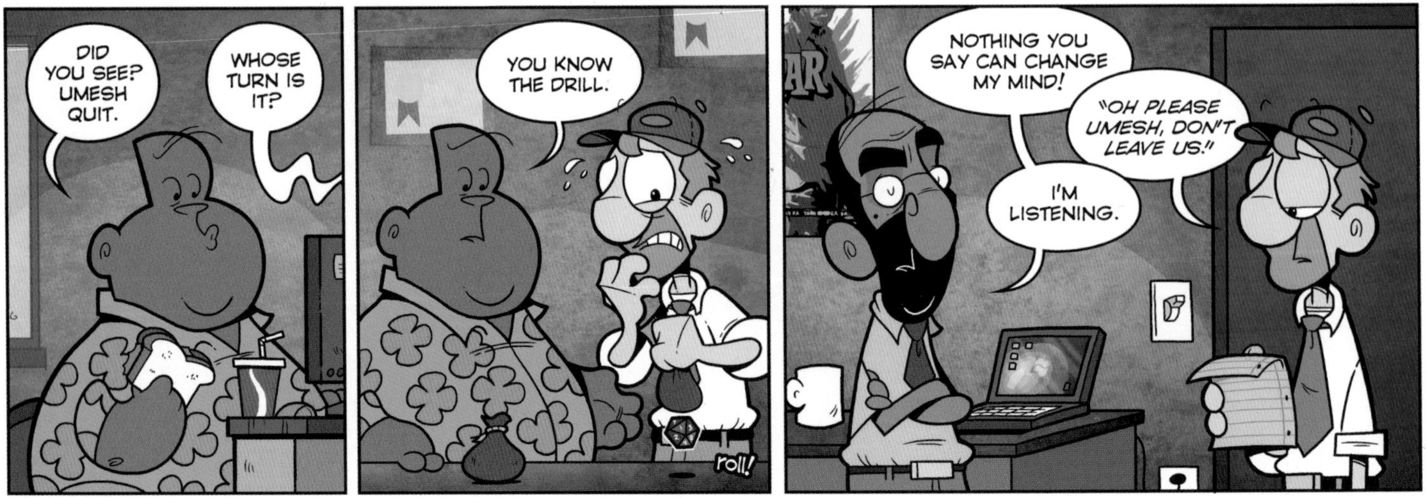
DID YOU SEE? UMESH QUIT.
WHOSE TURN IS IT?
YOU KNOW THE DRILL.
roll!
NOTHING YOU SAY CAN CHANGE MY MIND!
I'M LISTENING.
"OH PLEASE UMESH, DON'T LEAVE US."

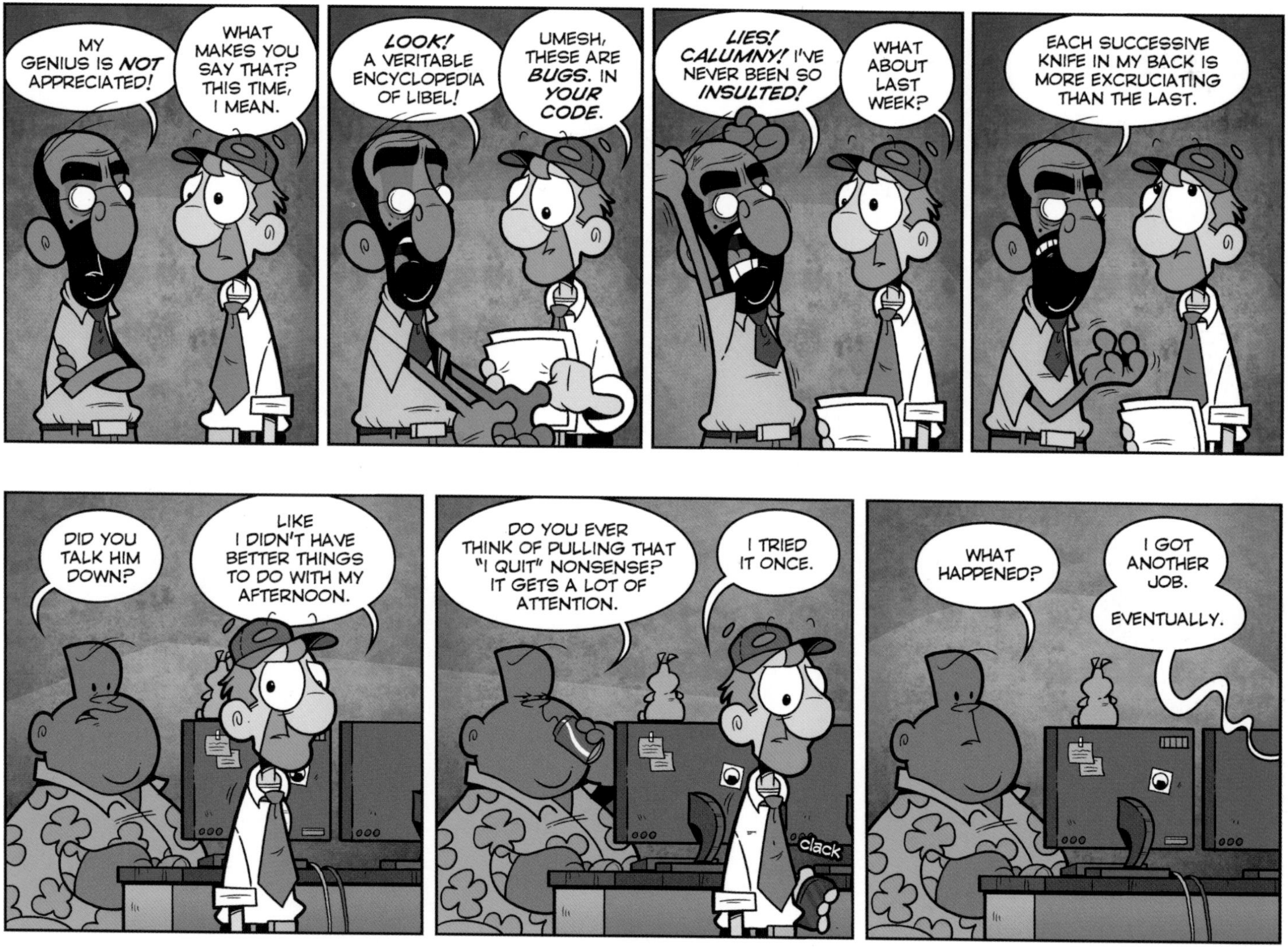
MY GENIUS IS *NOT* APPRECIATED!
WHAT MAKES YOU SAY THAT? THIS TIME, I MEAN.
LOOK! A VERITABLE ENCYCLOPEDIA OF LIBEL!
UMESH, THESE ARE *BUGS*. IN *YOUR CODE*.
LIES! CALUMNY! I'VE NEVER BEEN SO *INSULTED!*
WHAT ABOUT LAST WEEK?
EACH SUCCESSIVE KNIFE IN MY BACK IS MORE EXCRUCIATING THAN THE LAST.
DID YOU TALK HIM DOWN?
LIKE I DIDN'T HAVE BETTER THINGS TO DO WITH MY AFTERNOON.
DO YOU EVER THINK OF PULLING THAT "I QUIT" NONSENSE? IT GETS A LOT OF ATTENTION.
I TRIED IT ONCE.
clack
WHAT HAPPENED?
I GOT ANOTHER JOB.
EVENTUALLY.

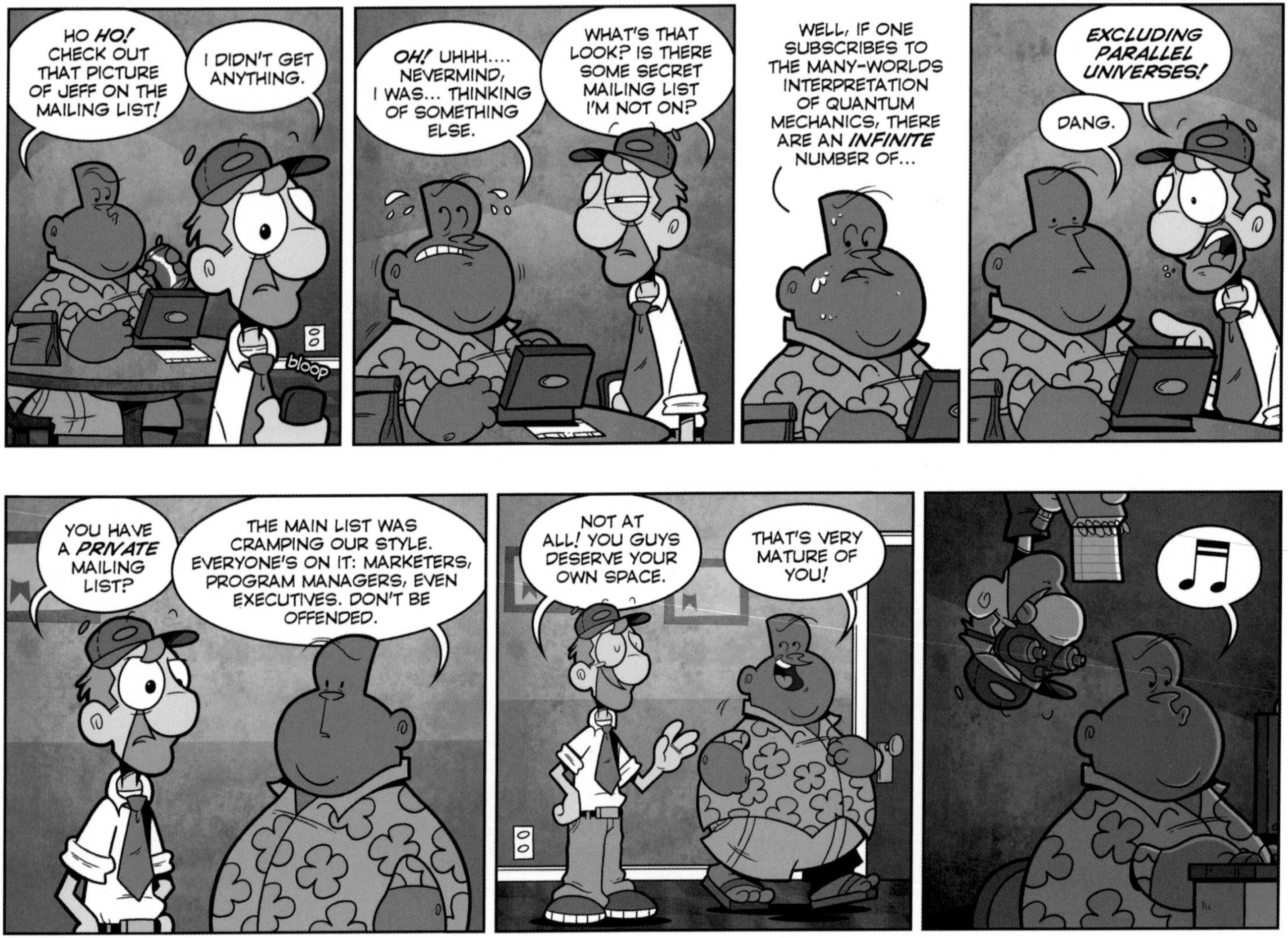
HO *HO!* CHECK OUT THAT PICTURE OF JEFF ON THE MAILING LIST!
I DIDN'T GET ANYTHING.
bloop
OH! UHHH.... NEVERMIND, I WAS... THINKING OF SOMETHING ELSE.
WHAT'S THAT LOOK? IS THERE SOME SECRET MAILING LIST I'M NOT ON?
WELL, IF ONE SUBSCRIBES TO THE MANY-WORLDS INTERPRETATION OF QUANTUM MECHANICS, THERE ARE AN *INFINITE* NUMBER OF...
EXCLUDING PARALLEL UNIVERSES!
DANG.
YOU HAVE A *PRIVATE* MAILING LIST?
THE MAIN LIST WAS CRAMPING OUR STYLE. EVERYONE'S ON IT: MARKETERS, PROGRAM MANAGERS, EVEN EXECUTIVES. DON'T BE OFFENDED.
NOT AT ALL! YOU GUYS DESERVE YOUR OWN SPACE.
THAT'S VERY MATURE OF YOU!

RUNTIME ERROR

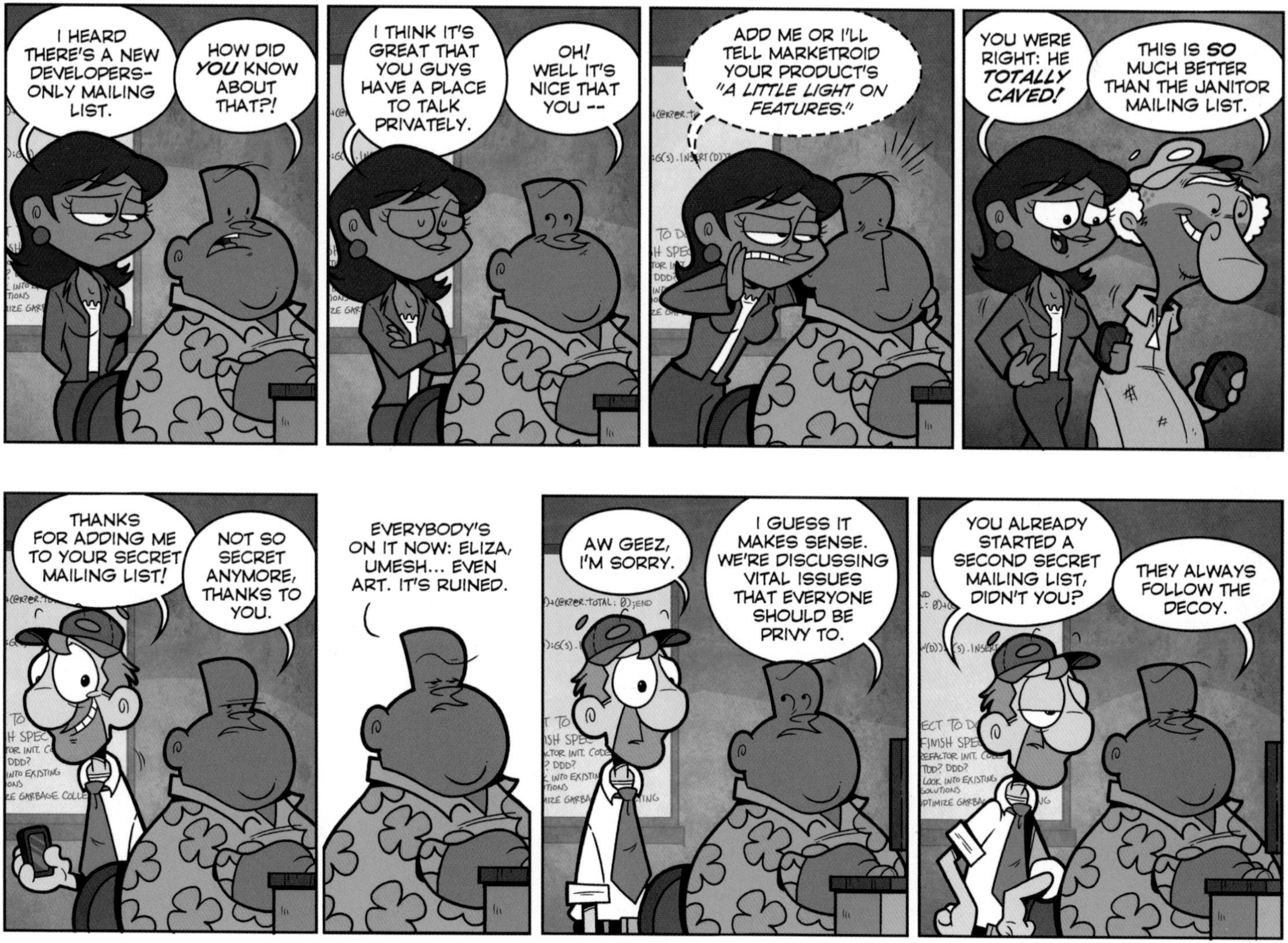
I HEARD THERE'S A NEW DEVELOPERS-ONLY MAILING LIST.
HOW DID *YOU* KNOW ABOUT THAT?!
I THINK IT'S GREAT THAT YOU GUYS HAVE A PLACE TO TALK PRIVATELY.
OH! WELL IT'S NICE THAT YOU --
ADD ME OR I'LL TELL MARKETROID YOUR PRODUCT'S *"A LITTLE LIGHT ON FEATURES."*
YOU WERE RIGHT: HE ***TOTALLY CAVED!***
THIS IS **SO** MUCH BETTER THAN THE JANITOR MAILING LIST.
THANKS FOR ADDING ME TO YOUR SECRET MAILING LIST!
NOT SO SECRET ANYMORE, THANKS TO YOU.
EVERYBODY'S ON IT NOW: ELIZA, UMESH... EVEN ART. IT'S RUINED.
AW GEEZ, I'M SORRY.
I GUESS IT MAKES SENSE. WE'RE DISCUSSING VITAL ISSUES THAT EVERYONE SHOULD BE PRIVY TO.
YOU ALREADY STARTED A SECOND SECRET MAILING LIST, DIDN'T YOU?
THEY ALWAYS FOLLOW THE DECOY.

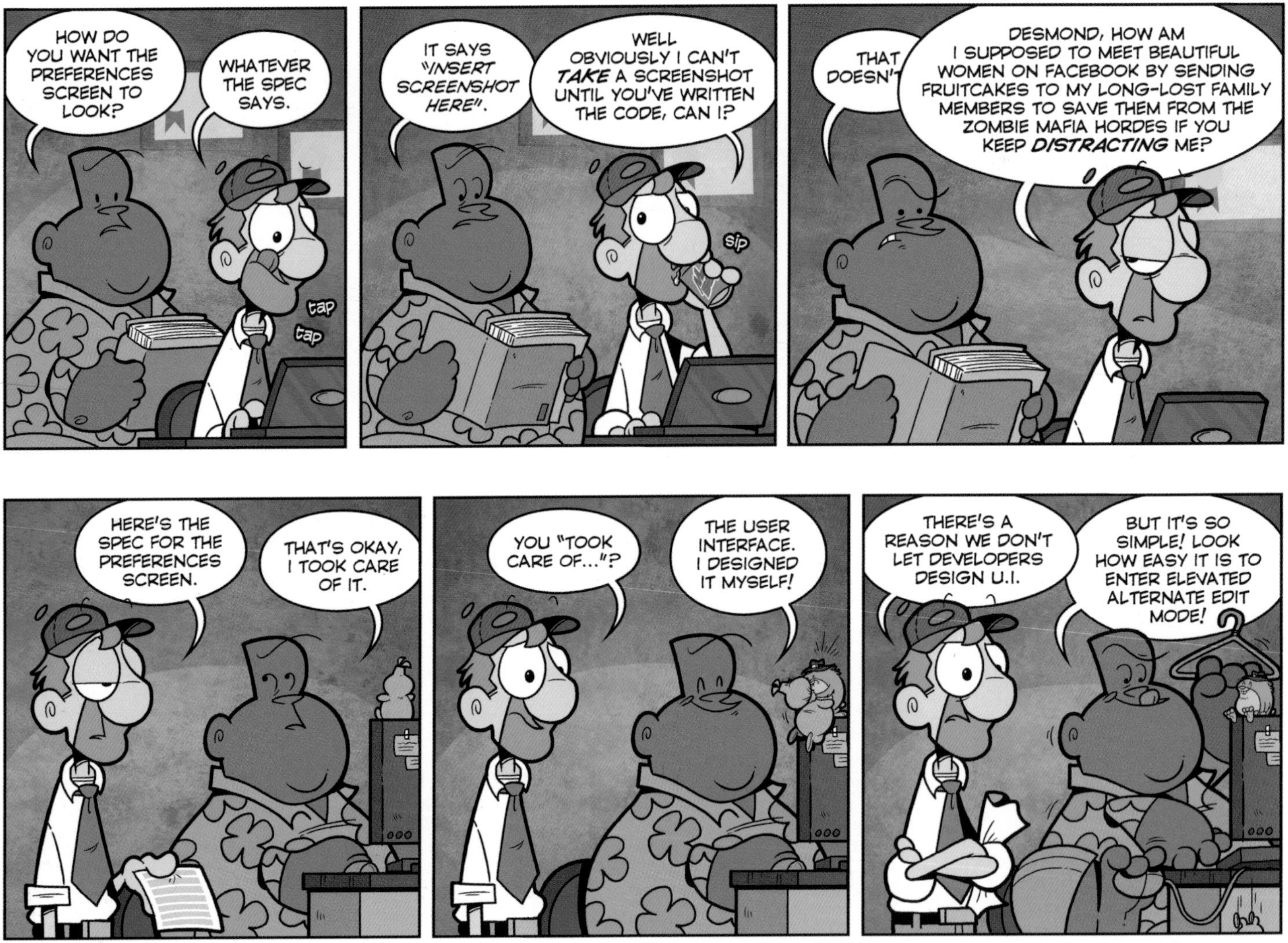
HOW DO YOU WANT THE PREFERENCES SCREEN TO LOOK?
WHATEVER THE SPEC SAYS.
tap
tap
IT SAYS "INSERT SCREENSHOT HERE".
WELL OBVIOUSLY I CAN'T *TAKE* A SCREENSHOT UNTIL YOU'VE WRITTEN THE CODE, CAN I?
sip
THAT DOESN'T
DESMOND, HOW AM I SUPPOSED TO MEET BEAUTIFUL WOMEN ON FACEBOOK BY SENDING FRUITCAKES TO MY LONG-LOST FAMILY MEMBERS TO SAVE THEM FROM THE ZOMBIE MAFIA HORDES IF YOU KEEP *DISTRACTING* ME?
HERE'S THE SPEC FOR THE PREFERENCES SCREEN.
THAT'S OKAY, I TOOK CARE OF IT.
YOU "TOOK CARE OF..."?
THE USER INTERFACE. I DESIGNED IT MYSELF!
THERE'S A REASON WE DON'T LET DEVELOPERS DESIGN U.I.
BUT IT'S SO SIMPLE! LOOK HOW EASY IT IS TO ENTER ELEVATED ALTERNATE EDIT MODE!

RUNTIME ERROR

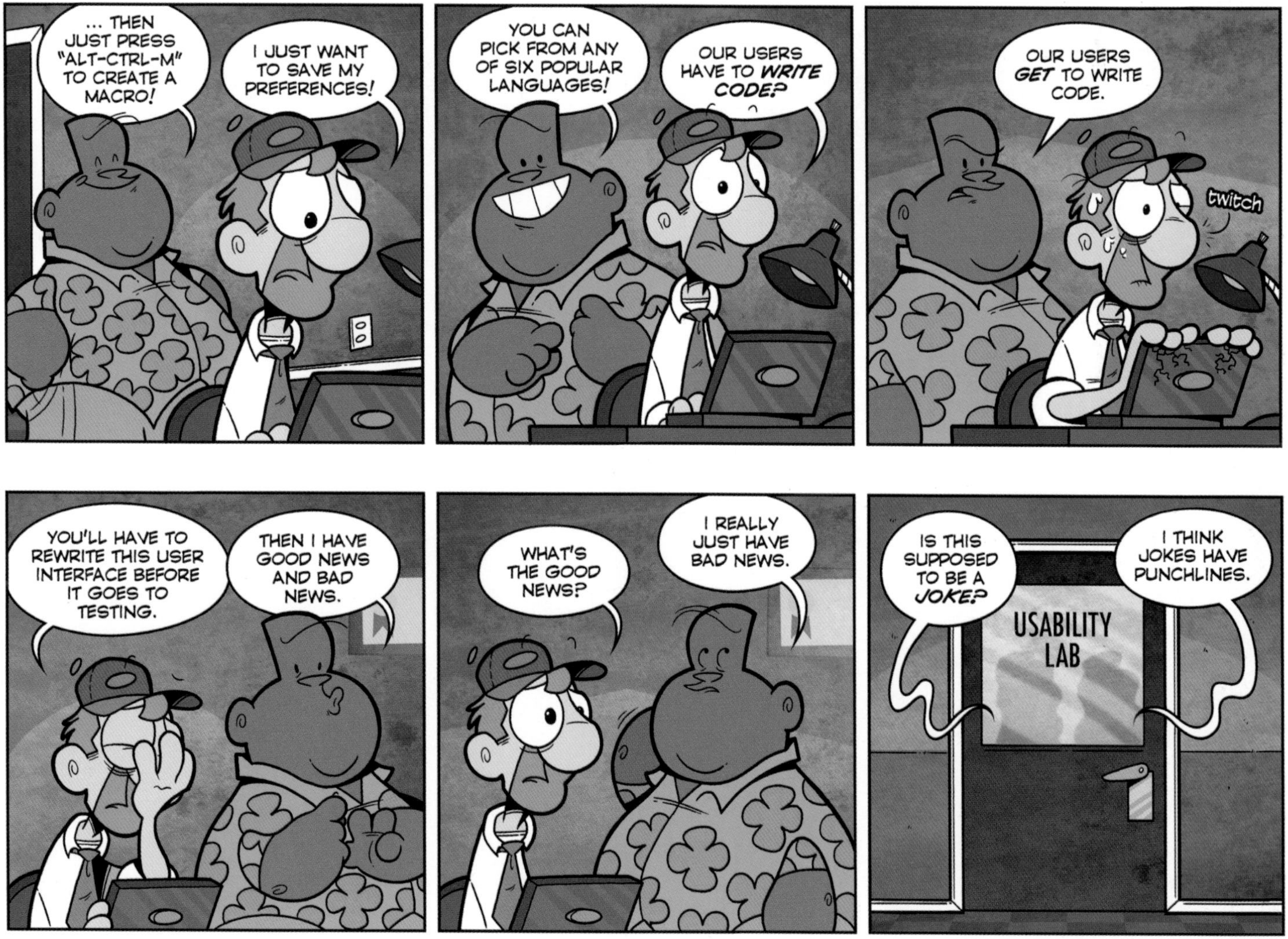

... THEN JUST PRESS "ALT-CTRL-M" TO CREATE A MACRO!
I JUST WANT TO SAVE MY PREFERENCES!
YOU CAN PICK FROM ANY OF SIX POPULAR LANGUAGES!
OUR USERS HAVE TO *WRITE CODE?*
OUR USERS *GET* TO WRITE CODE.
twitch
YOU'LL HAVE TO REWRITE THIS USER INTERFACE BEFORE IT GOES TO TESTING.
THEN I HAVE GOOD NEWS AND BAD NEWS.
WHAT'S THE GOOD NEWS?
I REALLY JUST HAVE BAD NEWS.
IS THIS SUPPOSED TO BE A *JOKE?*
USABILITY LAB
I THINK JOKES HAVE PUNCHLINES.

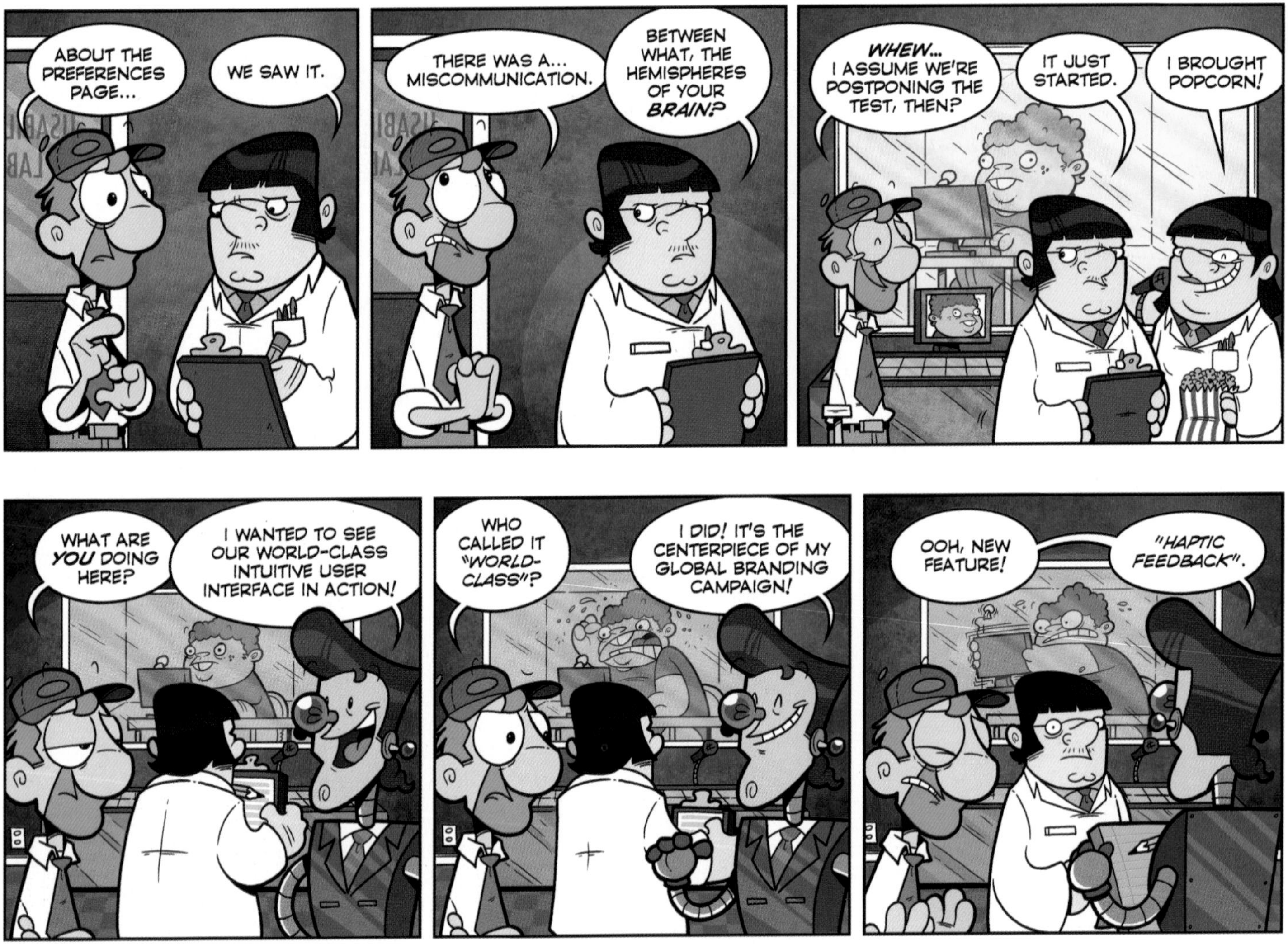
ABOUT THE PREFERENCES PAGE...
WE SAW IT.
THERE WAS A... MISCOMMUNICATION.
BETWEEN WHAT, THE HEMISPHERES OF YOUR *BRAIN?*
WHEW... I ASSUME WE'RE POSTPONING THE TEST, THEN?
IT JUST STARTED.
I BROUGHT POPCORN!
WHAT ARE *YOU* DOING HERE?
I WANTED TO SEE OUR WORLD-CLASS INTUITIVE USER INTERFACE IN ACTION!
WHO CALLED IT *"WORLD-CLASS"*?
I DID! IT'S THE CENTERPIECE OF MY GLOBAL BRANDING CAMPAIGN!
OOH, NEW FEATURE!
"HAPTIC FEEDBACK".

RUNTIME ERROR

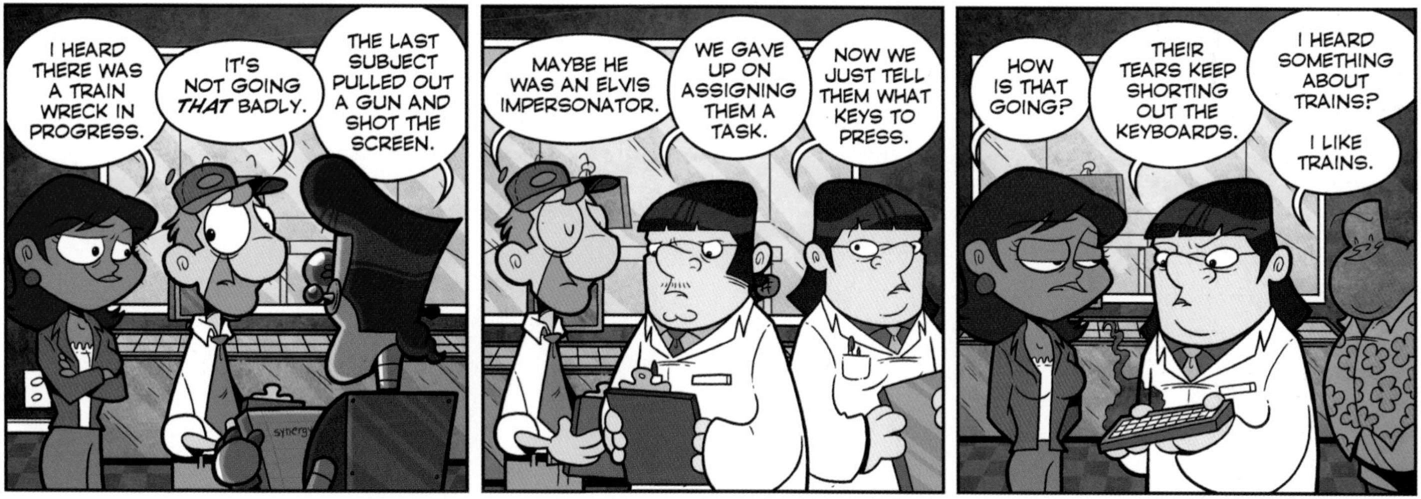
I HEARD THERE WAS A TRAIN WRECK IN PROGRESS.
IT'S NOT GOING *THAT* BADLY.
THE LAST SUBJECT PULLED OUT A GUN AND SHOT THE SCREEN.
MAYBE HE WAS AN ELVIS IMPERSONATOR.
WE GAVE UP ON ASSIGNING THEM A TASK.
NOW WE JUST TELL THEM WHAT KEYS TO PRESS.
HOW IS THAT GOING?
THEIR TEARS KEEP SHORTING OUT THE KEYBOARDS.
I HEARD SOMETHING ABOUT TRAINS?
I LIKE TRAINS.

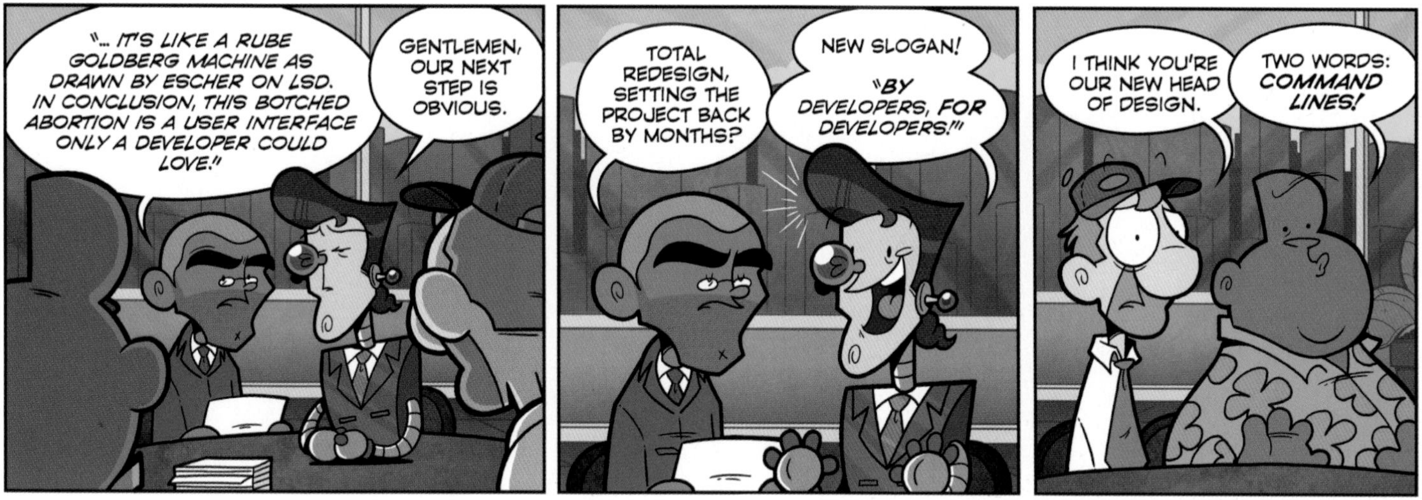
"... IT'S LIKE A RUBE GOLDBERG MACHINE AS DRAWN BY ESCHER ON LSD. IN CONCLUSION, THIS BOTCHED ABORTION IS A USER INTERFACE ONLY A DEVELOPER COULD LOVE."
GENTLEMEN, OUR NEXT STEP IS OBVIOUS.
TOTAL REDESIGN, SETTING THE PROJECT BACK BY MONTHS?
NEW SLOGAN!
"BY DEVELOPERS, FOR DEVELOPERS!"
I THINK YOU'RE OUR NEW HEAD OF DESIGN.
TWO WORDS: **COMMAND LINES!**

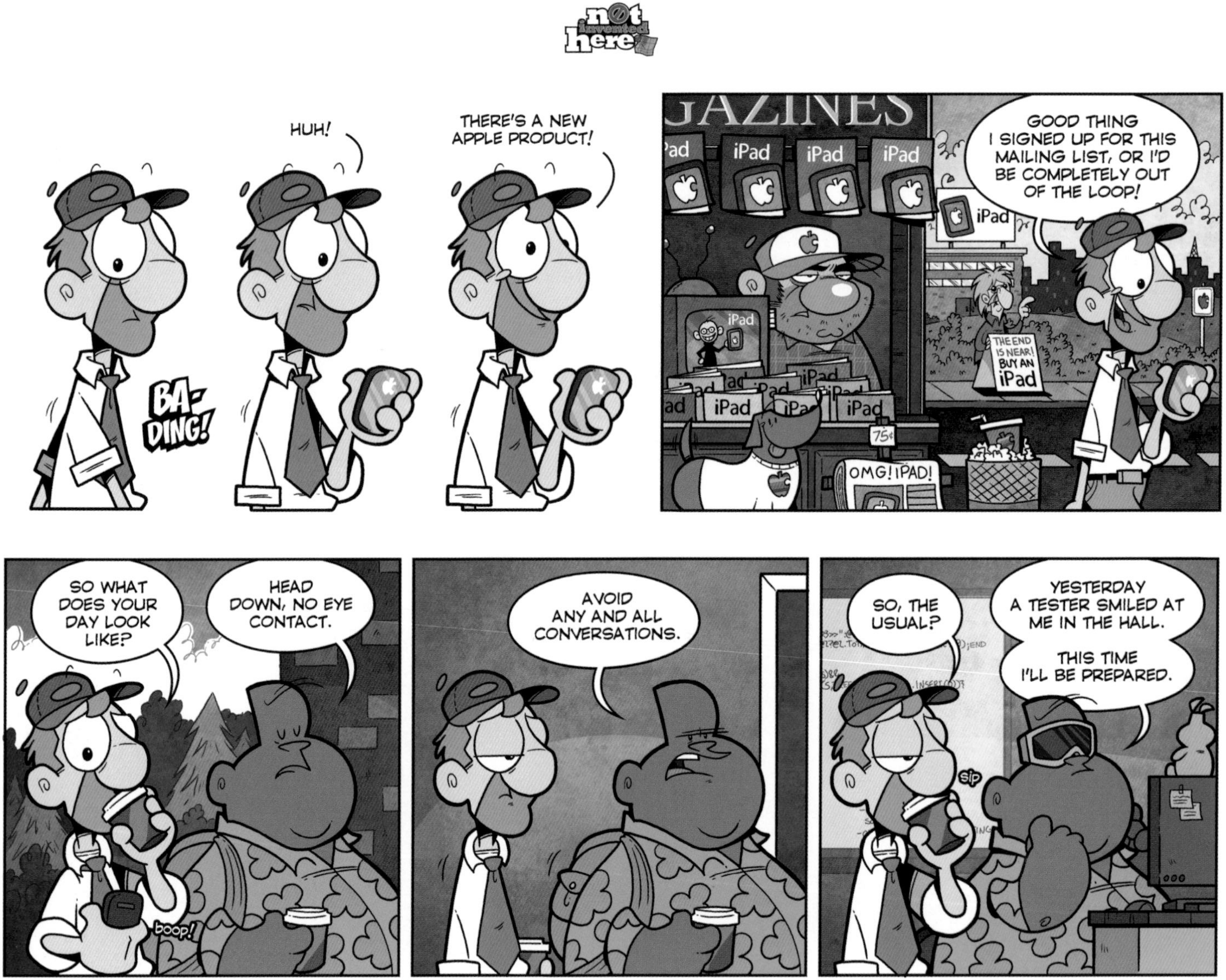
BA-DING!
HUH!
THERE'S A NEW APPLE PRODUCT!
GOOD THING I SIGNED UP FOR THIS MAILING LIST, OR I'D BE COMPLETELY OUT OF THE LOOP!
GAZINES
iPad
THE END IS NEAR! BUY AN iPad
75¢
OMG! IPAD!
SO WHAT DOES YOUR DAY LOOK LIKE?
HEAD DOWN, NO EYE CONTACT.
boop!
AVOID ANY AND ALL CONVERSATIONS.
SO, THE USUAL?
YESTERDAY A TESTER SMILED AT ME IN THE HALL.
THIS TIME I'LL BE PREPARED.
sip

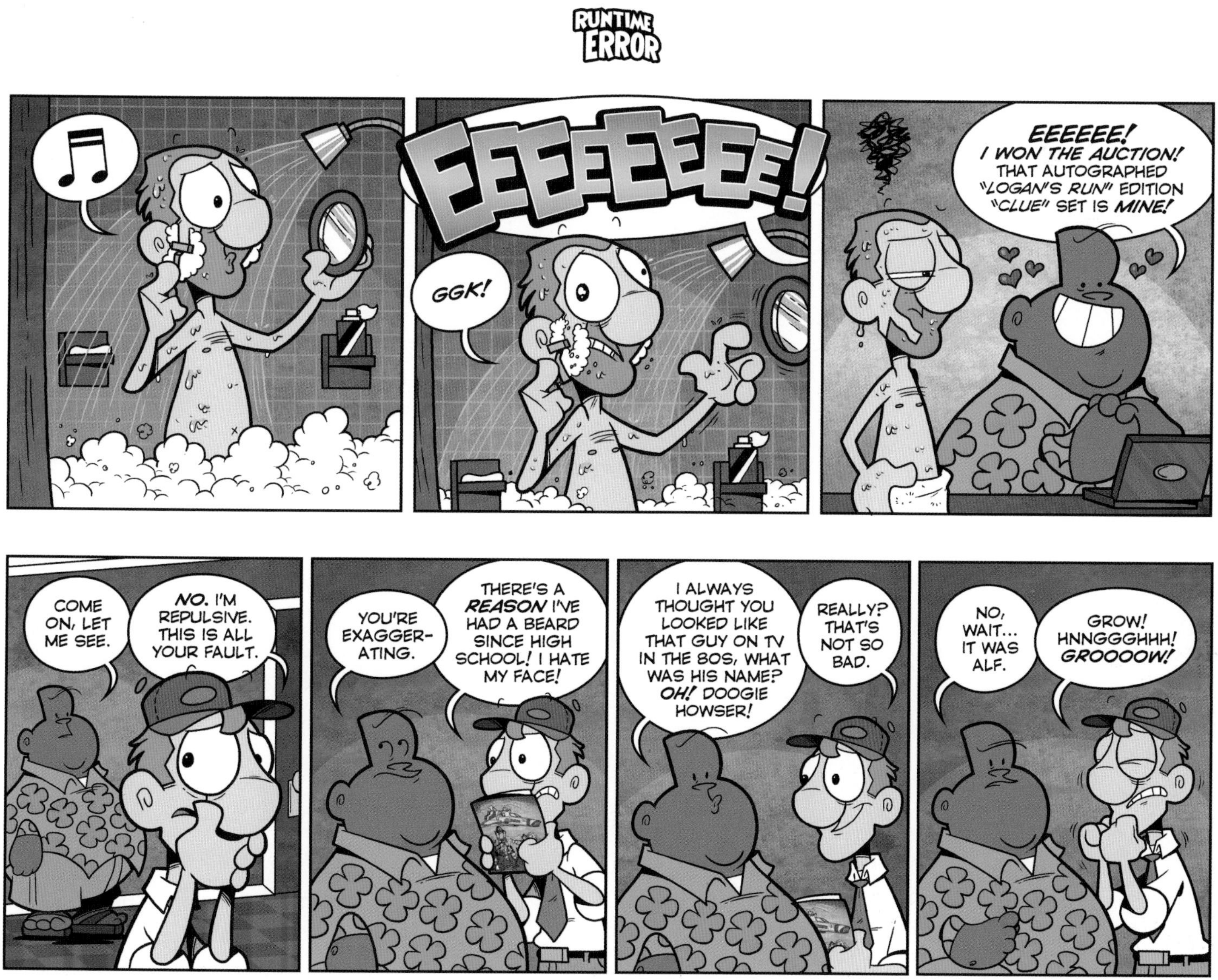
RUNTIME ERROR
EEEEEEEE!
GGK!
EEEEEE! I WON THE AUCTION! THAT AUTOGRAPHED "LOGAN'S RUN" EDITION "CLUE" SET IS MINE!
COME ON, LET ME SEE.
NO. I'M REPULSIVE. THIS IS ALL YOUR FAULT.
YOU'RE EXAGGER-ATING.
THERE'S A REASON I'VE HAD A BEARD SINCE HIGH SCHOOL! I HATE MY FACE!
I ALWAYS THOUGHT YOU LOOKED LIKE THAT GUY ON TV IN THE 80S, WHAT WAS HIS NAME? OH! DOOGIE HOWSER!
REALLY? THAT'S NOT SO BAD.
NO, WAIT... IT WAS ALF.
GROW! HNNGGGHHH! GROOOOW!

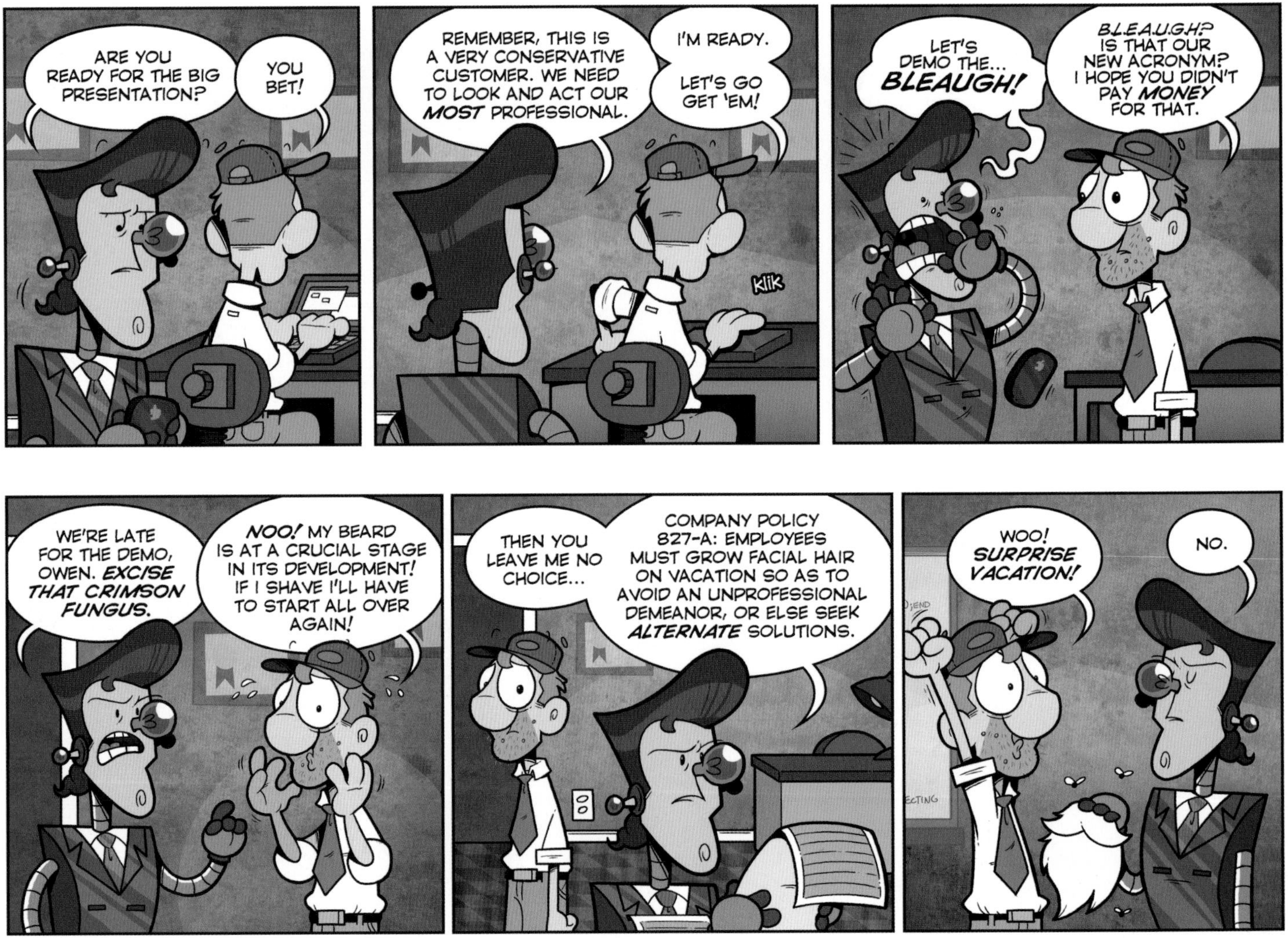
ARE YOU READY FOR THE BIG PRESENTATION?
YOU BET!
REMEMBER, THIS IS A VERY CONSERVATIVE CUSTOMER. WE NEED TO LOOK AND ACT OUR MOST PROFESSIONAL.
I'M READY.
LET'S GO GET 'EM!
KLIK
LET'S DEMO THE... BLEAUGH!
B.L.E.A.U.G.H? IS THAT OUR NEW ACRONYM? I HOPE YOU DIDN'T PAY MONEY FOR THAT.
WE'RE LATE FOR THE DEMO, OWEN. EXCISE THAT CRIMSON FUNGUS.
NOO! MY BEARD IS AT A CRUCIAL STAGE IN ITS DEVELOPMENT! IF I SHAVE I'LL HAVE TO START ALL OVER AGAIN!
THEN YOU LEAVE ME NO CHOICE...
COMPANY POLICY 827-A: EMPLOYEES MUST GROW FACIAL HAIR ON VACATION SO AS TO AVOID AN UNPROFESSIONAL DEMEANOR, OR ELSE SEEK ALTERNATE SOLUTIONS.
WOO! SURPRISE VACATION!
NO.

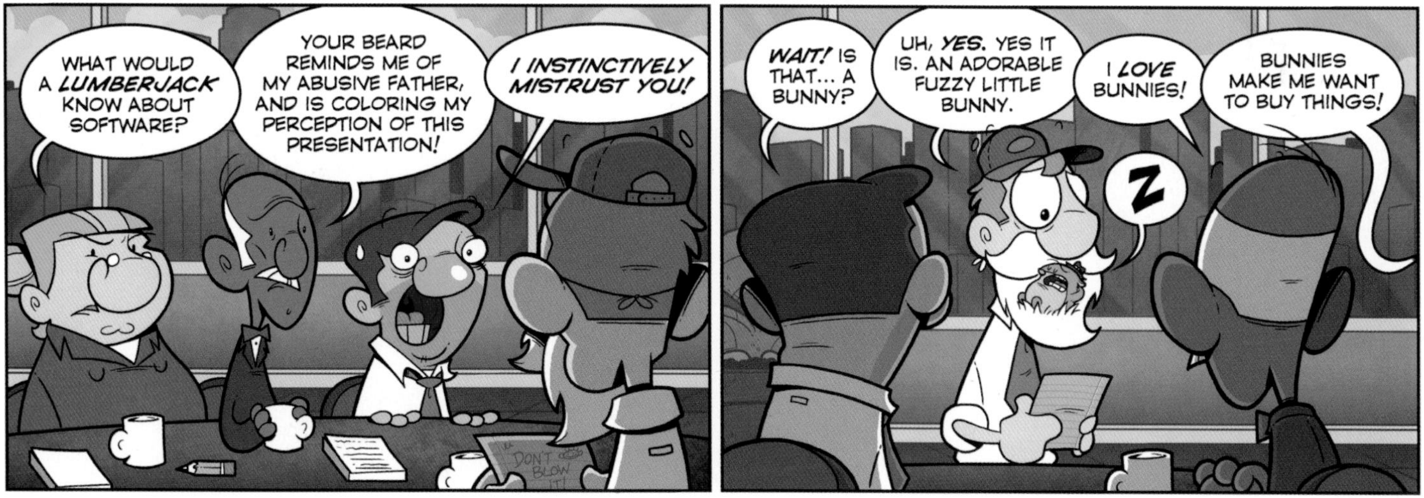
WHAT WOULD A *LUMBERJACK* KNOW ABOUT SOFTWARE?
YOUR BEARD REMINDS ME OF MY ABUSIVE FATHER, AND IS COLORING MY PERCEPTION OF THIS PRESENTATION!
I INSTINCTIVELY MISTRUST YOU!
DON'T BLOW IT!
WAIT! IS THAT... A BUNNY?
UH, *YES.* YES IT IS. AN ADORABLE FUZZY LITTLE BUNNY.
I *LOVE* BUNNIES!
BUNNIES MAKE ME WANT TO BUY THINGS!
Z

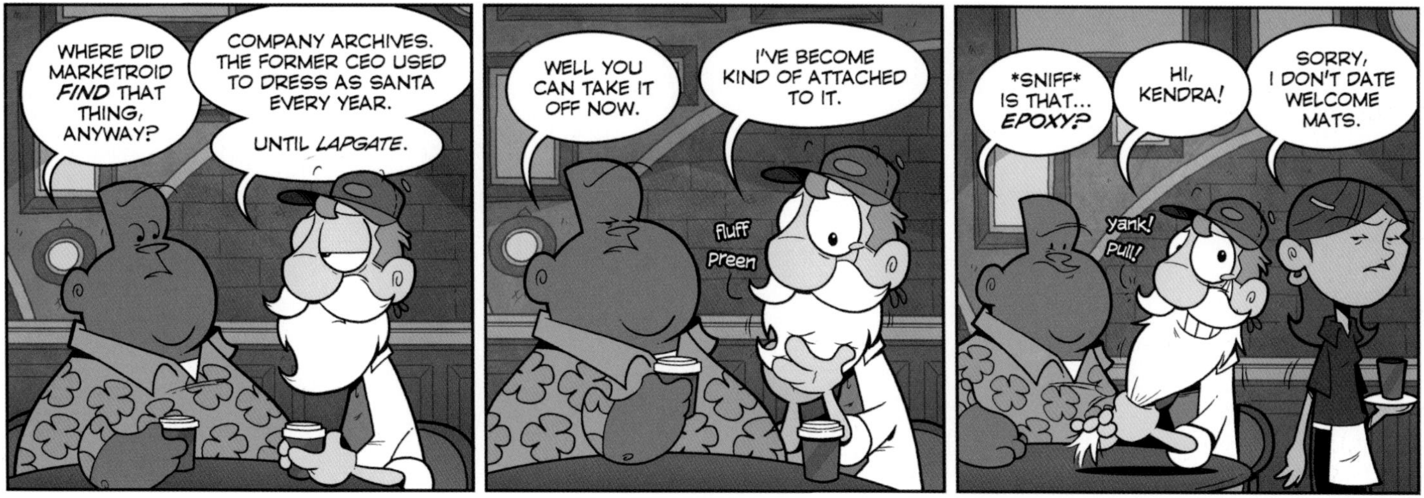
WHERE DID MARKETROID *FIND* THAT THING, ANYWAY?
COMPANY ARCHIVES. THE FORMER CEO USED TO DRESS AS SANTA EVERY YEAR.
UNTIL *LAPGATE*.
WELL YOU CAN TAKE IT OFF NOW.
I'VE BECOME KIND OF ATTACHED TO IT.
fluff
preen
SNIFF IS THAT... *EPOXY?*
HI, KENDRA!
SORRY, I DON'T DATE WELCOME MATS.
yank!
pull!

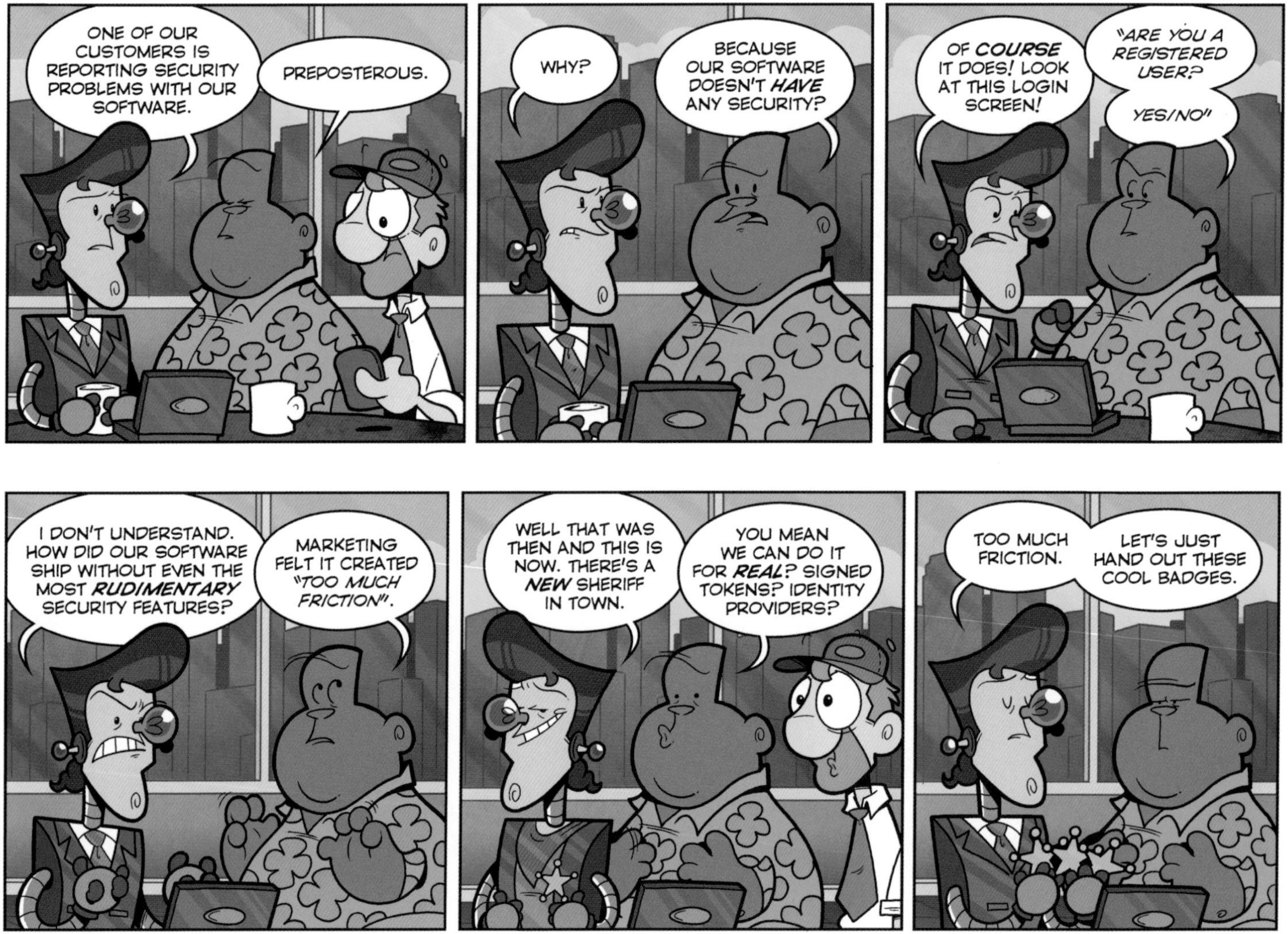
ONE OF OUR CUSTOMERS IS REPORTING SECURITY PROBLEMS WITH OUR SOFTWARE.
PREPOSTEROUS.
WHY?
BECAUSE OUR SOFTWARE DOESN'T *HAVE* ANY SECURITY?
OF *COURSE* IT DOES! LOOK AT THIS LOGIN SCREEN!
"ARE YOU A REGISTERED USER?
YES/NO"
I DON'T UNDERSTAND. HOW DID OUR SOFTWARE SHIP WITHOUT EVEN THE MOST *RUDIMENTARY* SECURITY FEATURES?
MARKETING FELT IT CREATED "TOO MUCH FRICTION".
WELL THAT WAS THEN AND THIS IS NOW. THERE'S A *NEW* SHERIFF IN TOWN.
YOU MEAN WE CAN DO IT FOR *REAL*? SIGNED TOKENS? IDENTITY PROVIDERS?
TOO MUCH FRICTION.
LET'S JUST HAND OUT THESE COOL BADGES.

RUNTIME ERROR

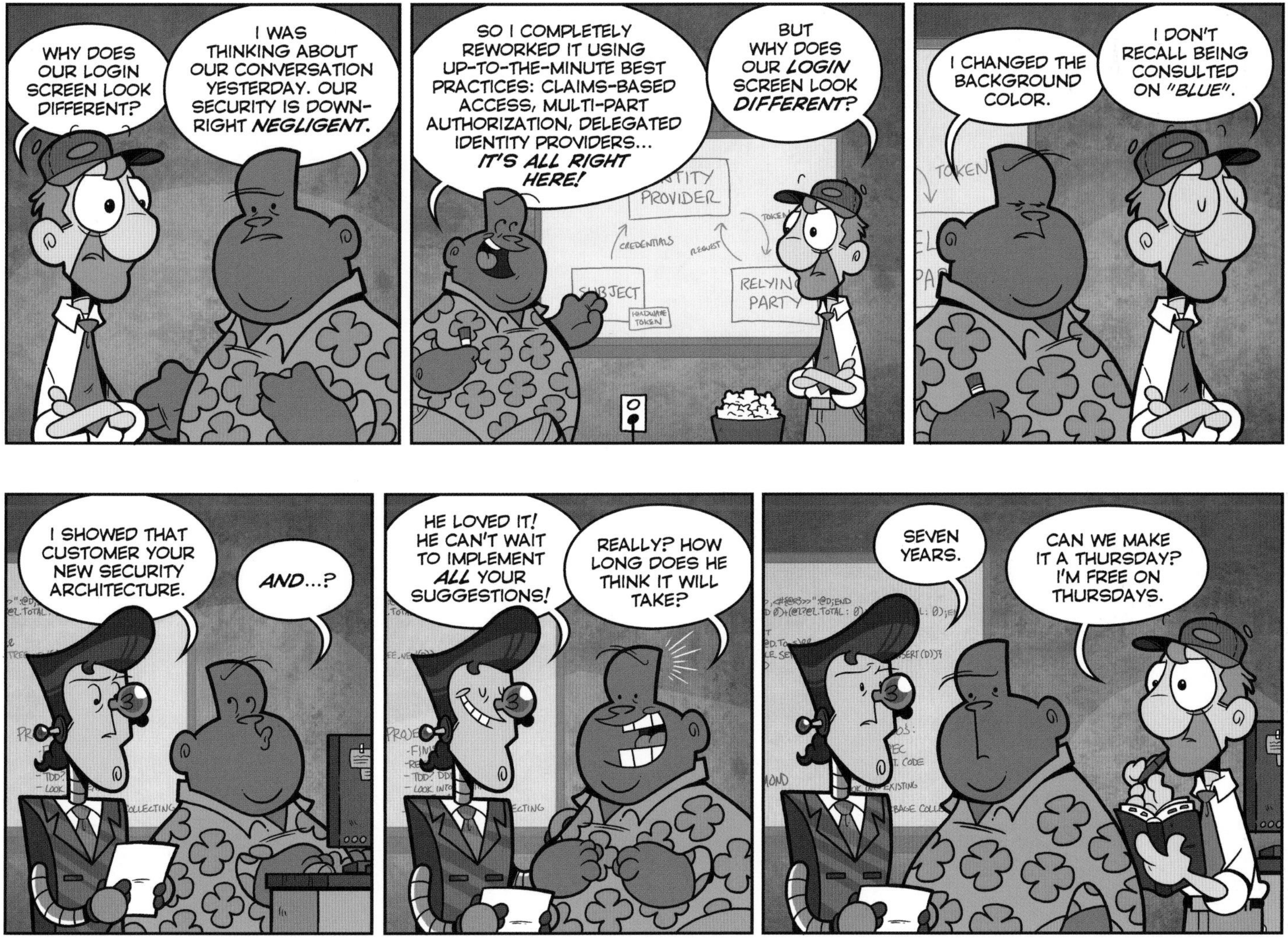
WHY DOES OUR LOGIN SCREEN LOOK DIFFERENT?
I WAS THINKING ABOUT OUR CONVERSATION YESTERDAY. OUR SECURITY IS DOWN-RIGHT *NEGLIGENT*.
SO I COMPLETELY REWORKED IT USING UP-TO-THE-MINUTE BEST PRACTICES: CLAIMS-BASED ACCESS, MULTI-PART AUTHORIZATION, DELEGATED IDENTITY PROVIDERS... *IT'S ALL RIGHT HERE!*
BUT WHY DOES OUR *LOGIN* SCREEN LOOK *DIFFERENT?*
I CHANGED THE BACKGROUND COLOR.
I DON'T RECALL BEING CONSULTED ON *"BLUE"*.
I SHOWED THAT CUSTOMER YOUR NEW SECURITY ARCHITECTURE.
AND...?
HE LOVED IT! HE CAN'T WAIT TO IMPLEMENT *ALL* YOUR SUGGESTIONS!
REALLY? HOW LONG DOES HE THINK IT WILL TAKE?
SEVEN YEARS.
CAN WE MAKE IT A THURSDAY? I'M FREE ON THURSDAYS.

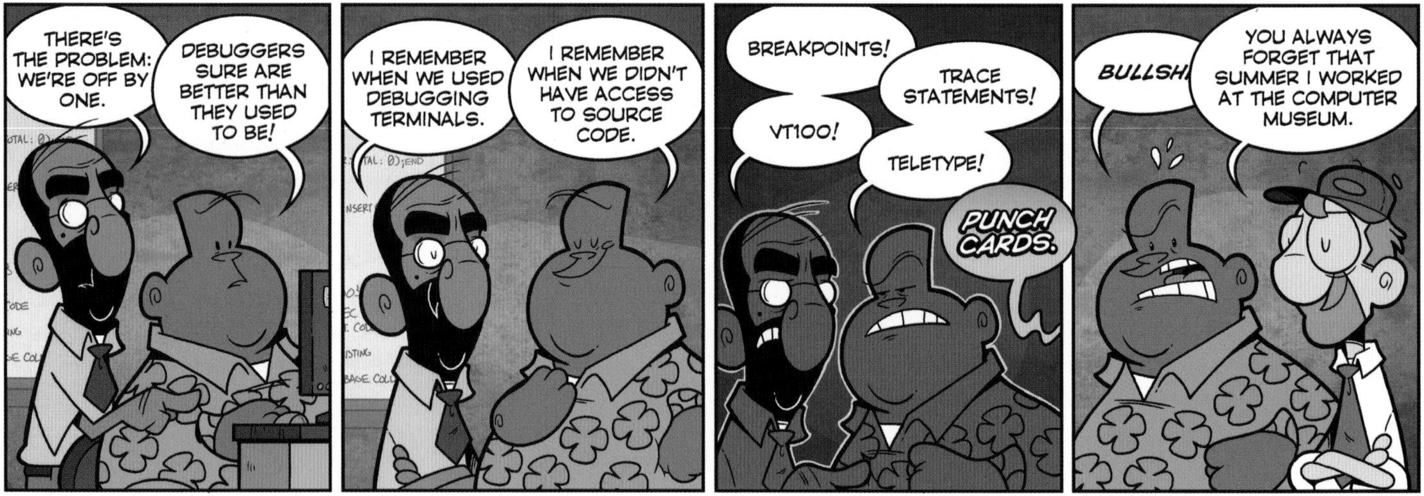
THERE'S THE PROBLEM: WE'RE OFF BY ONE.
DEBUGGERS SURE ARE BETTER THAN THEY USED TO BE!
I REMEMBER WHEN WE USED DEBUGGING TERMINALS.
I REMEMBER WHEN WE DIDN'T HAVE ACCESS TO SOURCE CODE.
BREAKPOINTS!
TRACE STATEMENTS!
VT100!
TELETYPE!
PUNCH CARDS.
BULLSH!
YOU ALWAYS FORGET THAT SUMMER I WORKED AT THE COMPUTER MUSEUM.

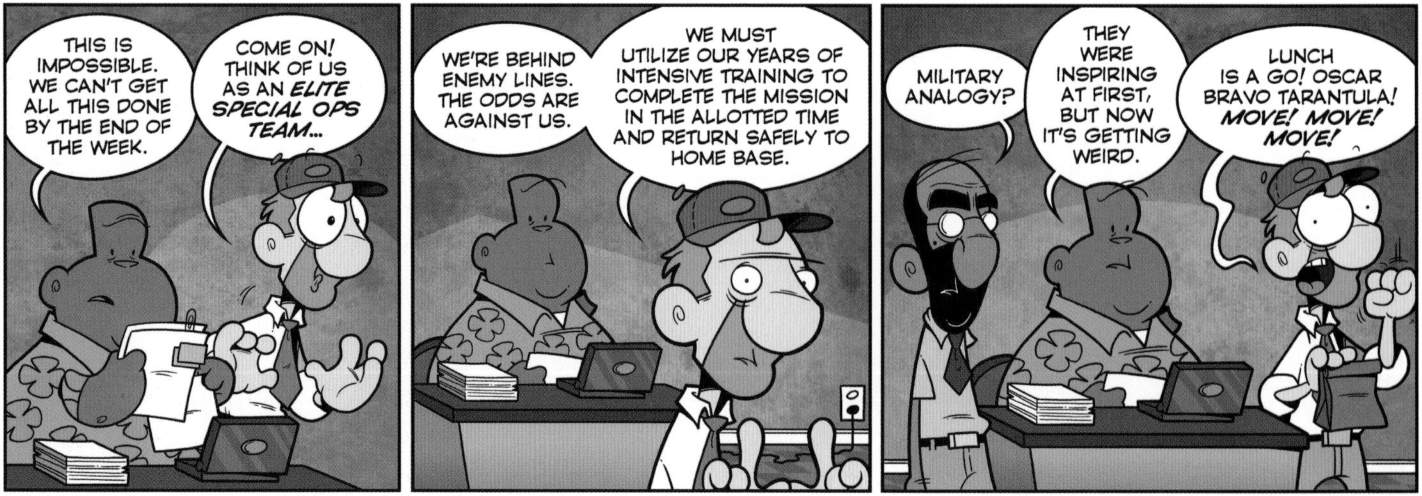
THIS IS IMPOSSIBLE. WE CAN'T GET ALL THIS DONE BY THE END OF THE WEEK.
COME ON! THINK OF US AS AN *ELITE SPECIAL OPS TEAM*...
WE'RE BEHIND ENEMY LINES. THE ODDS ARE AGAINST US.
WE MUST UTILIZE OUR YEARS OF INTENSIVE TRAINING TO COMPLETE THE MISSION IN THE ALLOTTED TIME AND RETURN SAFELY TO HOME BASE.
MILITARY ANALOGY?
THEY WERE INSPIRING AT FIRST, BUT NOW IT'S GETTING WEIRD.
LUNCH IS A *GO!* OSCAR BRAVO TARANTULA! ***MOVE! MOVE! MOVE!***

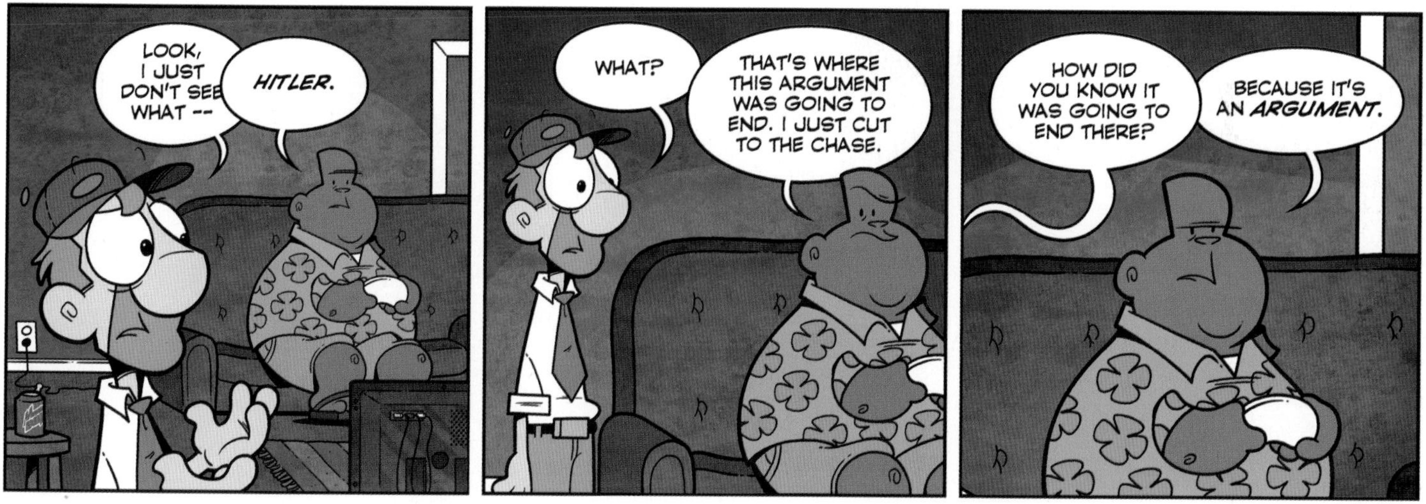
LOOK, I JUST DON'T SEE WHAT --
HITLER.
WHAT?
THAT'S WHERE THIS ARGUMENT WAS GOING TO END. I JUST CUT TO THE CHASE.
HOW DID YOU KNOW IT WAS GOING TO END THERE?
BECAUSE IT'S AN ARGUMENT.

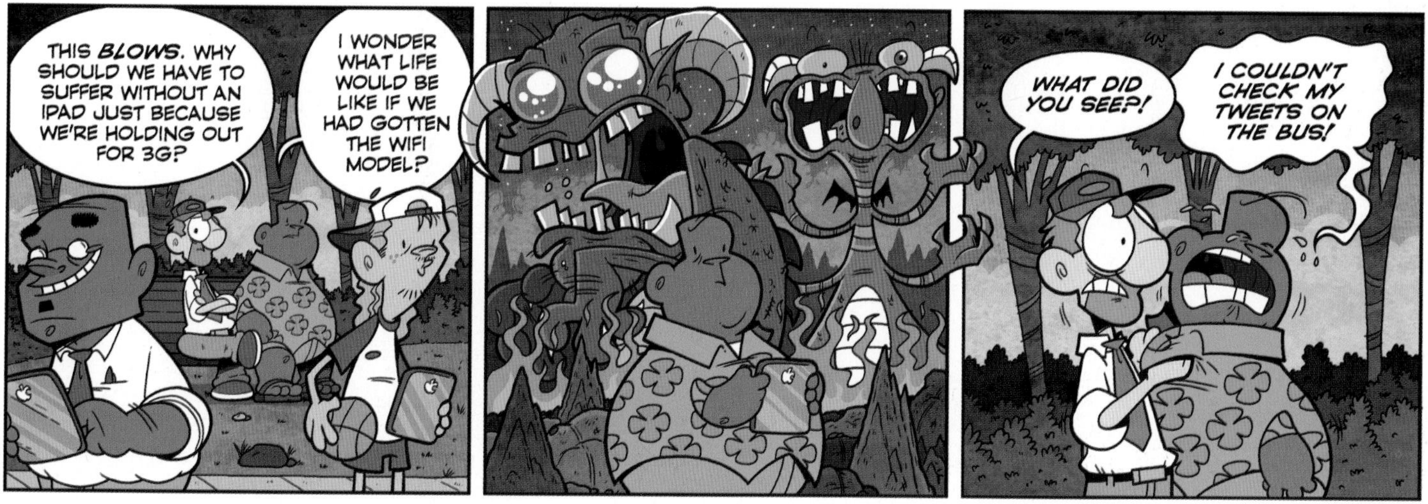
THIS BLOWS. WHY SHOULD WE HAVE TO SUFFER WITHOUT AN IPAD JUST BECAUSE WE'RE HOLDING OUT FOR 3G?
I WONDER WHAT LIFE WOULD BE LIKE IF WE HAD GOTTEN THE WIFI MODEL?
WHAT DID YOU SEE?!
I COULDN'T CHECK MY TWEETS ON THE BUS!

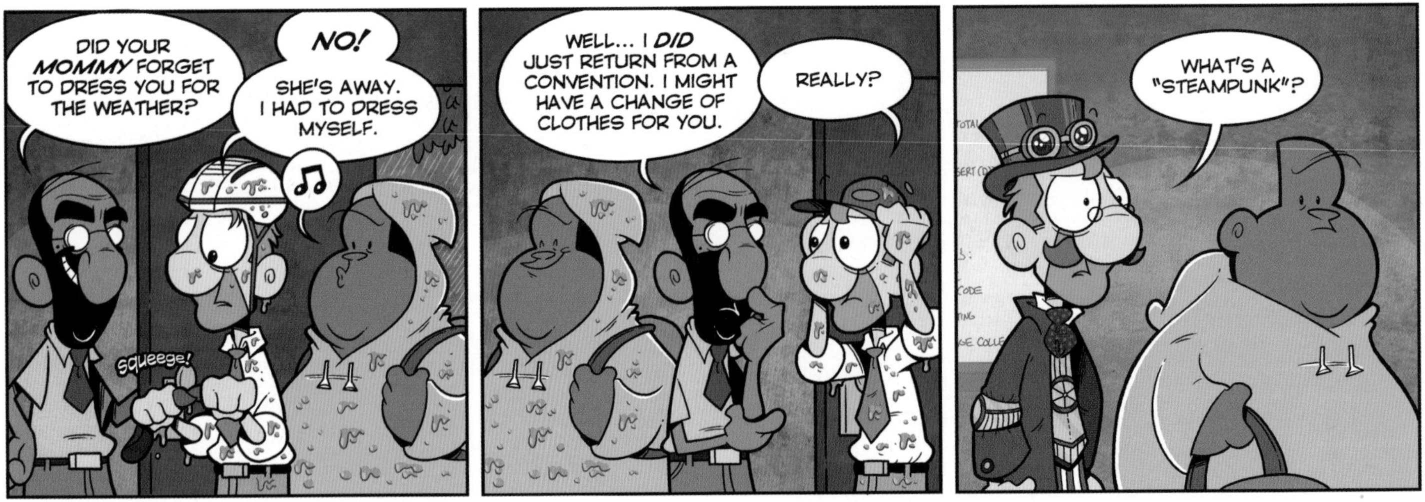
DID YOUR MOMMY FORGET TO DRESS YOU FOR THE WEATHER?
NO!
SHE'S AWAY. I HAD TO DRESS MYSELF.
squeege!
WELL... I DID JUST RETURN FROM A CONVENTION. I MIGHT HAVE A CHANGE OF CLOTHES FOR YOU.
REALLY?
WHAT'S A "STEAMPUNK"?

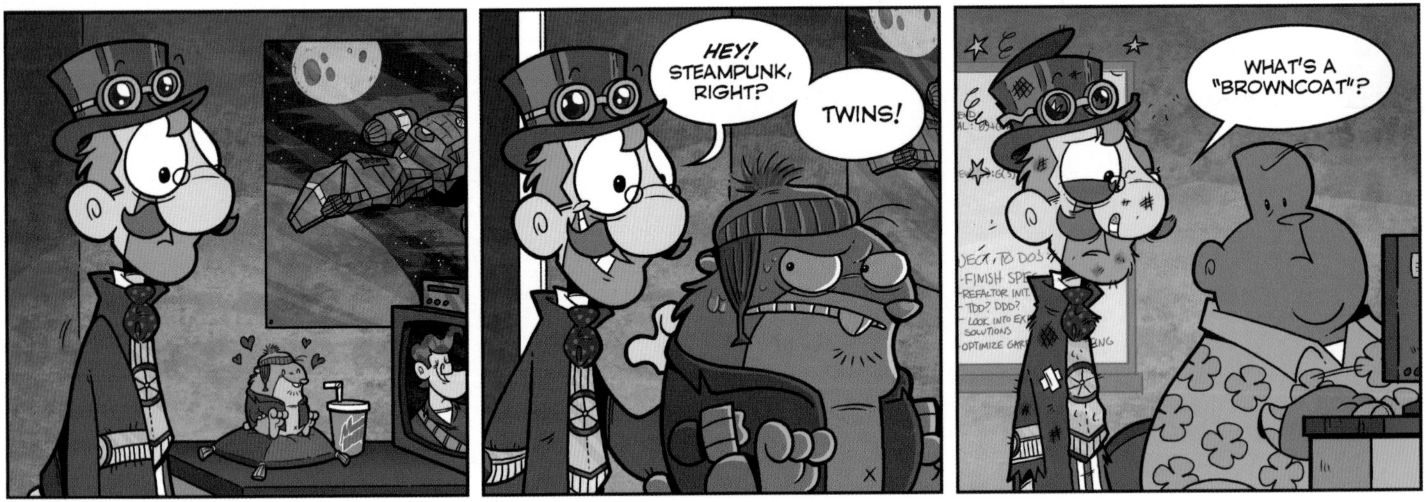
HEY! STEAMPUNK, RIGHT?
TWINS!
WHAT'S A "BROWNCOAT"?

RUNTIME ERROR

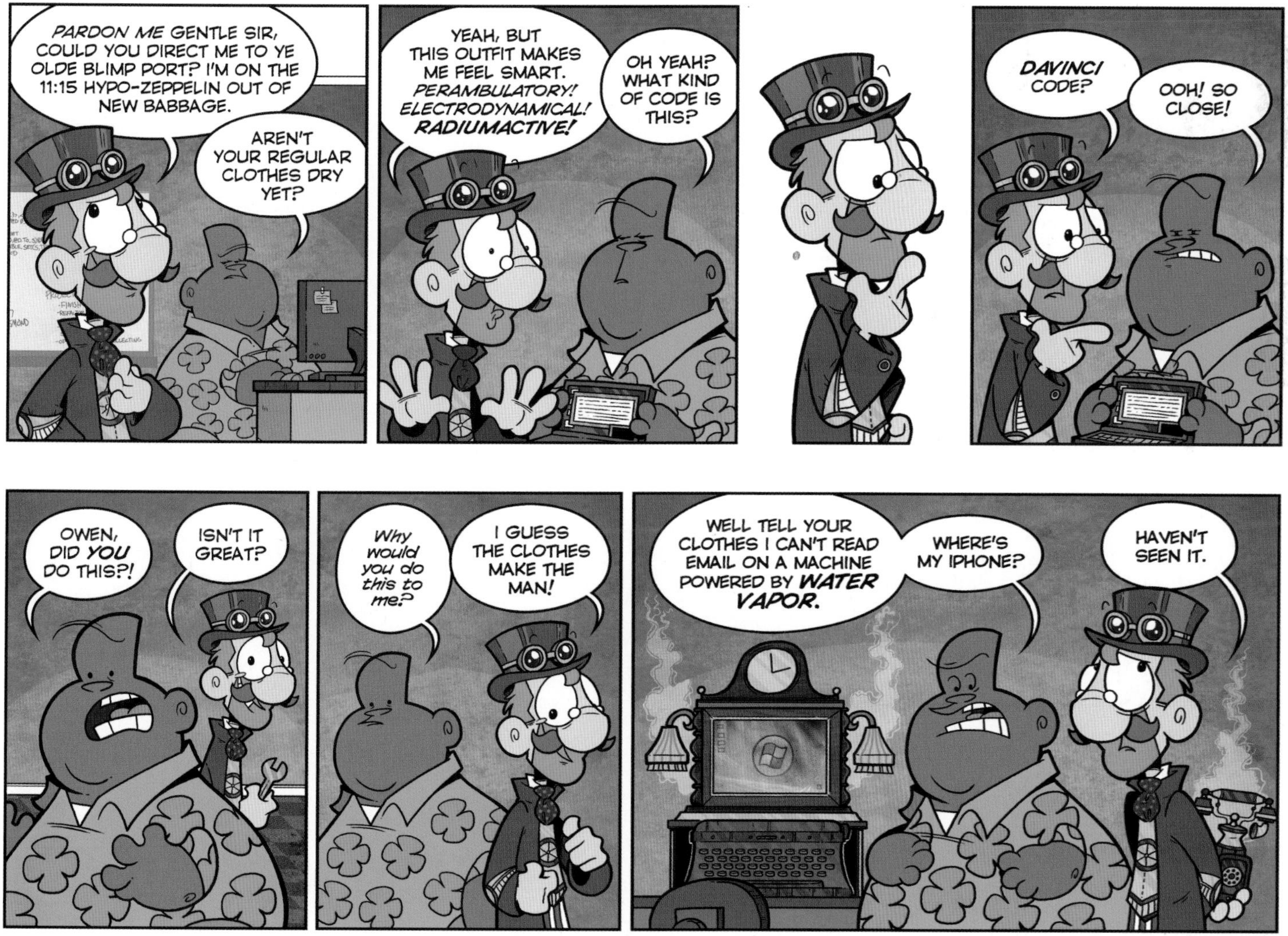
PARDON ME GENTLE SIR, COULD YOU DIRECT ME TO YE OLDE BLIMP PORT? I'M ON THE 11:15 HYPO-ZEPPELIN OUT OF NEW BABBAGE.
AREN'T YOUR REGULAR CLOTHES DRY YET?
YEAH, BUT THIS OUTFIT MAKES ME FEEL SMART. PERAMBULATORY! ELECTRODYNAMICAL! RADIUMACTIVE!
OH YEAH? WHAT KIND OF CODE IS THIS?
DAVINCI CODE?
OOH! SO CLOSE!
OWEN, DID YOU DO THIS?!
ISN'T IT GREAT?
Why would you do this to me?
I GUESS THE CLOTHES MAKE THE MAN!
WELL TELL YOUR CLOTHES I CAN'T READ EMAIL ON A MACHINE POWERED BY WATER VAPOR.
WHERE'S MY IPHONE?
HAVEN'T SEEN IT.

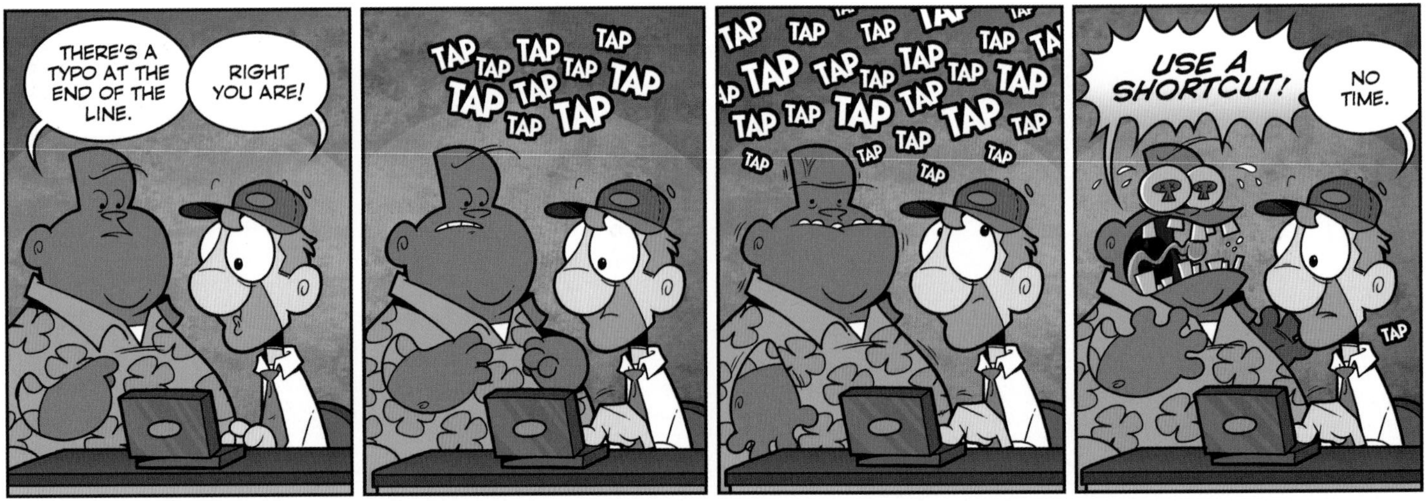
THERE'S A TYPO AT THE END OF THE LINE.
RIGHT YOU ARE!
TAP TAP TAP TAP TAP TAP TAP TAP TAP TAP TAP
TAP TAP TAP TAP TAP TAP TAP TAP TAP TAP TAP TAP TAP TAP TAP TAP TAP TAP TAP TAP TAP TAP TAP TAP TAP
USE A SHORTCUT!
NO TIME.
TAP

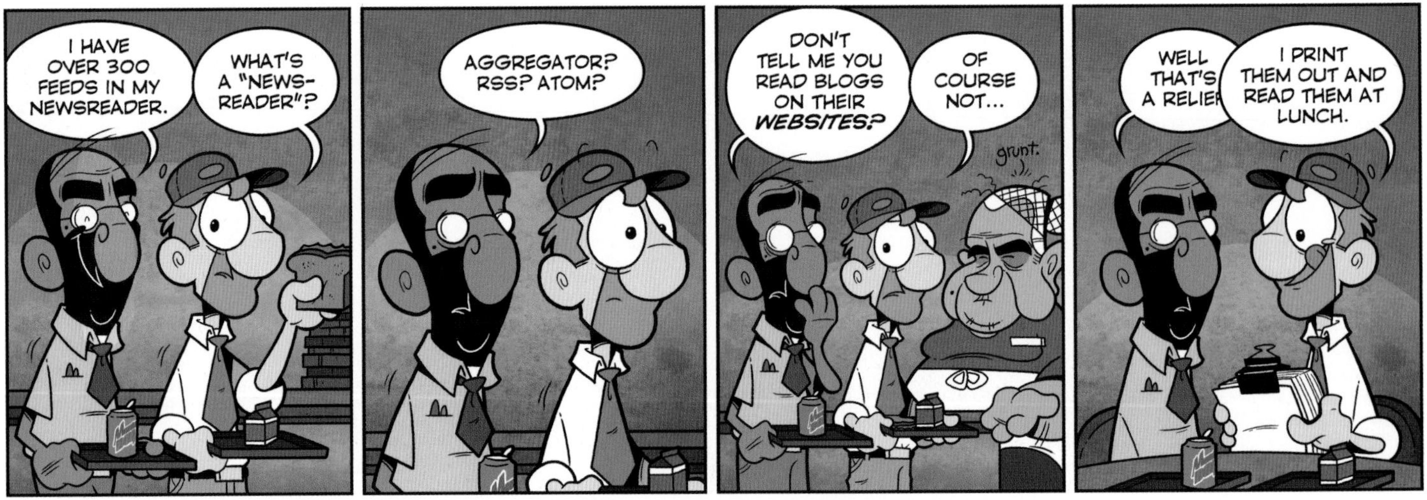
I HAVE OVER 300 FEEDS IN MY NEWSREADER.
WHAT'S A "NEWS-READER"?
AGGREGATOR? RSS? ATOM?
DON'T TELL ME YOU READ BLOGS ON THEIR *WEBSITES?*
OF COURSE NOT...
grunt.
WELL THAT'S A RELIE
I PRINT THEM OUT AND READ THEM AT LUNCH.

RUNTIME ERROR

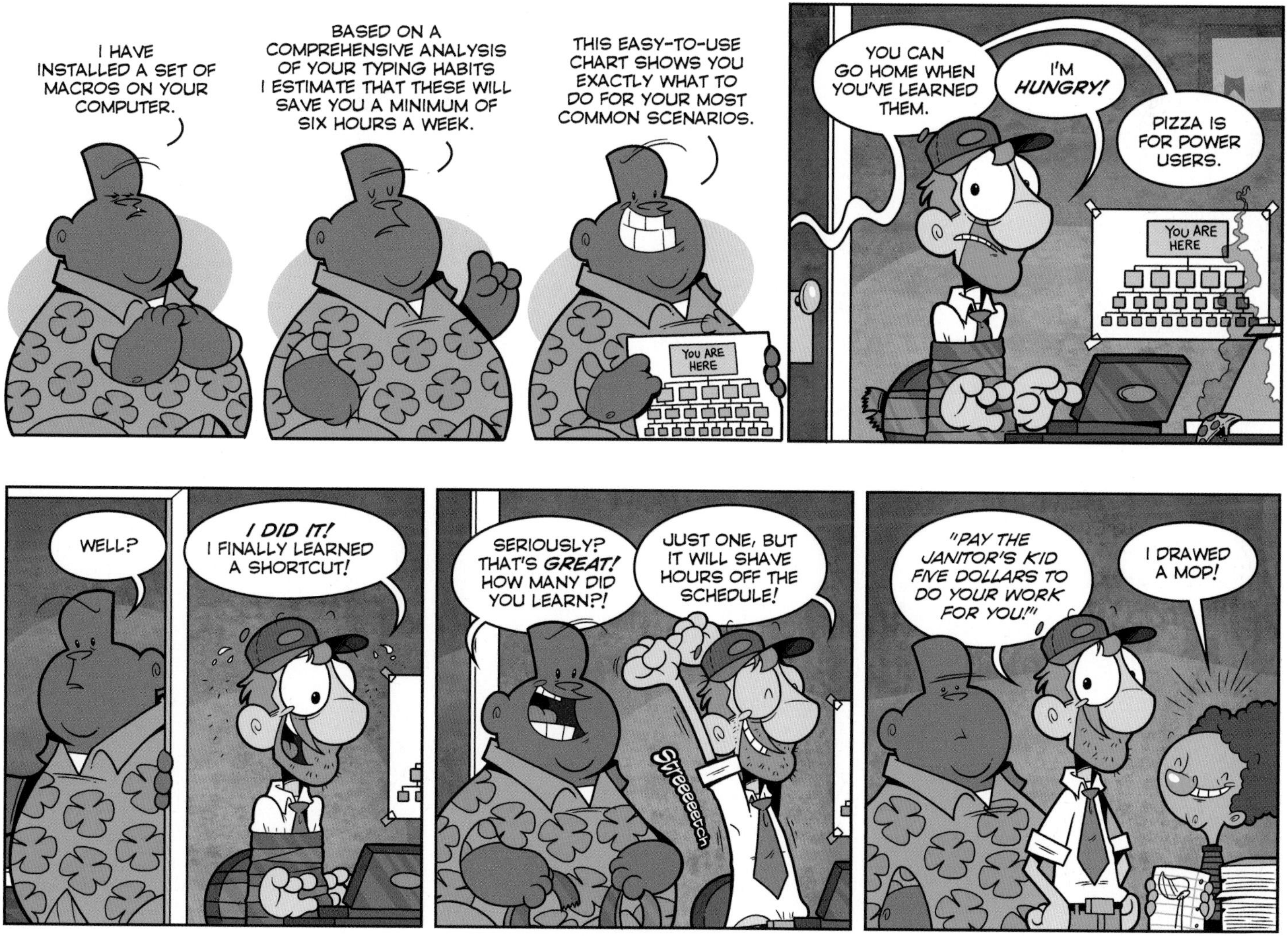
I HAVE INSTALLED A SET OF MACROS ON YOUR COMPUTER.
BASED ON A COMPREHENSIVE ANALYSIS OF YOUR TYPING HABITS I ESTIMATE THAT THESE WILL SAVE YOU A MINIMUM OF SIX HOURS A WEEK.
THIS EASY-TO-USE CHART SHOWS YOU EXACTLY WHAT TO DO FOR YOUR MOST COMMON SCENARIOS.
YOU ARE HERE
YOU CAN GO HOME WHEN YOU'VE LEARNED THEM.
I'M *HUNGRY!*
PIZZA IS FOR POWER USERS.
YOU ARE HERE
WELL?
I DID IT! I FINALLY LEARNED A SHORTCUT!
SERIOUSLY? THAT'S *GREAT!* HOW MANY DID YOU LEARN?!
JUST ONE, BUT IT WILL SHAVE HOURS OFF THE SCHEDULE!
Streeeeetch
"PAY THE JANITOR'S KID FIVE DOLLARS TO DO YOUR WORK FOR YOU!"
I DRAWED A MOP!

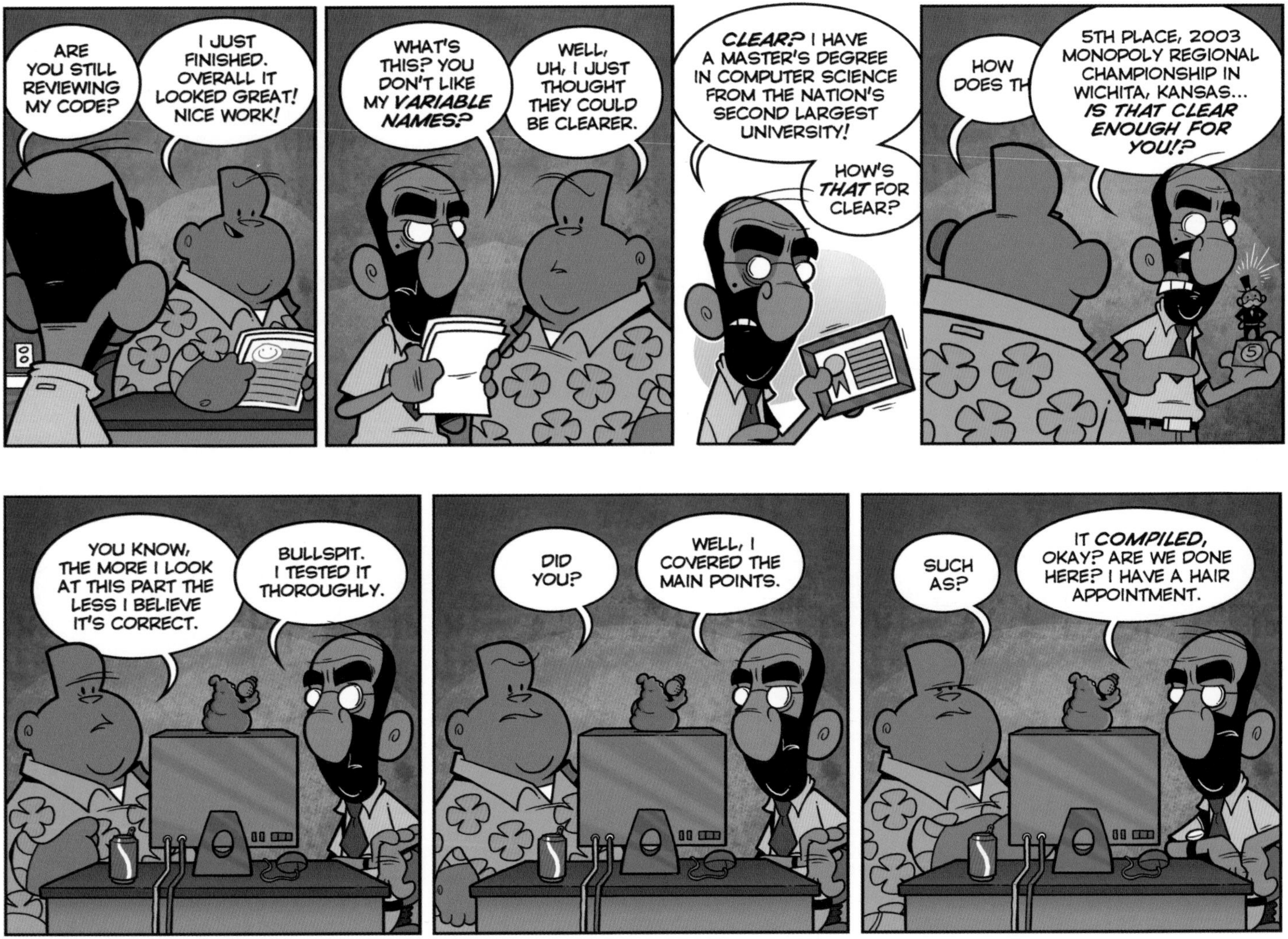
ARE YOU STILL REVIEWING MY CODE?
I JUST FINISHED. OVERALL IT LOOKED GREAT! NICE WORK!
WHAT'S THIS? YOU DON'T LIKE MY VARIABLE NAMES?
WELL, UH, I JUST THOUGHT THEY COULD BE CLEARER.
CLEAR? I HAVE A MASTER'S DEGREE IN COMPUTER SCIENCE FROM THE NATION'S SECOND LARGEST UNIVERSITY!
HOW'S THAT FOR CLEAR?
HOW DOES TH
5TH PLACE, 2003 MONOPOLY REGIONAL CHAMPIONSHIP IN WICHITA, KANSAS... IS THAT CLEAR ENOUGH FOR YOU!?
YOU KNOW, THE MORE I LOOK AT THIS PART THE LESS I BELIEVE IT'S CORRECT.
BULLSPIT. I TESTED IT THOROUGHLY.
DID YOU?
WELL, I COVERED THE MAIN POINTS.
SUCH AS?
IT COMPILED, OKAY? ARE WE DONE HERE? I HAVE A HAIR APPOINTMENT.

RUNTIME ERROR

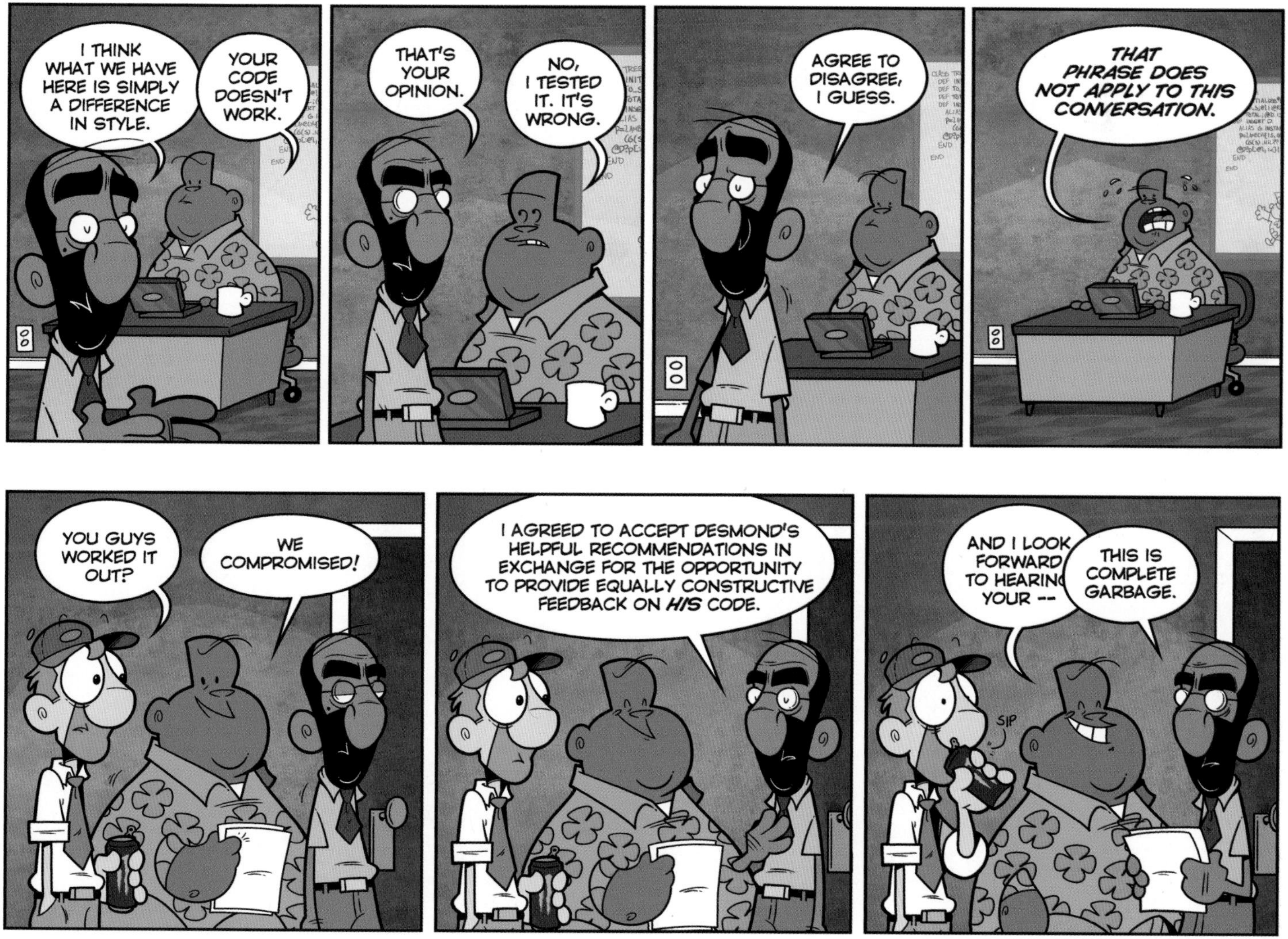
I THINK WHAT WE HAVE HERE IS SIMPLY A DIFFERENCE IN STYLE.
YOUR CODE DOESN'T WORK.
THAT'S YOUR OPINION.
NO, I TESTED IT. IT'S WRONG.
AGREE TO DISAGREE, I GUESS.
THAT *PHRASE DOES NOT APPLY TO THIS CONVERSATION.*
YOU GUYS WORKED IT OUT?
WE COMPROMISED!
I AGREED TO ACCEPT DESMOND'S HELPFUL RECOMMENDATIONS IN EXCHANGE FOR THE OPPORTUNITY TO PROVIDE EQUALLY CONSTRUCTIVE FEEDBACK ON *HIS* CODE.
AND I LOOK FORWARD TO HEARIN YOUR --
THIS IS COMPLETE GARBAGE.
SIP

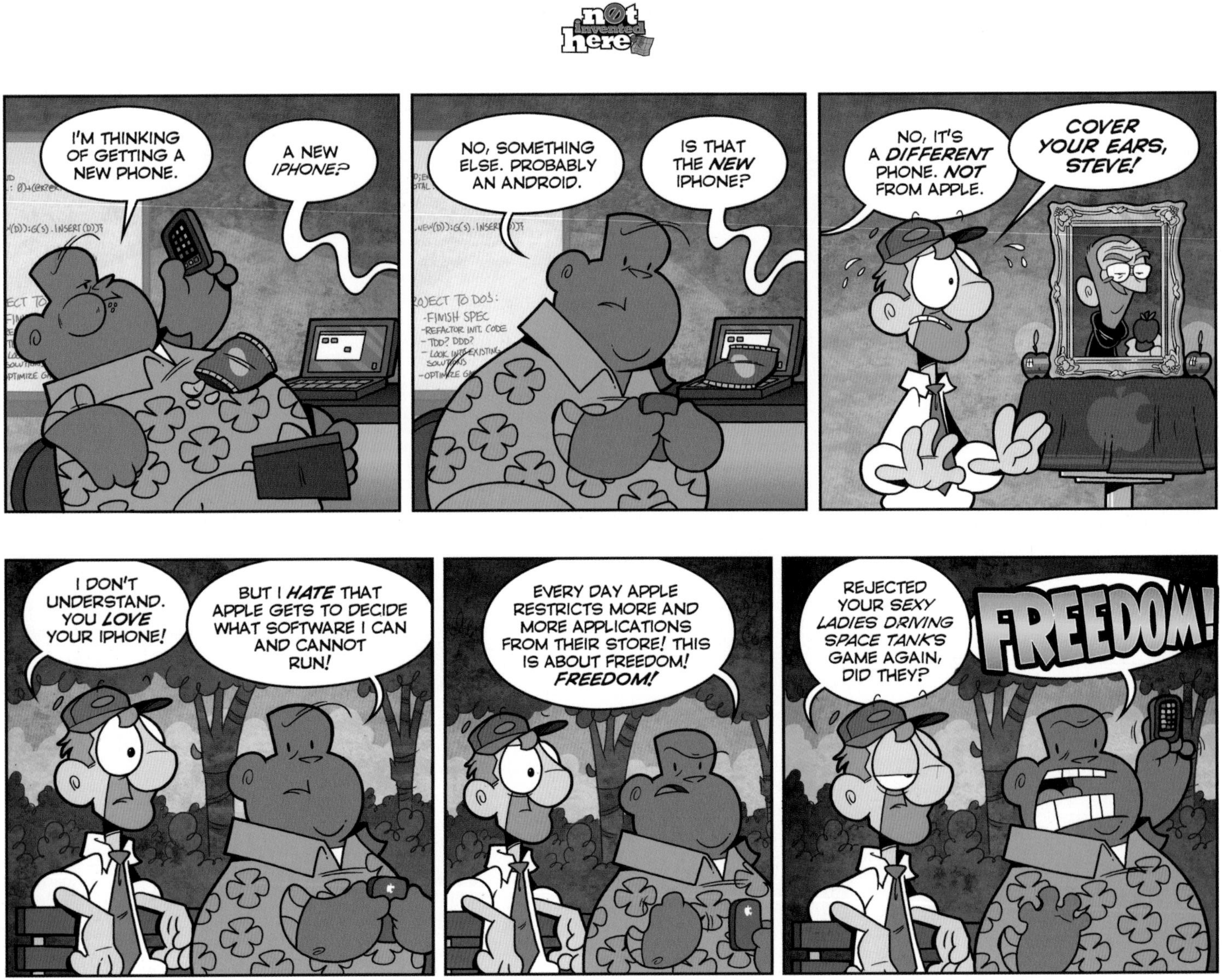
I'M THINKING OF GETTING A NEW PHONE.
A NEW *IPHONE?*
NO, SOMETHING ELSE. PROBABLY AN ANDROID.
IS THAT THE *NEW* IPHONE?
PROJECT TO DOS:
-FINISH SPEC
-REFACTOR INIT. CODE
NO, IT'S A *DIFFERENT* PHONE. *NOT* FROM APPLE.
COVER YOUR EARS, STEVE!
I DON'T UNDERSTAND. YOU *LOVE* YOUR IPHONE!
BUT I *HATE* THAT APPLE GETS TO DECIDE WHAT SOFTWARE I CAN AND CANNOT RUN!
EVERY DAY APPLE RESTRICTS MORE AND MORE APPLICATIONS FROM THEIR STORE! THIS IS ABOUT FREEDOM! *FREEDOM!*
REJECTED YOUR *SEXY LADIES DRIVING SPACE TANKS* GAME AGAIN, DID THEY?
FREEDOM!

RUNTIME ERROR

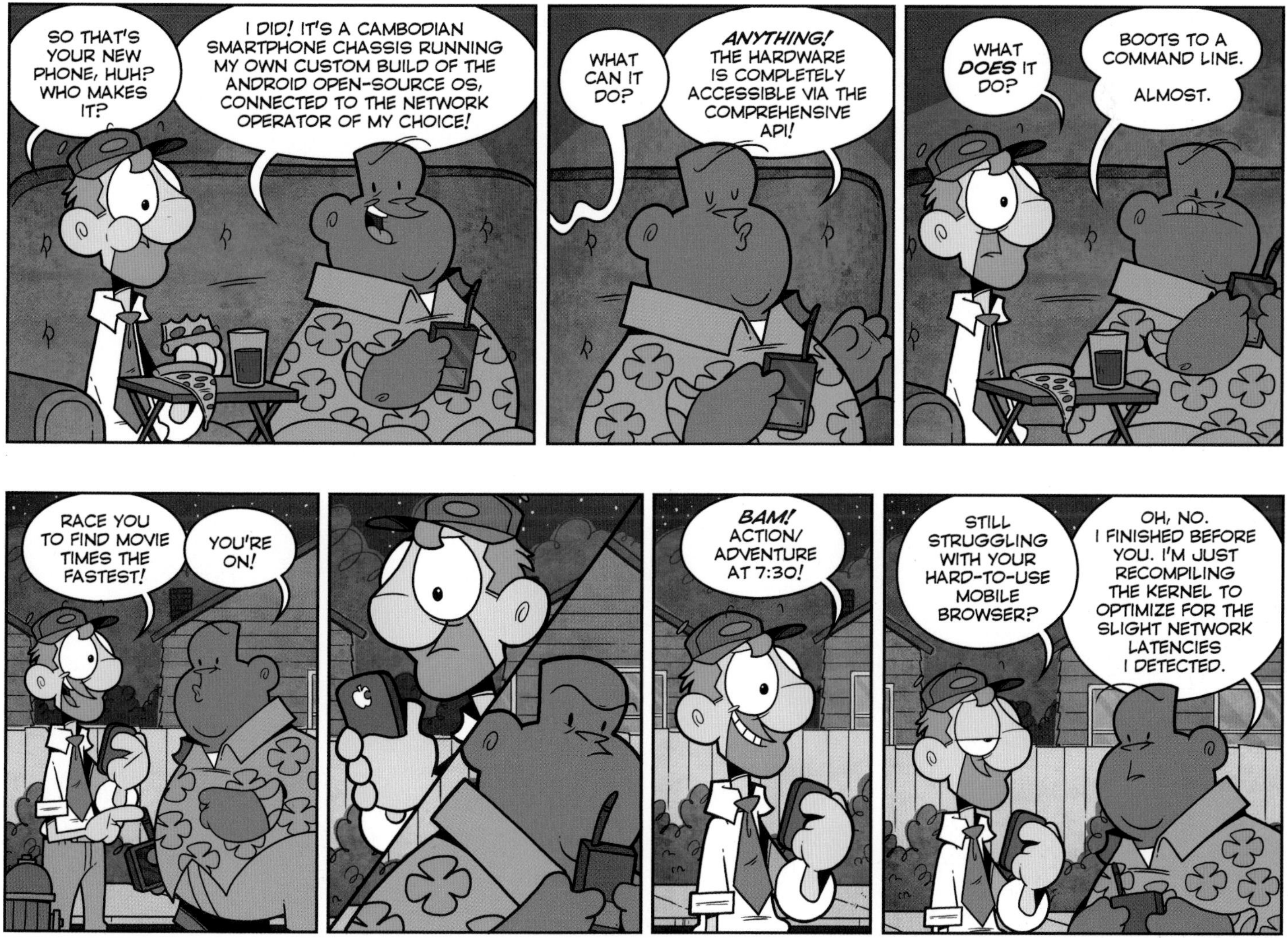
SO THAT'S YOUR NEW PHONE, HUH? WHO MAKES IT?
I DID! IT'S A CAMBODIAN SMARTPHONE CHASSIS RUNNING MY OWN CUSTOM BUILD OF THE ANDROID OPEN-SOURCE OS, CONNECTED TO THE NETWORK OPERATOR OF MY CHOICE!
WHAT CAN IT DO?
ANYTHING! THE HARDWARE IS COMPLETELY ACCESSIBLE VIA THE COMPREHENSIVE API!
WHAT DOES IT DO?
BOOTS TO A COMMAND LINE.
ALMOST.
RACE YOU TO FIND MOVIE TIMES THE FASTEST!
YOU'RE ON!
BAM! ACTION/ ADVENTURE AT 7:30!
STILL STRUGGLING WITH YOUR HARD-TO-USE MOBILE BROWSER?
OH, NO. I FINISHED BEFORE YOU. I'M JUST RECOMPILING THE KERNEL TO OPTIMIZE FOR THE SLIGHT NETWORK LATENCIES I DETECTED.

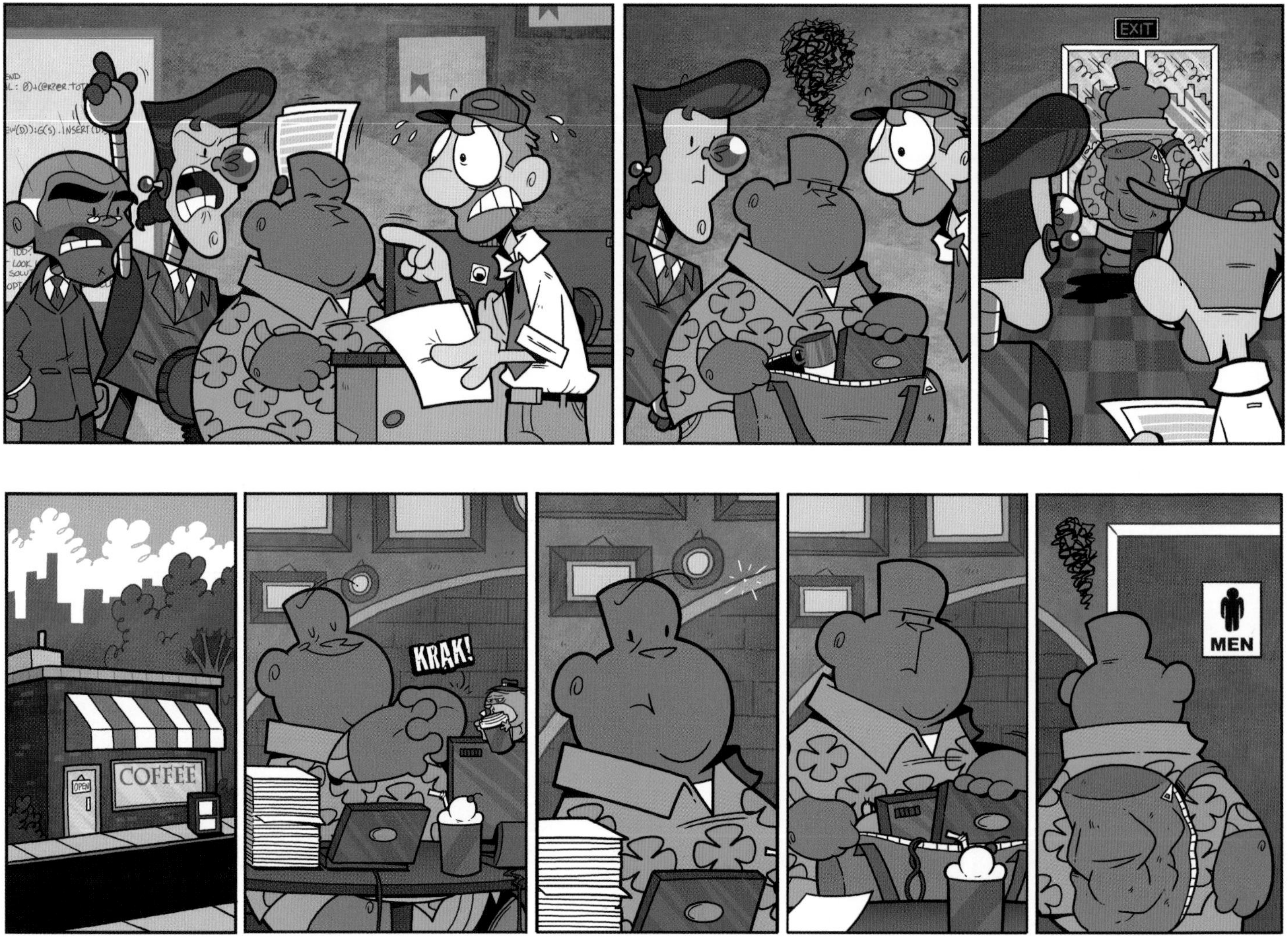
EXIT
OPEN
COFFEE
KRAK!
MEN

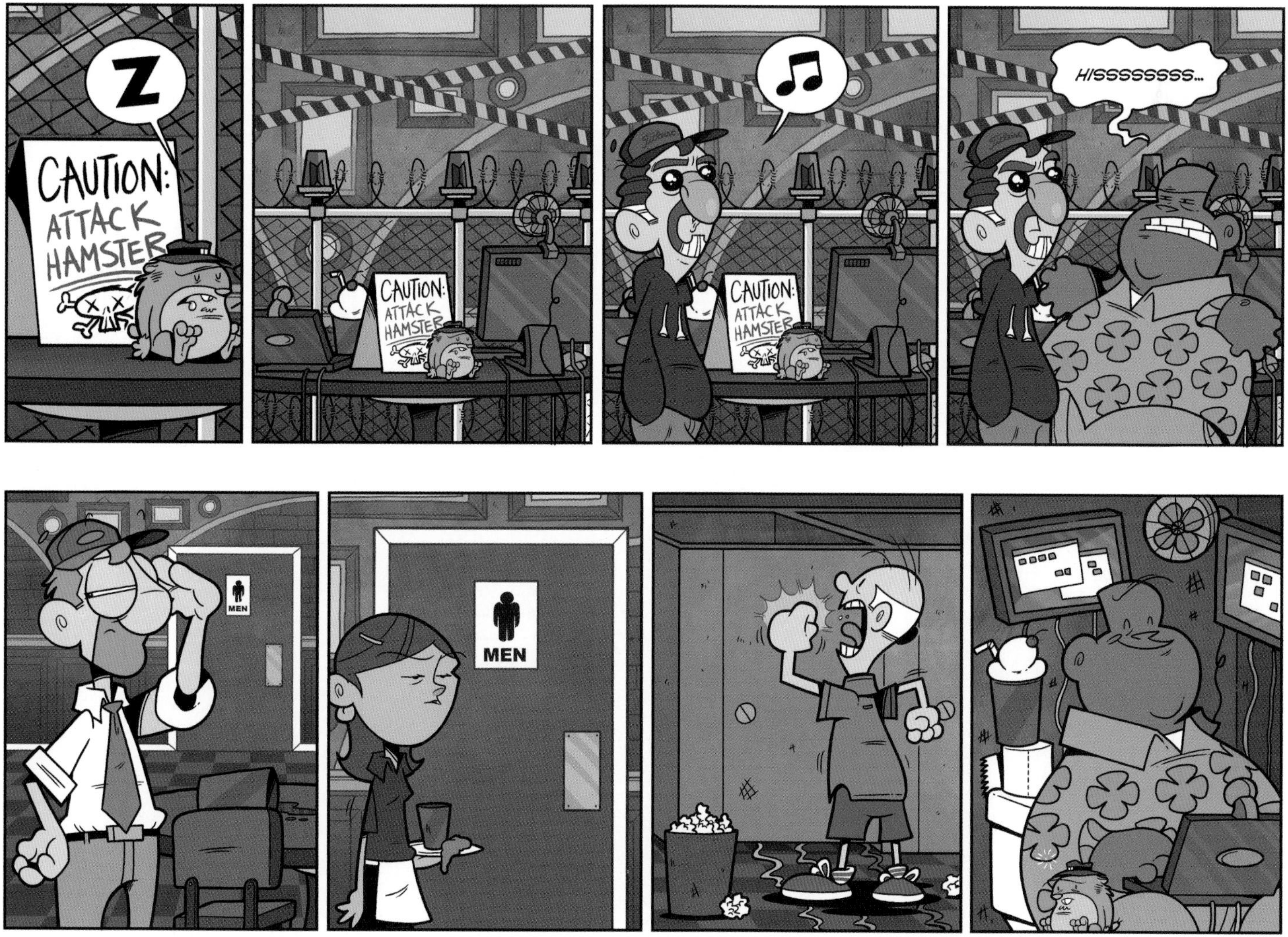
Z
CAUTION: ATTACK HAMSTER
CAUTION: ATTACK HAMSTER
CAUTION: ATTACK HAMSTER
HISSSSSSSS...
MEN
MEN

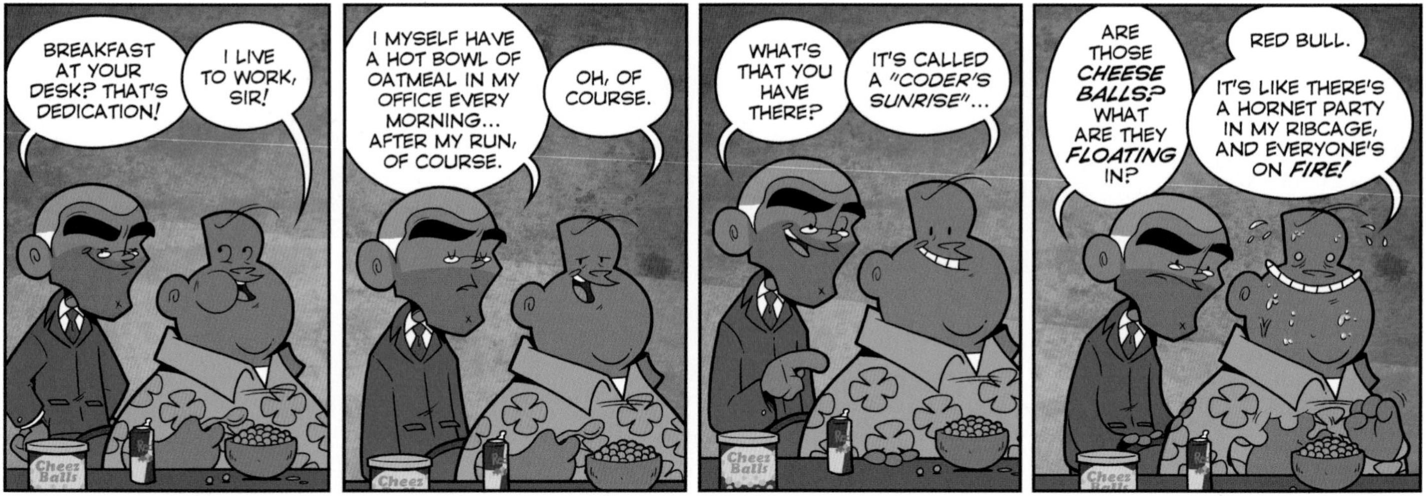
BREAKFAST AT YOUR DESK? THAT'S DEDICATION!
I LIVE TO WORK, SIR!
Cheez Balls
I MYSELF HAVE A HOT BOWL OF OATMEAL IN MY OFFICE EVERY MORNING... AFTER MY RUN, OF COURSE.
OH, OF COURSE.
WHAT'S THAT YOU HAVE THERE?
IT'S CALLED A "CODER'S SUNRISE"...
ARE THOSE CHEESE BALLS? WHAT ARE THEY FLOATING IN?
RED BULL.
IT'S LIKE THERE'S A HORNET PARTY IN MY RIBCAGE, AND EVERYONE'S ON FIRE!

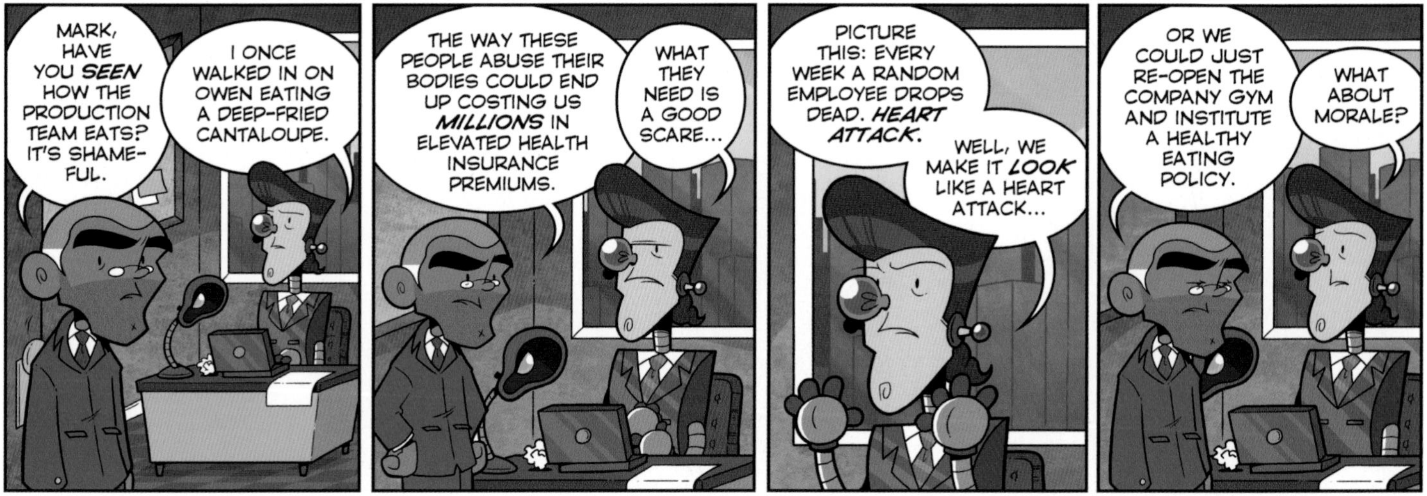
MARK, HAVE YOU SEEN HOW THE PRODUCTION TEAM EATS? IT'S SHAME-FUL.
I ONCE WALKED IN ON OWEN EATING A DEEP-FRIED CANTALOUPE.
THE WAY THESE PEOPLE ABUSE THEIR BODIES COULD END UP COSTING US MILLIONS IN ELEVATED HEALTH INSURANCE PREMIUMS.
WHAT THEY NEED IS A GOOD SCARE...
PICTURE THIS: EVERY WEEK A RANDOM EMPLOYEE DROPS DEAD. HEART ATTACK.
WELL, WE MAKE IT LOOK LIKE A HEART ATTACK...
OR WE COULD JUST RE-OPEN THE COMPANY GYM AND INSTITUTE A HEALTHY EATING POLICY.
WHAT ABOUT MORALE?

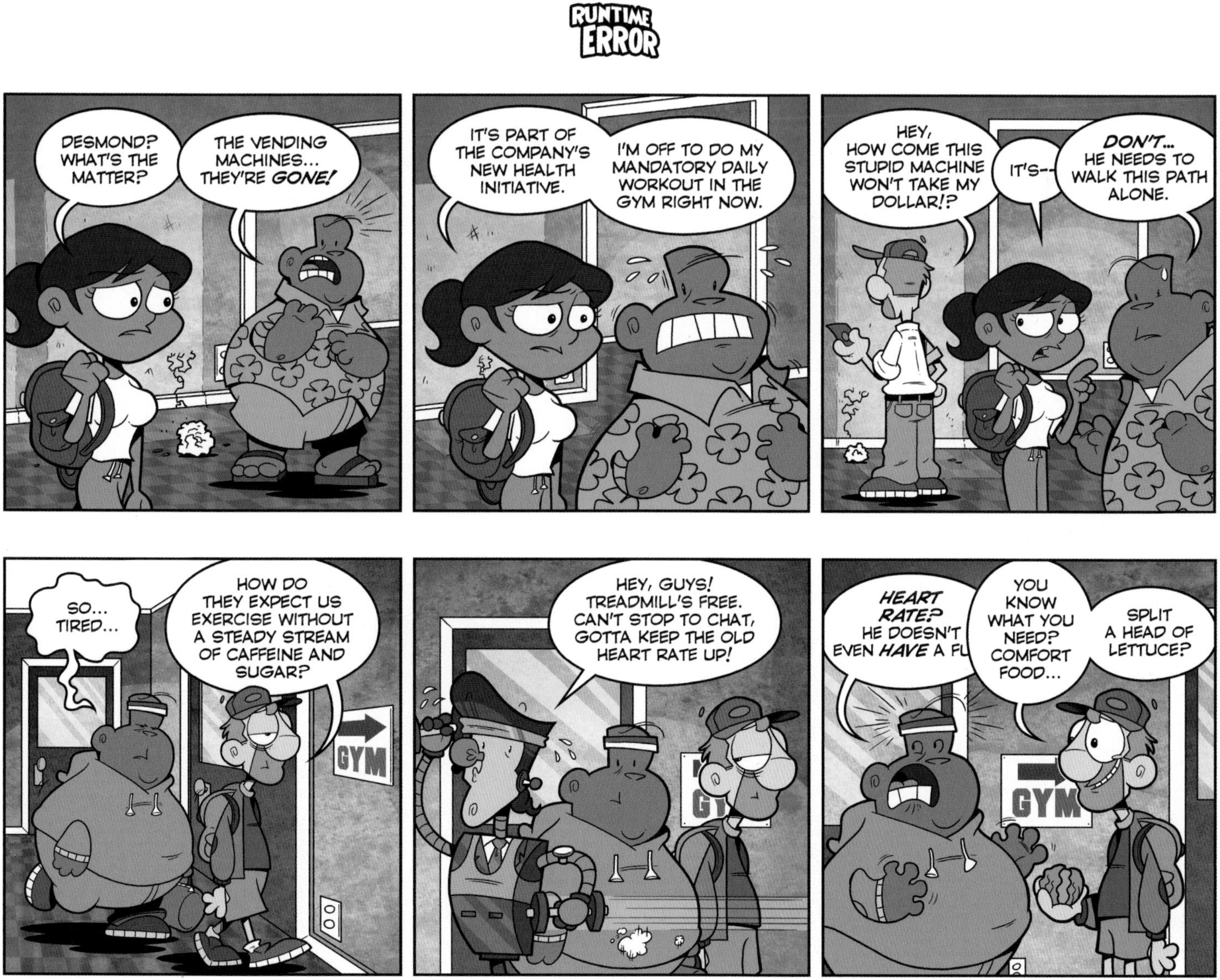
RUNTIME ERROR
DESMOND? WHAT'S THE MATTER?
THE VENDING MACHINES... THEY'RE GONE!
IT'S PART OF THE COMPANY'S NEW HEALTH INITIATIVE.
I'M OFF TO DO MY MANDATORY DAILY WORKOUT IN THE GYM RIGHT NOW.
HEY, HOW COME THIS STUPID MACHINE WON'T TAKE MY DOLLAR!?
IT'S--
DON'T... HE NEEDS TO WALK THIS PATH ALONE.
SO... TIRED...
HOW DO THEY EXPECT US EXERCISE WITHOUT A STEADY STREAM OF CAFFEINE AND SUGAR?
GYM
HEY, GUYS! TREADMILL'S FREE. CAN'T STOP TO CHAT, GOTTA KEEP THE OLD HEART RATE UP!
HEART RATE? HE DOESN'T EVEN HAVE A PU
YOU KNOW WHAT YOU NEED? COMFORT FOOD...
SPLIT A HEAD OF LETTUCE?
GYM

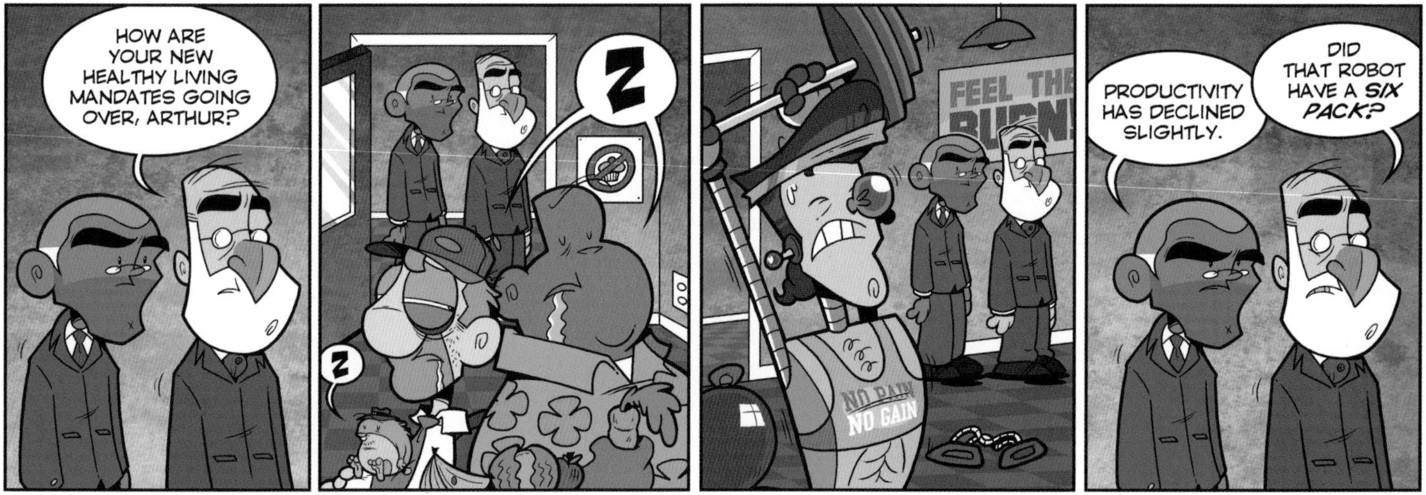
HOW ARE YOUR NEW HEALTHY LIVING MANDATES GOING OVER, ARTHUR?
Z
Z
FEEL THE
NO PAIN
NO GAIN
PRODUCTIVITY HAS DECLINED SLIGHTLY.
DID THAT ROBOT HAVE A *SIX PACK?*

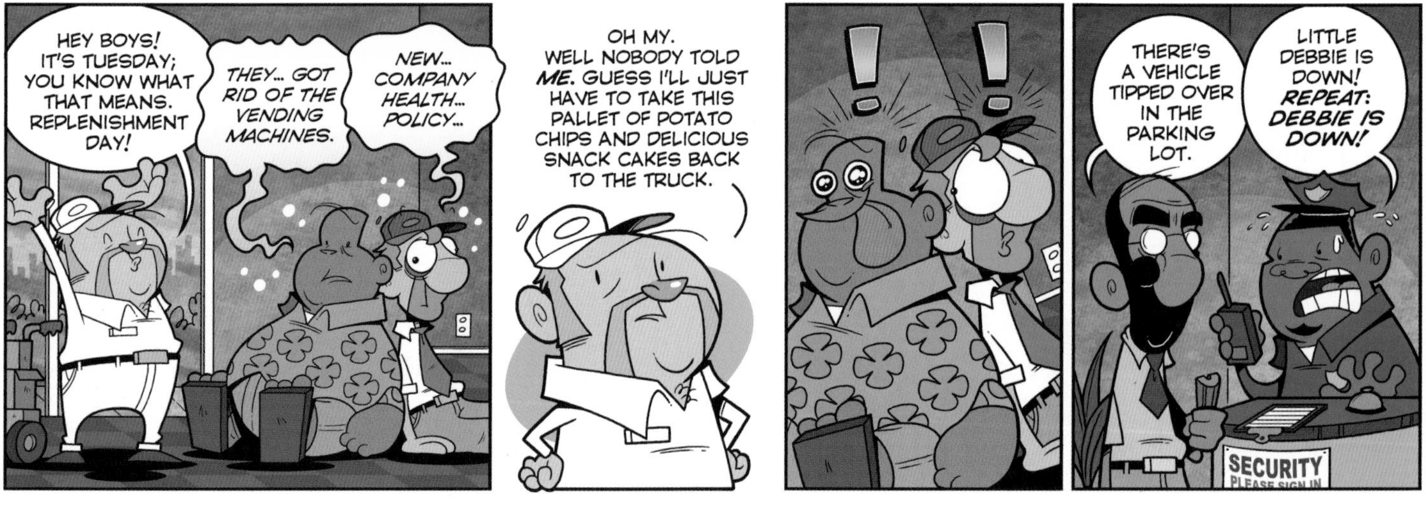
HEY BOYS! IT'S TUESDAY; YOU KNOW WHAT THAT MEANS. REPLENISHMENT DAY!
THEY... GOT RID OF THE VENDING MACHINES.
NEW... COMPANY HEALTH... POLICY...
OH MY. WELL NOBODY TOLD ***ME.*** GUESS I'LL JUST HAVE TO TAKE THIS PALLET OF POTATO CHIPS AND DELICIOUS SNACK CAKES BACK TO THE TRUCK.
!
!
THERE'S A VEHICLE TIPPED OVER IN THE PARKING LOT.
LITTLE DEBBIE IS DOWN! ***REPEAT: DEBBIE IS DOWN!***
SECURITY

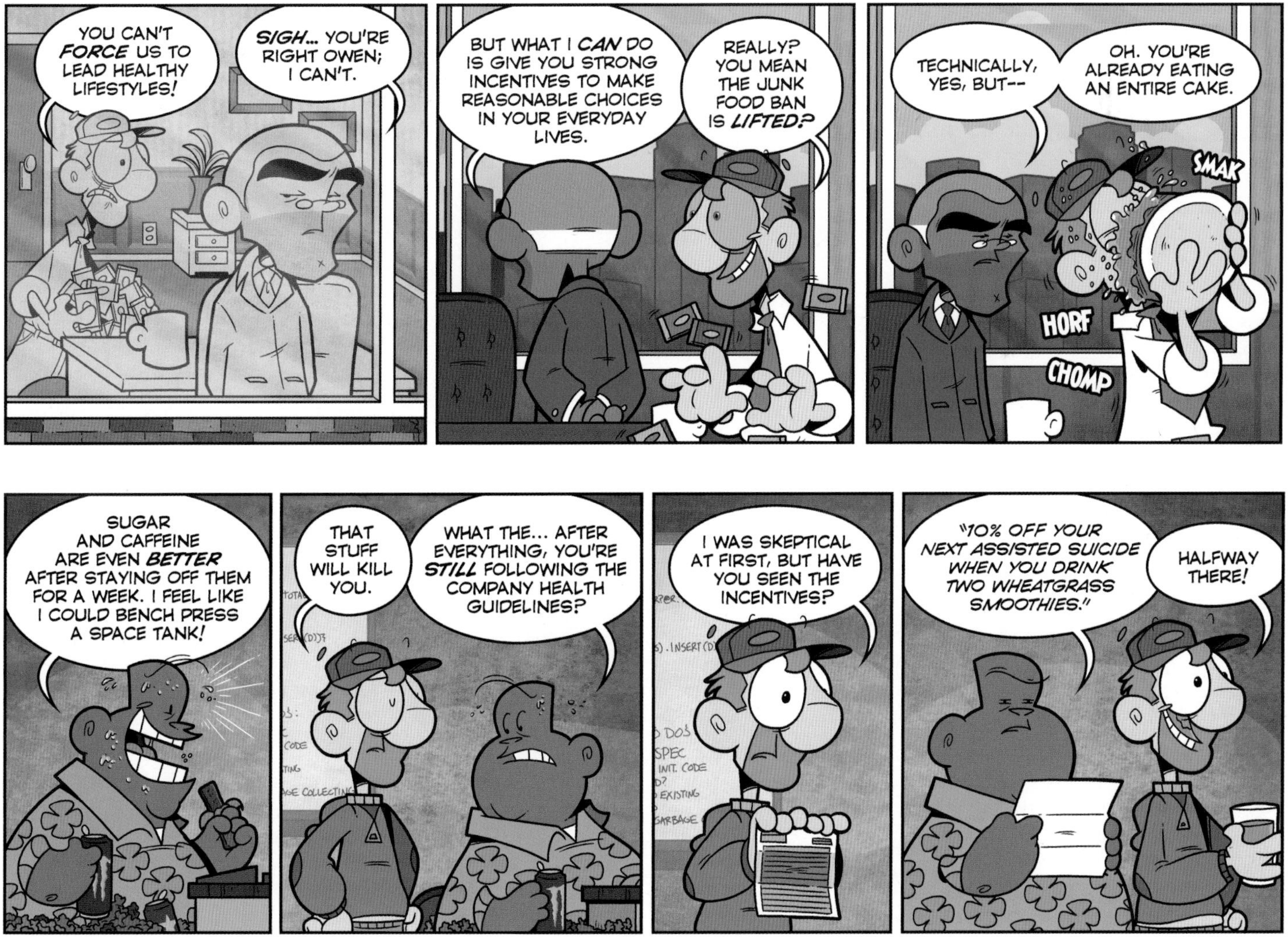
YOU CAN'T *FORCE* US TO LEAD HEALTHY LIFESTYLES!
SIGH... YOU'RE RIGHT OWEN; I CAN'T.
BUT WHAT I *CAN* DO IS GIVE YOU STRONG INCENTIVES TO MAKE REASONABLE CHOICES IN YOUR EVERYDAY LIVES.
REALLY? YOU MEAN THE JUNK FOOD BAN IS *LIFTED?*
TECHNICALLY, YES, BUT--
OH. YOU'RE ALREADY EATING AN ENTIRE CAKE.
SMAK
HORF
CHOMP
SUGAR AND CAFFEINE ARE EVEN *BETTER* AFTER STAYING OFF THEM FOR A WEEK. I FEEL LIKE I COULD BENCH PRESS A SPACE TANK!
THAT STUFF WILL KILL YOU.
WHAT THE... AFTER EVERYTHING, YOU'RE *STILL* FOLLOWING THE COMPANY HEALTH GUIDELINES?
I WAS SKEPTICAL AT FIRST, BUT HAVE YOU SEEN THE INCENTIVES?
"10% OFF YOUR NEXT ASSISTED SUICIDE WHEN YOU DRINK TWO WHEATGRASS SMOOTHIES."
HALFWAY THERE!

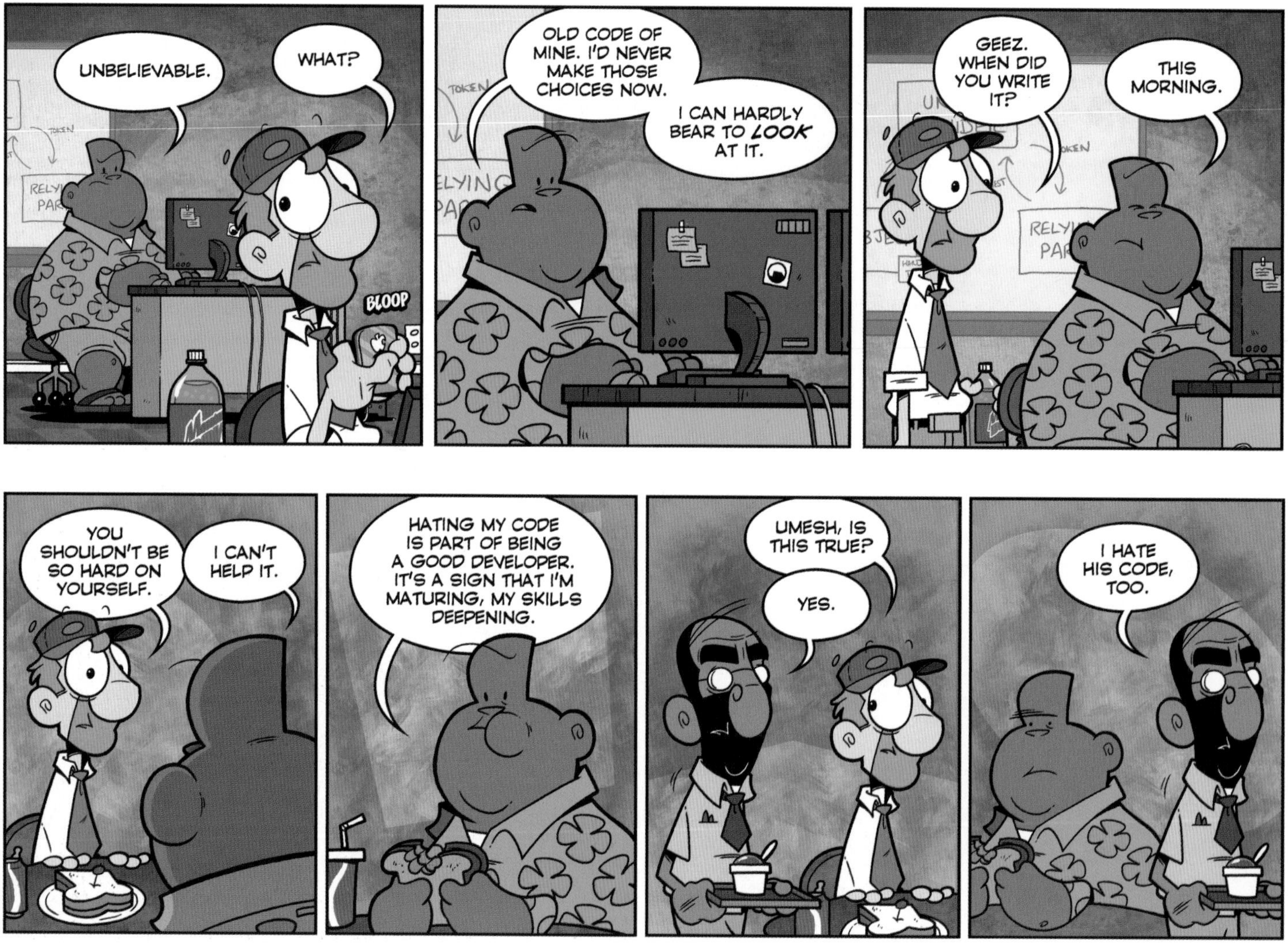
UNBELIEVABLE.
WHAT?
BLOOP
OLD CODE OF MINE. I'D NEVER MAKE THOSE CHOICES NOW.
I CAN HARDLY BEAR TO LOOK AT IT.
GEEZ. WHEN DID YOU WRITE IT?
THIS MORNING.
YOU SHOULDN'T BE SO HARD ON YOURSELF.
I CAN'T HELP IT.
HATING MY CODE IS PART OF BEING A GOOD DEVELOPER. IT'S A SIGN THAT I'M MATURING, MY SKILLS DEEPENING.
UMESH, IS THIS TRUE?
YES.
I HATE HIS CODE, TOO.

RUNTIME ERROR

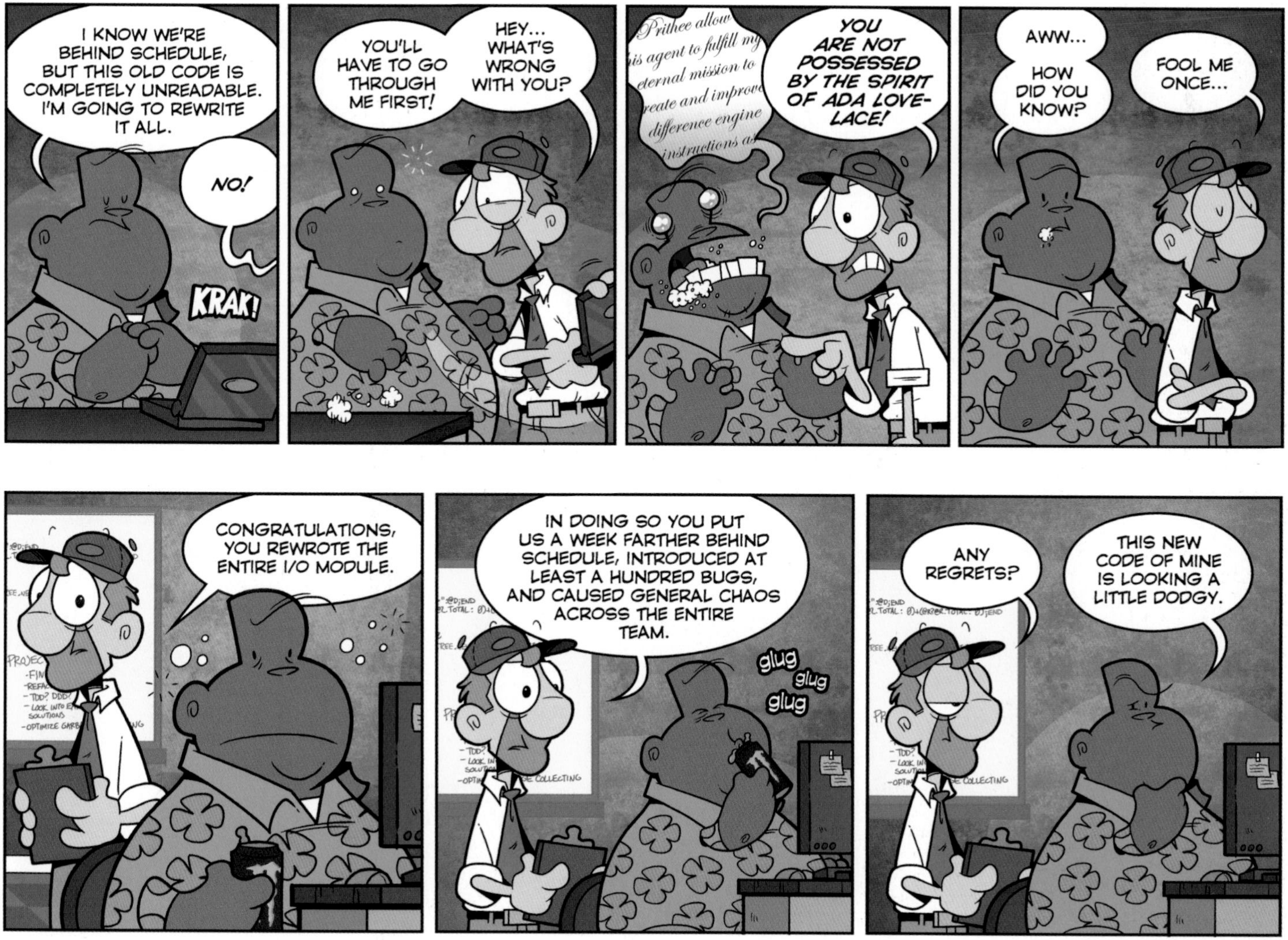

I KNOW WE'RE BEHIND SCHEDULE, BUT THIS OLD CODE IS COMPLETELY UNREADABLE. I'M GOING TO REWRITE IT ALL.
NO!
KRAK!
YOU'LL HAVE TO GO THROUGH ME FIRST!
HEY... WHAT'S WRONG WITH YOU?
Prithee allow is agent to fulfill my eternal mission to reate and improv difference engine instructions a
YOU ARE NOT POSSESSED BY THE SPIRIT OF ADA LOVE-LACE!
AWW... HOW DID YOU KNOW?
FOOL ME ONCE...
CONGRATULATIONS, YOU REWROTE THE ENTIRE I/O MODULE.
IN DOING SO YOU PUT US A WEEK FARTHER BEHIND SCHEDULE, INTRODUCED AT LEAST A HUNDRED BUGS, AND CAUSED GENERAL CHAOS ACROSS THE ENTIRE TEAM.
glug glug glug
ANY REGRETS?
THIS NEW CODE OF MINE IS LOOKING A LITTLE DODGY.

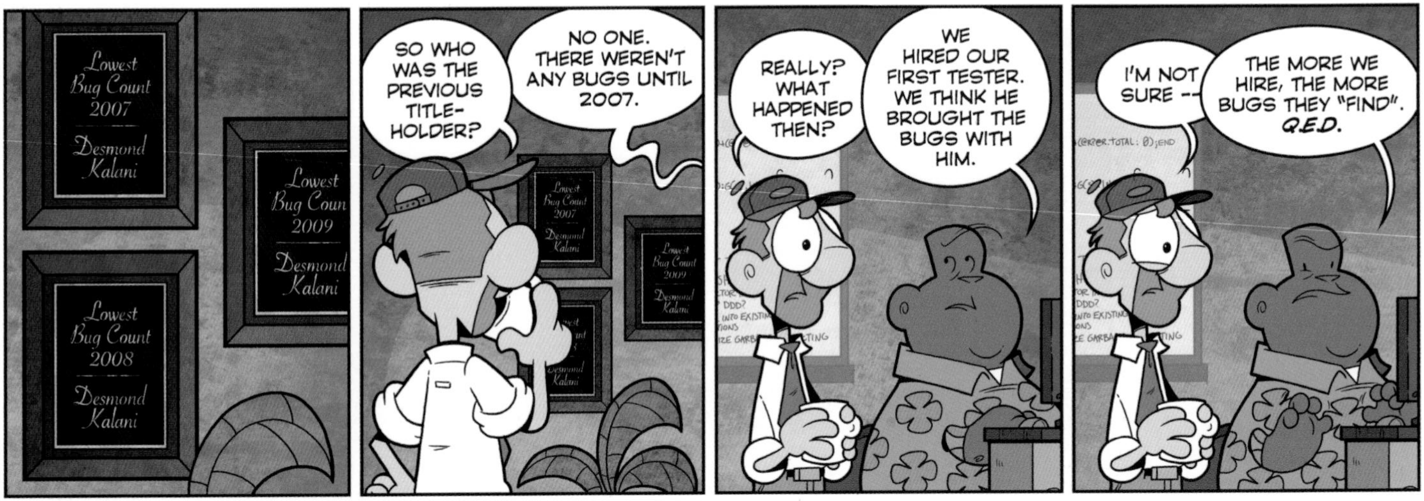
Lowest Bug Count 2007 Desmond Kalani
Lowest Bug Count 2009 Desmond Kalani
Lowest Bug Count 2008 Desmond Kalani
SO WHO WAS THE PREVIOUS TITLE-HOLDER?
NO ONE. THERE WEREN'T ANY BUGS UNTIL 2007.
REALLY? WHAT HAPPENED THEN?
WE HIRED OUR FIRST TESTER. WE THINK HE BROUGHT THE BUGS WITH HIM.
I'M NOT SURE --
THE MORE WE HIRE, THE MORE BUGS THEY "FIND". ***Q.E.D.***

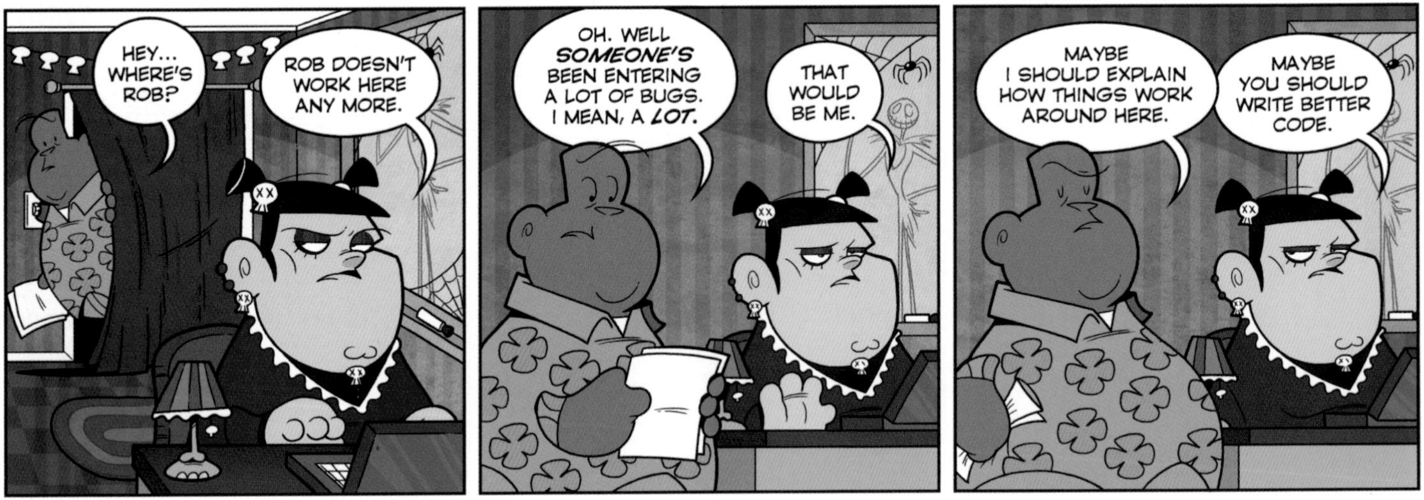
HEY... WHERE'S ROB?
ROB DOESN'T WORK HERE ANY MORE.
OH. WELL ***SOMEONE'S*** BEEN ENTERING A LOT OF BUGS. I MEAN, A ***LOT.***
THAT WOULD BE ME.
MAYBE I SHOULD EXPLAIN HOW THINGS WORK AROUND HERE.
MAYBE YOU SHOULD WRITE BETTER CODE.

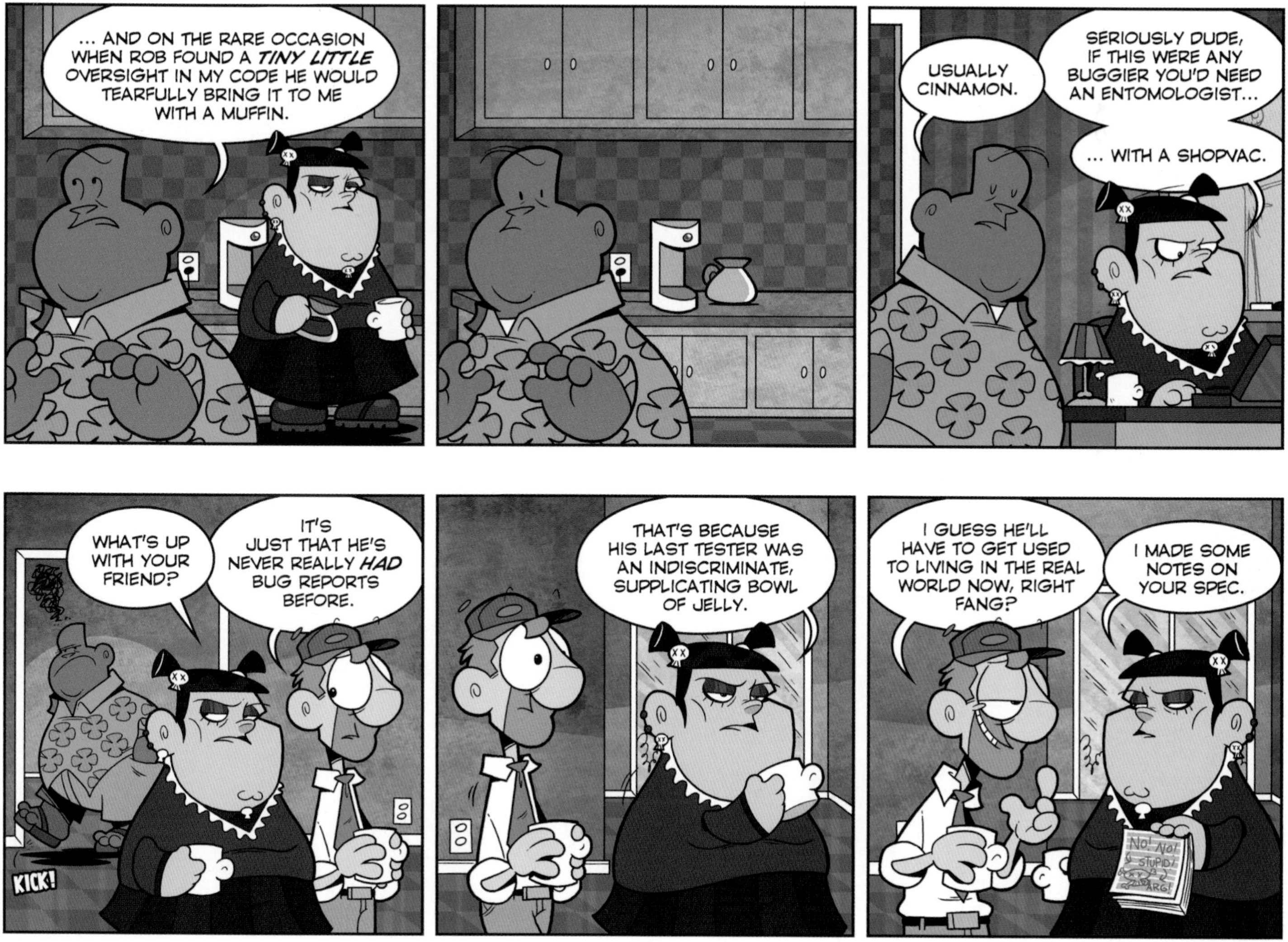
... AND ON THE RARE OCCASION WHEN ROB FOUND A *TINY LITTLE* OVERSIGHT IN MY CODE HE WOULD TEARFULLY BRING IT TO ME WITH A MUFFIN.
USUALLY CINNAMON.
SERIOUSLY DUDE, IF THIS WERE ANY BUGGIER YOU'D NEED AN ENTOMOLOGIST...
... WITH A SHOPVAC.
WHAT'S UP WITH YOUR FRIEND?
IT'S JUST THAT HE'S NEVER REALLY *HAD* BUG REPORTS BEFORE.
KICK!
THAT'S BECAUSE HIS LAST TESTER WAS AN INDISCRIMINATE, SUPPLICATING BOWL OF JELLY.
I GUESS HE'LL HAVE TO GET USED TO LIVING IN THE REAL WORLD NOW, RIGHT FANG?
I MADE SOME NOTES ON YOUR SPEC.
No! No!
STUPID!
ARG!

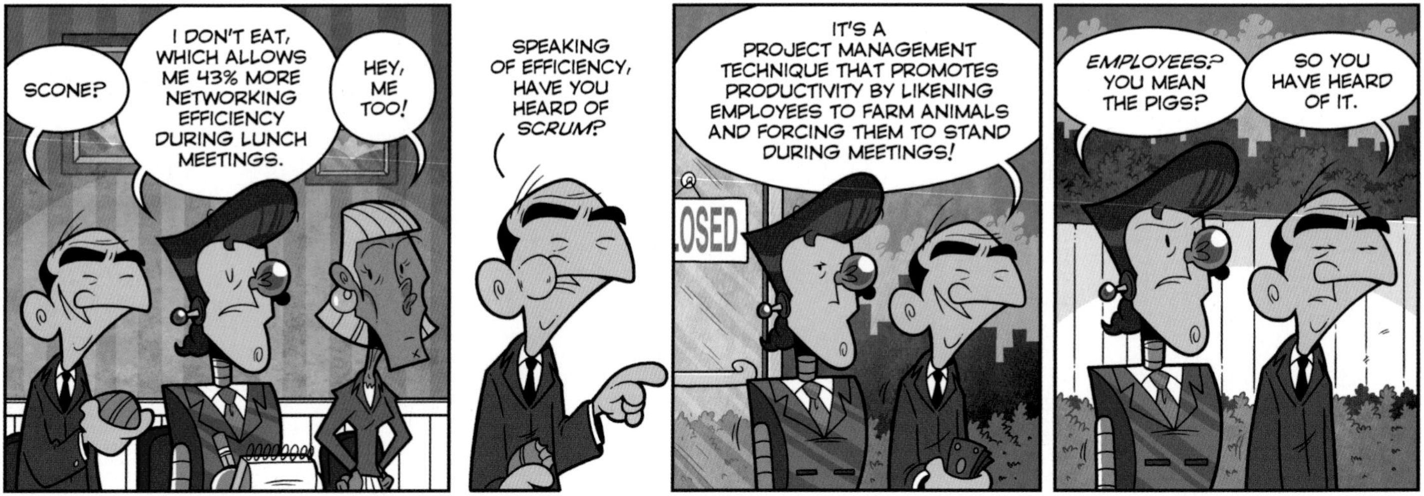
SCONE?
I DON'T EAT, WHICH ALLOWS ME 43% MORE NETWORKING EFFICIENCY DURING LUNCH MEETINGS.
HEY, ME TOO!
SPEAKING OF EFFICIENCY, HAVE YOU HEARD OF *SCRUM?*
IT'S A PROJECT MANAGEMENT TECHNIQUE THAT PROMOTES PRODUCTIVITY BY LIKENING EMPLOYEES TO FARM ANIMALS AND FORCING THEM TO STAND DURING MEETINGS!
LOSED
EMPLOYEES? YOU MEAN THE PIGS?
SO YOU HAVE HEARD OF IT.

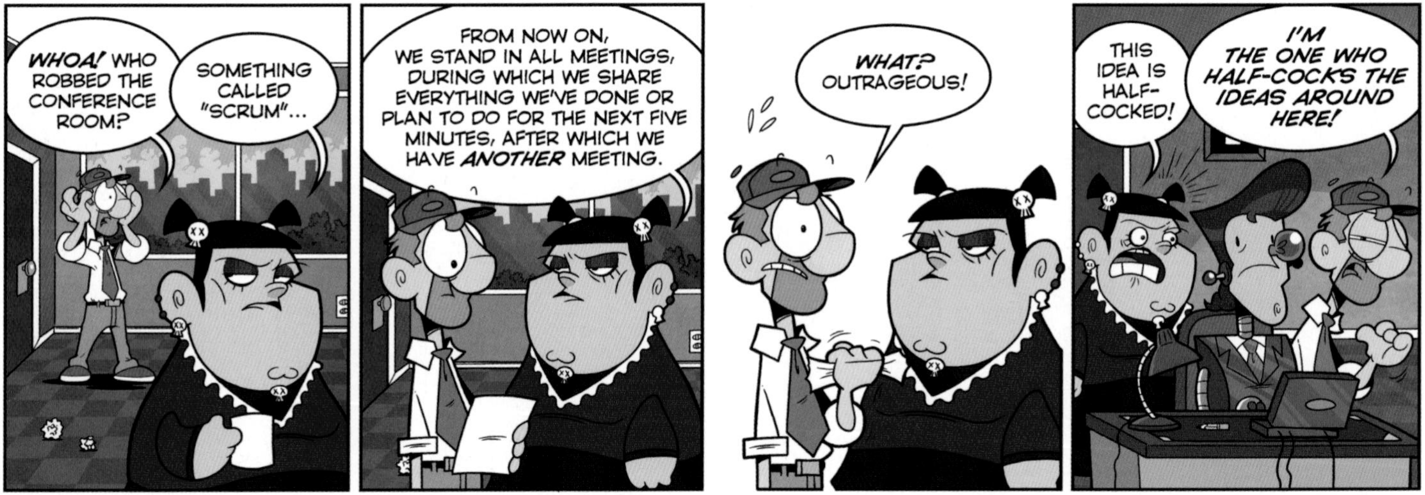
WHOA! WHO ROBBED THE CONFERENCE ROOM?
SOMETHING CALLED "SCRUM"...
FROM NOW ON, WE STAND IN ALL MEETINGS, DURING WHICH WE SHARE EVERYTHING WE'VE DONE OR PLAN TO DO FOR THE NEXT FIVE MINUTES, AFTER WHICH WE HAVE ***ANOTHER*** MEETING.
WHAT? OUTRAGEOUS!
THIS IDEA IS HALF-COCKED!
I'M THE ONE WHO HALF-COCKS THE IDEAS AROUND HERE!

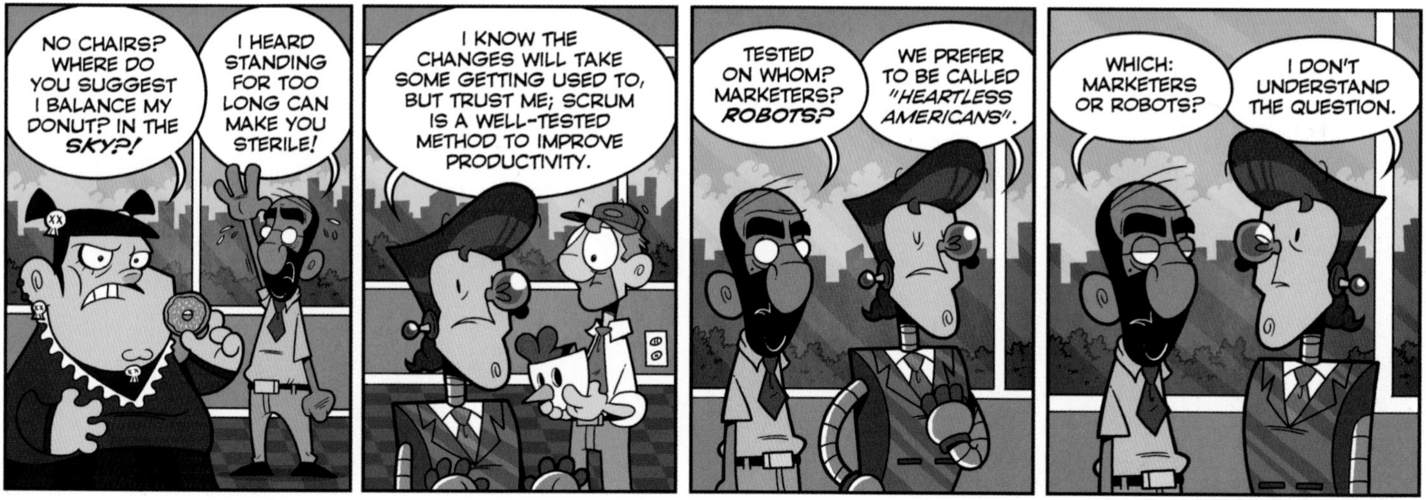
NO CHAIRS? WHERE DO YOU SUGGEST I BALANCE MY DONUT? IN THE *SKY?!*
I HEARD STANDING FOR TOO LONG CAN MAKE YOU STERILE!
I KNOW THE CHANGES WILL TAKE SOME GETTING USED TO, BUT TRUST ME; SCRUM IS A WELL-TESTED METHOD TO IMPROVE PRODUCTIVITY.
TESTED ON WHOM? MARKETERS? *ROBOTS?*
WE PREFER TO BE CALLED *"HEARTLESS AMERICANS"*.
WHICH: MARKETERS OR ROBOTS?
I DON'T UNDERSTAND THE QUESTION.

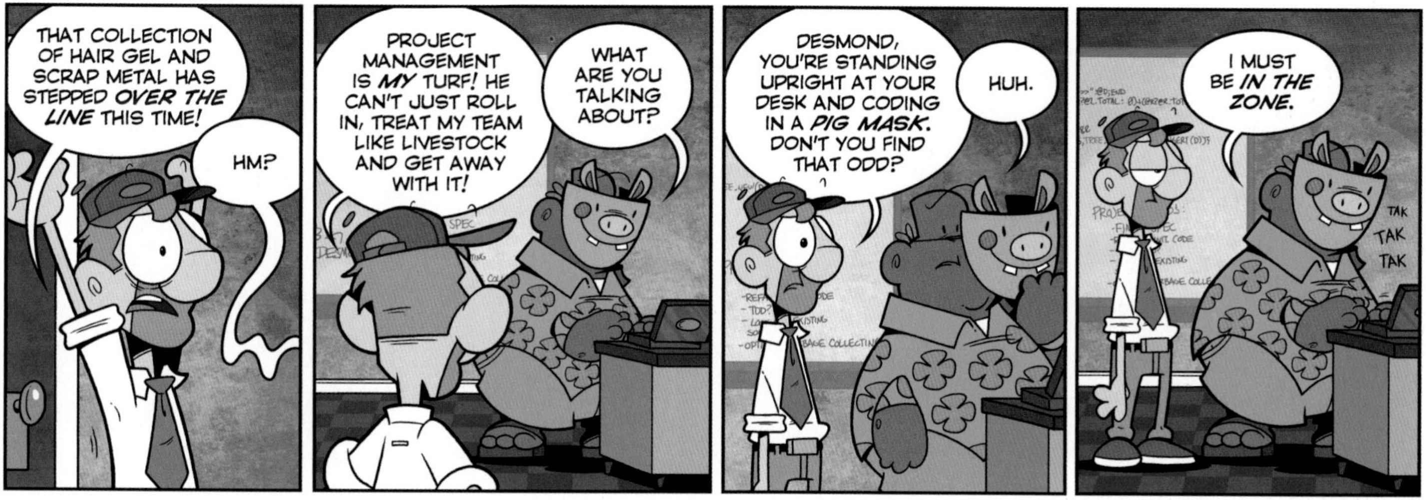
THAT COLLECTION OF HAIR GEL AND SCRAP METAL HAS STEPPED *OVER THE LINE* THIS TIME!
HM?
PROJECT MANAGEMENT IS *MY* TURF! HE CAN'T JUST ROLL IN, TREAT MY TEAM LIKE LIVESTOCK AND GET AWAY WITH IT!
WHAT ARE YOU TALKING ABOUT?
DESMOND, YOU'RE STANDING UPRIGHT AT YOUR DESK AND CODING IN A *PIG MASK*. DON'T YOU FIND THAT ODD?
HUH.
I MUST BE *IN THE ZONE*.
TAK
TAK
TAK

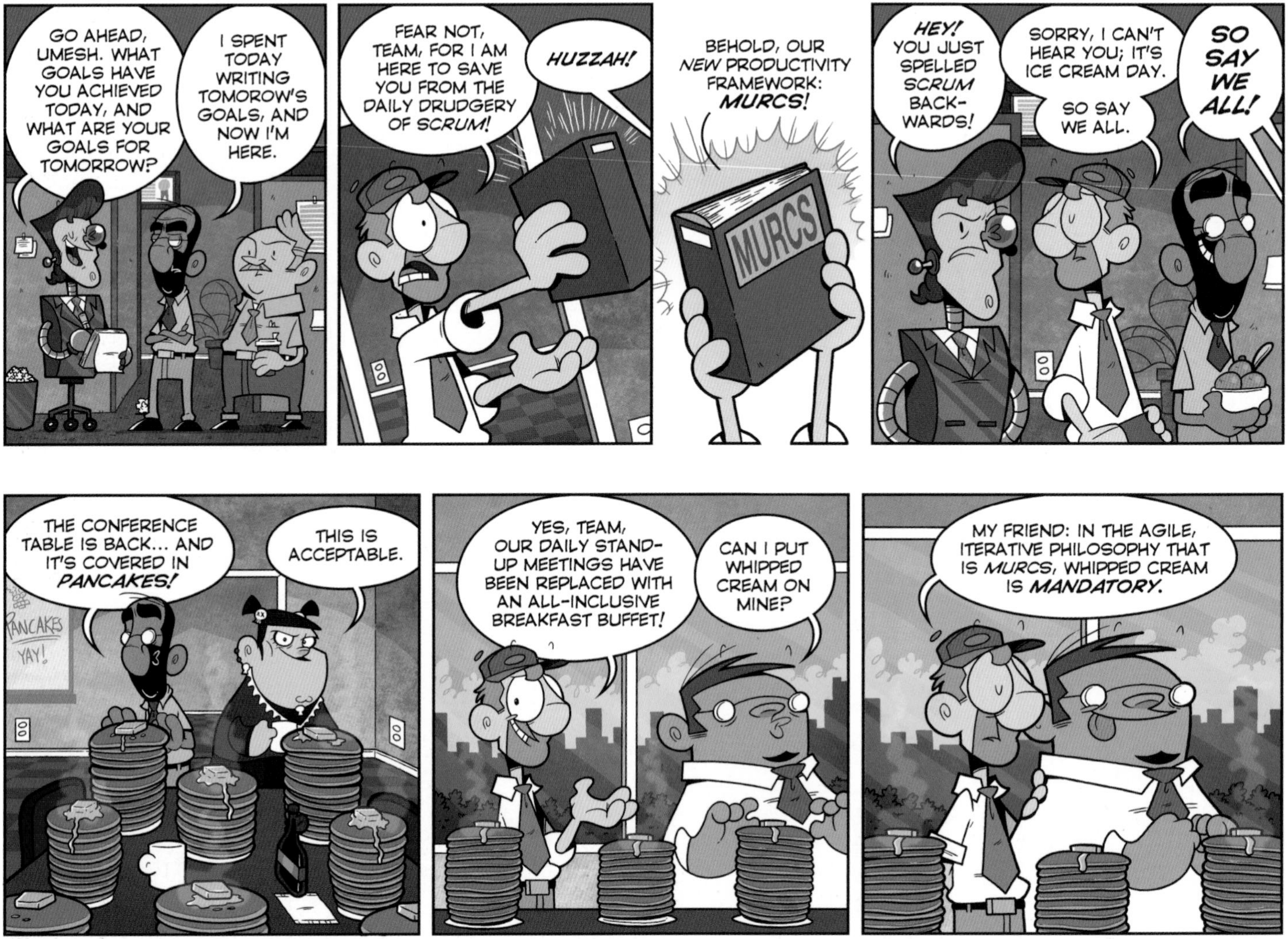
GO AHEAD, UMESH. WHAT GOALS HAVE YOU ACHIEVED TODAY, AND WHAT ARE YOUR GOALS FOR TOMORROW?
I SPENT TODAY WRITING TOMORROW'S GOALS, AND NOW I'M HERE.
FEAR NOT, TEAM, FOR I AM HERE TO SAVE YOU FROM THE DAILY DRUDGERY OF SCRUM!
HUZZAH!
BEHOLD, OUR NEW PRODUCTIVITY FRAMEWORK: MURCS!
MURCS
HEY! YOU JUST SPELLED SCRUM BACK-WARDS!
SORRY, I CAN'T HEAR YOU; IT'S ICE CREAM DAY.
SO SAY WE ALL.
SO SAY WE ALL!
THE CONFERENCE TABLE IS BACK... AND IT'S COVERED IN PANCAKES!
THIS IS ACCEPTABLE.
PANCAKES YAY!
YES, TEAM, OUR DAILY STAND-UP MEETINGS HAVE BEEN REPLACED WITH AN ALL-INCLUSIVE BREAKFAST BUFFET!
CAN I PUT WHIPPED CREAM ON MINE?
MY FRIEND: IN THE AGILE, ITERATIVE PHILOSOPHY THAT IS MURCS, WHIPPED CREAM IS MANDATORY.

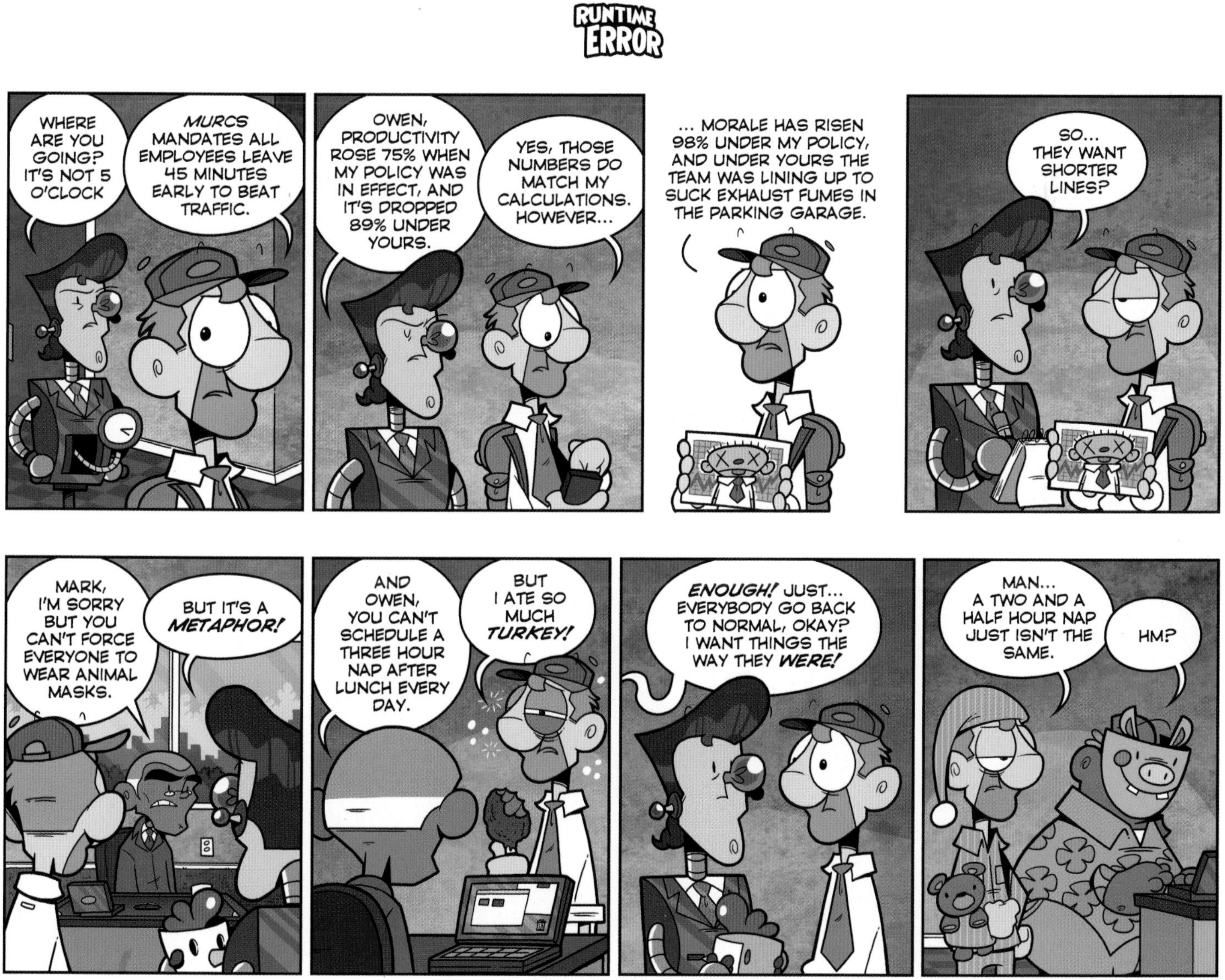
RUNTIME ERROR
WHERE ARE YOU GOING? IT'S NOT 5 O'CLOCK
MURCS MANDATES ALL EMPLOYEES LEAVE 45 MINUTES EARLY TO BEAT TRAFFIC.
OWEN, PRODUCTIVITY ROSE 75% WHEN MY POLICY WAS IN EFFECT, AND IT'S DROPPED 89% UNDER YOURS.
YES, THOSE NUMBERS DO MATCH MY CALCULATIONS. HOWEVER...
... MORALE HAS RISEN 98% UNDER MY POLICY, AND UNDER YOURS THE TEAM WAS LINING UP TO SUCK EXHAUST FUMES IN THE PARKING GARAGE.
SO... THEY WANT SHORTER LINES?
MARK, I'M SORRY BUT YOU CAN'T FORCE EVERYONE TO WEAR ANIMAL MASKS.
BUT IT'S A *METAPHOR!*
AND OWEN, YOU CAN'T SCHEDULE A THREE HOUR NAP AFTER LUNCH EVERY DAY.
BUT I ATE SO MUCH *TURKEY!*
ENOUGH! JUST... EVERYBODY GO BACK TO NORMAL, OKAY? I WANT THINGS THE WAY THEY *WERE!*
MAN... A TWO AND A HALF HOUR NAP JUST ISN'T THE SAME.
HM?

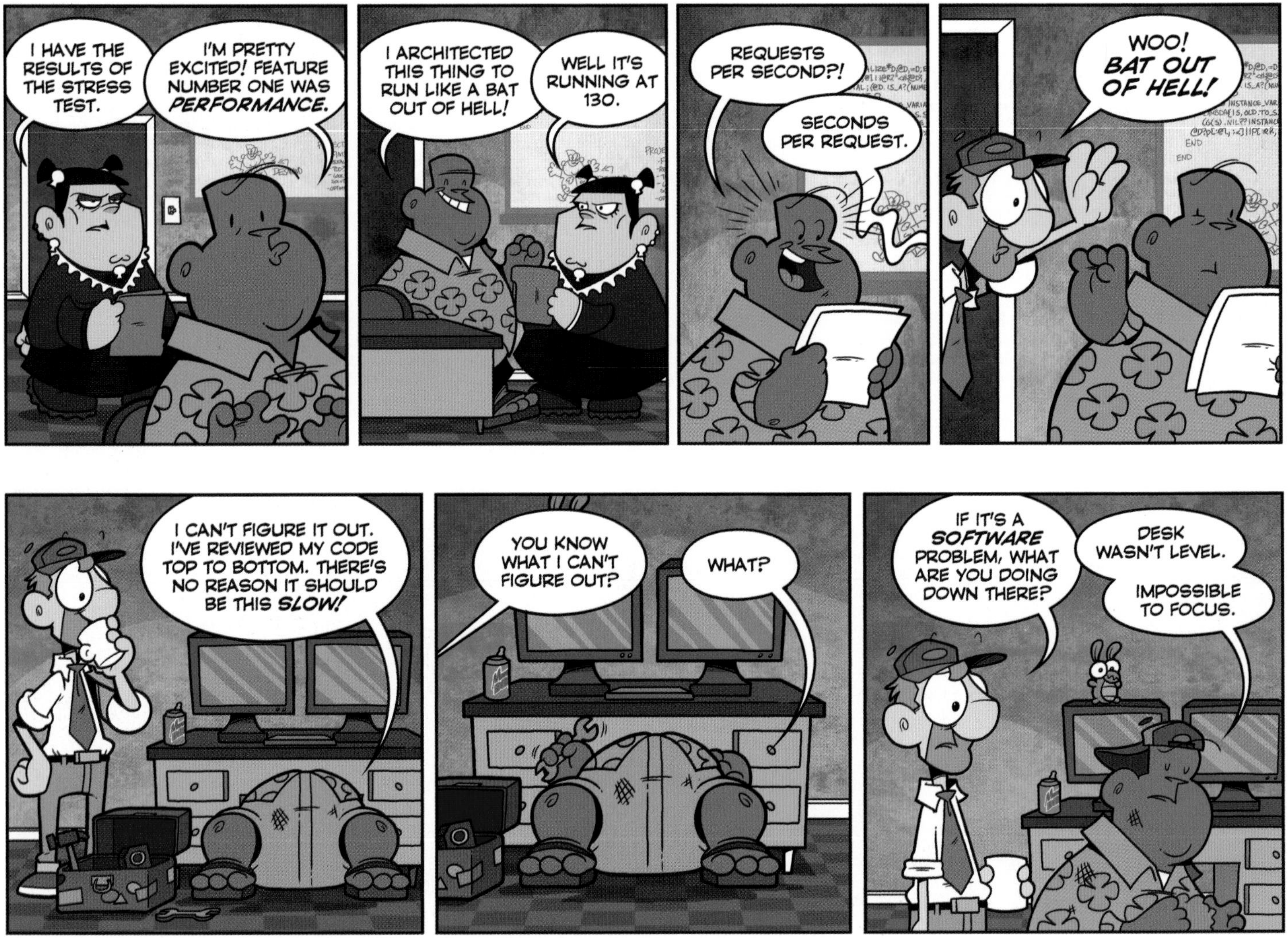
I HAVE THE RESULTS OF THE STRESS TEST.
I'M PRETTY EXCITED! FEATURE NUMBER ONE WAS *PERFORMANCE.*
I ARCHITECTED THIS THING TO RUN LIKE A BAT OUT OF HELL!
WELL IT'S RUNNING AT 130.
REQUESTS PER SECOND?!
SECONDS PER REQUEST.
WOO! *BAT OUT OF HELL!*
I CAN'T FIGURE IT OUT. I'VE REVIEWED MY CODE TOP TO BOTTOM. THERE'S NO REASON IT SHOULD BE THIS *SLOW!*
YOU KNOW WHAT I CAN'T FIGURE OUT?
WHAT?
IF IT'S A *SOFTWARE* PROBLEM, WHAT ARE YOU DOING DOWN THERE?
DESK WASN'T LEVEL.
IMPOSSIBLE TO FOCUS.

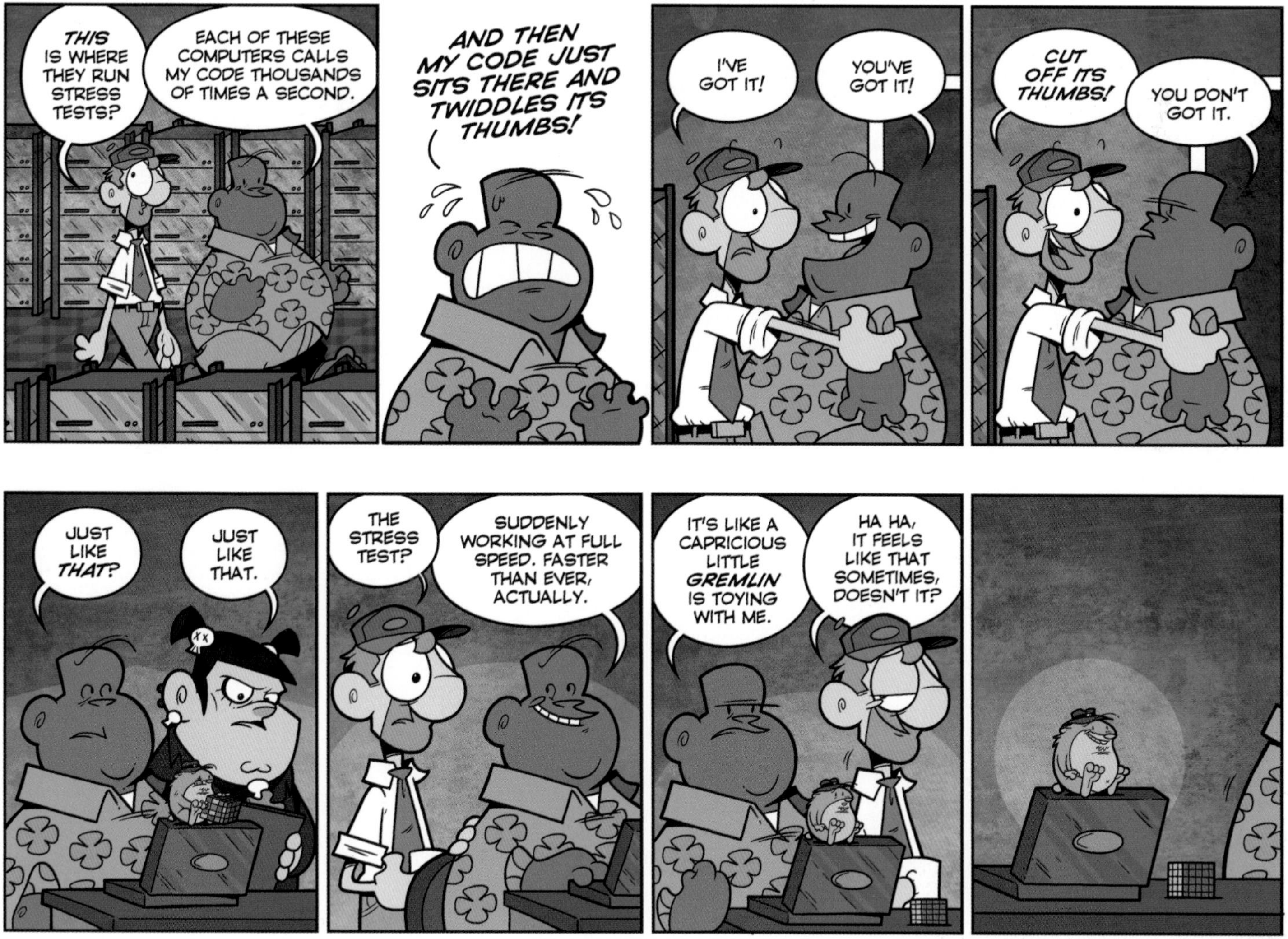
THIS IS WHERE THEY RUN STRESS TESTS?
EACH OF THESE COMPUTERS CALLS MY CODE THOUSANDS OF TIMES A SECOND.
AND THEN MY CODE JUST SITS THERE AND TWIDDLES ITS THUMBS!
I'VE GOT IT!
YOU'VE GOT IT!
CUT OFF ITS THUMBS!
YOU DON'T GOT IT.
JUST LIKE THAT?
JUST LIKE THAT.
THE STRESS TEST?
SUDDENLY WORKING AT FULL SPEED. FASTER THAN EVER, ACTUALLY.
IT'S LIKE A CAPRICIOUS LITTLE GREMLIN IS TOYING WITH ME.
HA HA, IT FEELS LIKE THAT SOMETIMES, DOESN'T IT?

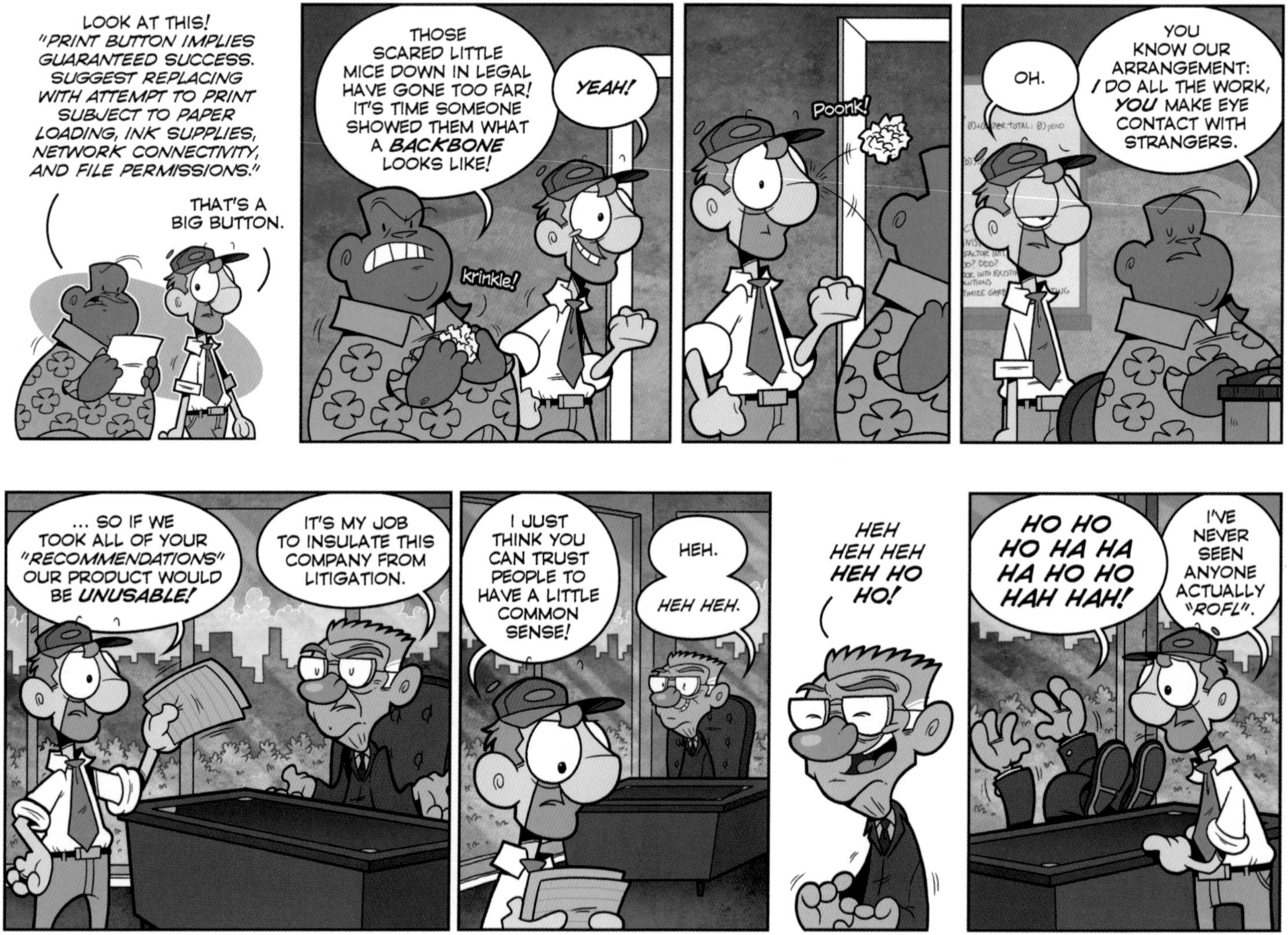
LOOK AT THIS! "PRINT BUTTON IMPLIES GUARANTEED SUCCESS. SUGGEST REPLACING WITH ATTEMPT TO PRINT SUBJECT TO PAPER LOADING, INK SUPPLIES, NETWORK CONNECTIVITY, AND FILE PERMISSIONS."
THAT'S A BIG BUTTON.
THOSE SCARED LITTLE MICE DOWN IN LEGAL HAVE GONE TOO FAR! IT'S TIME SOMEONE SHOWED THEM WHAT A BACKBONE LOOKS LIKE!
YEAH!
krinkle!
Poonk!
OH.
YOU KNOW OUR ARRANGEMENT: I DO ALL THE WORK, YOU MAKE EYE CONTACT WITH STRANGERS.
... SO IF WE TOOK ALL OF YOUR "RECOMMENDATIONS" OUR PRODUCT WOULD BE UNUSABLE!
IT'S MY JOB TO INSULATE THIS COMPANY FROM LITIGATION.
I JUST THINK YOU CAN TRUST PEOPLE TO HAVE A LITTLE COMMON SENSE!
HEH.
HEH HEH.
HEH HEH HEH HEH HO HO!
HO HO HO HA HA HA HO HO HAH HAH!
I'VE NEVER SEEN ANYONE ACTUALLY "ROFL".

RUNTIME ERROR

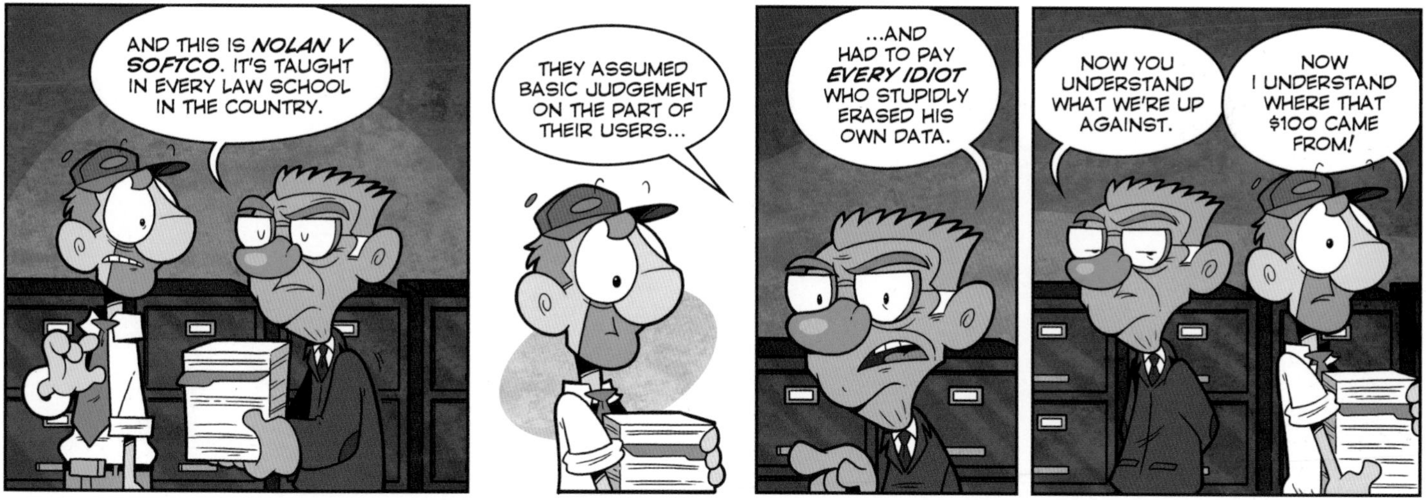

AND THIS IS *NOLAN V SOFTCO*. IT'S TAUGHT IN EVERY LAW SCHOOL IN THE COUNTRY.
THEY ASSUMED BASIC JUDGEMENT ON THE PART OF THEIR USERS...
...AND HAD TO PAY *EVERY IDIOT* WHO STUPIDLY ERASED HIS OWN DATA.
NOW YOU UNDERSTAND WHAT WE'RE UP AGAINST.
NOW I UNDERSTAND WHERE THAT $100 CAME FROM!

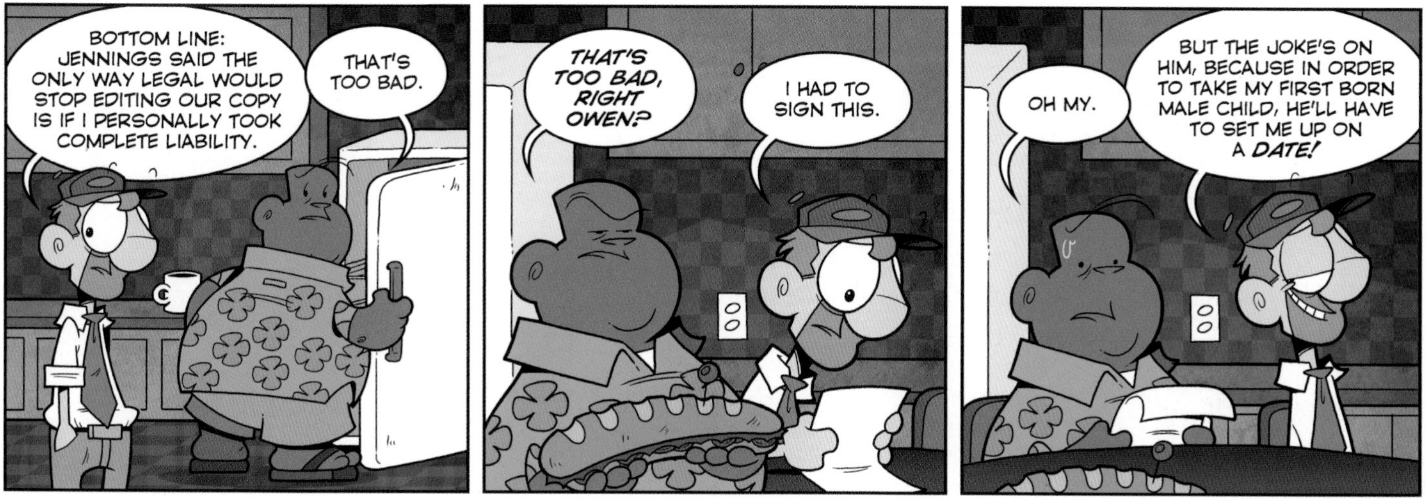

BOTTOM LINE: JENNINGS SAID THE ONLY WAY LEGAL WOULD STOP EDITING OUR COPY IS IF I PERSONALLY TOOK COMPLETE LIABILITY.
THAT'S TOO BAD.
THAT'S TOO BAD, RIGHT OWEN?
I HAD TO SIGN THIS.
OH MY.
BUT THE JOKE'S ON HIM, BECAUSE IN ORDER TO TAKE MY FIRST BORN MALE CHILD, HE'LL HAVE TO SET ME UP ON A *DATE!*

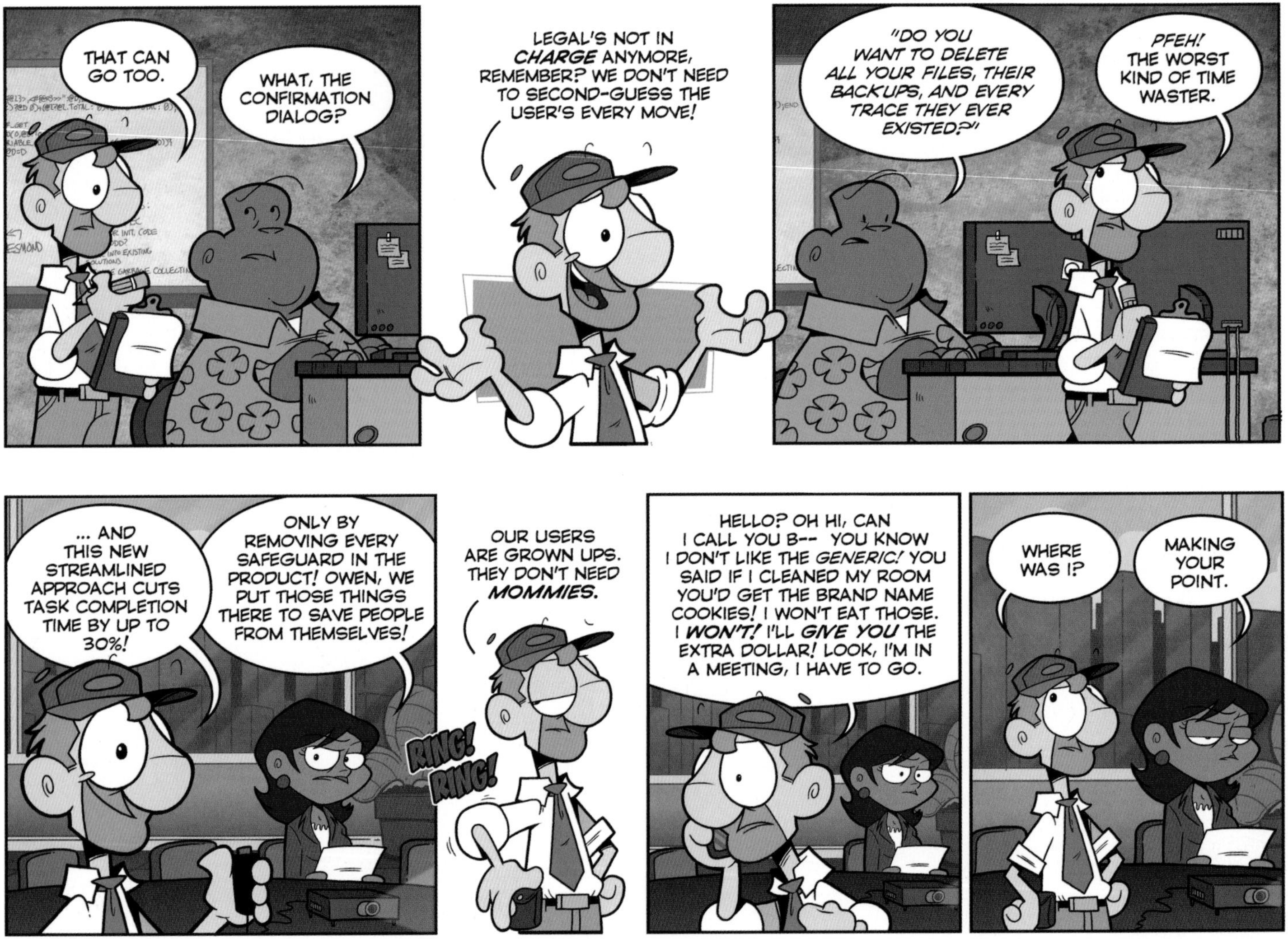
THAT CAN GO TOO.
WHAT, THE CONFIRMATION DIALOG?
LEGAL'S NOT IN *CHARGE* ANYMORE, REMEMBER? WE DON'T NEED TO SECOND-GUESS THE USER'S EVERY MOVE!
"DO YOU WANT TO DELETE ALL YOUR FILES, THEIR BACKUPS, AND EVERY TRACE THEY EVER EXISTED?"
PFEH! THE WORST KIND OF TIME WASTER.
... AND THIS NEW STREAMLINED APPROACH CUTS TASK COMPLETION TIME BY UP TO 30%!
ONLY BY REMOVING EVERY SAFEGUARD IN THE PRODUCT! OWEN, WE PUT THOSE THINGS THERE TO SAVE PEOPLE FROM THEMSELVES!
OUR USERS ARE GROWN UPS. THEY DON'T NEED ***MOMMIES.***
RING! RING!
HELLO? OH HI, CAN I CALL YOU B-- YOU KNOW I DON'T LIKE THE *GENERIC!* YOU SAID IF I CLEANED MY ROOM YOU'D GET THE BRAND NAME COOKIES! I WON'T EAT THOSE. I ***WON'T!*** I'LL ***GIVE YOU*** THE EXTRA DOLLAR! LOOK, I'M IN A MEETING, I HAVE TO GO.
WHERE WAS I?
MAKING YOUR POINT.

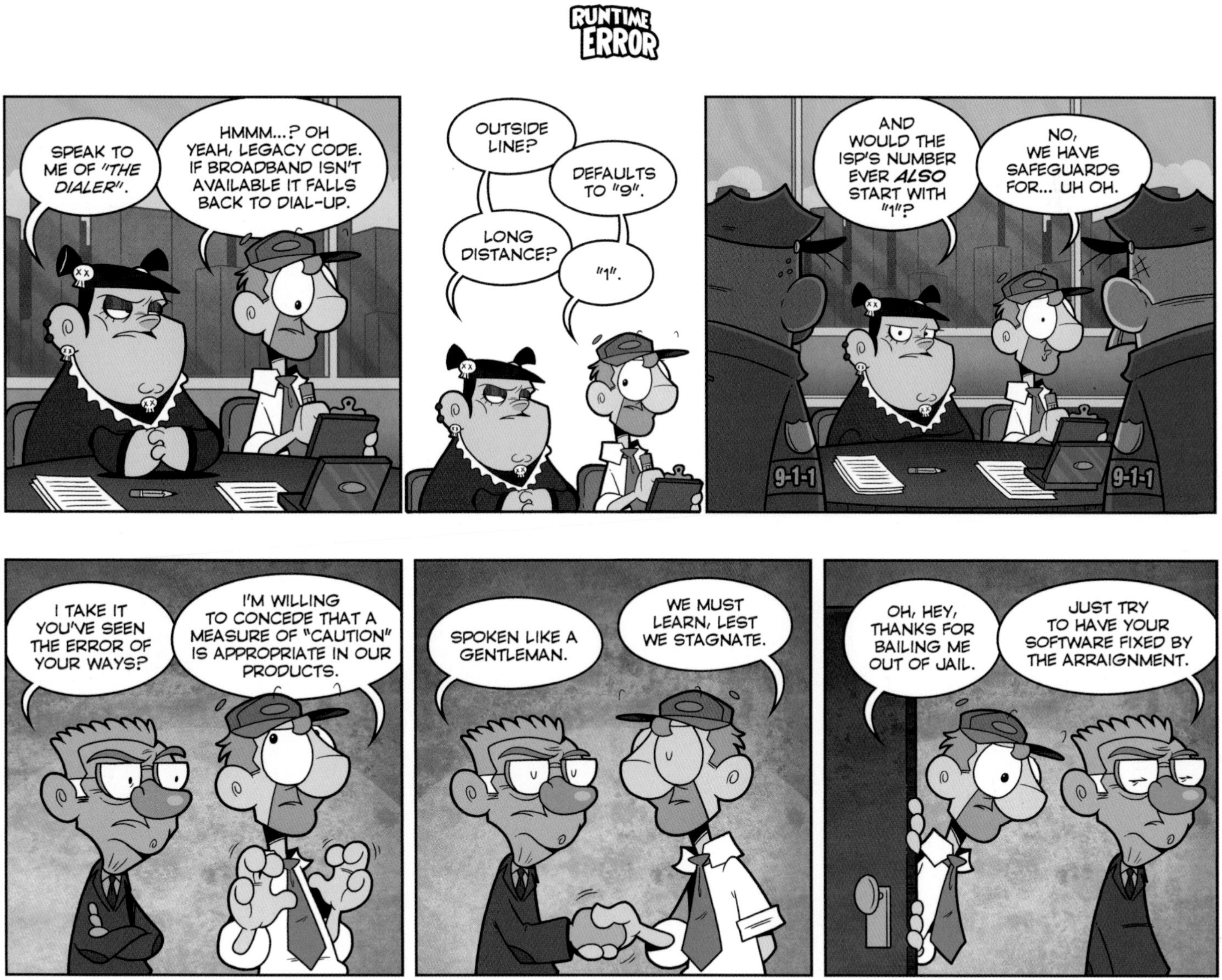
RUNTIME ERROR
SPEAK TO ME OF "THE DIALER".
HMMM...? OH YEAH, LEGACY CODE. IF BROADBAND ISN'T AVAILABLE IT FALLS BACK TO DIAL-UP.
OUTSIDE LINE?
DEFAULTS TO "9".
LONG DISTANCE?
"1".
AND WOULD THE ISP'S NUMBER EVER ALSO START WITH "1"?
NO, WE HAVE SAFEGUARDS FOR... UH OH.
9-1-1
9-1-1
I TAKE IT YOU'VE SEEN THE ERROR OF YOUR WAYS?
I'M WILLING TO CONCEDE THAT A MEASURE OF "CAUTION" IS APPROPRIATE IN OUR PRODUCTS.
SPOKEN LIKE A GENTLEMAN.
WE MUST LEARN, LEST WE STAGNATE.
OH, HEY, THANKS FOR BAILING ME OUT OF JAIL.
JUST TRY TO HAVE YOUR SOFTWARE FIXED BY THE ARRAIGNMENT.

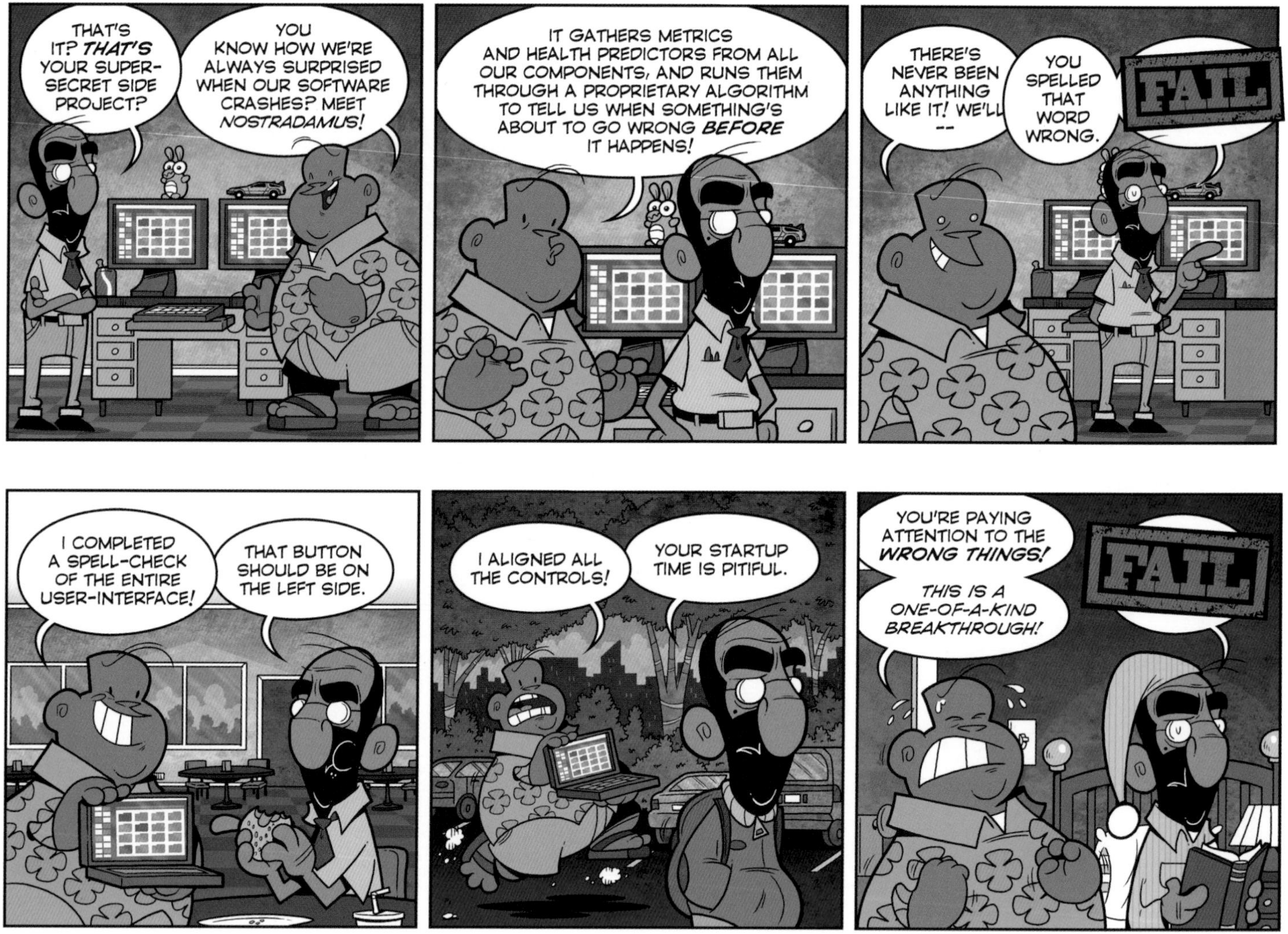
THAT'S IT? THAT'S YOUR SUPER-SECRET SIDE PROJECT?
YOU KNOW HOW WE'RE ALWAYS SURPRISED WHEN OUR SOFTWARE CRASHES? MEET NOSTRADAMUS!
IT GATHERS METRICS AND HEALTH PREDICTORS FROM ALL OUR COMPONENTS, AND RUNS THEM THROUGH A PROPRIETARY ALGORITHM TO TELL US WHEN SOMETHING'S ABOUT TO GO WRONG BEFORE IT HAPPENS!
THERE'S NEVER BEEN ANYTHING LIKE IT! WE'LL --
YOU SPELLED THAT WORD WRONG.
FAIL
I COMPLETED A SPELL-CHECK OF THE ENTIRE USER-INTERFACE!
THAT BUTTON SHOULD BE ON THE LEFT SIDE.
I ALIGNED ALL THE CONTROLS!
YOUR STARTUP TIME IS PITIFUL.
YOU'RE PAYING ATTENTION TO THE WRONG THINGS!
THIS IS A ONE-OF-A-KIND BREAKTHROUGH!
FAIL

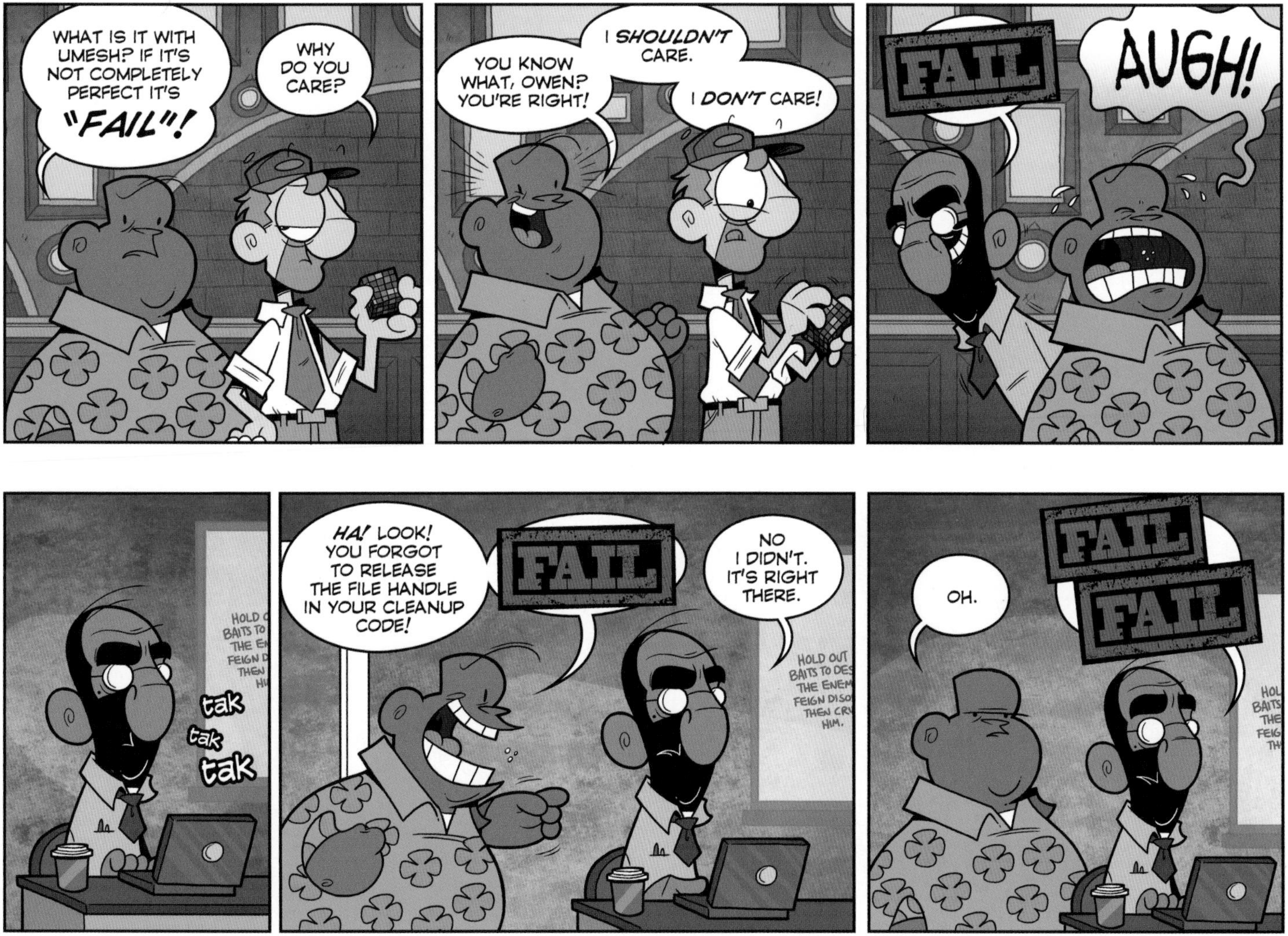
WHAT IS IT WITH UMESH? IF IT'S NOT COMPLETELY PERFECT IT'S "FAIL"!
WHY DO YOU CARE?
YOU KNOW WHAT, OWEN? YOU'RE RIGHT!
I SHOULDN'T CARE.
I DON'T CARE!
FAIL
AUGH!
tak
tak
tak
HA! LOOK! YOU FORGOT TO RELEASE THE FILE HANDLE IN YOUR CLEANUP CODE!
FAIL
NO I DIDN'T. IT'S RIGHT THERE.
HOLD OUT BAITS TO DES THE ENEM FEIGN DISO THEN CRY HIM.
OH.
FAIL
FAIL

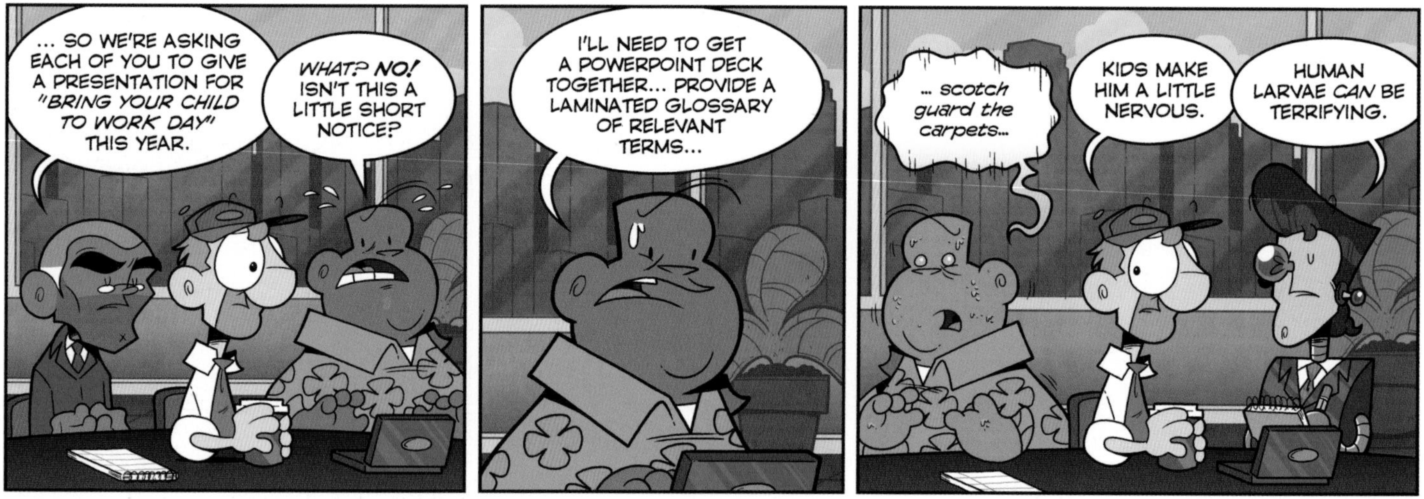
... SO WE'RE ASKING EACH OF YOU TO GIVE A PRESENTATION FOR "BRING YOUR CHILD TO WORK DAY" THIS YEAR.
WHAT? NO! ISN'T THIS A LITTLE SHORT NOTICE?
I'LL NEED TO GET A POWERPOINT DECK TOGETHER... PROVIDE A LAMINATED GLOSSARY OF RELEVANT TERMS...
... scotch guard the carpets...
KIDS MAKE HIM A LITTLE NERVOUS.
HUMAN LARVAE CAN BE TERRIFYING.

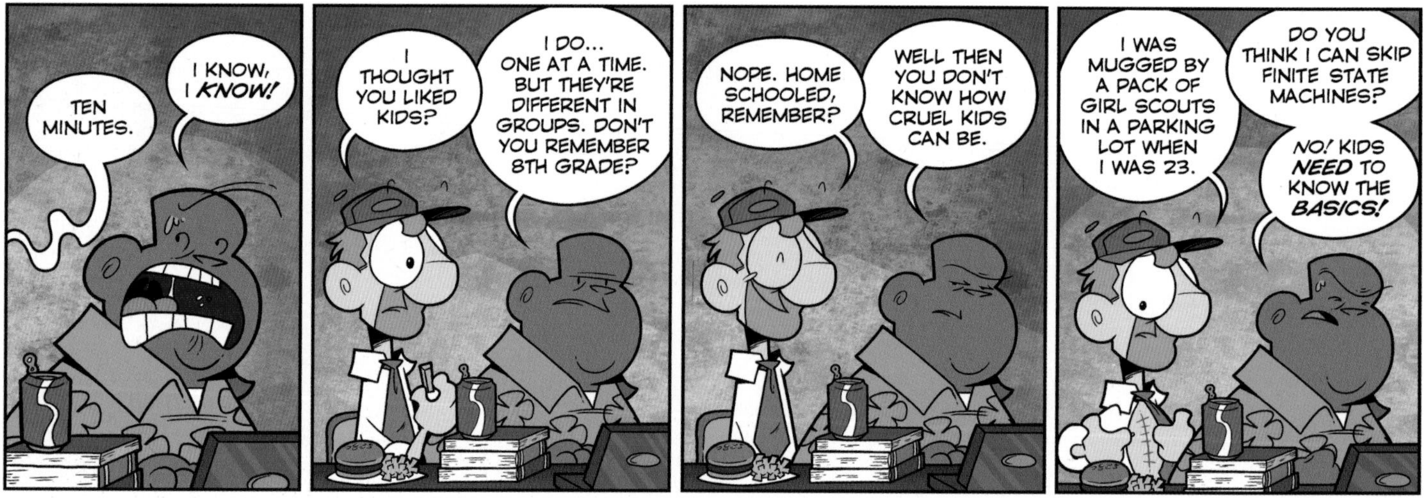
TEN MINUTES.
I KNOW, I KNOW!
I THOUGHT YOU LIKED KIDS?
I DO... ONE AT A TIME. BUT THEY'RE DIFFERENT IN GROUPS. DON'T YOU REMEMBER 8TH GRADE?
NOPE. HOME SCHOOLED, REMEMBER?
WELL THEN YOU DON'T KNOW HOW CRUEL KIDS CAN BE.
I WAS MUGGED BY A PACK OF GIRL SCOUTS IN A PARKING LOT WHEN I WAS 23.
DO YOU THINK I CAN SKIP FINITE STATE MACHINES?
NO! KIDS NEED TO KNOW THE BASICS!

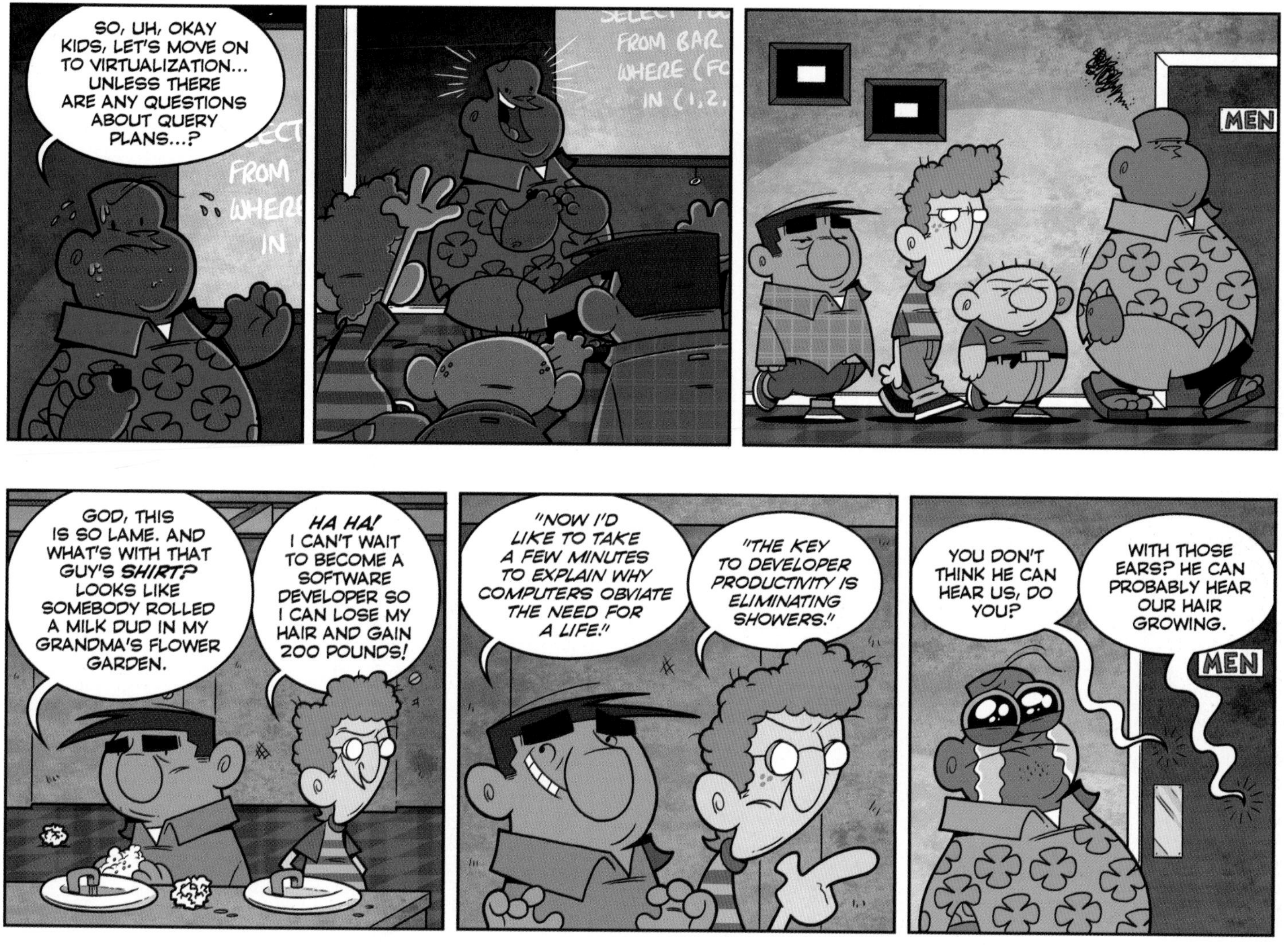
SO, UH, OKAY KIDS, LET'S MOVE ON TO VIRTUALIZATION... UNLESS THERE ARE ANY QUESTIONS ABOUT QUERY PLANS...?
MEN
GOD, THIS IS SO LAME. AND WHAT'S WITH THAT GUY'S SHIRT? LOOKS LIKE SOMEBODY ROLLED A MILK DUD IN MY GRANDMA'S FLOWER GARDEN.
HA HA! I CAN'T WAIT TO BECOME A SOFTWARE DEVELOPER SO I CAN LOSE MY HAIR AND GAIN 200 POUNDS!
"NOW I'D LIKE TO TAKE A FEW MINUTES TO EXPLAIN WHY COMPUTERS OBVIATE THE NEED FOR A LIFE."
"THE KEY TO DEVELOPER PRODUCTIVITY IS ELIMINATING SHOWERS."
YOU DON'T THINK HE CAN HEAR US, DO YOU?
WITH THOSE EARS? HE CAN PROBABLY HEAR OUR HAIR GROWING.
MEN

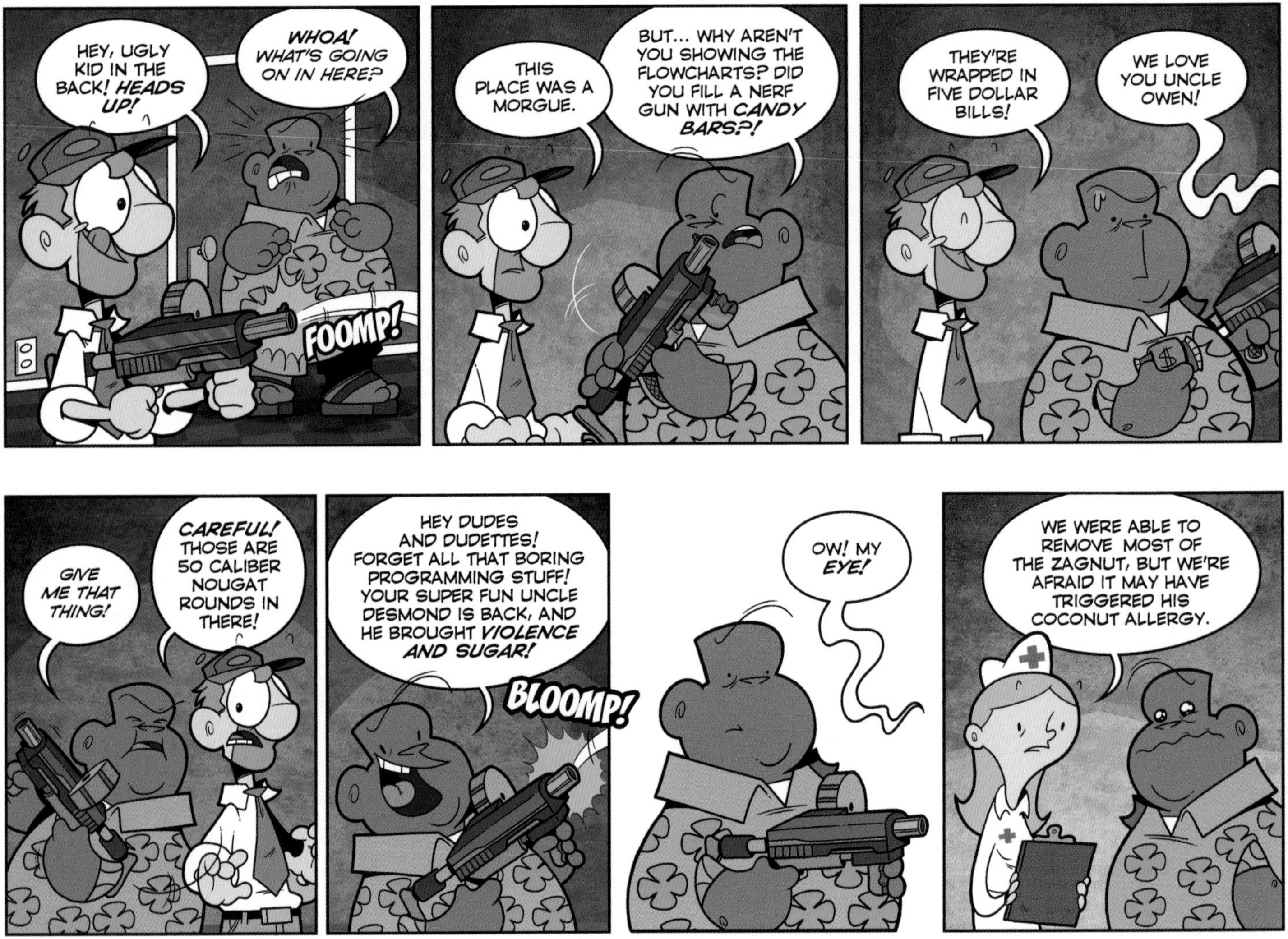
HEY, UGLY KID IN THE BACK! *HEADS UP!*
WHOA! WHAT'S GOING ON IN HERE?
FOOMP!
THIS PLACE WAS A MORGUE.
BUT... WHY AREN'T YOU SHOWING THE FLOWCHARTS? DID YOU FILL A NERF GUN WITH *CANDY BARS?!*
THEY'RE WRAPPED IN FIVE DOLLAR BILLS!
WE LOVE YOU UNCLE OWEN!
GIVE ME THAT THING!
CAREFUL! THOSE ARE 50 CALIBER NOUGAT ROUNDS IN THERE!
HEY DUDES AND DUDETTES! FORGET ALL THAT BORING PROGRAMMING STUFF! YOUR SUPER FUN UNCLE DESMOND IS BACK, AND HE BROUGHT *VIOLENCE AND SUGAR!*
BLOOMP!
OW! MY *EYE!*
WE WERE ABLE TO REMOVE MOST OF THE ZAGNUT, BUT WE'RE AFRAID IT MAY HAVE TRIGGERED HIS COCONUT ALLERGY.

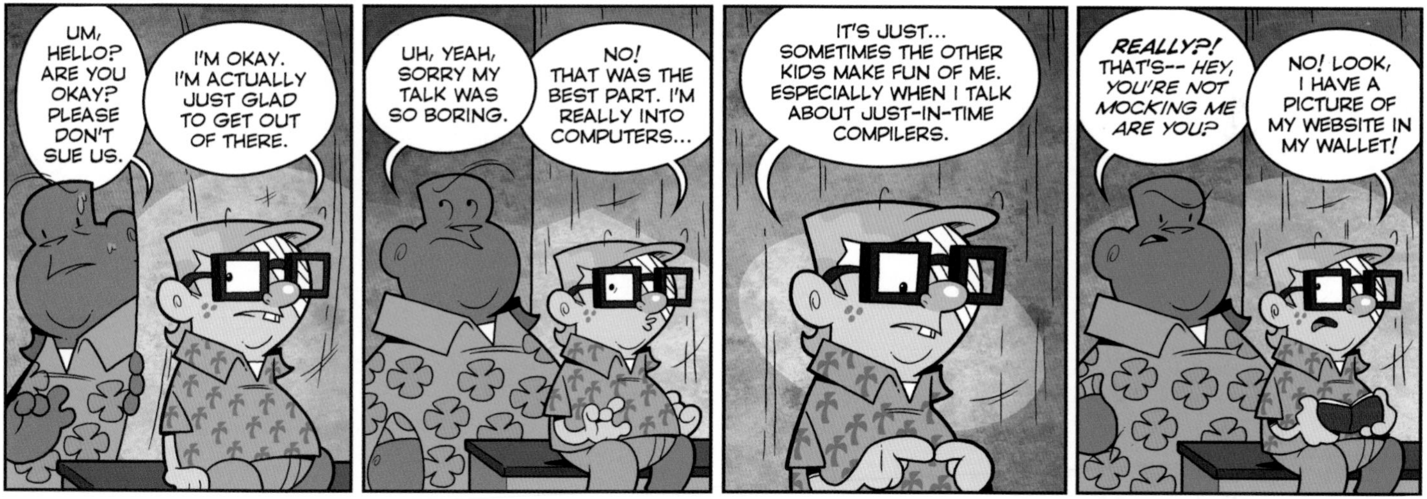
UM, HELLO? ARE YOU OKAY? PLEASE DON'T SUE US.
I'M OKAY. I'M ACTUALLY JUST GLAD TO GET OUT OF THERE.
UH, YEAH, SORRY MY TALK WAS SO BORING.
NO! THAT WAS THE BEST PART. I'M REALLY INTO COMPUTERS...
IT'S JUST... SOMETIMES THE OTHER KIDS MAKE FUN OF ME. ESPECIALLY WHEN I TALK ABOUT JUST-IN-TIME COMPILERS.
REALLY?! THAT'S-- HEY, YOU'RE NOT MOCKING ME ARE YOU?
NO! LOOK, I HAVE A PICTURE OF MY WEBSITE IN MY WALLET!

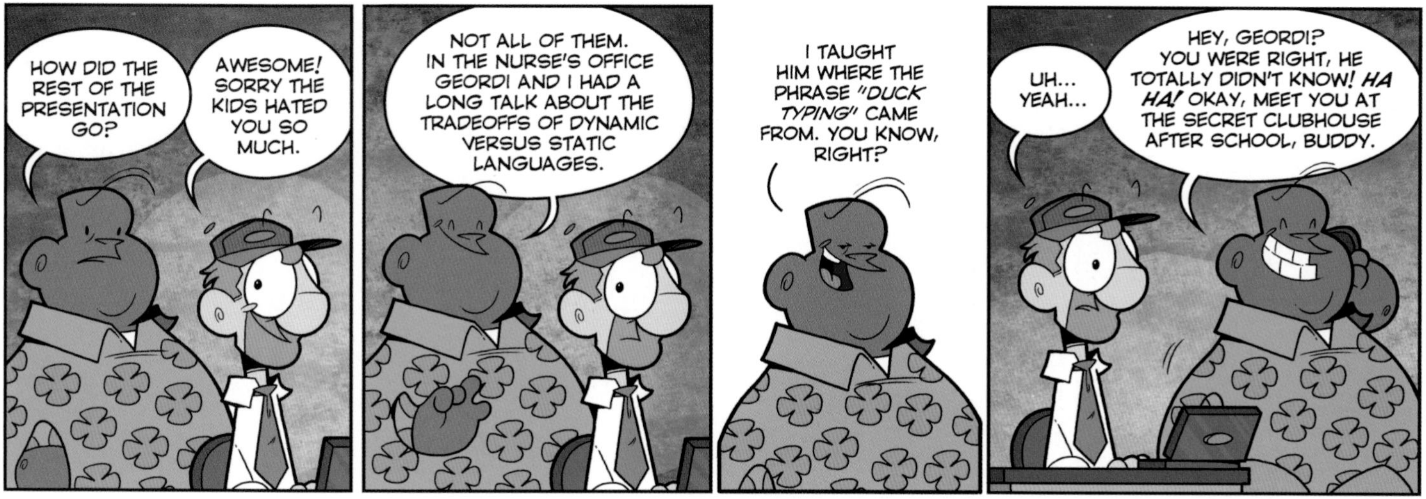
HOW DID THE REST OF THE PRESENTATION GO?
AWESOME! SORRY THE KIDS HATED YOU SO MUCH.
NOT ALL OF THEM. IN THE NURSE'S OFFICE GEORDI AND I HAD A LONG TALK ABOUT THE TRADEOFFS OF DYNAMIC VERSUS STATIC LANGUAGES.
I TAUGHT HIM WHERE THE PHRASE "DUCK TYPING" CAME FROM. YOU KNOW, RIGHT?
UH... YEAH...
HEY, GEORDI? YOU WERE RIGHT, HE TOTALLY DIDN'T KNOW! HA HA! OKAY, MEET YOU AT THE SECRET CLUBHOUSE AFTER SCHOOL, BUDDY.

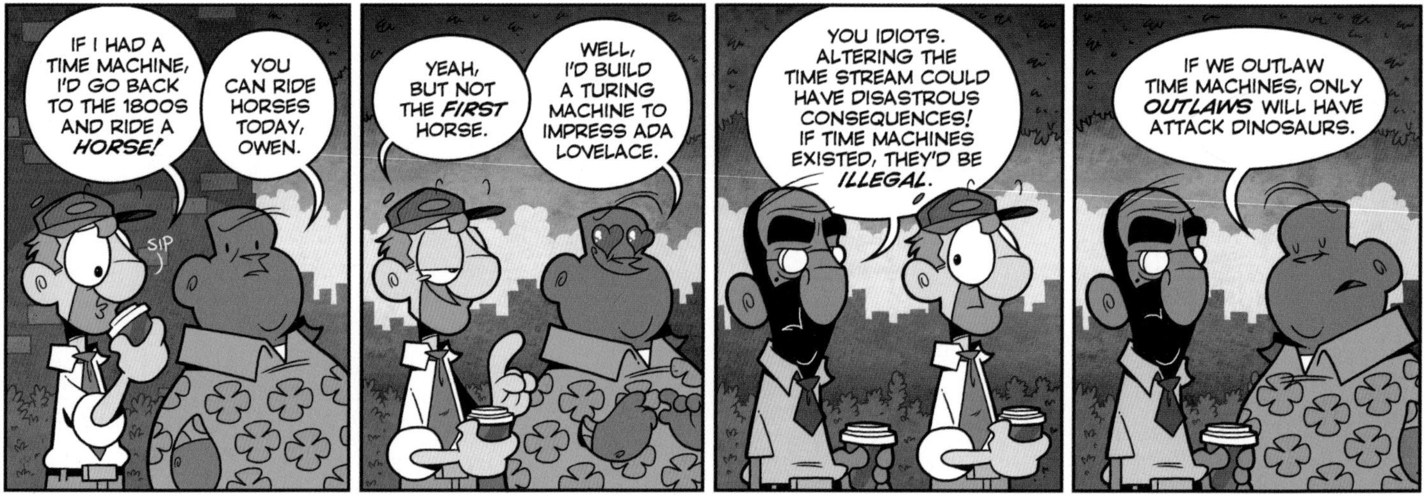
IF I HAD A TIME MACHINE, I'D GO BACK TO THE 1800S AND RIDE A *HORSE!*
YOU CAN RIDE HORSES TODAY, OWEN.
SIP
YEAH, BUT NOT THE *FIRST* HORSE.
WELL, I'D BUILD A TURING MACHINE TO IMPRESS ADA LOVELACE.
YOU IDIOTS. ALTERING THE TIME STREAM COULD HAVE DISASTROUS CONSEQUENCES! IF TIME MACHINES EXISTED, THEY'D BE *ILLEGAL*.
IF WE OUTLAW TIME MACHINES, ONLY *OUTLAWS* WILL HAVE ATTACK DINOSAURS.

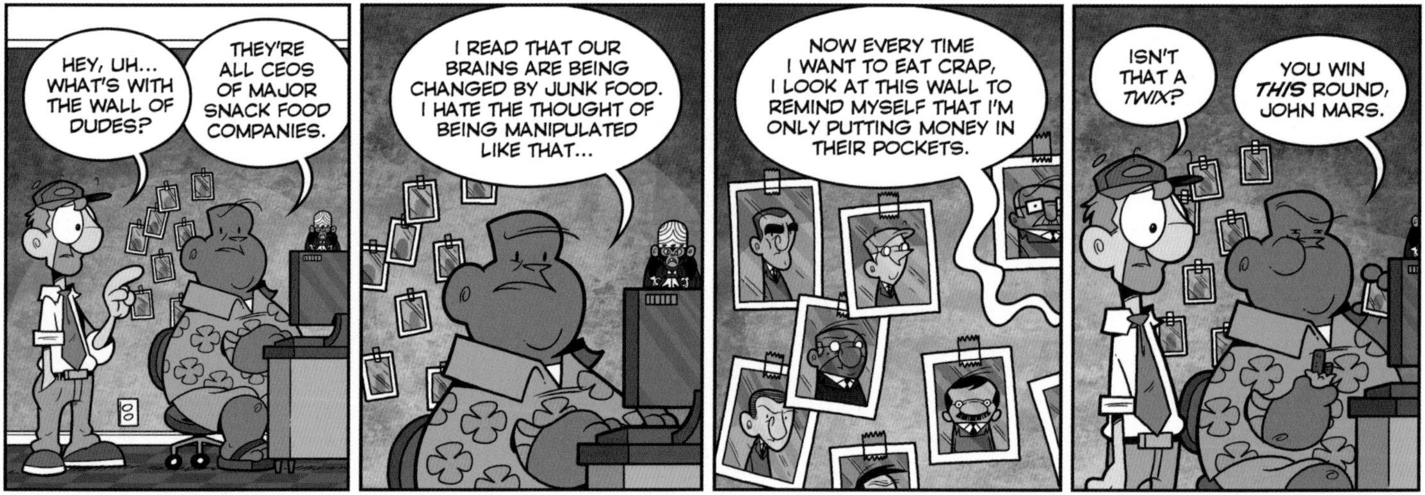
HEY, UH... WHAT'S WITH THE WALL OF DUDES?
THEY'RE ALL CEOS OF MAJOR SNACK FOOD COMPANIES.
I READ THAT OUR BRAINS ARE BEING CHANGED BY JUNK FOOD. I HATE THE THOUGHT OF BEING MANIPULATED LIKE THAT...
NOW EVERY TIME I WANT TO EAT CRAP, I LOOK AT THIS WALL TO REMIND MYSELF THAT I'M ONLY PUTTING MONEY IN THEIR POCKETS.
ISN'T THAT A *TWIX*?
YOU WIN *THIS* ROUND, JOHN MARS.

RUNTIME ERROR

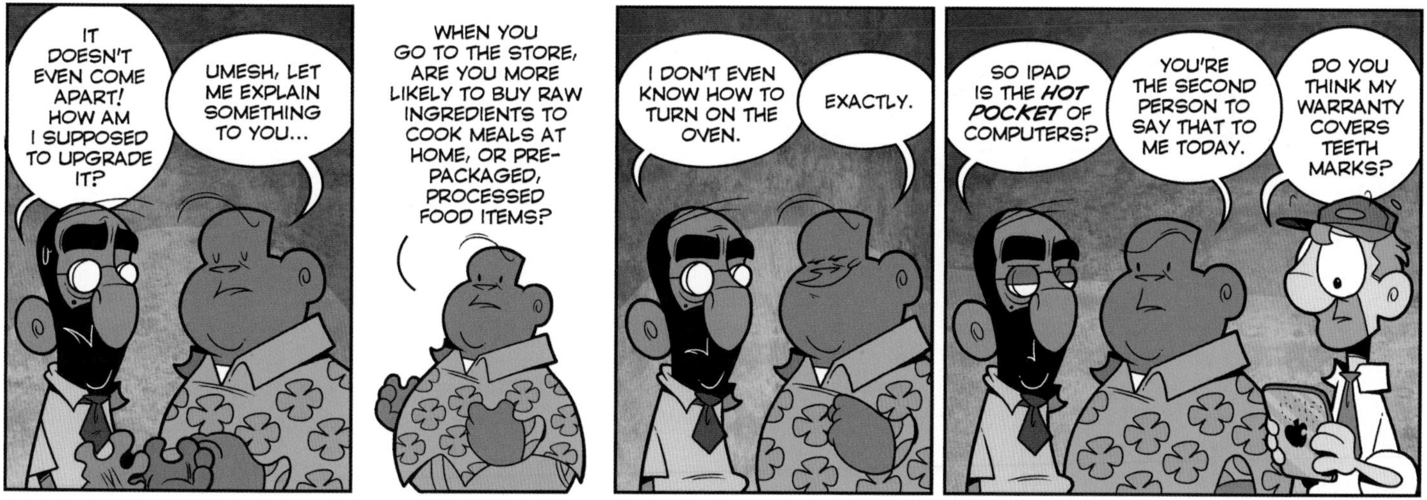
IT DOESN'T EVEN COME APART! HOW AM I SUPPOSED TO UPGRADE IT?
UMESH, LET ME EXPLAIN SOMETHING TO YOU...
WHEN YOU GO TO THE STORE, ARE YOU MORE LIKELY TO BUY RAW INGREDIENTS TO COOK MEALS AT HOME, OR PRE-PACKAGED, PROCESSED FOOD ITEMS?
I DON'T EVEN KNOW HOW TO TURN ON THE OVEN.
EXACTLY.
SO IPAD IS THE *HOT POCKET* OF COMPUTERS?
YOU'RE THE SECOND PERSON TO SAY THAT TO ME TODAY.
DO YOU THINK MY WARRANTY COVERS TEETH MARKS?

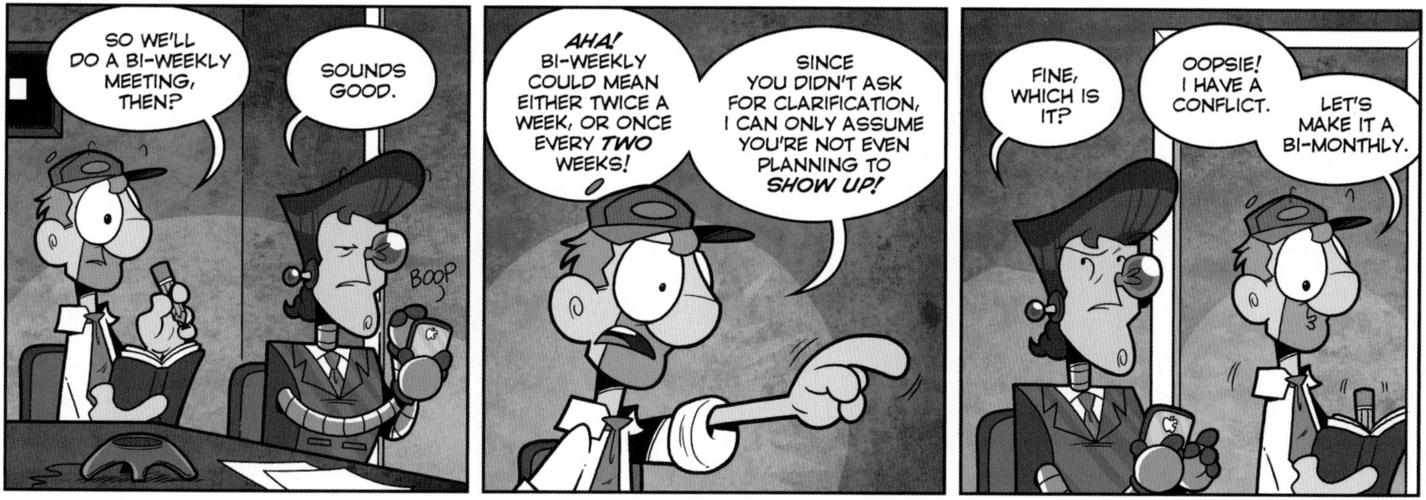
SO WE'LL DO A BI-WEEKLY MEETING, THEN?
SOUNDS GOOD.
BOOP
AHA! BI-WEEKLY COULD MEAN EITHER TWICE A WEEK, OR ONCE EVERY *TWO* WEEKS!
SINCE YOU DIDN'T ASK FOR CLARIFICATION, I CAN ONLY ASSUME YOU'RE NOT EVEN PLANNING TO *SHOW UP!*
FINE, WHICH IS IT?
OOPSIE! I HAVE A CONFLICT.
LET'S MAKE IT A BI-MONTHLY.

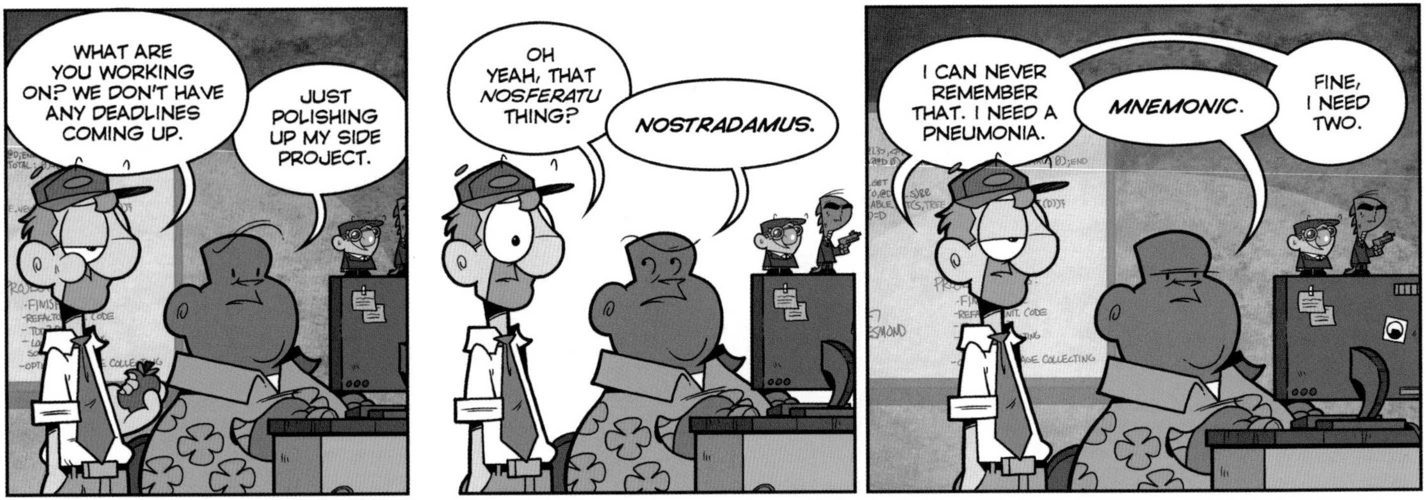
WHAT ARE YOU WORKING ON? WE DON'T HAVE ANY DEADLINES COMING UP.
JUST POLISHING UP MY SIDE PROJECT.
OH YEAH, THAT *NOSFERATU* THING?
NOSTRADAMUS.
I CAN NEVER REMEMBER THAT. I NEED A PNEUMONIA.
MNEMONIC.
FINE, I NEED TWO.

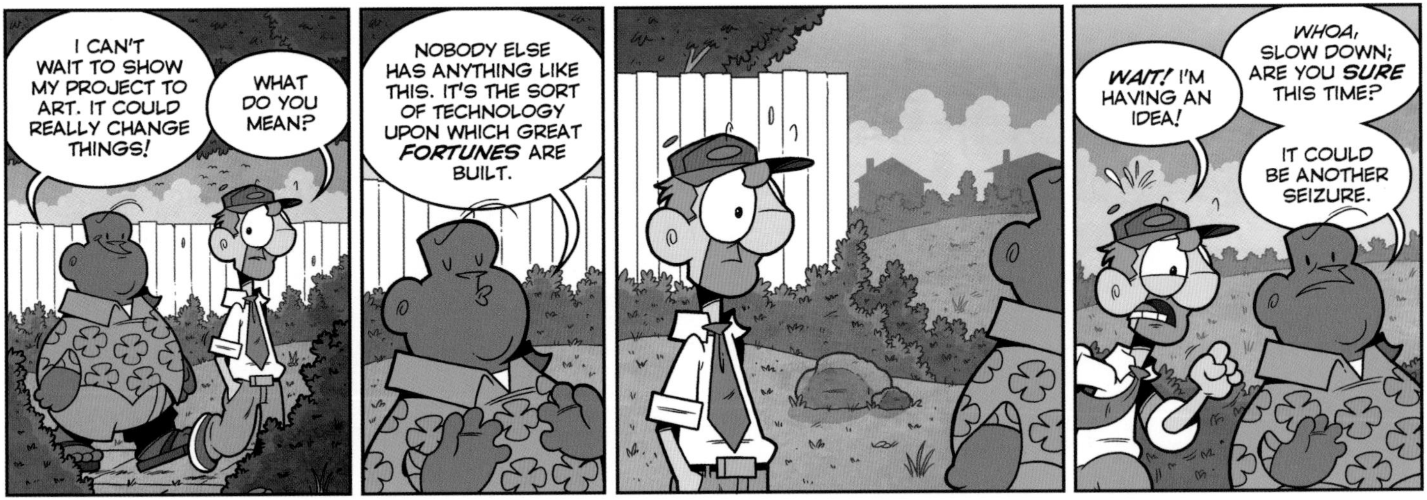
I CAN'T WAIT TO SHOW MY PROJECT TO ART. IT COULD REALLY CHANGE THINGS*!*
WHAT DO YOU MEAN?
NOBODY ELSE HAS ANYTHING LIKE THIS. IT'S THE SORT OF TECHNOLOGY UPON WHICH GREAT ***FORTUNES*** ARE BUILT.
WAIT! I'M HAVING AN IDEA*!*
WHOA, SLOW DOWN; ARE YOU ***SURE*** THIS TIME?
IT COULD BE ANOTHER SEIZURE.

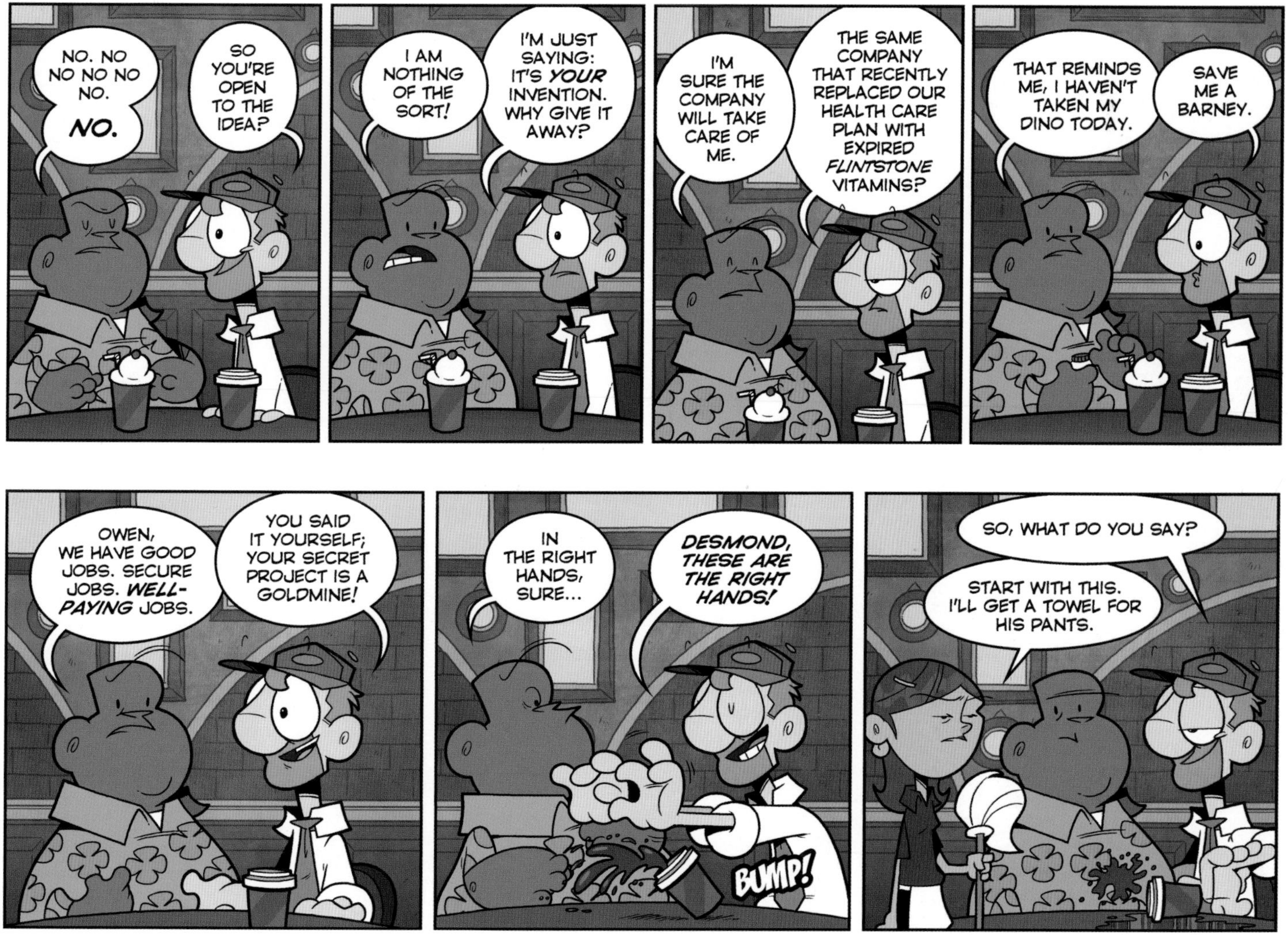

NO. NO NO NO NO NO. *NO.*
SO YOU'RE OPEN TO THE IDEA?
I AM NOTHING OF THE SORT!
I'M JUST SAYING: IT'S *YOUR* INVENTION. WHY GIVE IT AWAY?
I'M SURE THE COMPANY WILL TAKE CARE OF ME.
THE SAME COMPANY THAT RECENTLY REPLACED OUR HEALTH CARE PLAN WITH EXPIRED *FLINTSTONE* VITAMINS?
THAT REMINDS ME, I HAVEN'T TAKEN MY DINO TODAY.
SAVE ME A BARNEY.
OWEN, WE HAVE GOOD JOBS. SECURE JOBS. *WELL-PAYING* JOBS.
YOU SAID IT YOURSELF; YOUR SECRET PROJECT IS A GOLDMINE!
IN THE RIGHT HANDS, SURE...
DESMOND, THESE ARE THE RIGHT HANDS!
BUMP!
SO, WHAT DO YOU SAY?
START WITH THIS. I'LL GET A TOWEL FOR HIS PANTS.

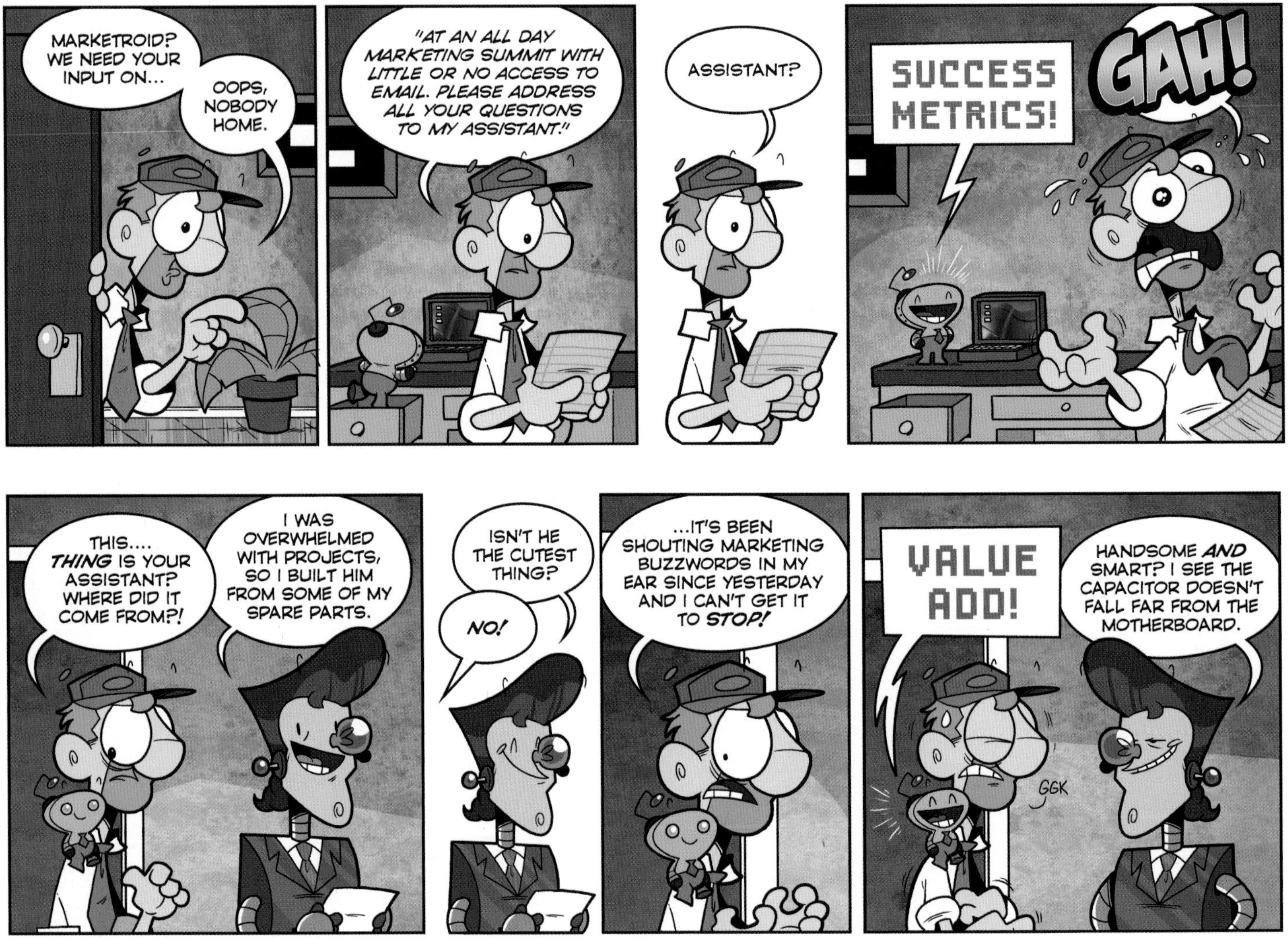

MARKETROID? WE NEED YOUR INPUT ON...
OOPS, NOBODY HOME.
"AT AN ALL DAY MARKETING SUMMIT WITH LITTLE OR NO ACCESS TO EMAIL. PLEASE ADDRESS ALL YOUR QUESTIONS TO MY ASSISTANT."
ASSISTANT?
SUCCESS METRICS!
GAH!
THIS.... *THING* IS YOUR ASSISTANT? WHERE DID IT COME FROM?!
I WAS OVERWHELMED WITH PROJECTS, SO I BUILT HIM FROM SOME OF MY SPARE PARTS.
ISN'T HE THE CUTEST THING?
NO!
...IT'S BEEN SHOUTING MARKETING BUZZWORDS IN MY EAR SINCE YESTERDAY AND I CAN'T GET IT TO *STOP!*
VALUE ADD!
GGK
HANDSOME *AND* SMART? I SEE THE CAPACITOR DOESN'T FALL FAR FROM THE MOTHERBOARD.

RUNTIME ERROR

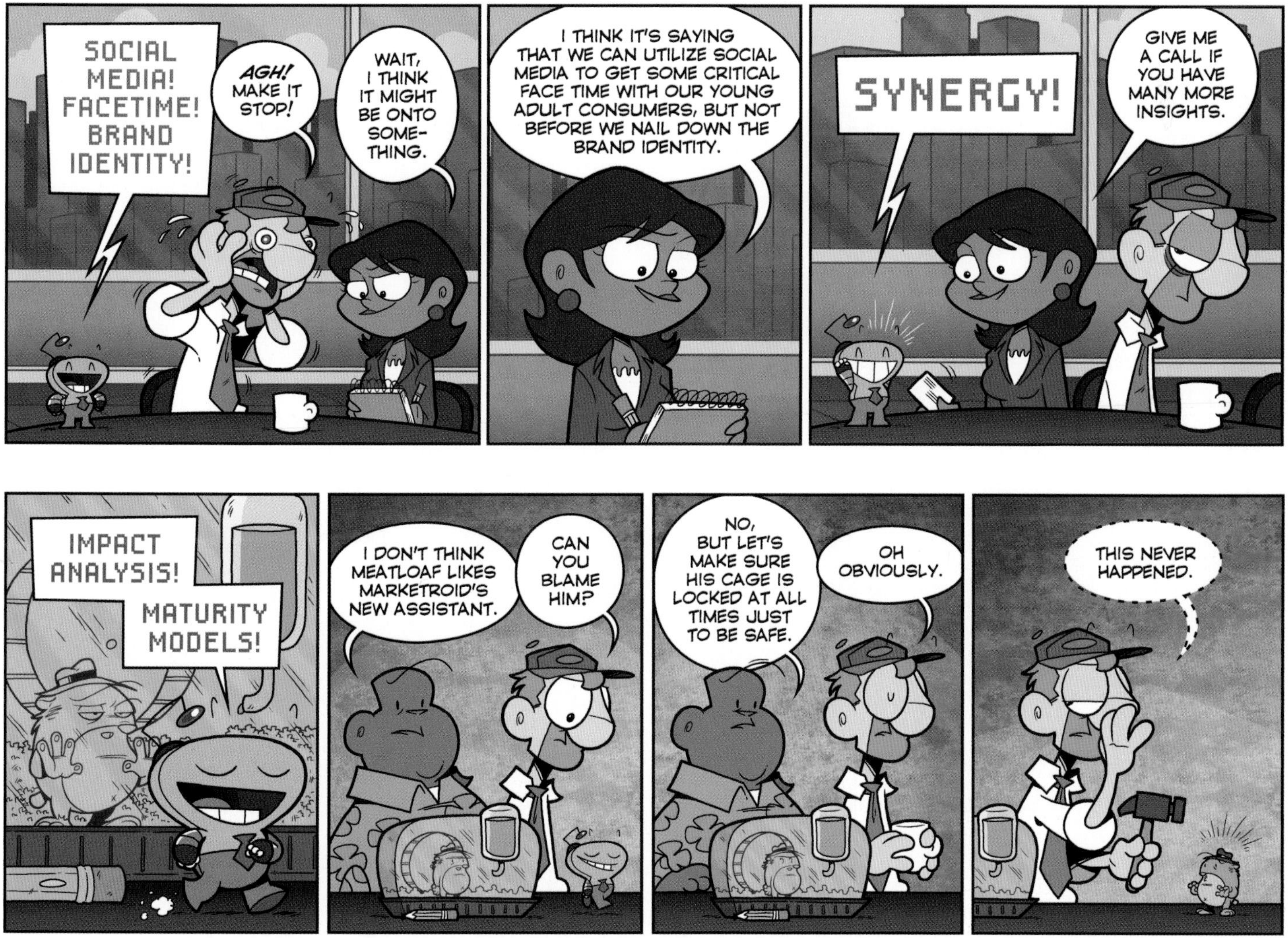
SOCIAL MEDIA! FACETIME! BRAND IDENTITY!
AGH! MAKE IT STOP!
WAIT, I THINK IT MIGHT BE ONTO SOME-THING.
I THINK IT'S SAYING THAT WE CAN UTILIZE SOCIAL MEDIA TO GET SOME CRITICAL FACE TIME WITH OUR YOUNG ADULT CONSUMERS, BUT NOT BEFORE WE NAIL DOWN THE BRAND IDENTITY.
SYNERGY!
GIVE ME A CALL IF YOU HAVE MANY MORE INSIGHTS.
IMPACT ANALYSIS!
MATURITY MODELS!
I DON'T THINK MEATLOAF LIKES MARKETROID'S NEW ASSISTANT.
CAN YOU BLAME HIM?
NO, BUT LET'S MAKE SURE HIS CAGE IS LOCKED AT ALL TIMES JUST TO BE SAFE.
OH OBVIOUSLY.
THIS NEVER HAPPENED.

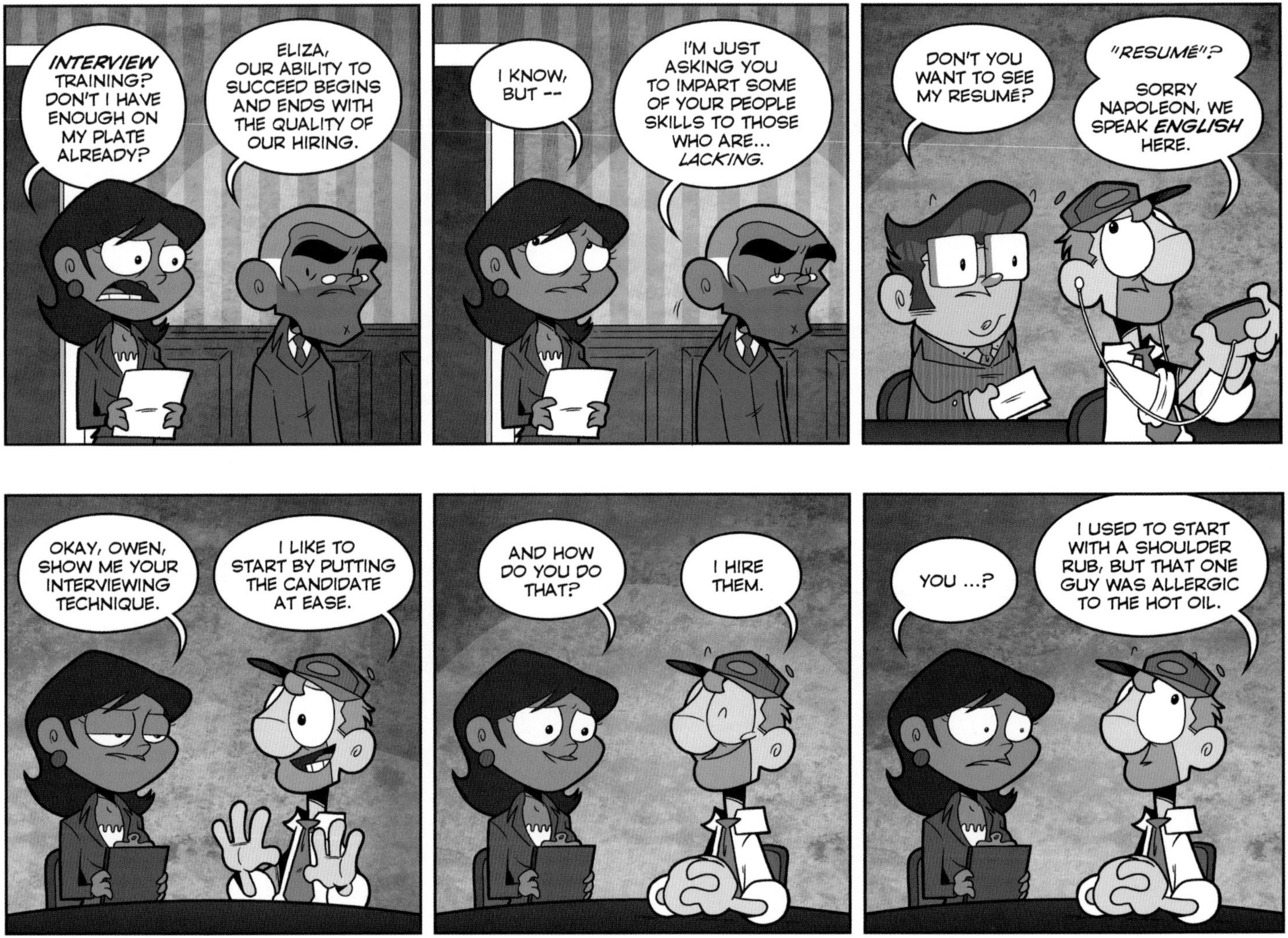
INTERVIEW TRAINING? DON'T I HAVE ENOUGH ON MY PLATE ALREADY?
ELIZA, OUR ABILITY TO SUCCEED BEGINS AND ENDS WITH THE QUALITY OF OUR HIRING.
I KNOW, BUT --
I'M JUST ASKING YOU TO IMPART SOME OF YOUR PEOPLE SKILLS TO THOSE WHO ARE... LACKING.
DON'T YOU WANT TO SEE MY RESUMÉ?
"RESUMÉ"? SORRY NAPOLEON, WE SPEAK ENGLISH HERE.
OKAY, OWEN, SHOW ME YOUR INTERVIEWING TECHNIQUE.
I LIKE TO START BY PUTTING THE CANDIDATE AT EASE.
AND HOW DO YOU DO THAT?
I HIRE THEM.
YOU ...?
I USED TO START WITH A SHOULDER RUB, BUT THAT ONE GUY WAS ALLERGIC TO THE HOT OIL.

RUNTIME ERROR

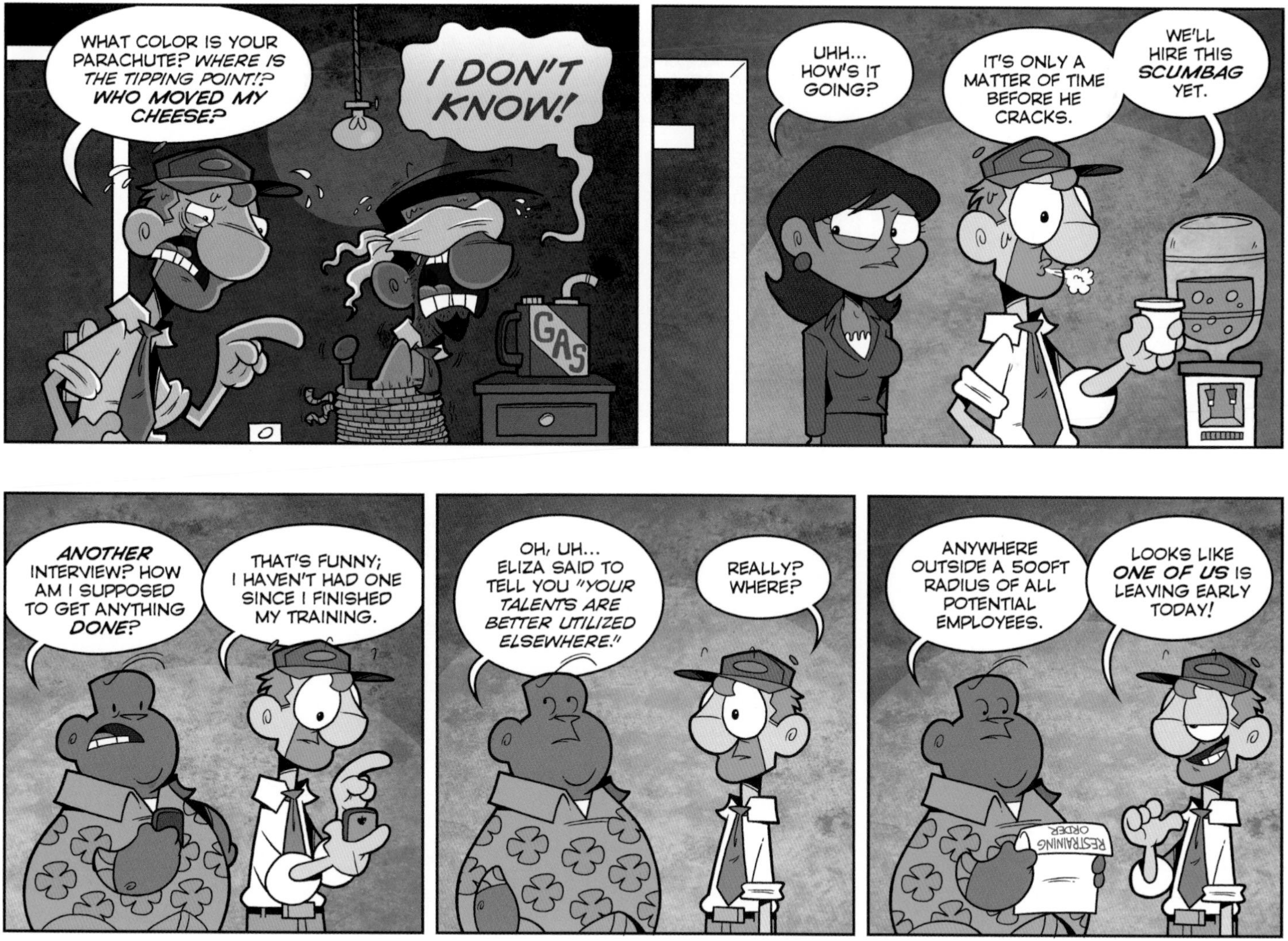

WHAT COLOR IS YOUR PARACHUTE? *WHERE IS THE TIPPING POINT!?* ***WHO MOVED MY CHEESE?***
I DON'T KNOW!
GAS
UHH... HOW'S IT GOING?
IT'S ONLY A MATTER OF TIME BEFORE HE CRACKS.
WE'LL HIRE THIS ***SCUMBAG*** YET.
ANOTHER INTERVIEW? HOW AM I SUPPOSED TO GET ANYTHING ***DONE***?
THAT'S FUNNY; I HAVEN'T HAD ONE SINCE I FINISHED MY TRAINING.
OH, UH... ELIZA SAID TO TELL YOU *"YOUR TALENTS ARE BETTER UTILIZED ELSEWHERE."*
REALLY? WHERE?
ANYWHERE OUTSIDE A 500FT RADIUS OF ALL POTENTIAL EMPLOYEES.
RESTRAINING ORDER
LOOKS LIKE ***ONE OF US*** IS LEAVING EARLY TODAY!

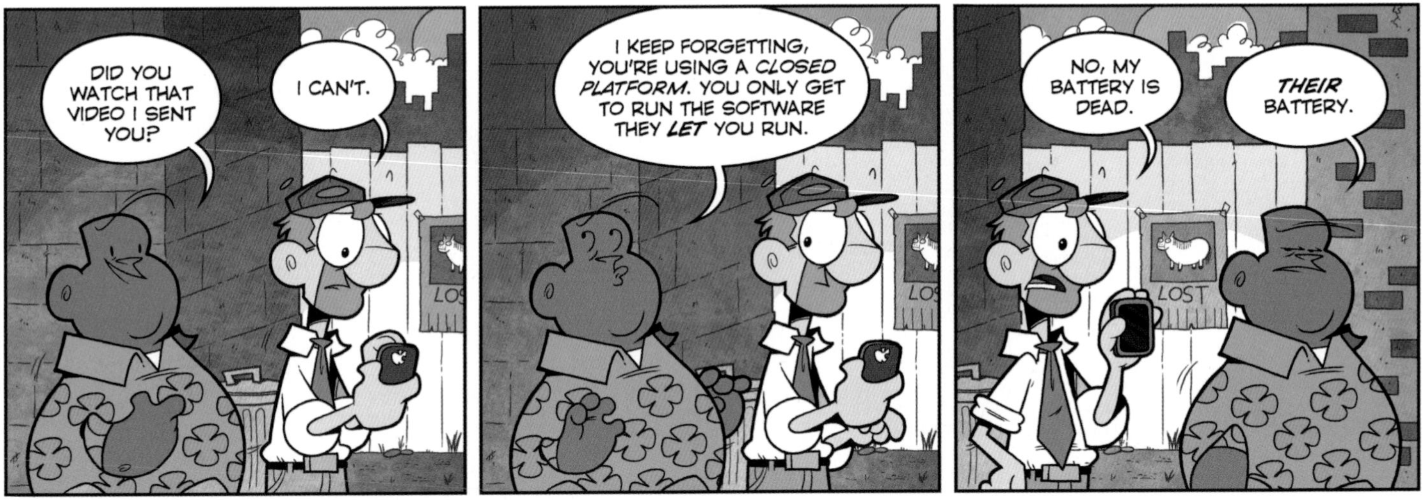
DID YOU WATCH THAT VIDEO I SENT YOU?
I CAN'T.
I KEEP FORGETTING, YOU'RE USING A *CLOSED PLATFORM*. YOU ONLY GET TO RUN THE SOFTWARE THEY ***LET*** YOU RUN.
NO, MY BATTERY IS DEAD.
THEIR BATTERY.
LOST

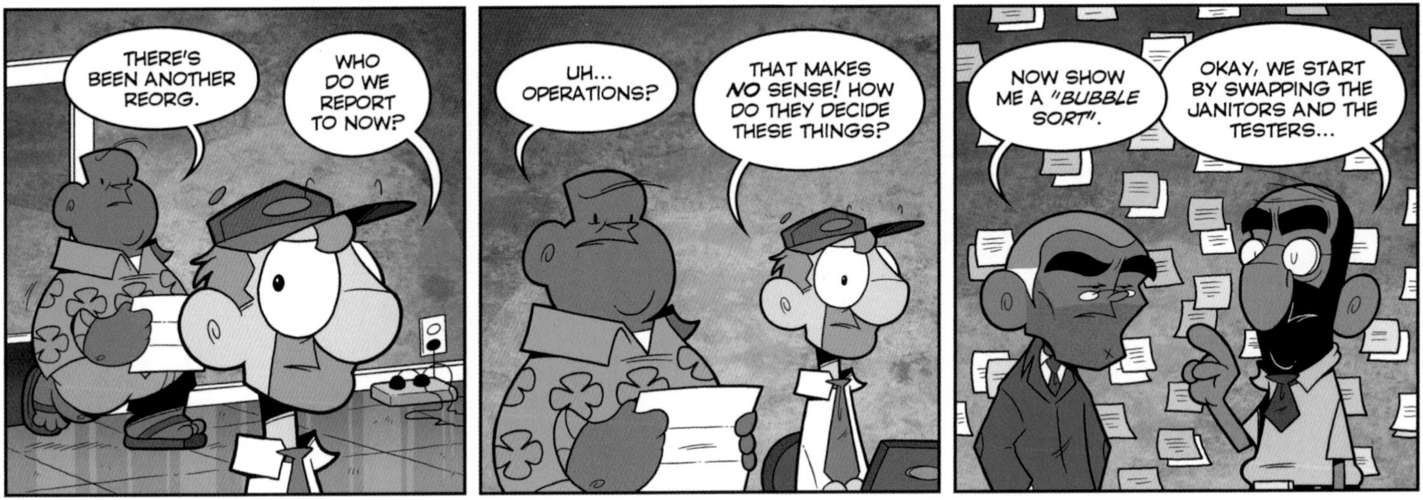
THERE'S BEEN ANOTHER REORG.
WHO DO WE REPORT TO NOW?
UH... OPERATIONS?
THAT MAKES ***NO*** SENSE! HOW DO THEY DECIDE THESE THINGS?
NOW SHOW ME A *"BUBBLE SORT"*.
OKAY, WE START BY SWAPPING THE JANITORS AND THE TESTERS...

RUNTIME ERROR

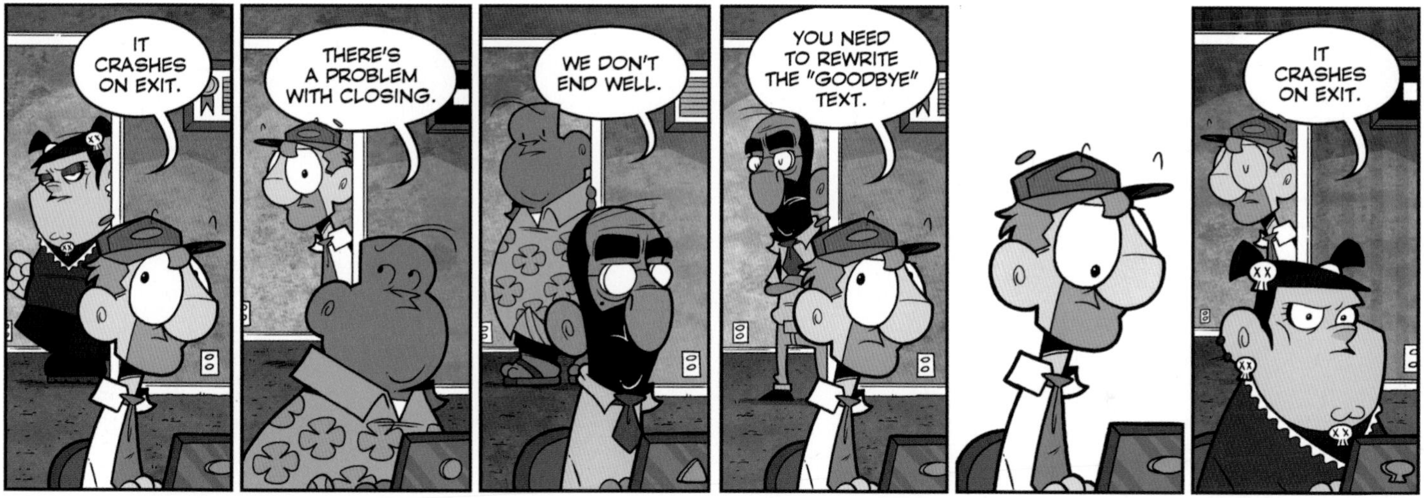
IT CRASHES ON EXIT.
THERE'S A PROBLEM WITH CLOSING.
WE DON'T END WELL.
YOU NEED TO REWRITE THE "GOODBYE" TEXT.
IT CRASHES ON EXIT.

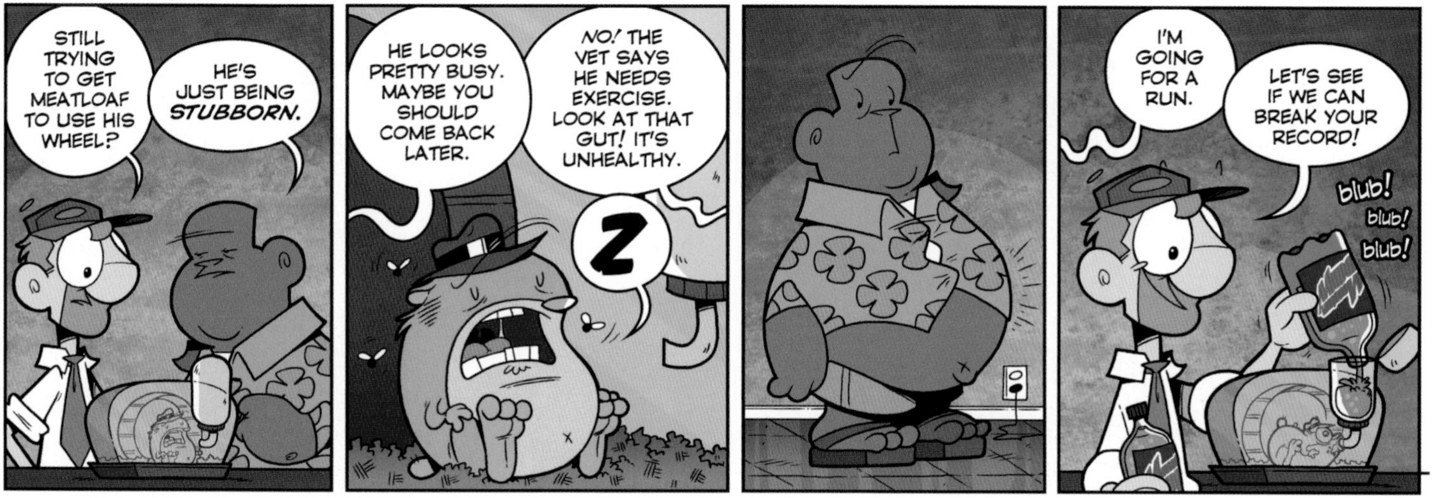
STILL TRYING TO GET MEATLOAF TO USE HIS WHEEL?
HE'S JUST BEING STUBBORN.
HE LOOKS PRETTY BUSY. MAYBE YOU SHOULD COME BACK LATER.
NO! THE VET SAYS HE NEEDS EXERCISE. LOOK AT THAT GUT! IT'S UNHEALTHY.
Z
I'M GOING FOR A RUN.
LET'S SEE IF WE CAN BREAK YOUR RECORD!
blub!
blub!
blub!

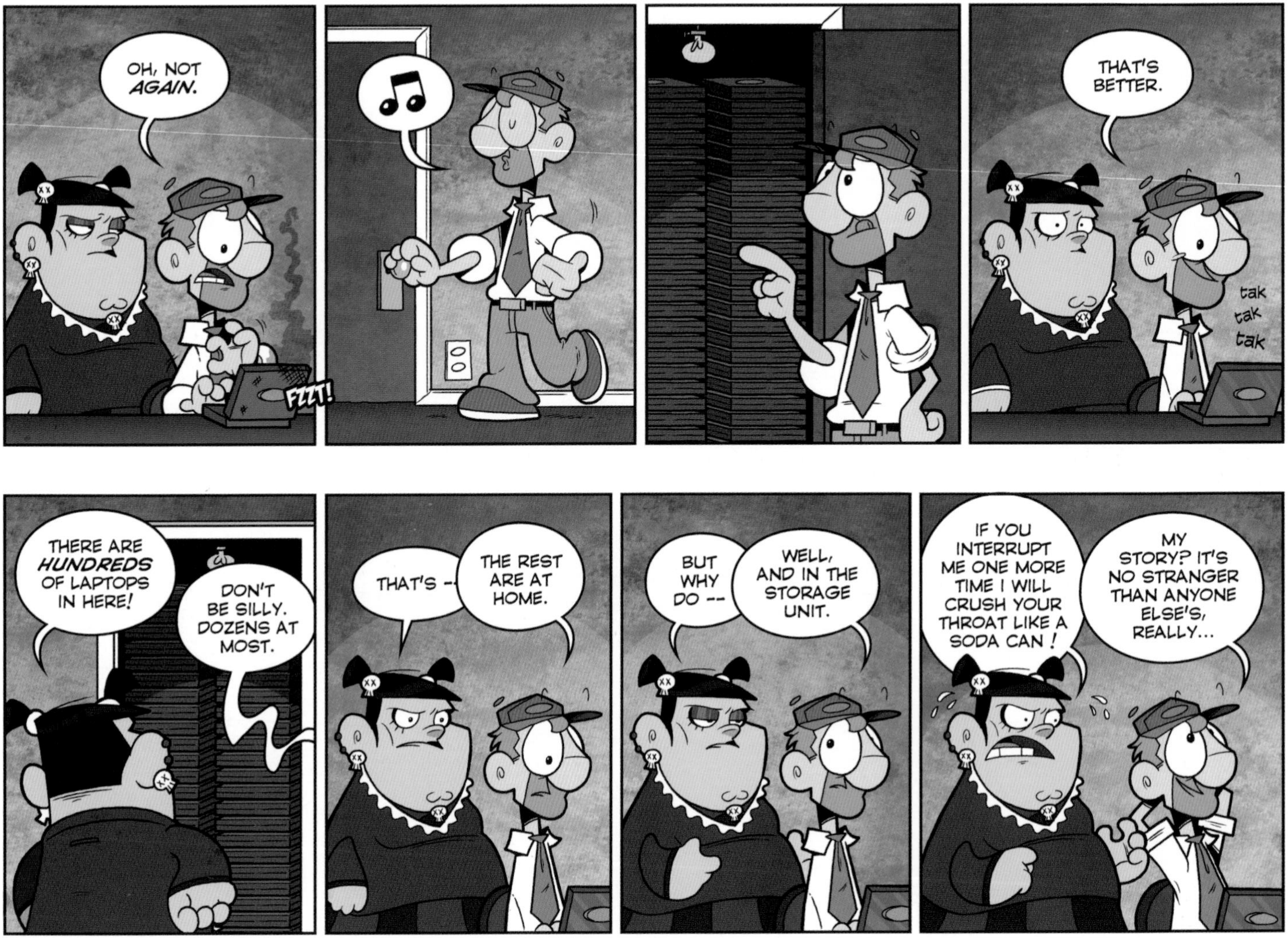
OH, NOT *AGAIN*.
FZZT!
THAT'S BETTER.
tak tak tak
THERE ARE *HUNDREDS* OF LAPTOPS IN HERE!
DON'T BE SILLY. DOZENS AT MOST.
THAT'S --
THE REST ARE AT HOME.
BUT WHY DO --
WELL, AND IN THE STORAGE UNIT.
IF YOU INTERRUPT ME ONE MORE TIME I WILL CRUSH YOUR THROAT LIKE A SODA CAN!
MY STORY? IT'S NO STRANGER THAN ANYONE ELSE'S, REALLY...

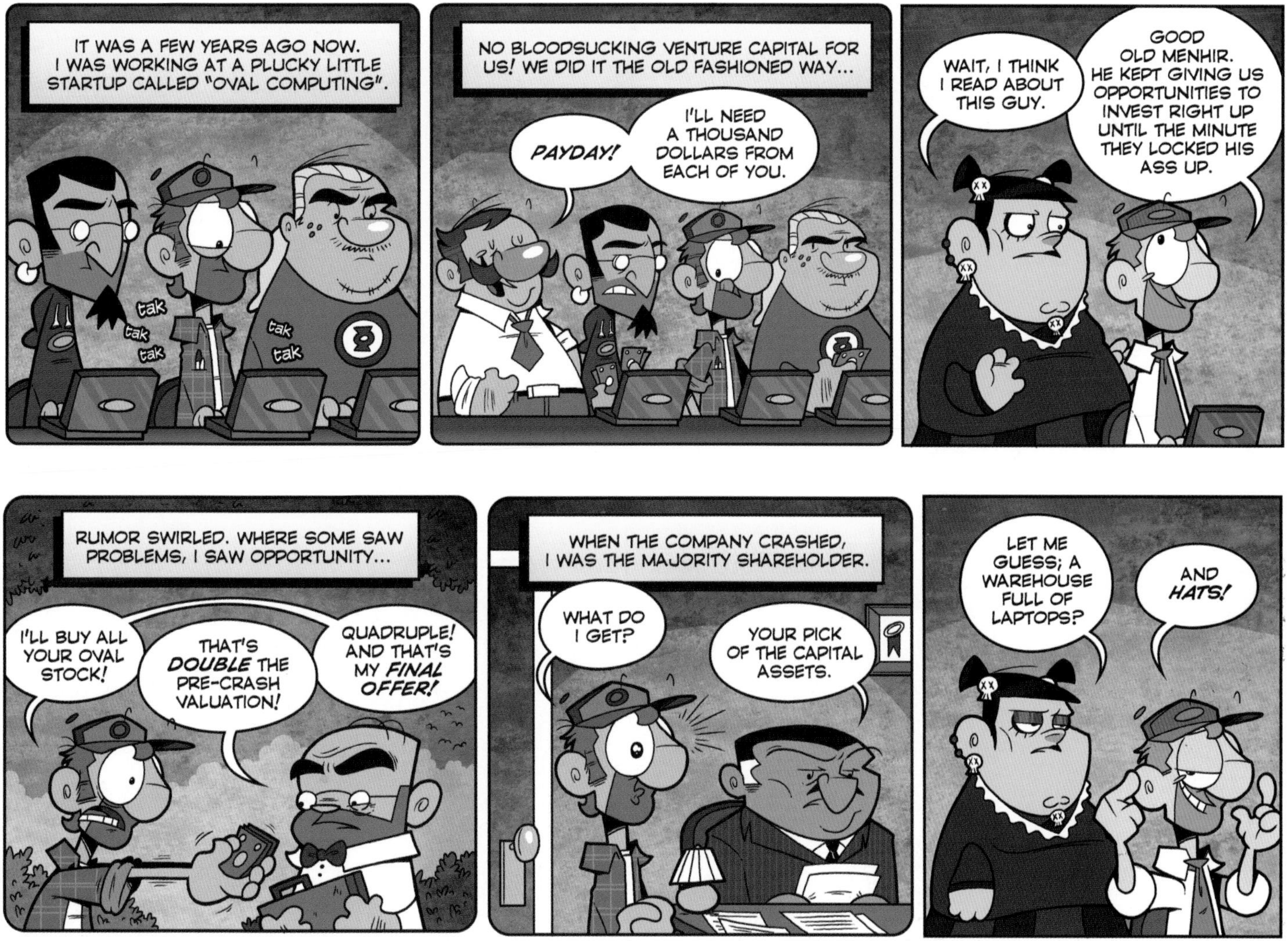
IT WAS A FEW YEARS AGO NOW. I WAS WORKING AT A PLUCKY LITTLE STARTUP CALLED "OVAL COMPUTING".
tak
tak
tak
tak
tak
NO BLOODSUCKING VENTURE CAPITAL FOR US! WE DID IT THE OLD FASHIONED WAY...
PAYDAY!
I'LL NEED A THOUSAND DOLLARS FROM EACH OF YOU.
WAIT, I THINK I READ ABOUT THIS GUY.
GOOD OLD MENHIR. HE KEPT GIVING US OPPORTUNITIES TO INVEST RIGHT UP UNTIL THE MINUTE THEY LOCKED HIS ASS UP.
RUMOR SWIRLED. WHERE SOME SAW PROBLEMS, I SAW OPPORTUNITY...
I'LL BUY ALL YOUR OVAL STOCK!
THAT'S DOUBLE THE PRE-CRASH VALUATION!
QUADRUPLE! AND THAT'S MY FINAL OFFER!
WHEN THE COMPANY CRASHED, I WAS THE MAJORITY SHAREHOLDER.
WHAT DO I GET?
YOUR PICK OF THE CAPITAL ASSETS.
LET ME GUESS; A WAREHOUSE FULL OF LAPTOPS?
AND HATS!

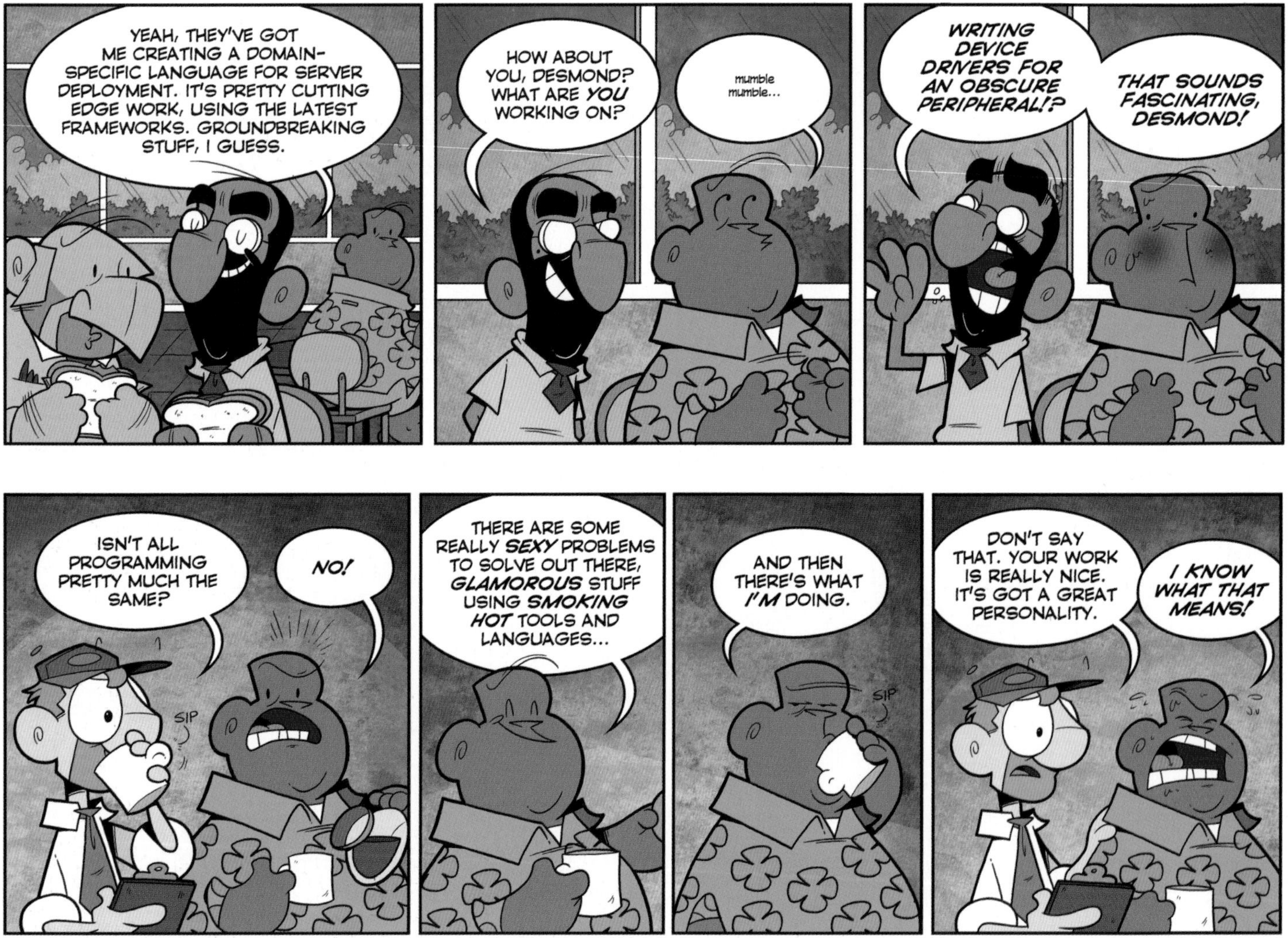
YEAH, THEY'VE GOT ME CREATING A DOMAIN-SPECIFIC LANGUAGE FOR SERVER DEPLOYMENT. IT'S PRETTY CUTTING EDGE WORK, USING THE LATEST FRAMEWORKS. GROUNDBREAKING STUFF, I GUESS.
HOW ABOUT YOU, DESMOND? WHAT ARE *YOU* WORKING ON?
mumble mumble...
WRITING DEVICE DRIVERS FOR AN OBSCURE PERIPHERAL!?
THAT SOUNDS FASCINATING, DESMOND!
ISN'T ALL PROGRAMMING PRETTY MUCH THE SAME?
SIP
NO!
THERE ARE SOME REALLY ***SEXY*** PROBLEMS TO SOLVE OUT THERE, ***GLAMOROUS*** STUFF USING ***SMOKING HOT*** TOOLS AND LANGUAGES...
AND THEN THERE'S WHAT ***I'M*** DOING.
SIP
DON'T SAY THAT. YOUR WORK IS REALLY NICE. IT'S GOT A GREAT PERSONALITY.
I KNOW WHAT THAT MEANS!

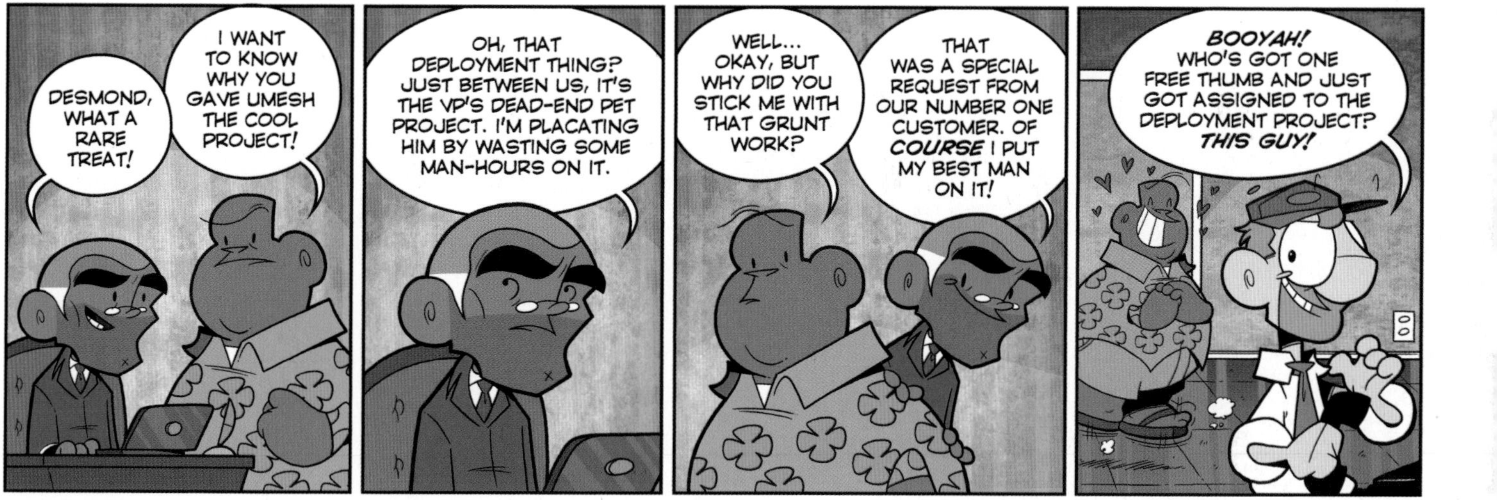
DESMOND, WHAT A RARE TREAT!
I WANT TO KNOW WHY YOU GAVE UMESH THE COOL PROJECT!
OH, THAT DEPLOYMENT THING? JUST BETWEEN US, IT'S THE VP'S DEAD-END PET PROJECT. I'M PLACATING HIM BY WASTING SOME MAN-HOURS ON IT.
WELL... OKAY, BUT WHY DID YOU STICK ME WITH THAT GRUNT WORK?
THAT WAS A SPECIAL REQUEST FROM OUR NUMBER ONE CUSTOMER. OF COURSE I PUT MY BEST MAN ON IT!
BOOYAH! WHO'S GOT ONE FREE THUMB AND JUST GOT ASSIGNED TO THE DEPLOYMENT PROJECT? THIS GUY!

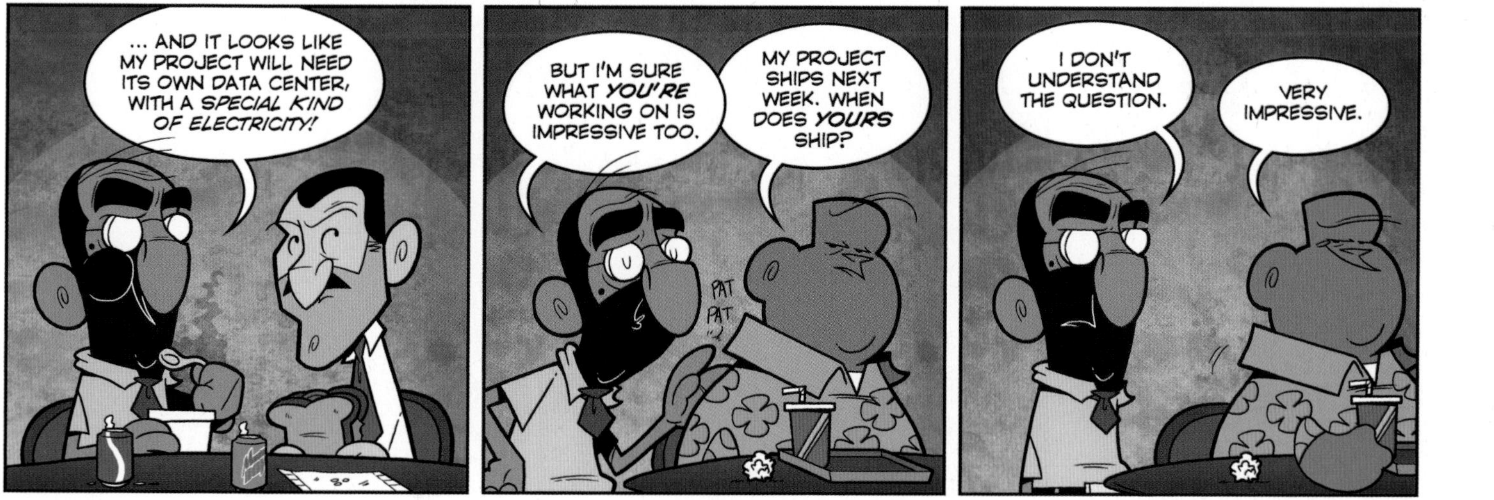
... AND IT LOOKS LIKE MY PROJECT WILL NEED ITS OWN DATA CENTER, WITH A SPECIAL KIND OF ELECTRICITY!
BUT I'M SURE WHAT YOU'RE WORKING ON IS IMPRESSIVE TOO.
PAT PAT
MY PROJECT SHIPS NEXT WEEK. WHEN DOES YOURS SHIP?
I DON'T UNDERSTAND THE QUESTION.
VERY IMPRESSIVE.

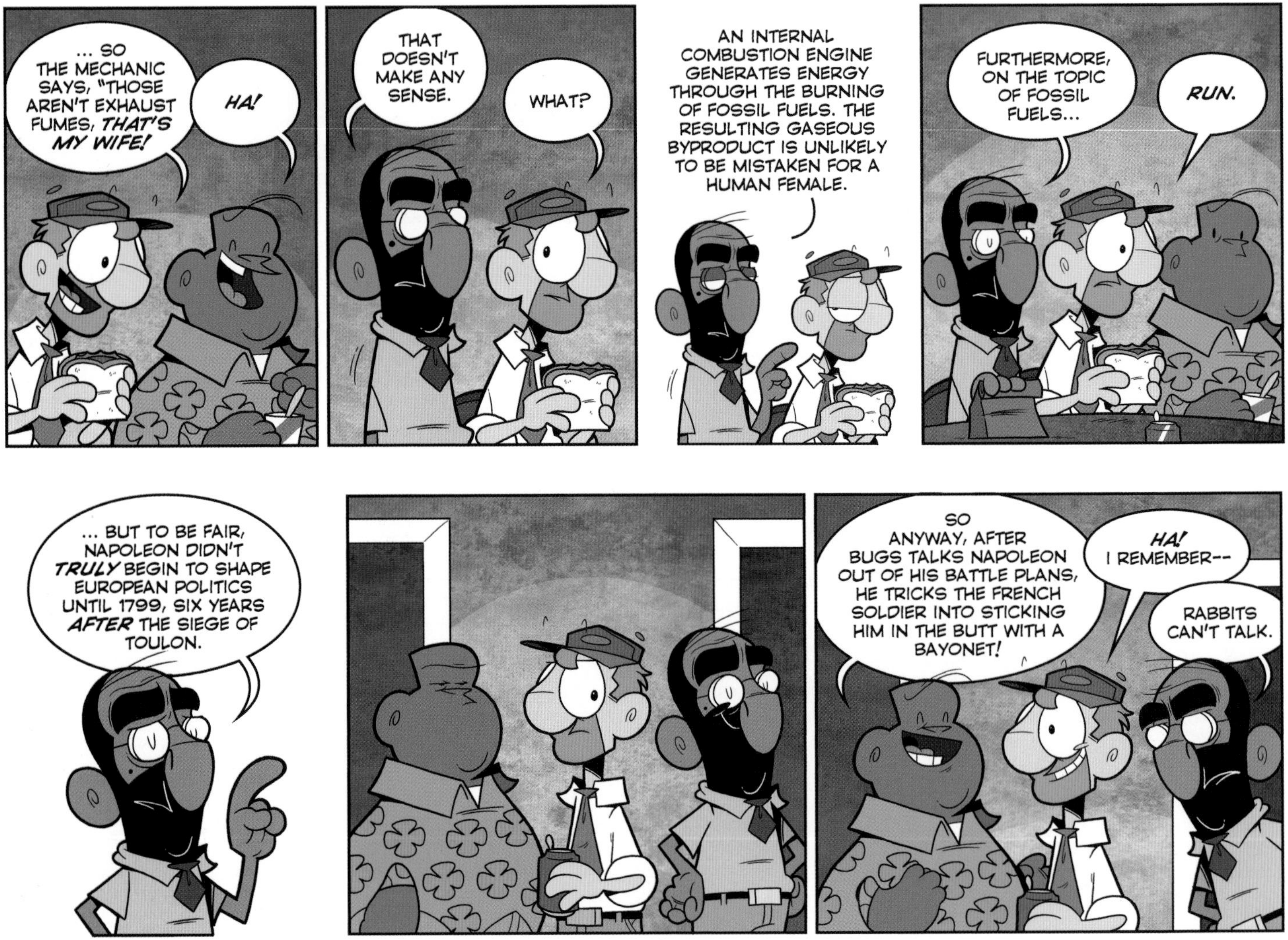
... SO THE MECHANIC SAYS, "THOSE AREN'T EXHAUST FUMES, *THAT'S MY WIFE!*
HA!
THAT DOESN'T MAKE ANY SENSE.
WHAT?
AN INTERNAL COMBUSTION ENGINE GENERATES ENERGY THROUGH THE BURNING OF FOSSIL FUELS. THE RESULTING GASEOUS BYPRODUCT IS UNLIKELY TO BE MISTAKEN FOR A HUMAN FEMALE.
FURTHERMORE, ON THE TOPIC OF FOSSIL FUELS...
RUN.
... BUT TO BE FAIR, NAPOLEON DIDN'T *TRULY* BEGIN TO SHAPE EUROPEAN POLITICS UNTIL 1799, SIX YEARS *AFTER* THE SIEGE OF TOULON.
SO ANYWAY, AFTER BUGS TALKS NAPOLEON OUT OF HIS BATTLE PLANS, HE TRICKS THE FRENCH SOLDIER INTO STICKING HIM IN THE BUTT WITH A BAYONET!
HA! I REMEMBER--
RABBITS CAN'T TALK.

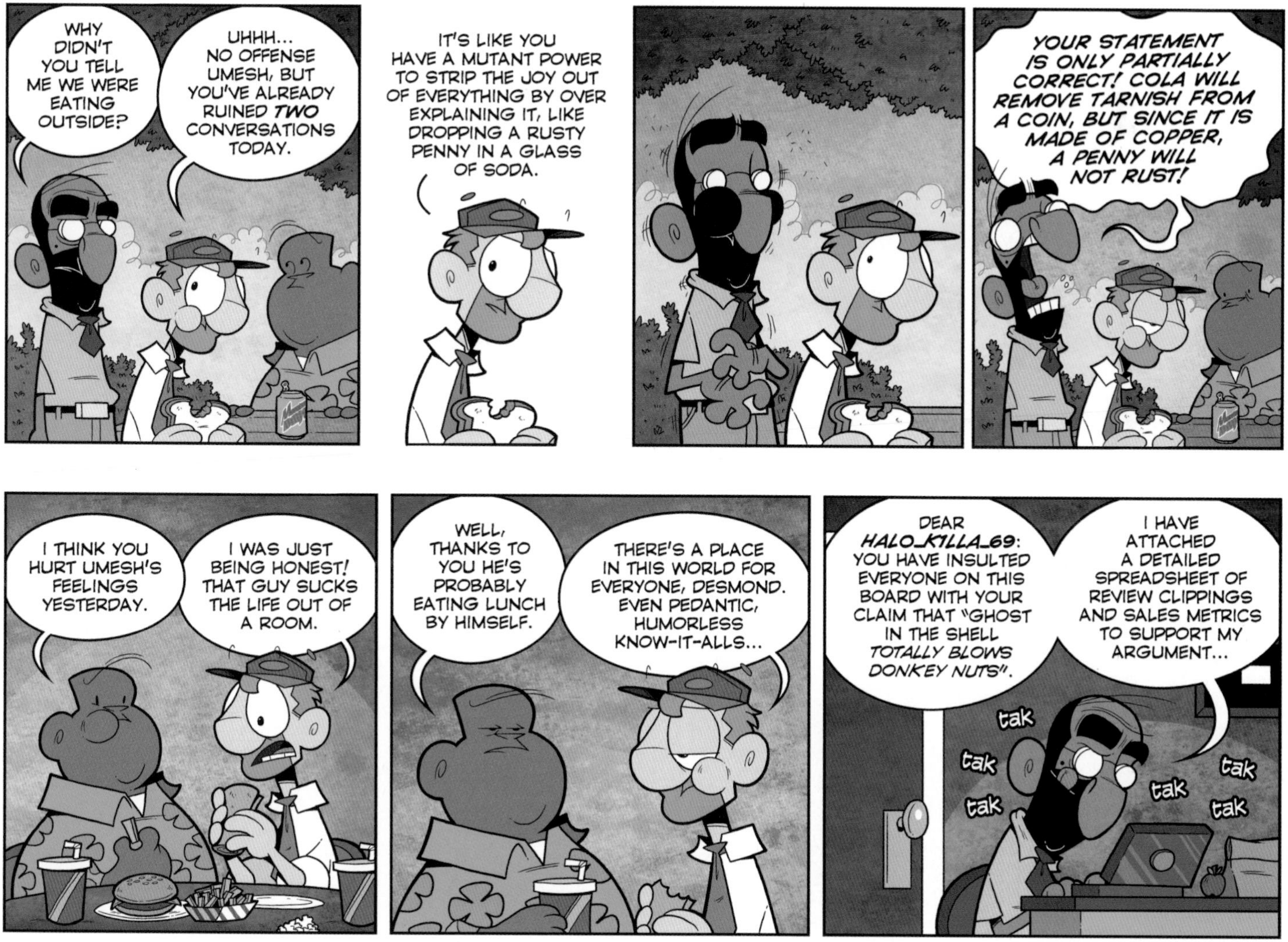
WHY DIDN'T YOU TELL ME WE WERE EATING OUTSIDE?
UHHH... NO OFFENSE UMESH, BUT YOU'VE ALREADY RUINED *TWO* CONVERSATIONS TODAY.
IT'S LIKE YOU HAVE A MUTANT POWER TO STRIP THE JOY OUT OF EVERYTHING BY OVER EXPLAINING IT, LIKE DROPPING A RUSTY PENNY IN A GLASS OF SODA.
YOUR STATEMENT IS ONLY PARTIALLY CORRECT! COLA WILL REMOVE TARNISH FROM A COIN, BUT SINCE IT IS MADE OF COPPER, A PENNY WILL NOT RUST!
I THINK YOU HURT UMESH'S FEELINGS YESTERDAY.
I WAS JUST BEING HONEST! THAT GUY SUCKS THE LIFE OUT OF A ROOM.
WELL, THANKS TO YOU HE'S PROBABLY EATING LUNCH BY HIMSELF.
THERE'S A PLACE IN THIS WORLD FOR EVERYONE, DESMOND. EVEN PEDANTIC, HUMORLESS KNOW-IT-ALLS...
DEAR *HALO_K1LLA_69*: YOU HAVE INSULTED EVERYONE ON THIS BOARD WITH YOUR CLAIM THAT "GHOST IN THE SHELL *TOTALLY BLOWS DONKEY NUTS*".
I HAVE ATTACHED A DETAILED SPREADSHEET OF REVIEW CLIPPINGS AND SALES METRICS TO SUPPORT MY ARGUMENT...
tak tak tak tak tak tak

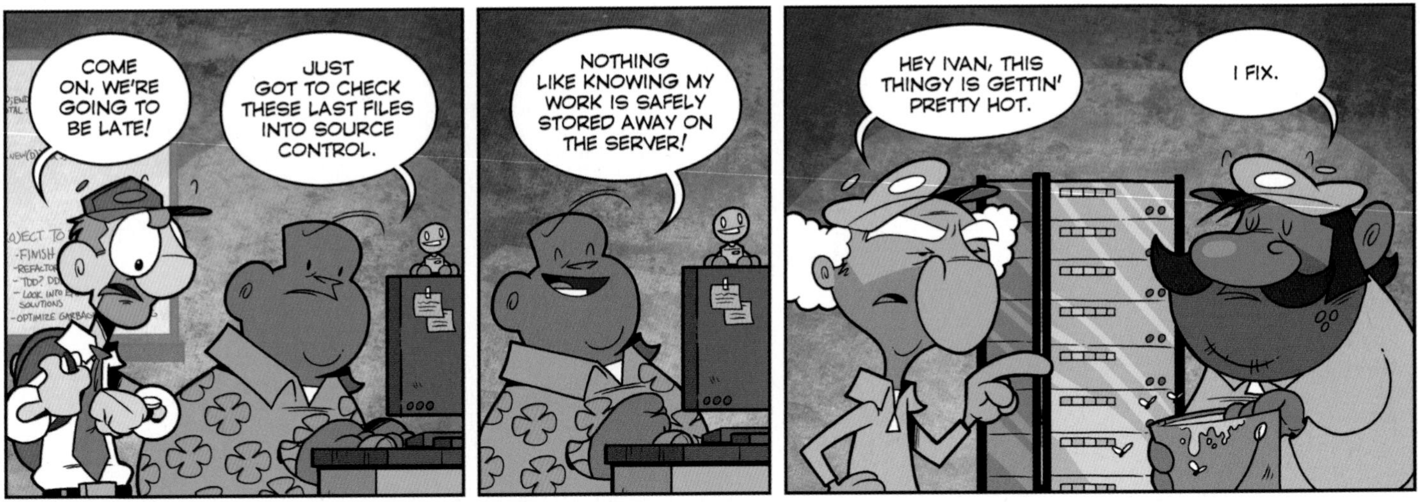
COME ON, WE'RE GOING TO BE LATE!
JUST GOT TO CHECK THESE LAST FILES INTO SOURCE CONTROL.
NOTHING LIKE KNOWING MY WORK IS SAFELY STORED AWAY ON THE SERVER!
HEY IVAN, THIS THINGY IS GETTIN' PRETTY HOT.
I FIX.

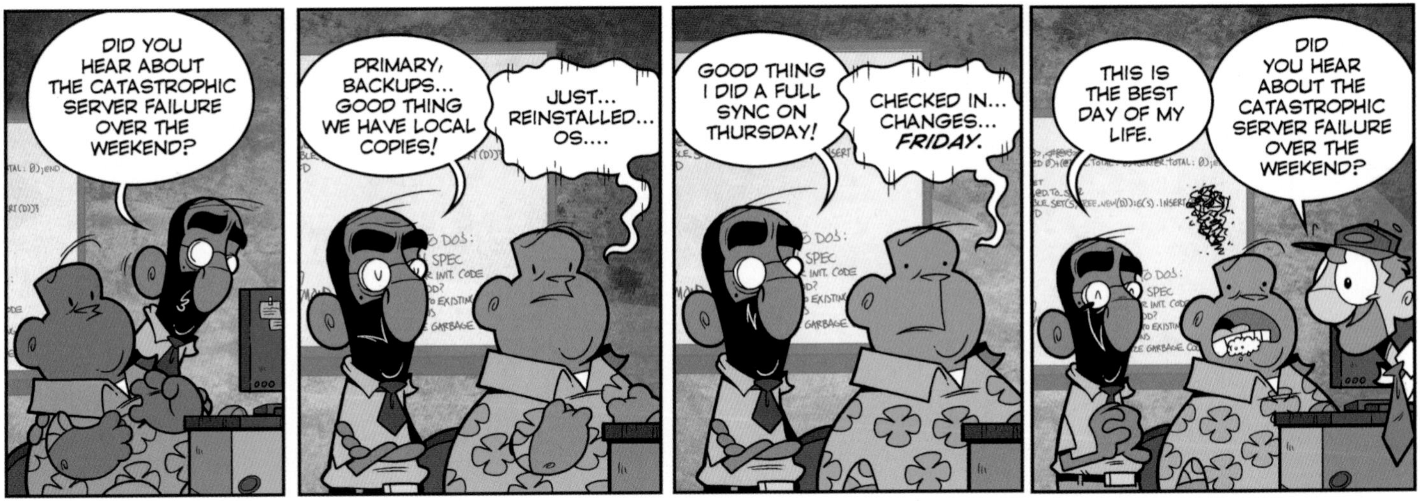
DID YOU HEAR ABOUT THE CATASTROPHIC SERVER FAILURE OVER THE WEEKEND?
PRIMARY, BACKUPS... GOOD THING WE HAVE LOCAL COPIES!
JUST... REINSTALLED... OS....
GOOD THING I DID A FULL SYNC ON THURSDAY!
CHECKED IN... CHANGES... FRIDAY.
THIS IS THE BEST DAY OF MY LIFE.
DID YOU HEAR ABOUT THE CATASTROPHIC SERVER FAILURE OVER THE WEEKEND?

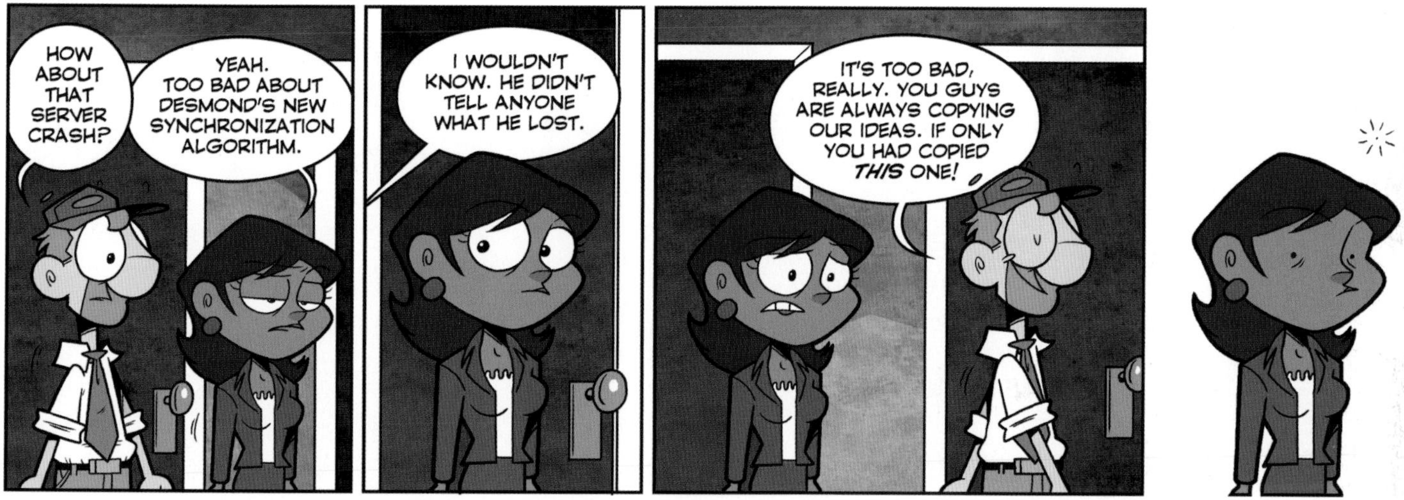
HOW ABOUT THAT SERVER CRASH?
YEAH. TOO BAD ABOUT DESMOND'S NEW SYNCHRONIZATION ALGORITHM.
I WOULDN'T KNOW. HE DIDN'T TELL ANYONE WHAT HE LOST.
IT'S TOO BAD, REALLY. YOU GUYS ARE ALWAYS COPYING OUR IDEAS. IF ONLY YOU HAD COPIED *THIS* ONE!

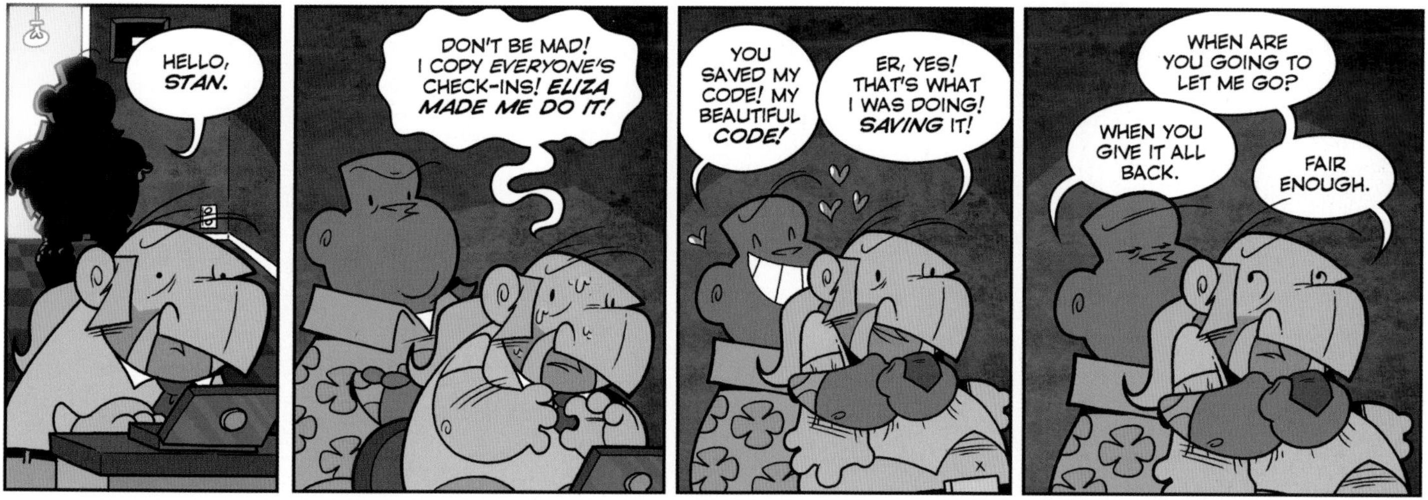
HELLO, *STAN.*
DON'T BE MAD! I COPY *EVERYONE'S* CHECK-INS! *ELIZA MADE ME DO IT!*
YOU SAVED MY CODE! MY BEAUTIFUL *CODE!*
ER, YES! THAT'S WHAT I WAS DOING! *SAVING* IT!
WHEN ARE YOU GOING TO LET ME GO?
WHEN YOU GIVE IT ALL BACK.
FAIR ENOUGH.

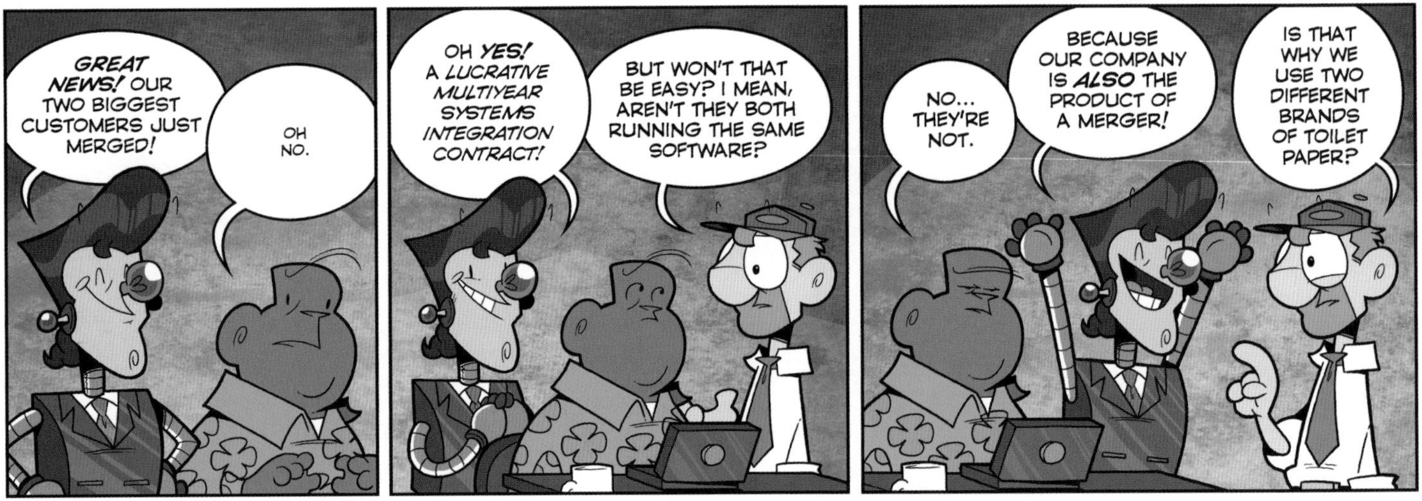
GREAT NEWS! OUR TWO BIGGEST CUSTOMERS JUST MERGED!
OH NO.
OH YES! A LUCRATIVE MULTIYEAR SYSTEMS INTEGRATION CONTRACT!
BUT WON'T THAT BE EASY? I MEAN, AREN'T THEY BOTH RUNNING THE SAME SOFTWARE?
NO... THEY'RE NOT.
BECAUSE OUR COMPANY IS ALSO THE PRODUCT OF A MERGER!
IS THAT WHY WE USE TWO DIFFERENT BRANDS OF TOILET PAPER?

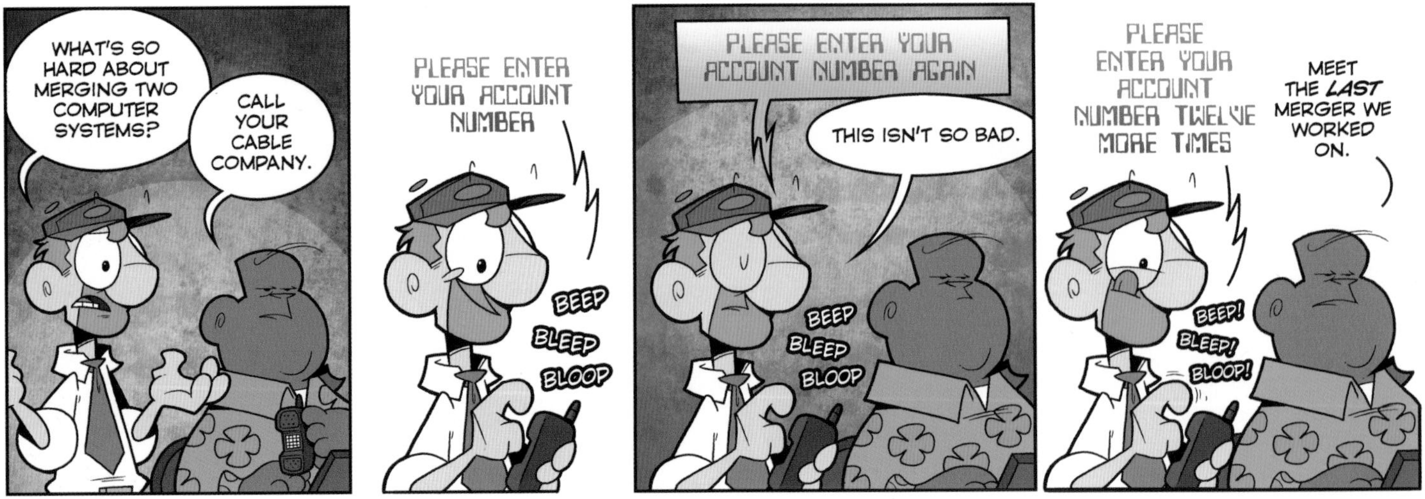
WHAT'S SO HARD ABOUT MERGING TWO COMPUTER SYSTEMS?
CALL YOUR CABLE COMPANY.
PLEASE ENTER YOUR ACCOUNT NUMBER
BEEP
BLEEP
BLOOP
PLEASE ENTER YOUR ACCOUNT NUMBER AGAIN
THIS ISN'T SO BAD.
BEEP
BLEEP
BLOOP
PLEASE ENTER YOUR ACCOUNT NUMBER TWELVE MORE TIMES
MEET THE LAST MERGER WE WORKED ON.
BEEP!
BLEEP!
BLOOP!

RUNTIME ERROR

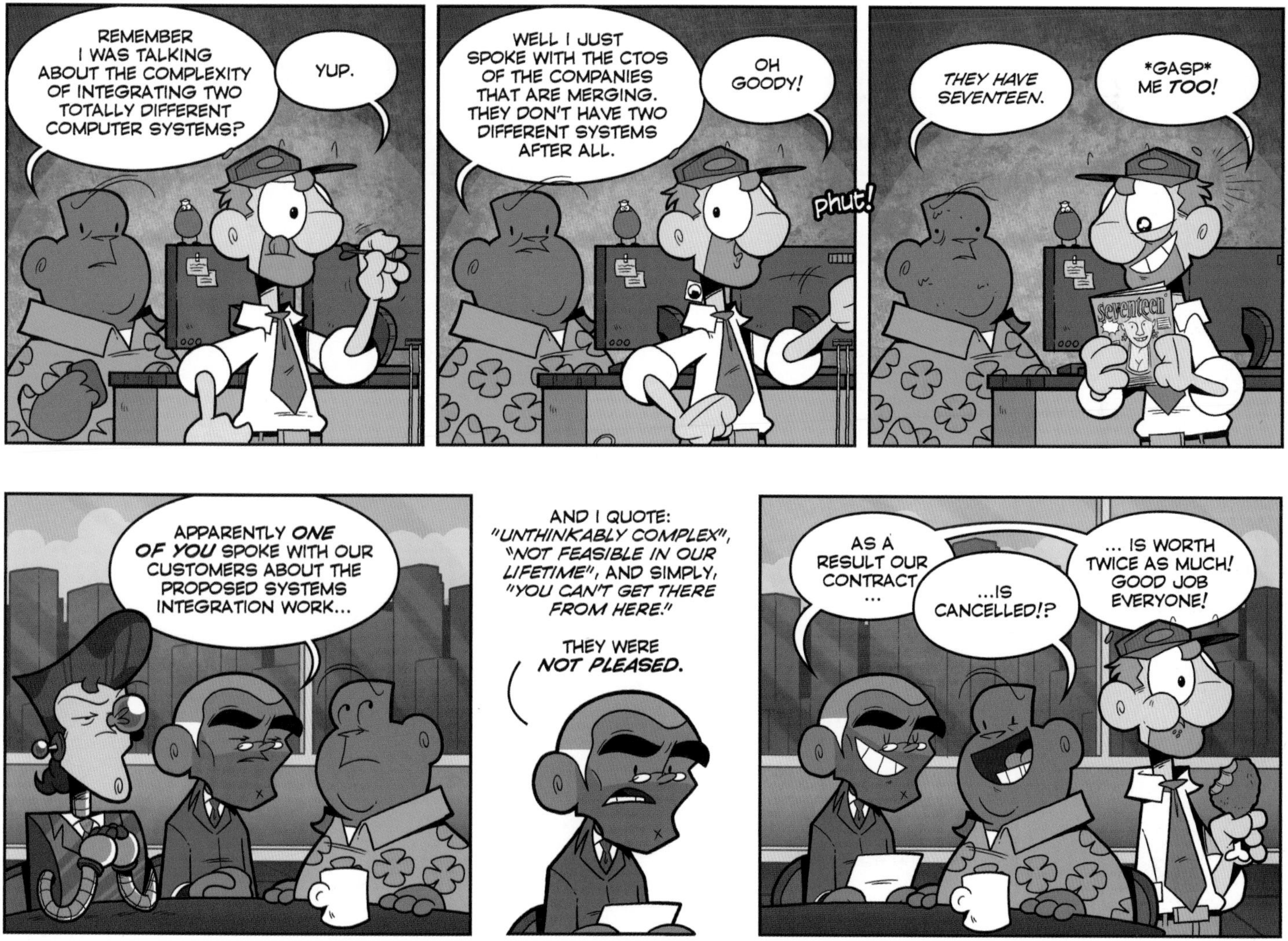
REMEMBER I WAS TALKING ABOUT THE COMPLEXITY OF INTEGRATING TWO TOTALLY DIFFERENT COMPUTER SYSTEMS?
YUP.
WELL I JUST SPOKE WITH THE CTOS OF THE COMPANIES THAT ARE MERGING. THEY DON'T HAVE TWO DIFFERENT SYSTEMS AFTER ALL.
OH GOODY!
phut!
THEY HAVE SEVENTEEN.
GASP ME TOO!
Seventeen
APPARENTLY ONE OF YOU SPOKE WITH OUR CUSTOMERS ABOUT THE PROPOSED SYSTEMS INTEGRATION WORK...
AND I QUOTE: "UNTHINKABLY COMPLEX", "NOT FEASIBLE IN OUR LIFETIME", AND SIMPLY, "YOU CAN'T GET THERE FROM HERE."
THEY WERE NOT PLEASED.
AS A RESULT OUR CONTRACT ...
...IS CANCELLED!?
... IS WORTH TWICE AS MUCH! GOOD JOB EVERYONE!

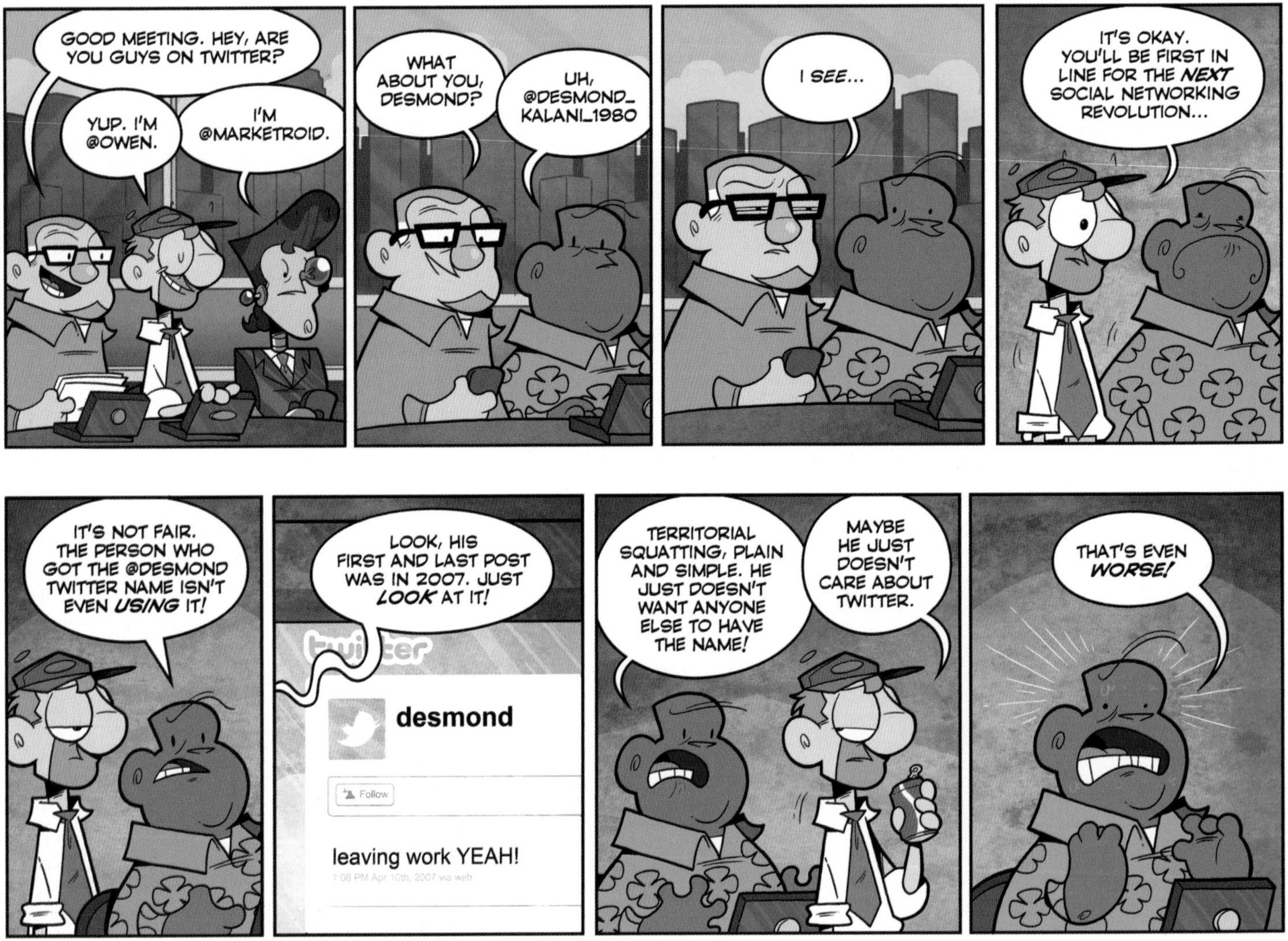

GOOD MEETING. HEY, ARE YOU GUYS ON TWITTER?
YUP. I'M @OWEN.
I'M @MARKETROID.
WHAT ABOUT YOU, DESMOND?
UH, @DESMOND_KALANI_1980
I *SEE*...
IT'S OKAY. YOU'LL BE FIRST IN LINE FOR THE *NEXT* SOCIAL NETWORKING REVOLUTION...
IT'S NOT FAIR. THE PERSON WHO GOT THE @DESMOND TWITTER NAME ISN'T EVEN *USING* IT!
LOOK, HIS FIRST AND LAST POST WAS IN 2007. JUST *LOOK* AT IT!
desmond
Follow
leaving work YEAH!
1:06 PM Apr 10th, 2007 via web
TERRITORIAL SQUATTING, PLAIN AND SIMPLE. HE JUST DOESN'T WANT ANYONE ELSE TO HAVE THE NAME!
MAYBE HE JUST DOESN'T CARE ABOUT TWITTER.
THAT'S EVEN *WORSE!*

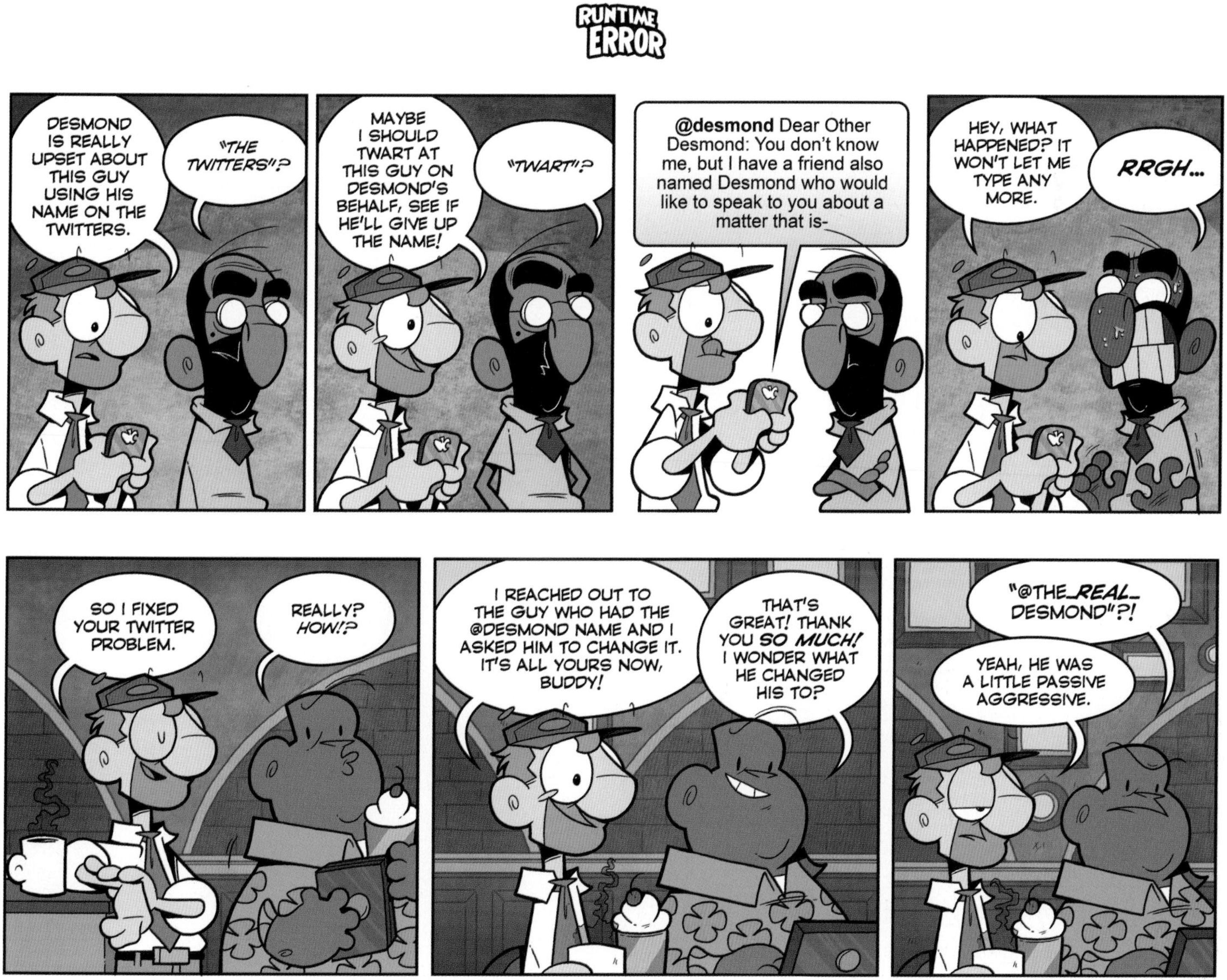
RUNTIME ERROR
DESMOND IS REALLY UPSET ABOUT THIS GUY USING HIS NAME ON THE TWITTERS.
"THE TWITTERS"?
MAYBE I SHOULD TWART AT THIS GUY ON DESMOND'S BEHALF, SEE IF HE'LL GIVE UP THE NAME!
"TWART"?
@desmond Dear Other Desmond: You don't know me, but I have a friend also named Desmond who would like to speak to you about a matter that is-
HEY, WHAT HAPPENED? IT WON'T LET ME TYPE ANY MORE.
RRGH...
SO I FIXED YOUR TWITTER PROBLEM.
REALLY? HOW!?
I REACHED OUT TO THE GUY WHO HAD THE @DESMOND NAME AND I ASKED HIM TO CHANGE IT. IT'S ALL YOURS NOW, BUDDY!
THAT'S GREAT! THANK YOU SO MUCH! I WONDER WHAT HE CHANGED HIS TO?
"@THE_REAL_DESMOND"?!
YEAH, HE WAS A LITTLE PASSIVE AGGRESSIVE.

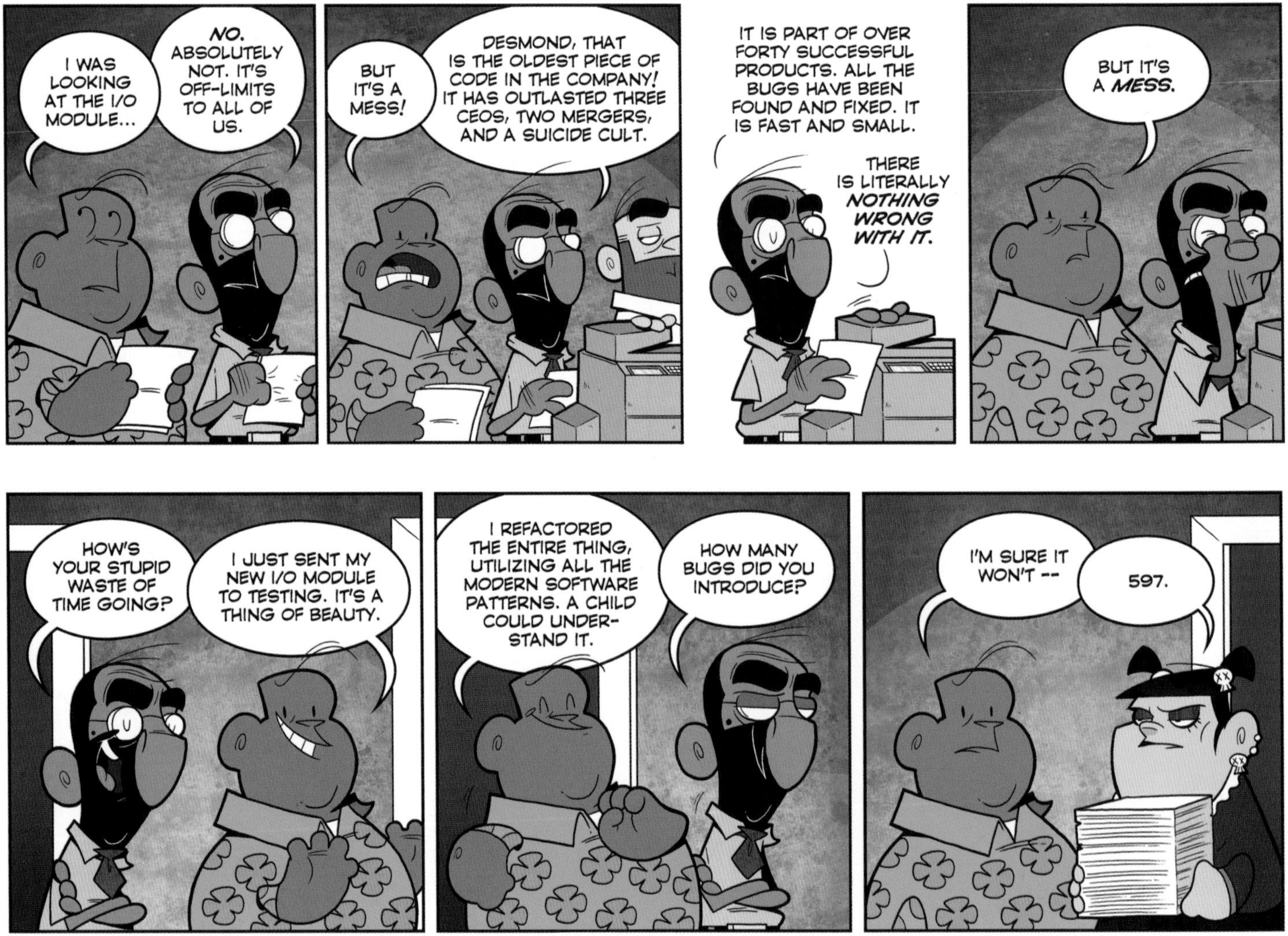
I WAS LOOKING AT THE I/O MODULE...
NO. ABSOLUTELY NOT. IT'S OFF-LIMITS TO ALL OF US.
BUT IT'S A MESS!
DESMOND, THAT IS THE OLDEST PIECE OF CODE IN THE COMPANY! IT HAS OUTLASTED THREE CEOS, TWO MERGERS, AND A SUICIDE CULT.
IT IS PART OF OVER FORTY SUCCESSFUL PRODUCTS. ALL THE BUGS HAVE BEEN FOUND AND FIXED. IT IS FAST AND SMALL.
THERE IS LITERALLY NOTHING WRONG WITH IT.
BUT IT'S A MESS.
HOW'S YOUR STUPID WASTE OF TIME GOING?
I JUST SENT MY NEW I/O MODULE TO TESTING. IT'S A THING OF BEAUTY.
I REFACTORED THE ENTIRE THING, UTILIZING ALL THE MODERN SOFTWARE PATTERNS. A CHILD COULD UNDER-STAND IT.
HOW MANY BUGS DID YOU INTRODUCE?
I'M SURE IT WON'T --
597.

RUNTIME ERROR

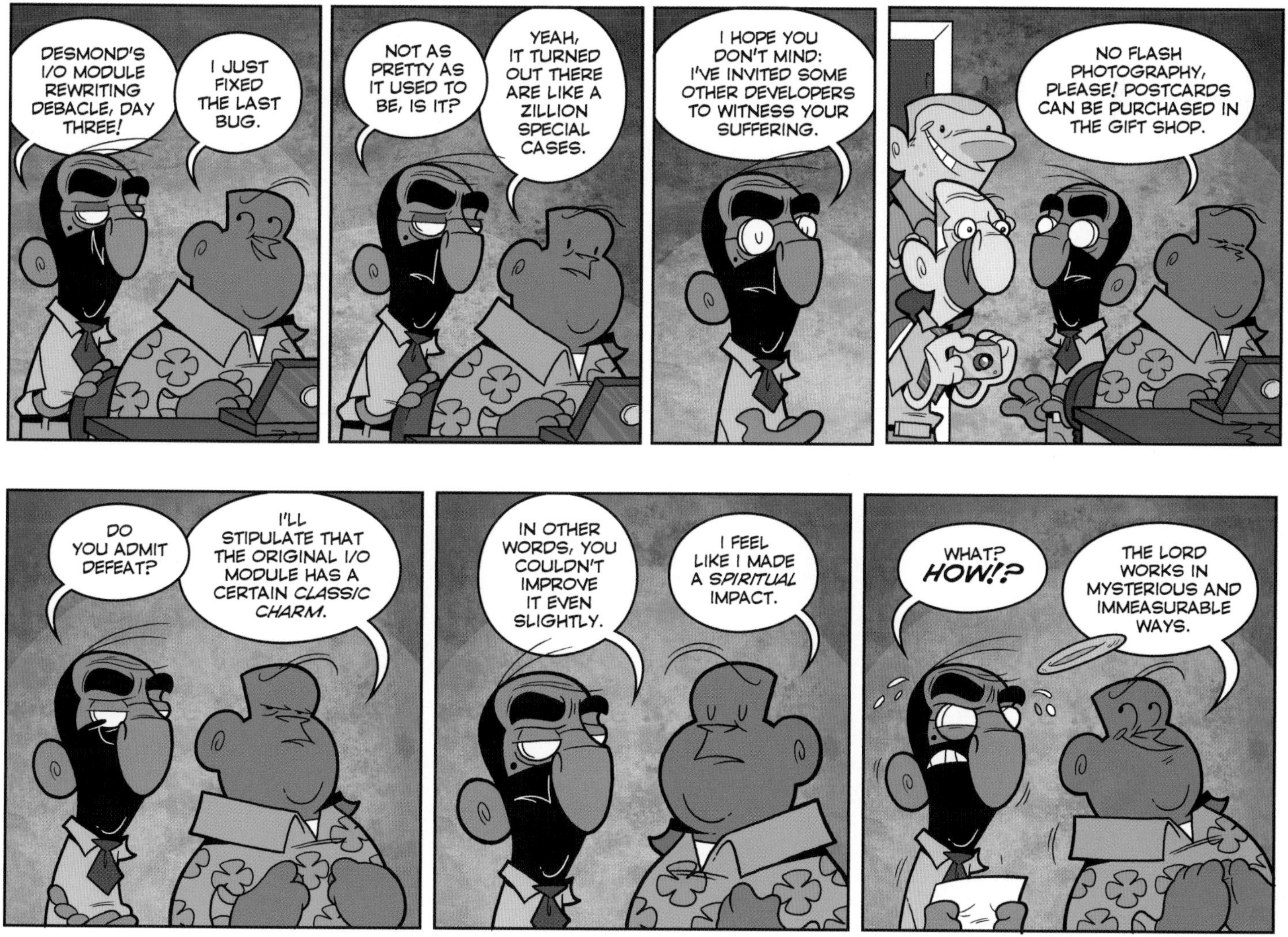

DESMOND'S I/O MODULE REWRITING DEBACLE, DAY THREE!
I JUST FIXED THE LAST BUG.
NOT AS PRETTY AS IT USED TO BE, IS IT?
YEAH, IT TURNED OUT THERE ARE LIKE A ZILLION SPECIAL CASES.
I HOPE YOU DON'T MIND: I'VE INVITED SOME OTHER DEVELOPERS TO WITNESS YOUR SUFFERING.
NO FLASH PHOTOGRAPHY, PLEASE! POSTCARDS CAN BE PURCHASED IN THE GIFT SHOP.
DO YOU ADMIT DEFEAT?
I'LL STIPULATE THAT THE ORIGINAL I/O MODULE HAS A CERTAIN *CLASSIC CHARM*.
IN OTHER WORDS, YOU COULDN'T IMPROVE IT EVEN SLIGHTLY.
I FEEL LIKE I MADE A *SPIRITUAL* IMPACT.
WHAT? ***HOW!?***
THE LORD WORKS IN MYSTERIOUS AND IMMEASURABLE WAYS.

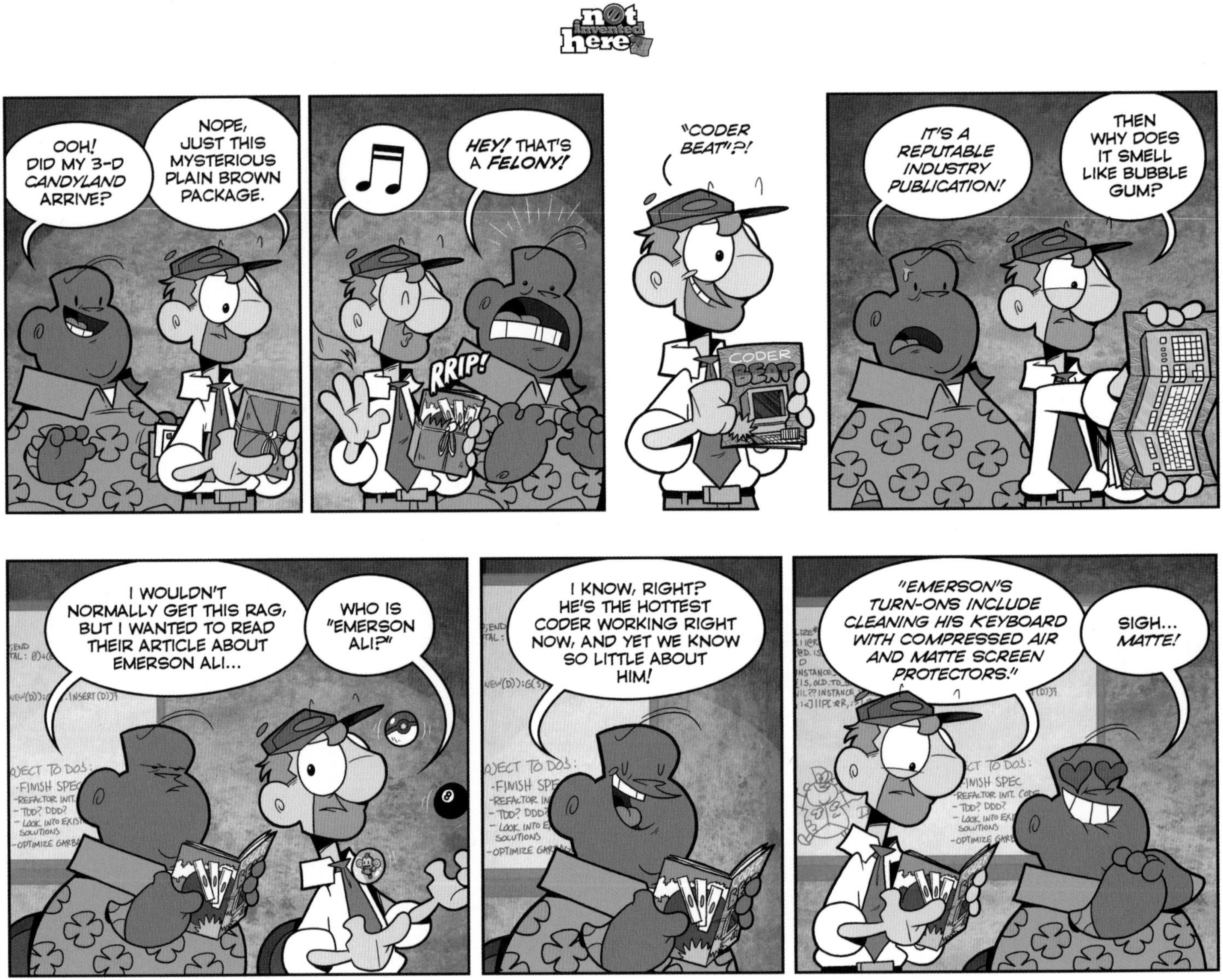
not invented here
OOH! DID MY 3-D CANDYLAND ARRIVE?
NOPE, JUST THIS MYSTERIOUS PLAIN BROWN PACKAGE.
♫
HEY! THAT'S A FELONY!
RRIP!
"CODER BEAT"?!
CODER BEAT
IT'S A REPUTABLE INDUSTRY PUBLICATION!
THEN WHY DOES IT SMELL LIKE BUBBLE GUM?
I WOULDN'T NORMALLY GET THIS RAG, BUT I WANTED TO READ THEIR ARTICLE ABOUT EMERSON ALI...
WHO IS "EMERSON ALI?"
I KNOW, RIGHT? HE'S THE HOTTEST CODER WORKING RIGHT NOW, AND YET WE KNOW SO LITTLE ABOUT HIM!
"EMERSON'S TURN-ONS INCLUDE CLEANING HIS KEYBOARD WITH COMPRESSED AIR AND MATTE SCREEN PROTECTORS."
SIGH... MATTE!

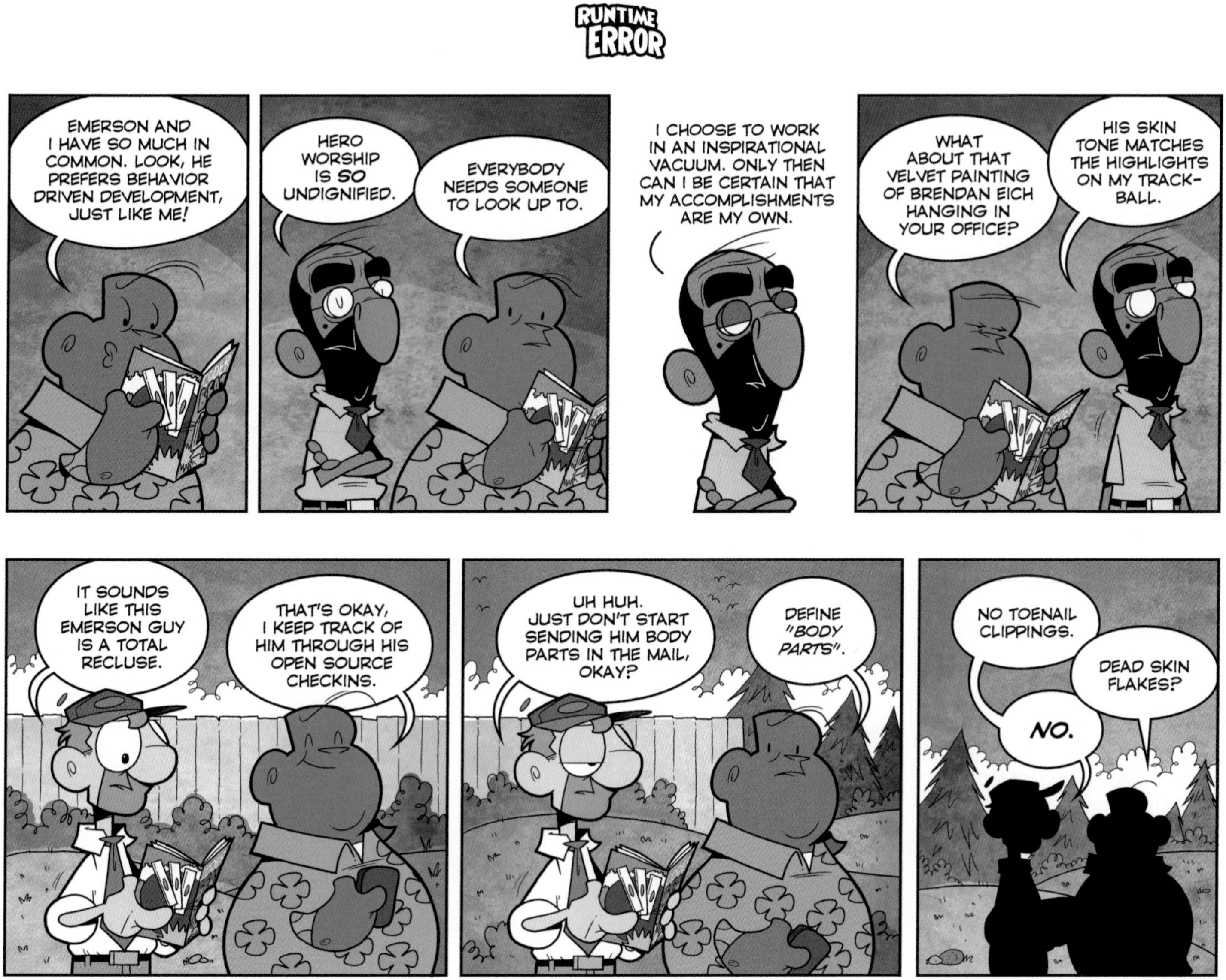
RUNTIME ERROR
EMERSON AND I HAVE SO MUCH IN COMMON. LOOK, HE PREFERS BEHAVIOR DRIVEN DEVELOPMENT, JUST LIKE ME!
HERO WORSHIP IS SO UNDIGNIFIED.
EVERYBODY NEEDS SOMEONE TO LOOK UP TO.
I CHOOSE TO WORK IN AN INSPIRATIONAL VACUUM. ONLY THEN CAN I BE CERTAIN THAT MY ACCOMPLISHMENTS ARE MY OWN.
WHAT ABOUT THAT VELVET PAINTING OF BRENDAN EICH HANGING IN YOUR OFFICE?
HIS SKIN TONE MATCHES THE HIGHLIGHTS ON MY TRACK-BALL.
IT SOUNDS LIKE THIS EMERSON GUY IS A TOTAL RECLUSE.
THAT'S OKAY, I KEEP TRACK OF HIM THROUGH HIS OPEN SOURCE CHECKINS.
UH HUH. JUST DON'T START SENDING HIM BODY PARTS IN THE MAIL, OKAY?
DEFINE "BODY PARTS".
NO TOENAIL CLIPPINGS.
DEAD SKIN FLAKES?
NO.

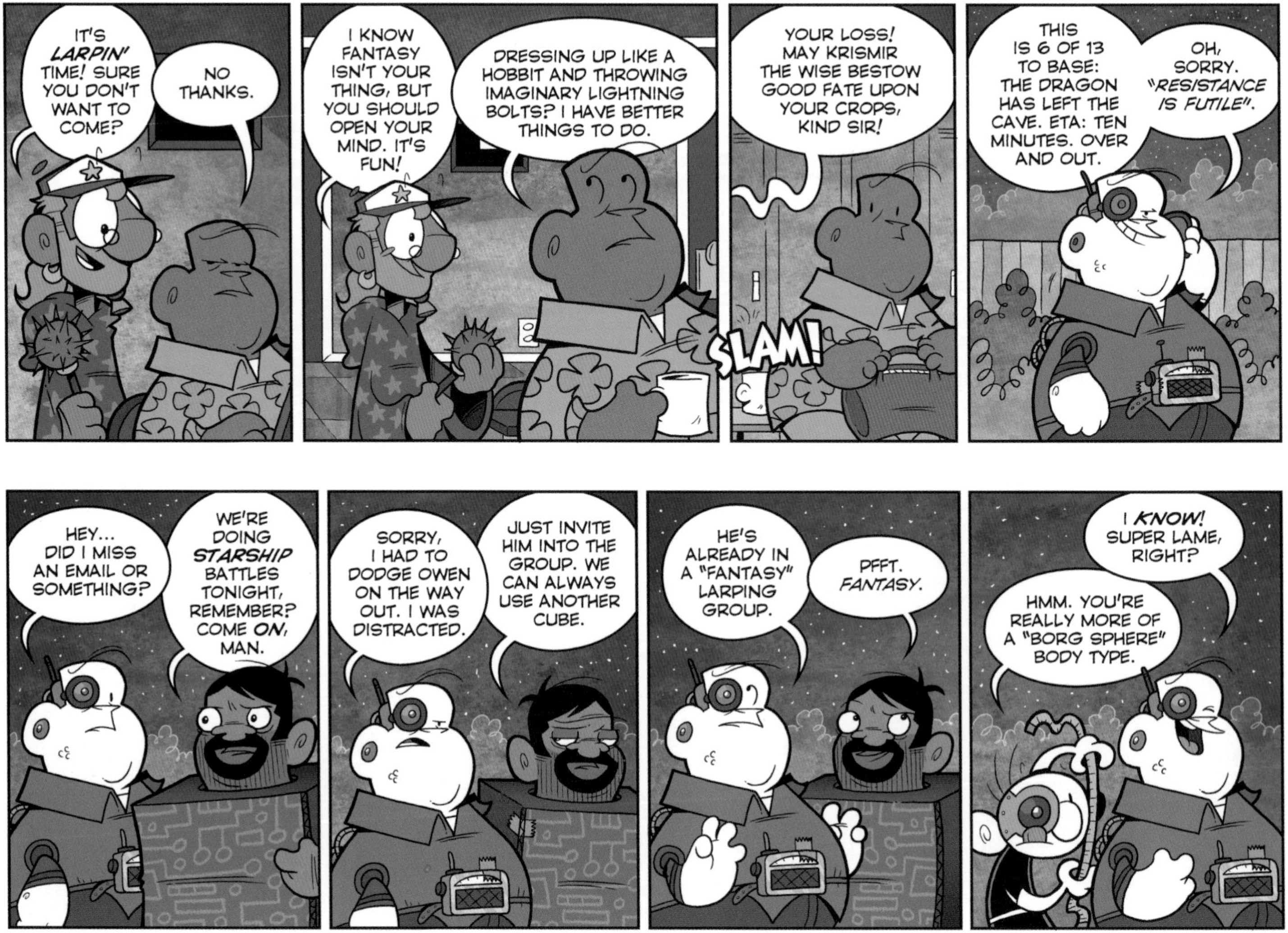

IT'S LARPIN' TIME! SURE YOU DON'T WANT TO COME?
NO THANKS.
I KNOW FANTASY ISN'T YOUR THING, BUT YOU SHOULD OPEN YOUR MIND. IT'S FUN!
DRESSING UP LIKE A HOBBIT AND THROWING IMAGINARY LIGHTNING BOLTS? I HAVE BETTER THINGS TO DO.
YOUR LOSS! MAY KRISMIR THE WISE BESTOW GOOD FATE UPON YOUR CROPS, KIND SIR!
SLAM!
THIS IS 6 OF 13 TO BASE: THE DRAGON HAS LEFT THE CAVE. ETA: TEN MINUTES. OVER AND OUT.
OH, SORRY. "RESISTANCE IS FUTILE".
HEY... DID I MISS AN EMAIL OR SOMETHING?
WE'RE DOING STARSHIP BATTLES TONIGHT, REMEMBER? COME ON, MAN.
SORRY, I HAD TO DODGE OWEN ON THE WAY OUT. I WAS DISTRACTED.
JUST INVITE HIM INTO THE GROUP. WE CAN ALWAYS USE ANOTHER CUBE.
HE'S ALREADY IN A "FANTASY" LARPING GROUP.
PFFT. FANTASY.
I KNOW! SUPER LAME, RIGHT?
HMM. YOU'RE REALLY MORE OF A "BORG SPHERE" BODY TYPE.

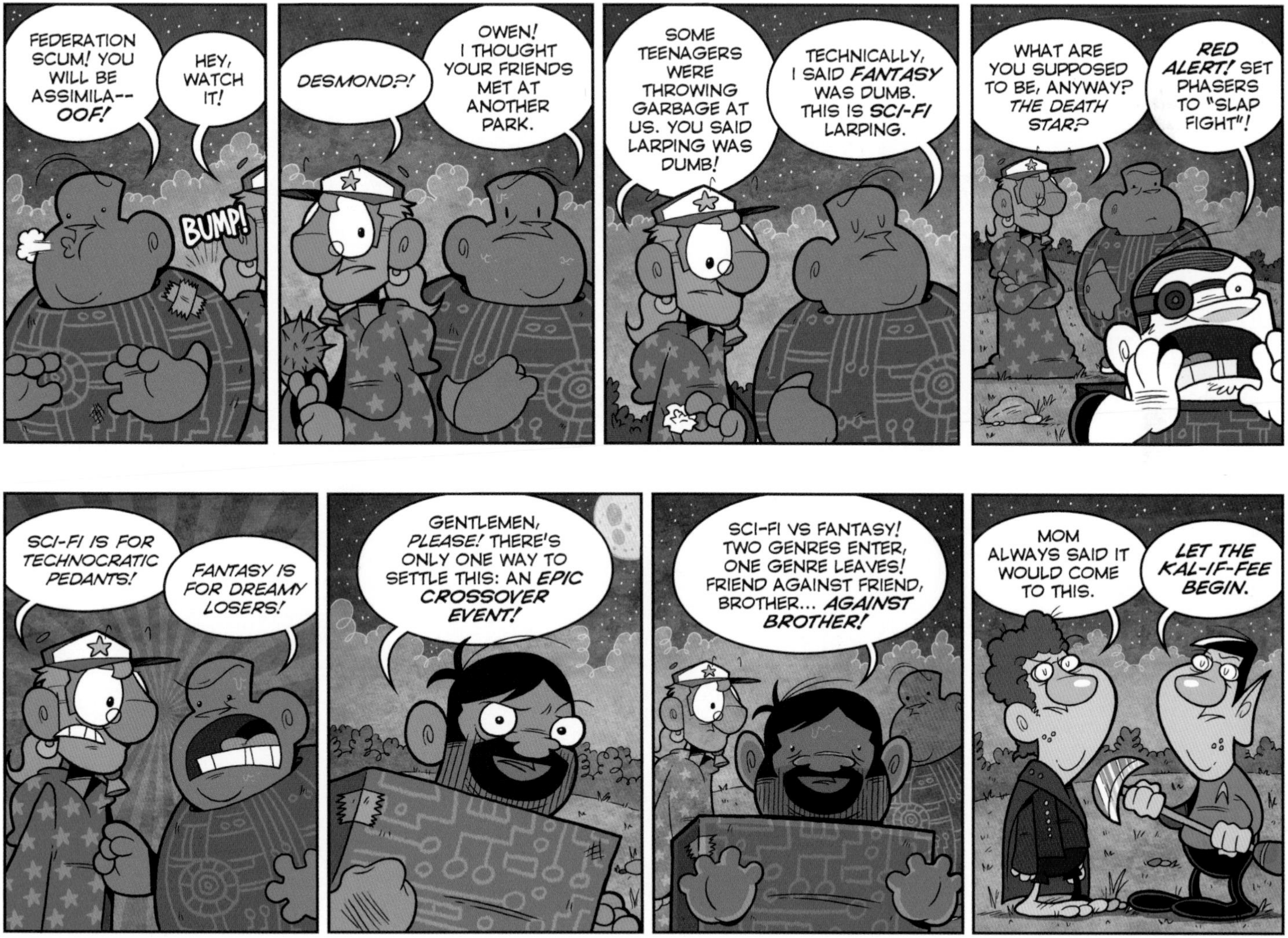
FEDERATION SCUM! YOU WILL BE ASSIMILA-- OOF!
HEY, WATCH IT!
BUMP!
DESMOND?!
OWEN! I THOUGHT YOUR FRIENDS MET AT ANOTHER PARK.
SOME TEENAGERS WERE THROWING GARBAGE AT US. YOU SAID LARPING WAS DUMB!
TECHNICALLY, I SAID FANTASY WAS DUMB. THIS IS SCI-FI LARPING.
WHAT ARE YOU SUPPOSED TO BE, ANYWAY? THE DEATH STAR?
RED ALERT! SET PHASERS TO "SLAP FIGHT"!
SCI-FI IS FOR TECHNOCRATIC PEDANTS!
FANTASY IS FOR DREAMY LOSERS!
GENTLEMEN, PLEASE! THERE'S ONLY ONE WAY TO SETTLE THIS: AN EPIC CROSSOVER EVENT!
SCI-FI VS FANTASY! TWO GENRES ENTER, ONE GENRE LEAVES! FRIEND AGAINST FRIEND, BROTHER... AGAINST BROTHER!
MOM ALWAYS SAID IT WOULD COME TO THIS.
LET THE KAL-IF-FEE BEGIN.

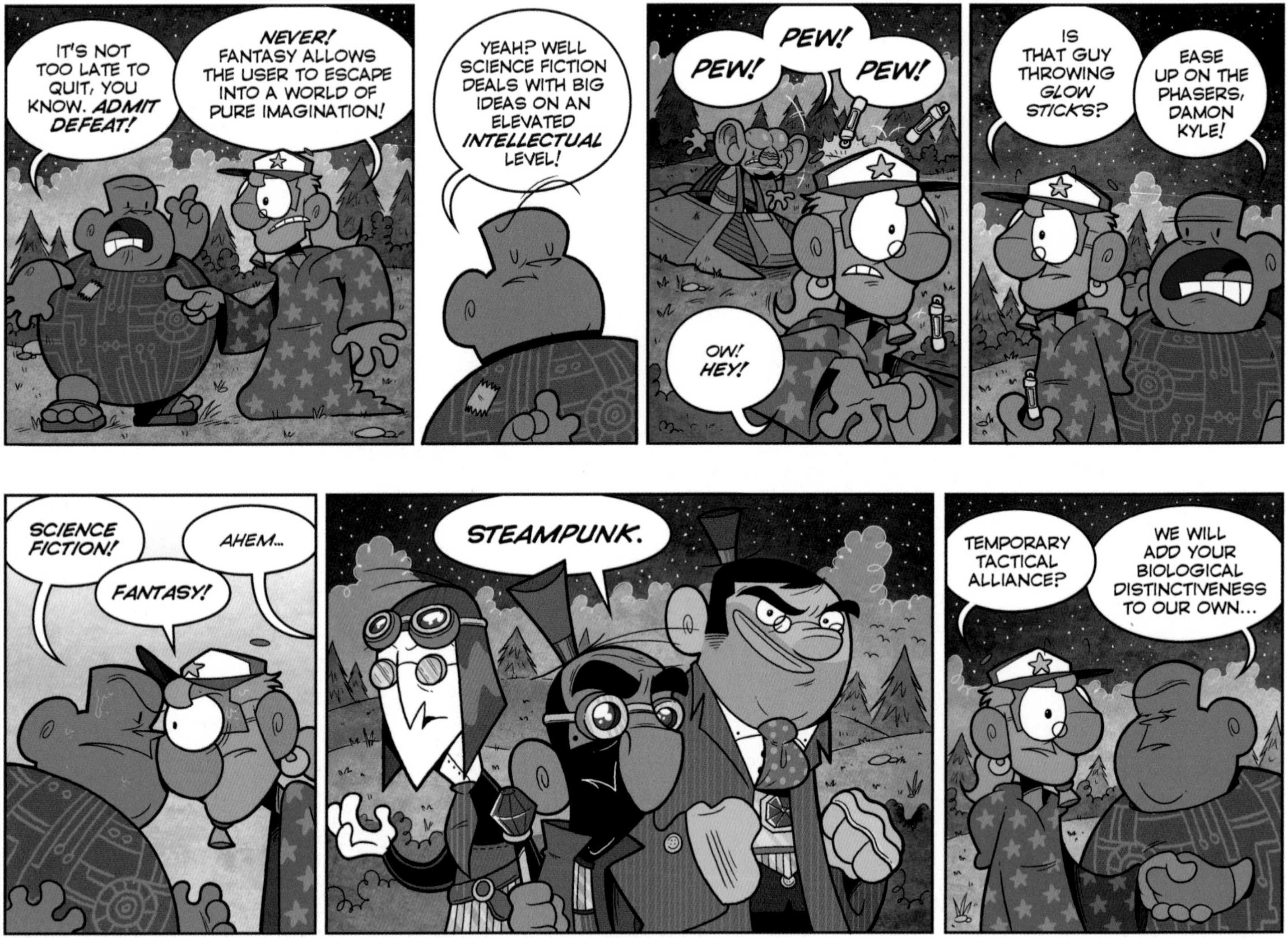
IT'S NOT TOO LATE TO QUIT, YOU KNOW. ADMIT DEFEAT!
NEVER! FANTASY ALLOWS THE USER TO ESCAPE INTO A WORLD OF PURE IMAGINATION!
YEAH? WELL SCIENCE FICTION DEALS WITH BIG IDEAS ON AN ELEVATED INTELLECTUAL LEVEL!
PEW!
PEW!
PEW!
OW! HEY!
IS THAT GUY THROWING GLOW STICKS?
EASE UP ON THE PHASERS, DAMON KYLE!
SCIENCE FICTION!
FANTASY!
AHEM...
STEAMPUNK.
TEMPORARY TACTICAL ALLIANCE?
WE WILL ADD YOUR BIOLOGICAL DISTINCTIVENESS TO OUR OWN...

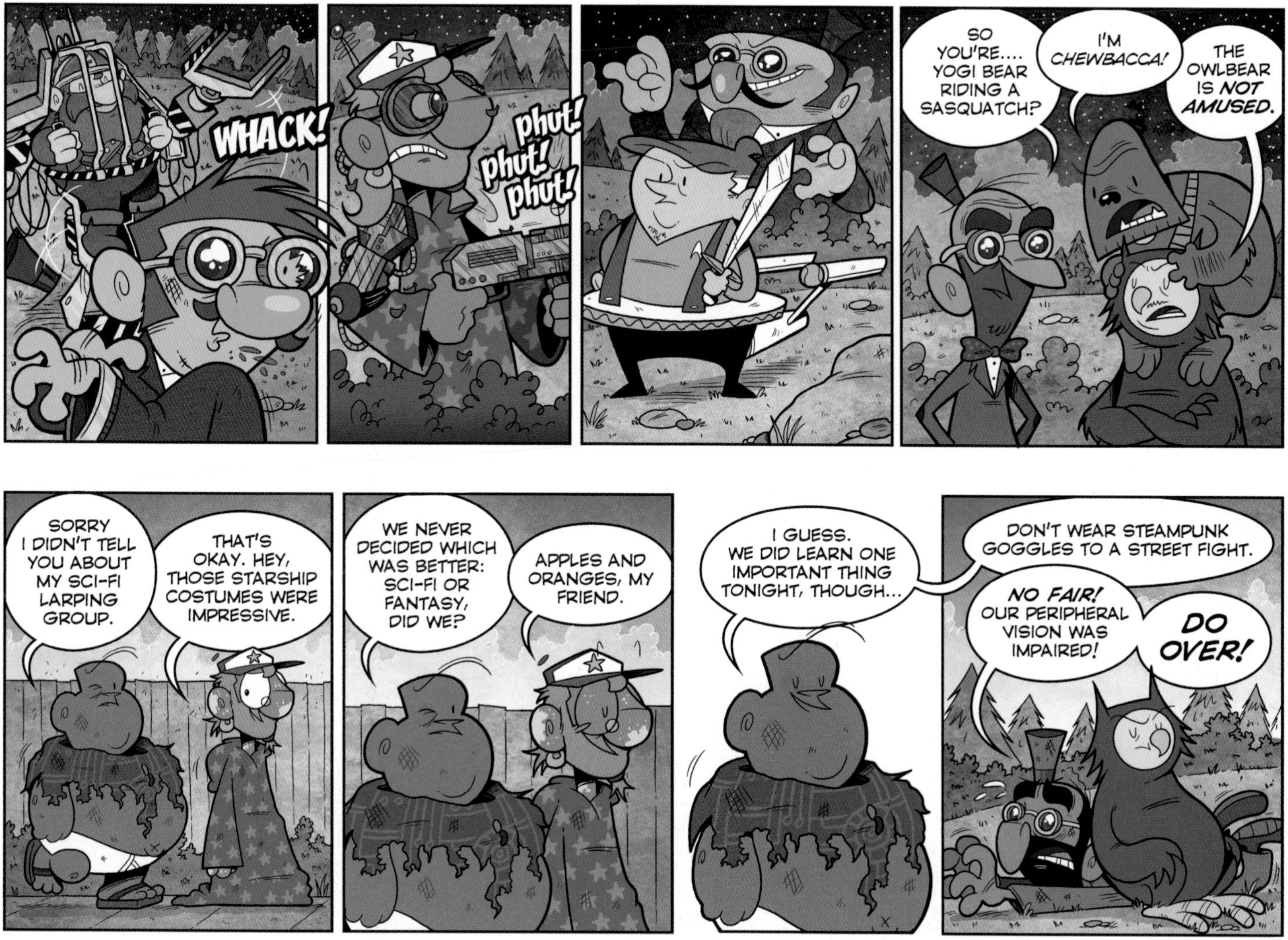
WHACK!
phut! phut! phut!
SO YOU'RE.... YOGI BEAR RIDING A SASQUATCH?
I'M CHEWBACCA!
THE OWLBEAR IS NOT AMUSED.
SORRY I DIDN'T TELL YOU ABOUT MY SCI-FI LARPING GROUP.
THAT'S OKAY. HEY, THOSE STARSHIP COSTUMES WERE IMPRESSIVE.
WE NEVER DECIDED WHICH WAS BETTER: SCI-FI OR FANTASY, DID WE?
APPLES AND ORANGES, MY FRIEND.
I GUESS. WE DID LEARN ONE IMPORTANT THING TONIGHT, THOUGH...
DON'T WEAR STEAMPUNK GOGGLES TO A STREET FIGHT.
NO FAIR! OUR PERIPHERAL VISION WAS IMPAIRED!
DO OVER!

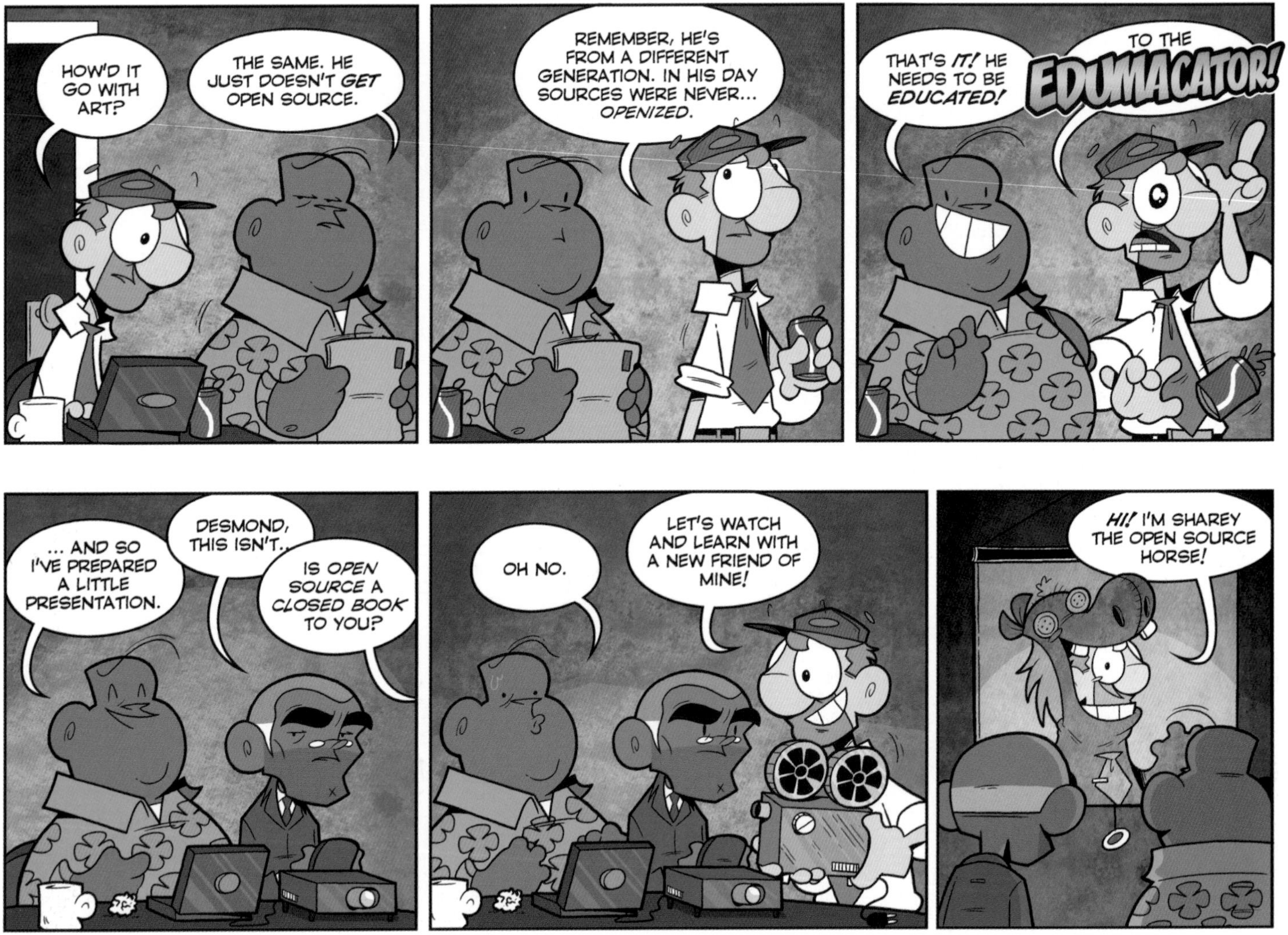
HOW'D IT GO WITH ART?
THE SAME. HE JUST DOESN'T *GET* OPEN SOURCE.
REMEMBER, HE'S FROM A DIFFERENT GENERATION. IN HIS DAY SOURCES WERE NEVER... *OPENIZED.*
THAT'S *IT!* HE NEEDS TO BE *EDUCATED!*
TO THE
EDUMACATOR!
... AND SO I'VE PREPARED A LITTLE PRESENTATION.
DESMOND, THIS ISN'T...
IS *OPEN* SOURCE A *CLOSED BOOK* TO YOU?
OH NO.
LET'S WATCH AND LEARN WITH A NEW FRIEND OF MINE!
HI! I'M SHAREY THE OPEN SOURCE HORSE!

RUNTIME ERROR

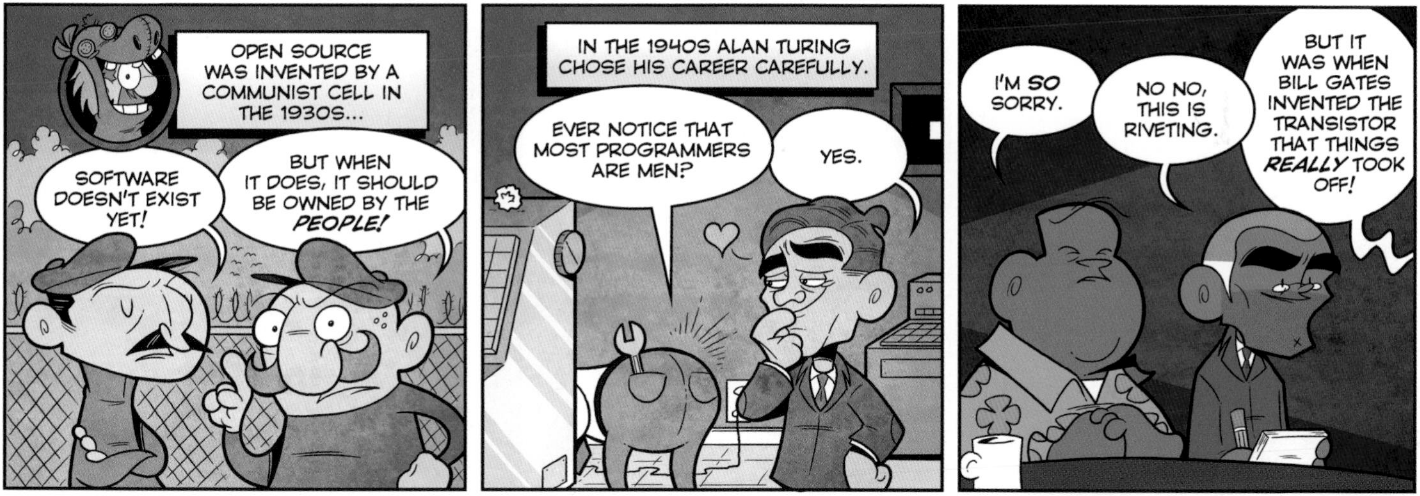
OPEN SOURCE WAS INVENTED BY A COMMUNIST CELL IN THE 1930S...
SOFTWARE DOESN'T EXIST YET!
BUT WHEN IT DOES, IT SHOULD BE OWNED BY THE *PEOPLE!*
IN THE 1940S ALAN TURING CHOSE HIS CAREER CAREFULLY.
EVER NOTICE THAT MOST PROGRAMMERS ARE MEN?
YES.
I'M *SO* SORRY.
NO NO, THIS IS RIVETING.
BUT IT WAS WHEN BILL GATES INVENTED THE TRANSISTOR THAT THINGS *REALLY* TOOK OFF!

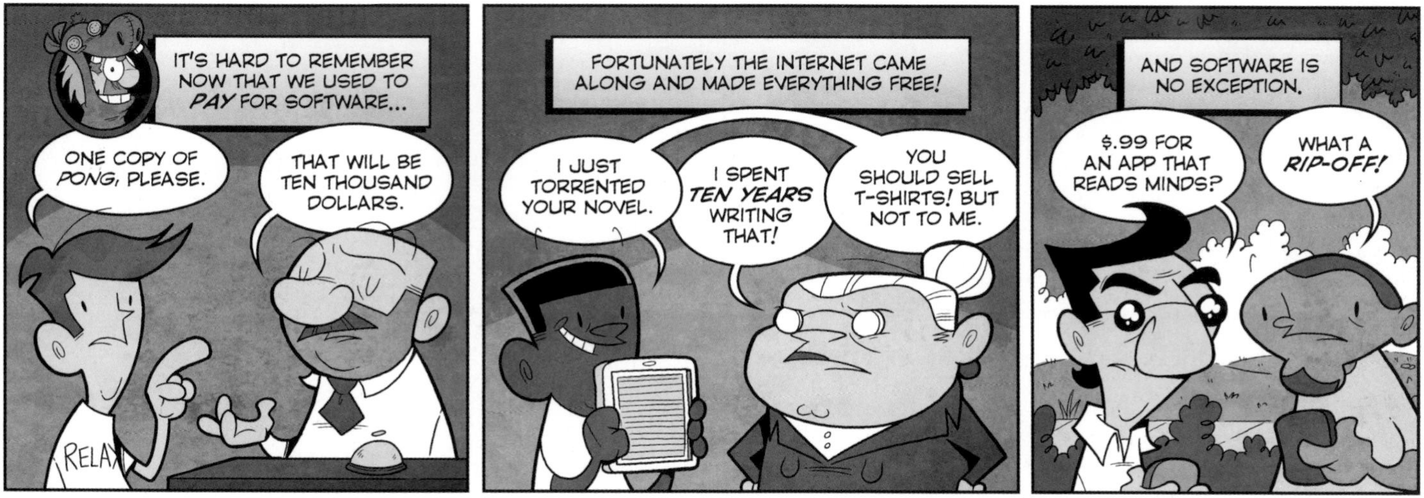
IT'S HARD TO REMEMBER NOW THAT WE USED TO *PAY* FOR SOFTWARE...
ONE COPY OF *PONG*, PLEASE.
THAT WILL BE TEN THOUSAND DOLLARS.
RELAX
FORTUNATELY THE INTERNET CAME ALONG AND MADE EVERYTHING FREE!
I JUST TORRENTED YOUR NOVEL.
I SPENT *TEN YEARS* WRITING THAT!
YOU SHOULD SELL T-SHIRTS! BUT NOT TO ME.
AND SOFTWARE IS NO EXCEPTION.
$.99 FOR AN APP THAT READS MINDS?
WHAT A *RIP-OFF!*

OPEN SOURCE SOFTWARE IS CREATED BY A "HIVE MIND".

IF (X =4) THEN

STOP HOGGING THE GLORY, *ETHAN.*

WHEN A PROJECT IS DEEMED COMPLETE IT IS RELEASED ONTO THE INTERNET IN THE FORM OF A COMPUTER VIRUS.

SHOULD I OPEN THIS FILE?

IT WOULD BE RUDE *NOT* TO!

AND BECAUSE THE SOURCES ARE FREELY AVAILABLE, YOU CAN CHANGE YOUR PROGRAM IF YOU DON'T LIKE IT!

MY WORD PROCESSOR KEEPS CRASHING.

HAVE YOU PROFILED THE MEMORY MANAGEMENT SUBSYSTEM?

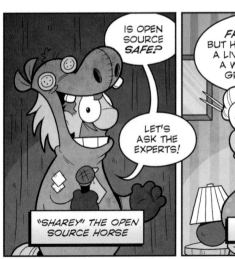

IS OPEN SOURCE *SAFE?*

LET'S ASK THE EXPERTS!

"SHAREY" THE OPEN SOURCE HORSE

FREE SOFTWARE? BUT HOW WILL YOU MAKE A LIVING AND ATTRACT A WIFE AND GIVE ME GRANDCHILDREN?

OWEN'S MOM!

HOMEMAKER

MY ENTIRE *LIFE* RUNS ON OPEN SOURCE. BUT THEN I DON'T HAVE MUCH OF A LIFE.

STUDENT

SO YOU'RE, WHAT, A *HORSE* NOW? HAVE SOME *DIGNITY*, MAN.

PROGRAMMER

RUNTIME ERROR

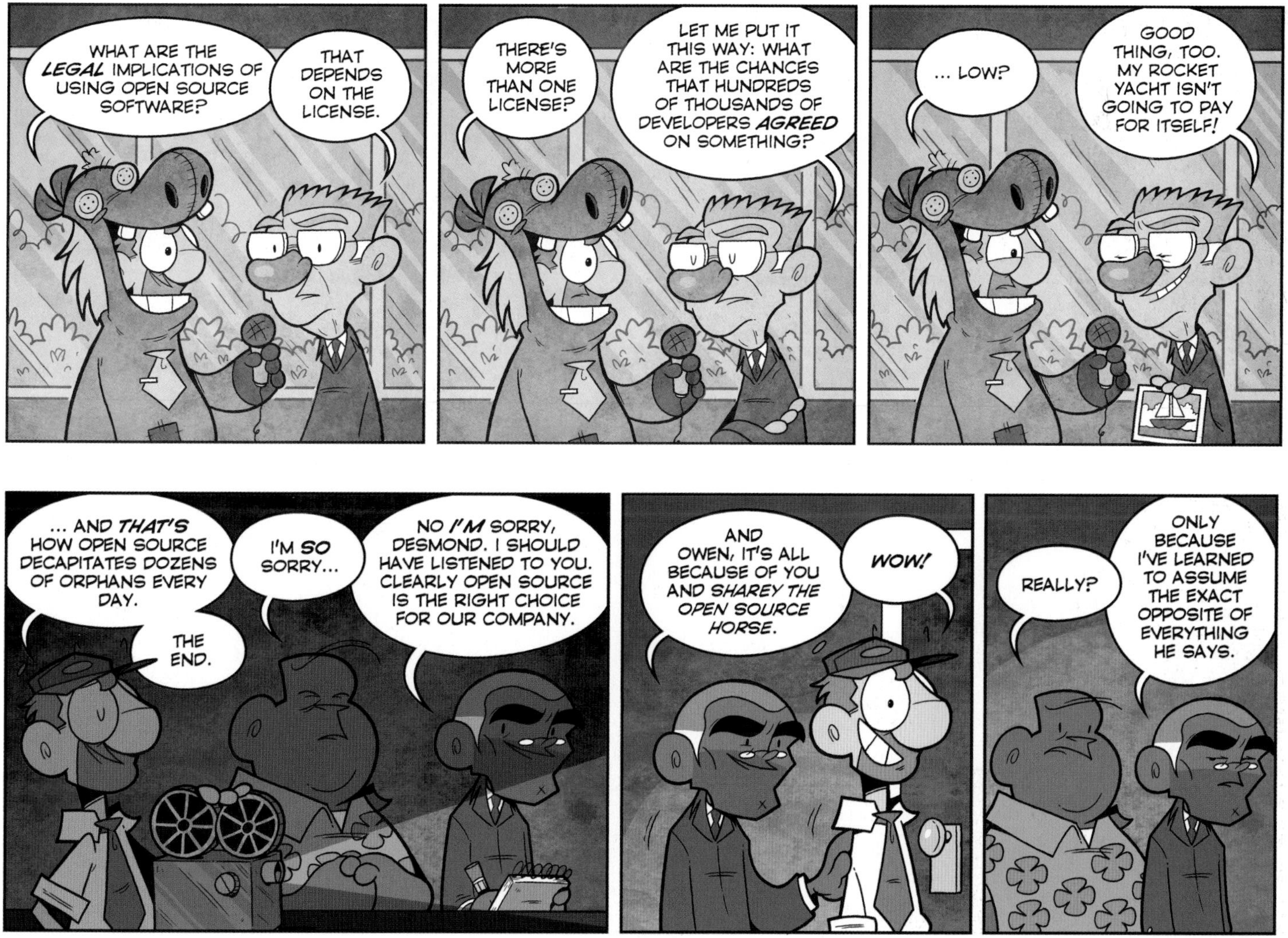
WHAT ARE THE *LEGAL* IMPLICATIONS OF USING OPEN SOURCE SOFTWARE?
THAT DEPENDS ON THE LICENSE.
THERE'S MORE THAN ONE LICENSE?
LET ME PUT IT THIS WAY: WHAT ARE THE CHANCES THAT HUNDREDS OF THOUSANDS OF DEVELOPERS *AGREED* ON SOMETHING?
... LOW?
GOOD THING, TOO. MY ROCKET YACHT ISN'T GOING TO PAY FOR ITSELF!
... AND *THAT'S* HOW OPEN SOURCE DECAPITATES DOZENS OF ORPHANS EVERY DAY.
THE END.
I'M *SO* SORRY...
NO *I'M* SORRY, DESMOND. I SHOULD HAVE LISTENED TO YOU. CLEARLY OPEN SOURCE IS THE RIGHT CHOICE FOR OUR COMPANY.
AND OWEN, IT'S ALL BECAUSE OF YOU AND *SHAREY THE OPEN SOURCE HORSE*.
WOW!
REALLY?
ONLY BECAUSE I'VE LEARNED TO ASSUME THE EXACT OPPOSITE OF EVERYTHING HE SAYS.

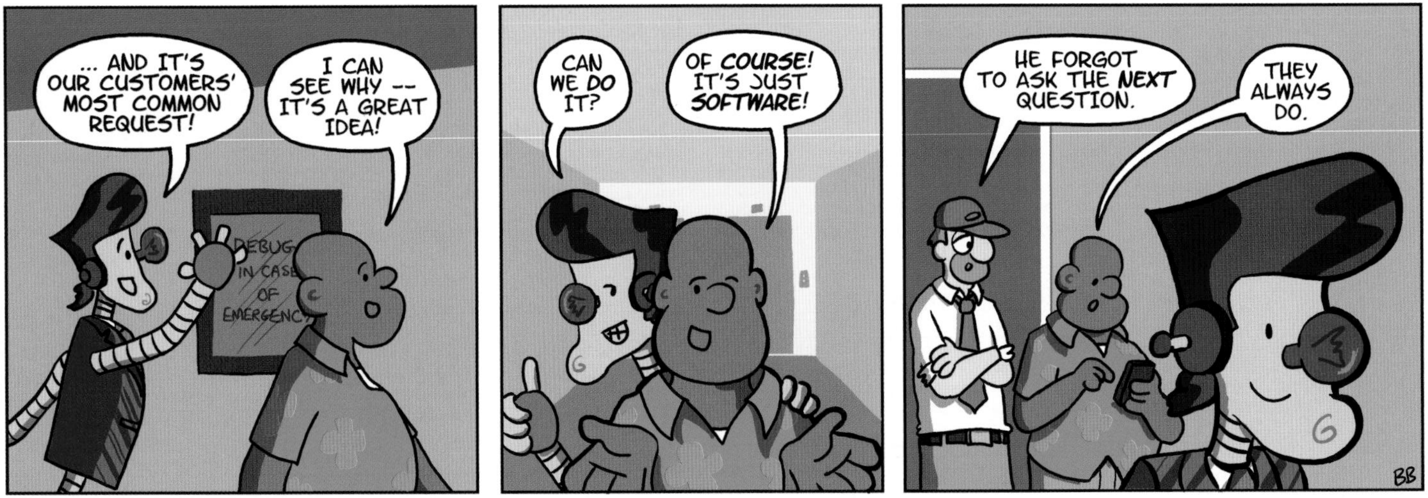
... AND IT'S OUR CUSTOMERS' MOST COMMON REQUEST!
I CAN SEE WHY -- IT'S A GREAT IDEA!
CAN WE DO IT?
OF COURSE! IT'S JUST SOFTWARE!
HE FORGOT TO ASK THE NEXT QUESTION.
THEY ALWAYS DO.
BB

It's not just you, these strips really do look different. They were drawn by Bill.

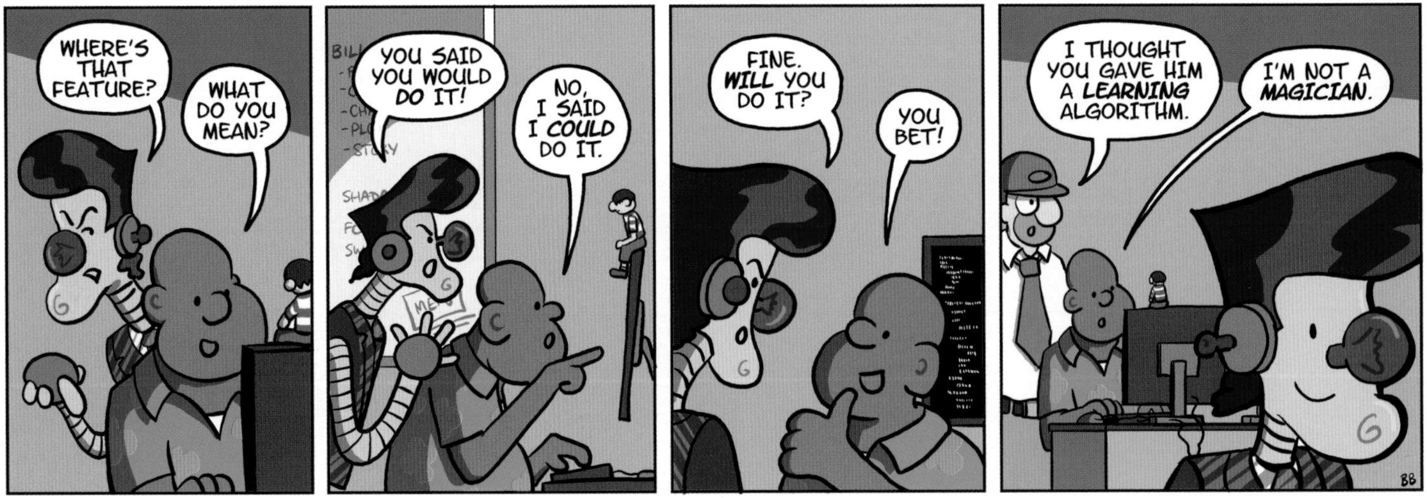
WHERE'S THAT FEATURE?
WHAT DO YOU MEAN?
YOU SAID YOU WOULD DO IT!
NO, I SAID I COULD DO IT.
FINE. WILL YOU DO IT?
YOU BET!
I THOUGHT YOU GAVE HIM A LEARNING ALGORITHM.
I'M NOT A MAGICIAN.
BB

RUNTIME ERROR

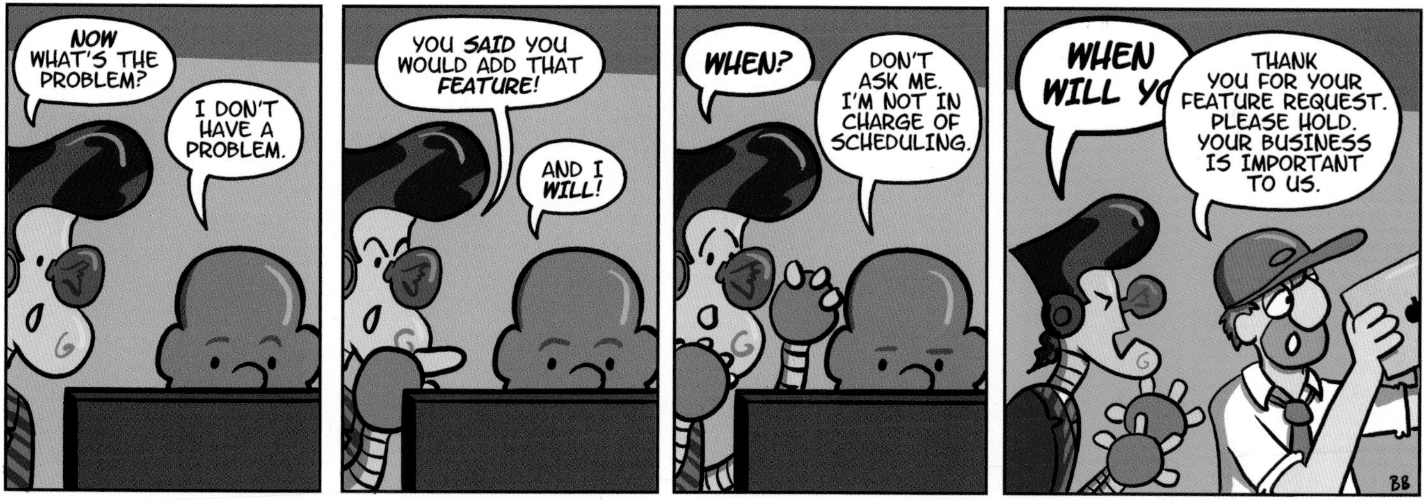
NOW WHAT'S THE PROBLEM?
I DON'T HAVE A PROBLEM.
YOU SAID YOU WOULD ADD THAT FEATURE!
AND I WILL!
WHEN?
DON'T ASK ME. I'M NOT IN CHARGE OF SCHEDULING.
WHEN WILL YO
THANK YOU FOR YOUR FEATURE REQUEST. PLEASE HOLD. YOUR BUSINESS IS IMPORTANT TO US.
BB

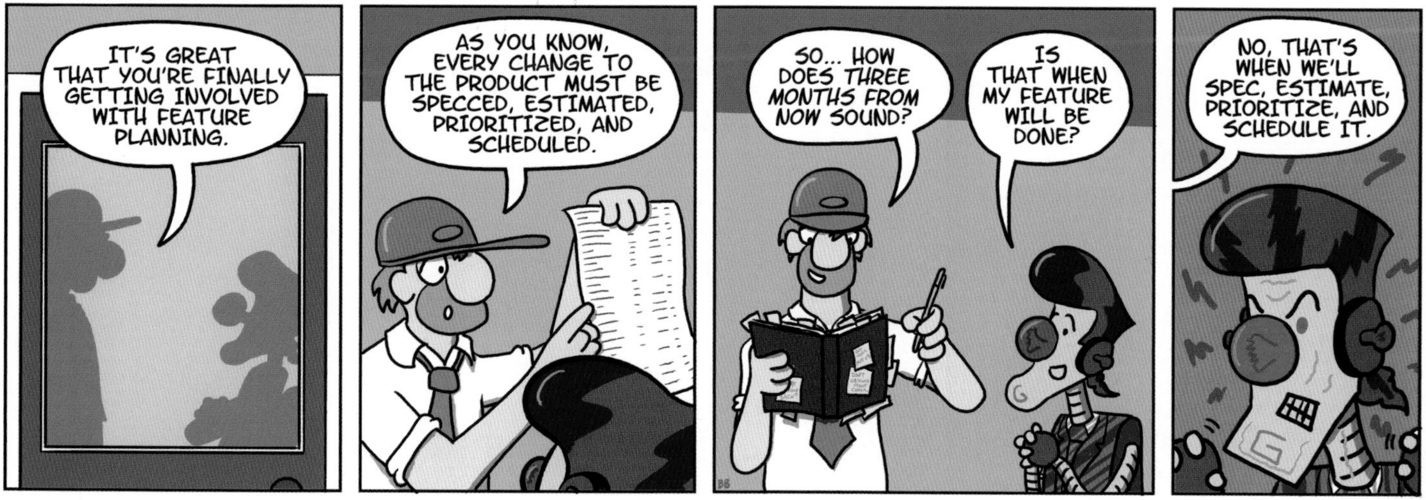
IT'S GREAT THAT YOU'RE FINALLY GETTING INVOLVED WITH FEATURE PLANNING.
AS YOU KNOW, EVERY CHANGE TO THE PRODUCT MUST BE SPECCED, ESTIMATED, PRIORITIZED, AND SCHEDULED.
SO... HOW DOES THREE MONTHS FROM NOW SOUND?
IS THAT WHEN MY FEATURE WILL BE DONE?
NO, THAT'S WHEN WE'LL SPEC, ESTIMATE, PRIORITIZE, AND SCHEDULE IT.
BB

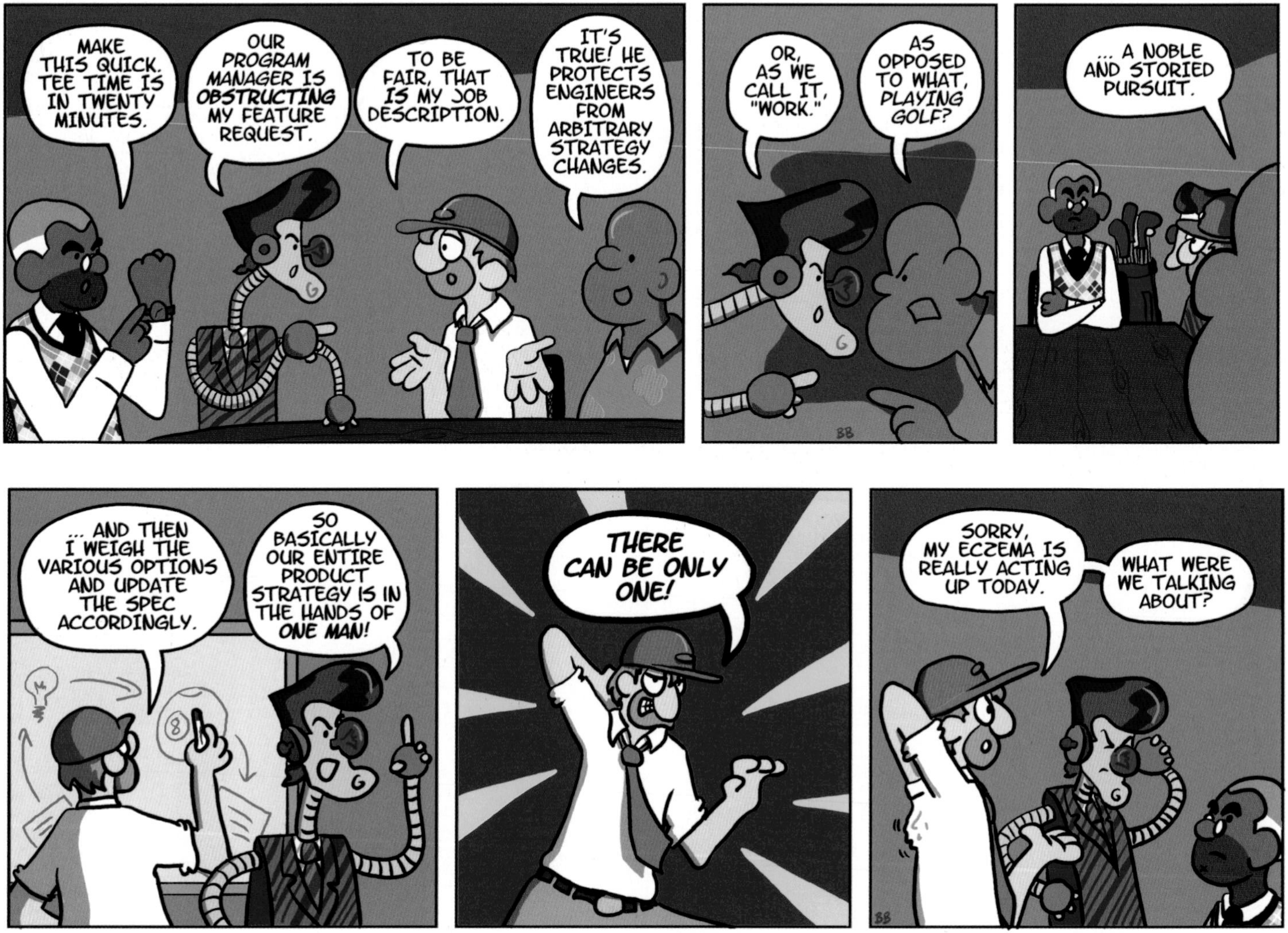
MAKE THIS QUICK. TEE TIME IS IN TWENTY MINUTES.
OUR PROGRAM MANAGER IS OBSTRUCTING MY FEATURE REQUEST.
TO BE FAIR, THAT IS MY JOB DESCRIPTION.
IT'S TRUE! HE PROTECTS ENGINEERS FROM ARBITRARY STRATEGY CHANGES.
OR, AS WE CALL IT, "WORK."
AS OPPOSED TO WHAT, PLAYING GOLF?
... A NOBLE AND STORIED PURSUIT.
... AND THEN I WEIGH THE VARIOUS OPTIONS AND UPDATE THE SPEC ACCORDINGLY.
SO BASICALLY OUR ENTIRE PRODUCT STRATEGY IS IN THE HANDS OF ONE MAN!
THERE CAN BE ONLY ONE!
SORRY, MY ECZEMA IS REALLY ACTING UP TODAY.
WHAT WERE WE TALKING ABOUT?

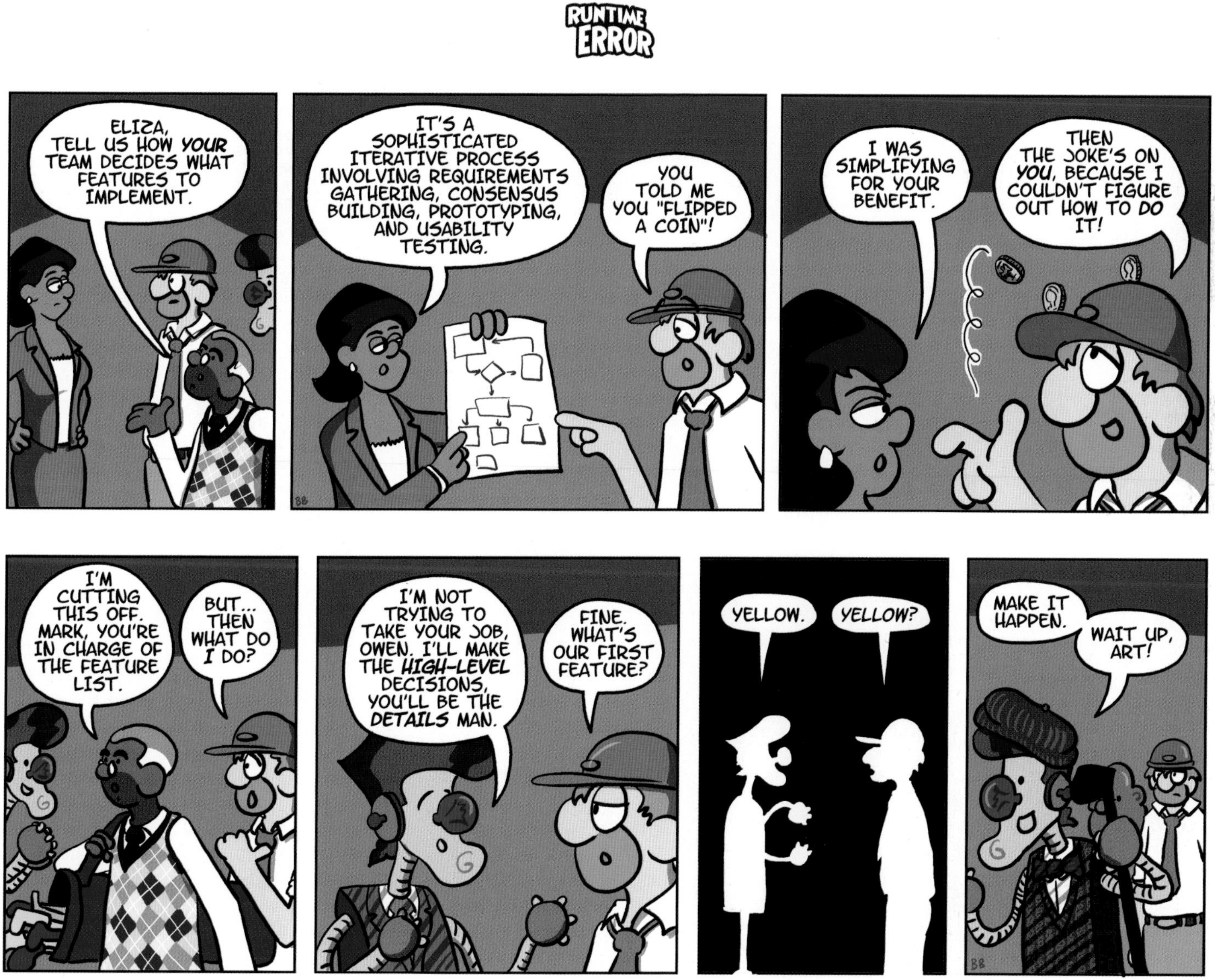
RUNTIME ERROR
ELIZA, TELL US HOW *YOUR* TEAM DECIDES WHAT FEATURES TO IMPLEMENT.
IT'S A SOPHISTICATED ITERATIVE PROCESS INVOLVING REQUIREMENTS GATHERING, CONSENSUS BUILDING, PROTOTYPING, AND USABILITY TESTING.
YOU TOLD ME YOU "FLIPPED A COIN"!
I WAS SIMPLIFYING FOR YOUR BENEFIT.
THEN THE JOKE'S ON *YOU*, BECAUSE I COULDN'T FIGURE OUT HOW TO *DO* IT!
I'M CUTTING THIS OFF. MARK, YOU'RE IN CHARGE OF THE FEATURE LIST.
BUT... THEN WHAT DO *I* DO?
I'M NOT TRYING TO TAKE YOUR JOB, OWEN. I'LL MAKE THE ***HIGH-LEVEL*** DECISIONS, YOU'LL BE THE ***DETAILS*** MAN.
FINE. WHAT'S OUR FIRST FEATURE?
YELLOW.
YELLOW?
MAKE IT HAPPEN.
WAIT UP, ART!

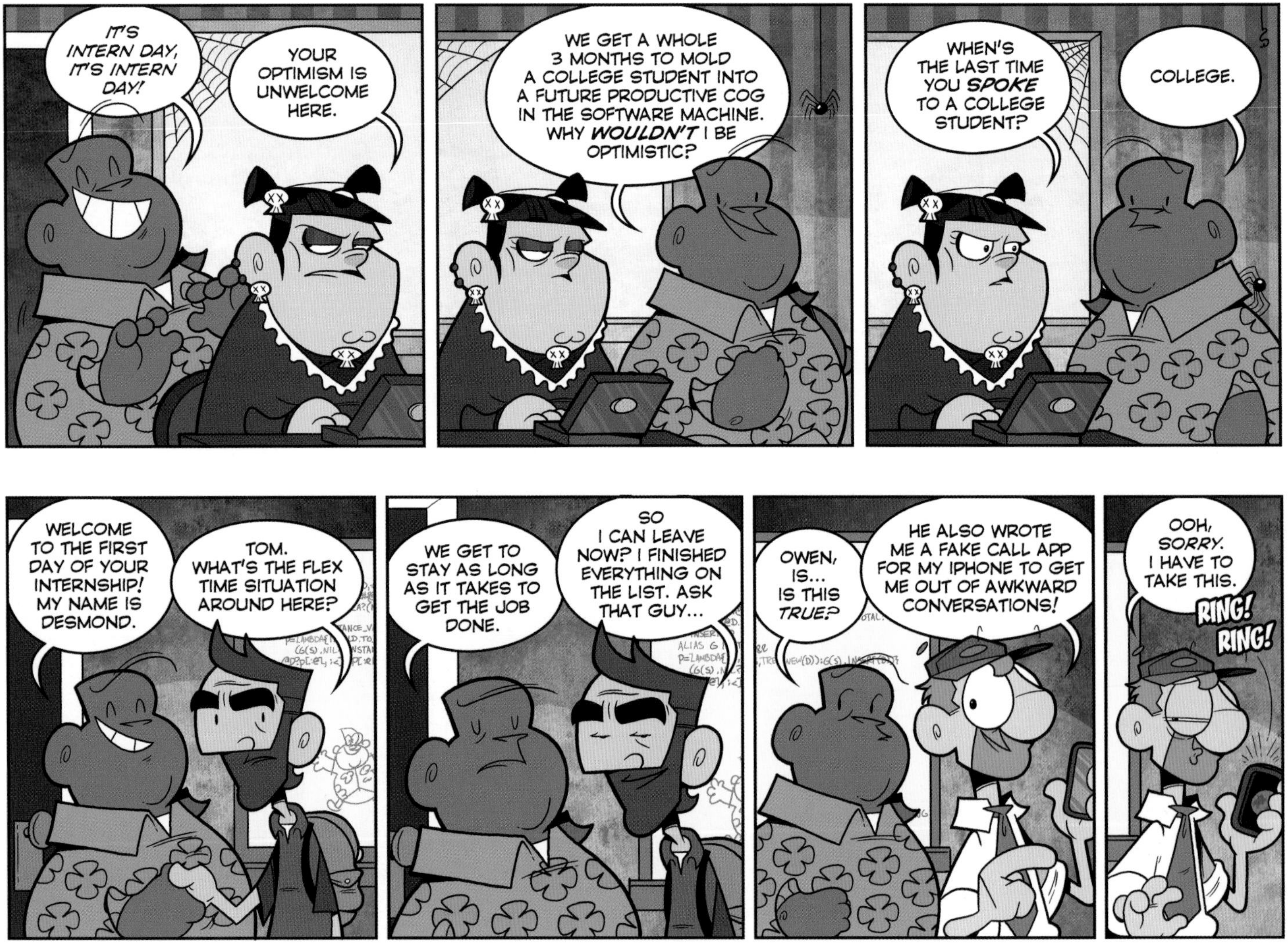
IT'S INTERN DAY, IT'S INTERN DAY!
YOUR OPTIMISM IS UNWELCOME HERE.
WE GET A WHOLE 3 MONTHS TO MOLD A COLLEGE STUDENT INTO A FUTURE PRODUCTIVE COG IN THE SOFTWARE MACHINE. WHY *WOULDN'T* I BE OPTIMISTIC?
WHEN'S THE LAST TIME YOU *SPOKE* TO A COLLEGE STUDENT?
COLLEGE.
WELCOME TO THE FIRST DAY OF YOUR INTERNSHIP! MY NAME IS DESMOND.
TOM. WHAT'S THE FLEX TIME SITUATION AROUND HERE?
WE GET TO STAY AS LONG AS IT TAKES TO GET THE JOB DONE.
SO I CAN LEAVE NOW? I FINISHED EVERYTHING ON THE LIST. ASK THAT GUY...
OWEN, IS... IS THIS *TRUE?*
HE ALSO WROTE ME A FAKE CALL APP FOR MY IPHONE TO GET ME OUT OF AWKWARD CONVERSATIONS!
OOH, *SORRY.* I HAVE TO TAKE THIS.
RING! RING!

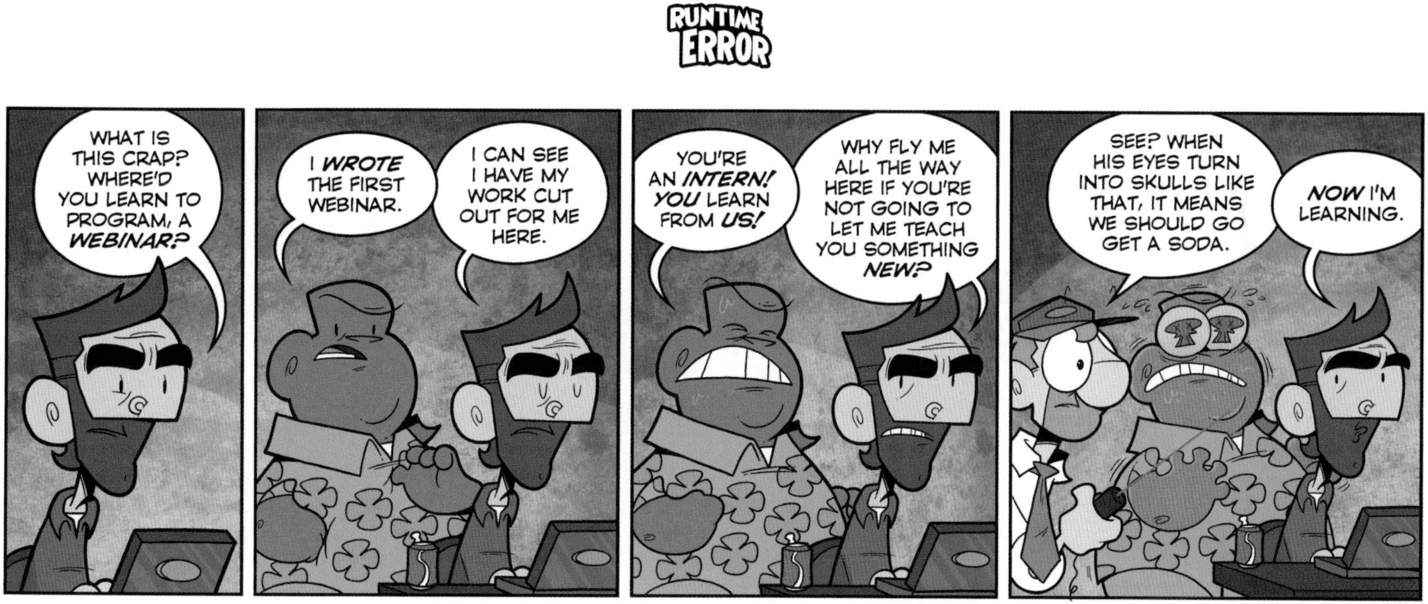
RUNTIME ERROR
WHAT IS THIS CRAP? WHERE'D YOU LEARN TO PROGRAM, A WEBINAR?
I WROTE THE FIRST WEBINAR.
I CAN SEE I HAVE MY WORK CUT OUT FOR ME HERE.
YOU'RE AN INTERN! YOU LEARN FROM US!
WHY FLY ME ALL THE WAY HERE IF YOU'RE NOT GOING TO LET ME TEACH YOU SOMETHING NEW?
SEE? WHEN HIS EYES TURN INTO SKULLS LIKE THAT, IT MEANS WE SHOULD GO GET A SODA.
NOW I'M LEARNING.

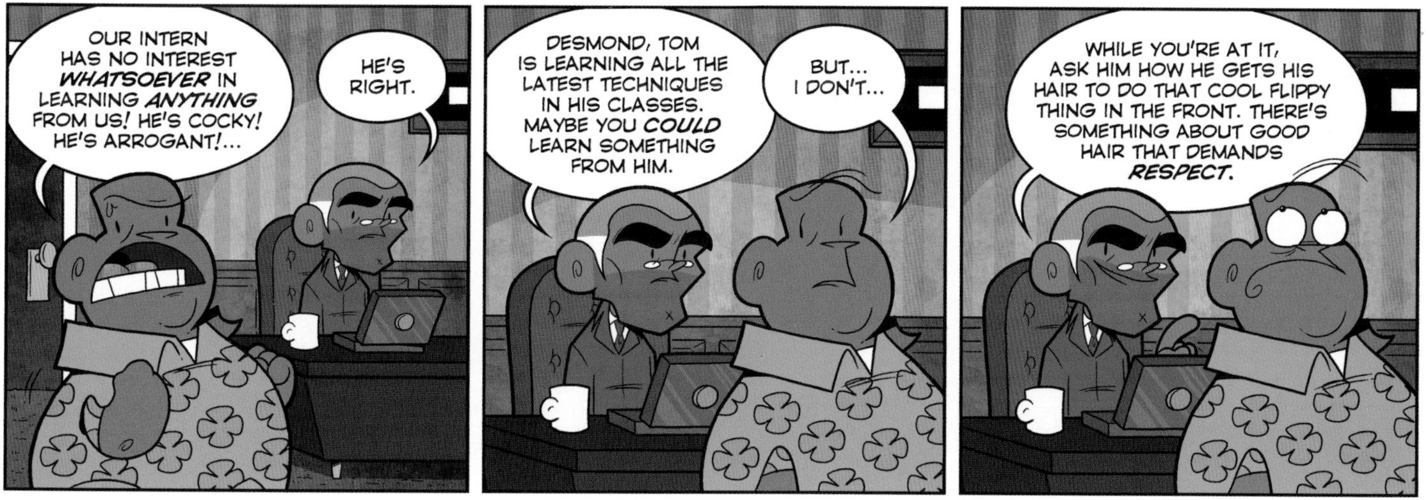
OUR INTERN HAS NO INTEREST WHATSOEVER IN LEARNING ANYTHING FROM US! HE'S COCKY! HE'S ARROGANT!...
HE'S RIGHT.
DESMOND, TOM IS LEARNING ALL THE LATEST TECHNIQUES IN HIS CLASSES. MAYBE YOU COULD LEARN SOMETHING FROM HIM.
BUT... I DON'T...
WHILE YOU'RE AT IT, ASK HIM HOW HE GETS HIS HAIR TO DO THAT COOL FLIPPY THING IN THE FRONT. THERE'S SOMETHING ABOUT GOOD HAIR THAT DEMANDS RESPECT.

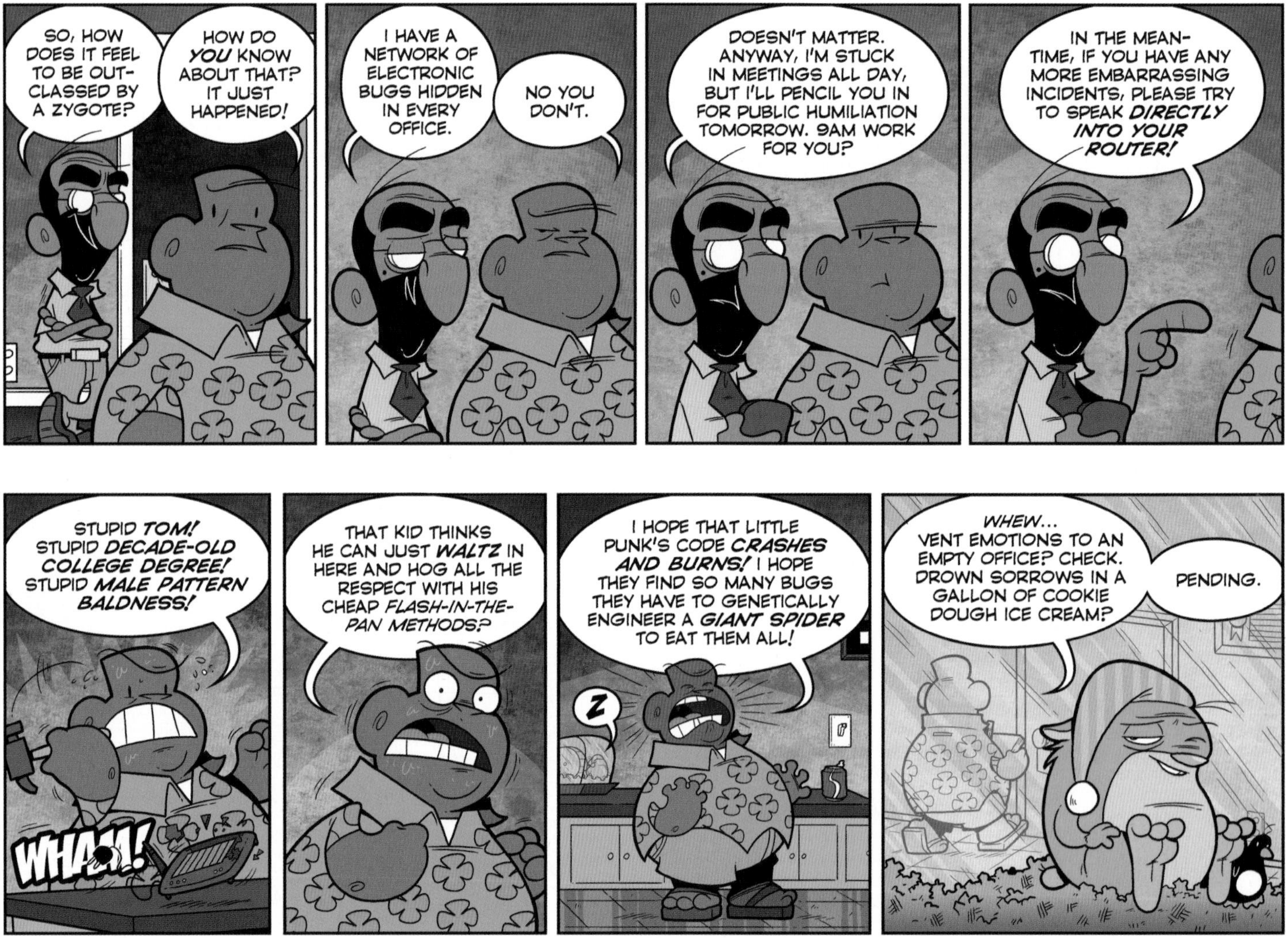
SO, HOW DOES IT FEEL TO BE OUT-CLASSED BY A ZYGOTE?
HOW DO YOU KNOW ABOUT THAT? IT JUST HAPPENED!
I HAVE A NETWORK OF ELECTRONIC BUGS HIDDEN IN EVERY OFFICE.
NO YOU DON'T.
DOESN'T MATTER. ANYWAY, I'M STUCK IN MEETINGS ALL DAY, BUT I'LL PENCIL YOU IN FOR PUBLIC HUMILIATION TOMORROW. 9AM WORK FOR YOU?
IN THE MEAN-TIME, IF YOU HAVE ANY MORE EMBARRASSING INCIDENTS, PLEASE TRY TO SPEAK DIRECTLY INTO YOUR ROUTER!
STUPID TOM! STUPID DECADE-OLD COLLEGE DEGREE! STUPID MALE PATTERN BALDNESS!
WHAM!
THAT KID THINKS HE CAN JUST WALTZ IN HERE AND HOG ALL THE RESPECT WITH HIS CHEAP FLASH-IN-THE-PAN METHODS?
I HOPE THAT LITTLE PUNK'S CODE CRASHES AND BURNS! I HOPE THEY FIND SO MANY BUGS THEY HAVE TO GENETICALLY ENGINEER A GIANT SPIDER TO EAT THEM ALL!
Z
WHEW... VENT EMOTIONS TO AN EMPTY OFFICE? CHECK. DROWN SORROWS IN A GALLON OF COOKIE DOUGH ICE CREAM?
PENDING.

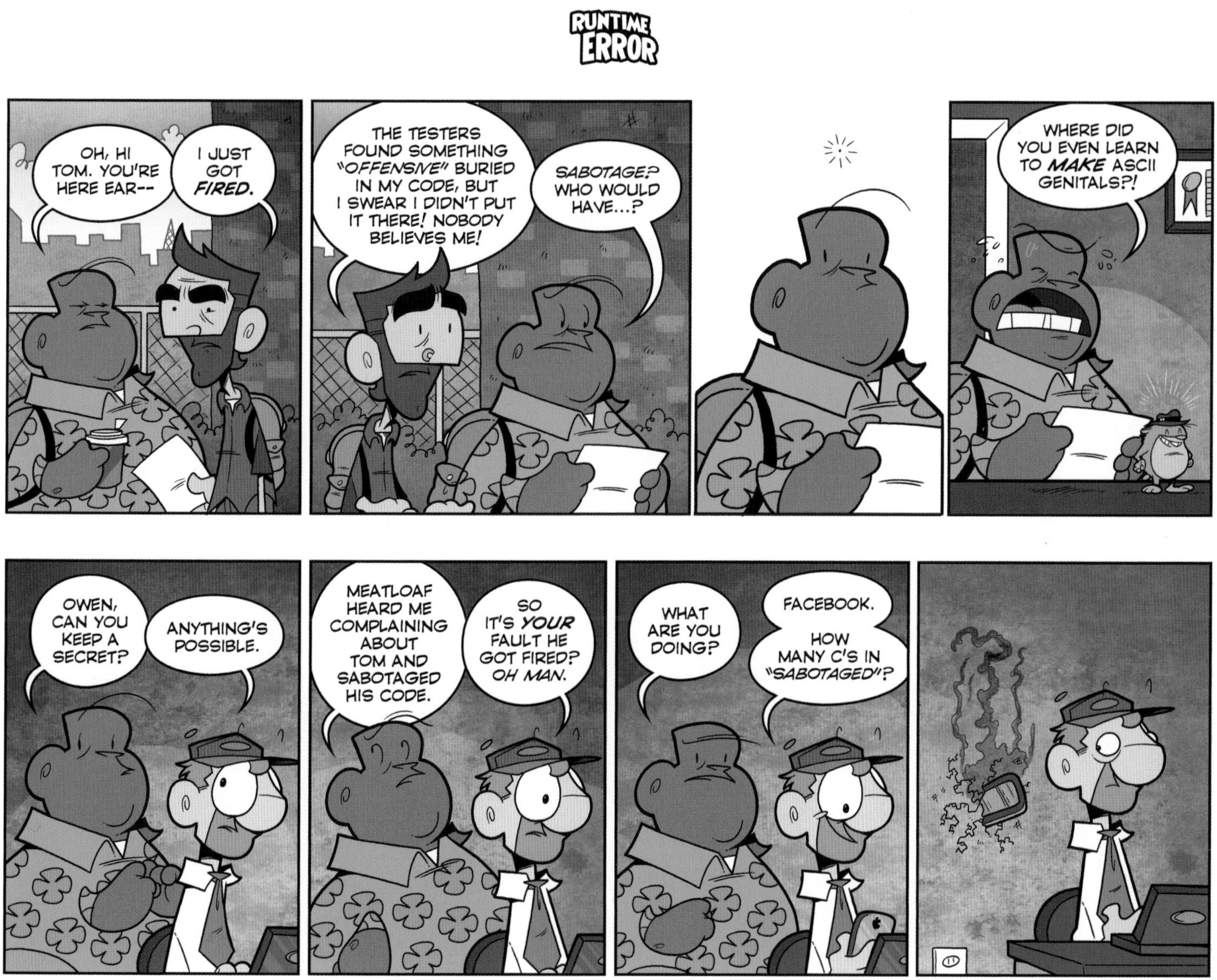
RUNTIME ERROR
OH, HI TOM. YOU'RE HERE EAR--
I JUST GOT FIRED.
THE TESTERS FOUND SOMETHING "OFFENSIVE" BURIED IN MY CODE, BUT I SWEAR I DIDN'T PUT IT THERE! NOBODY BELIEVES ME!
SABOTAGE? WHO WOULD HAVE...?
WHERE DID YOU EVEN LEARN TO MAKE ASCII GENITALS?!
OWEN, CAN YOU KEEP A SECRET?
ANYTHING'S POSSIBLE.
MEATLOAF HEARD ME COMPLAINING ABOUT TOM AND SABOTAGED HIS CODE.
SO IT'S YOUR FAULT HE GOT FIRED? OH MAN.
WHAT ARE YOU DOING?
FACEBOOK.
HOW MANY C'S IN "SABOTAGED"?

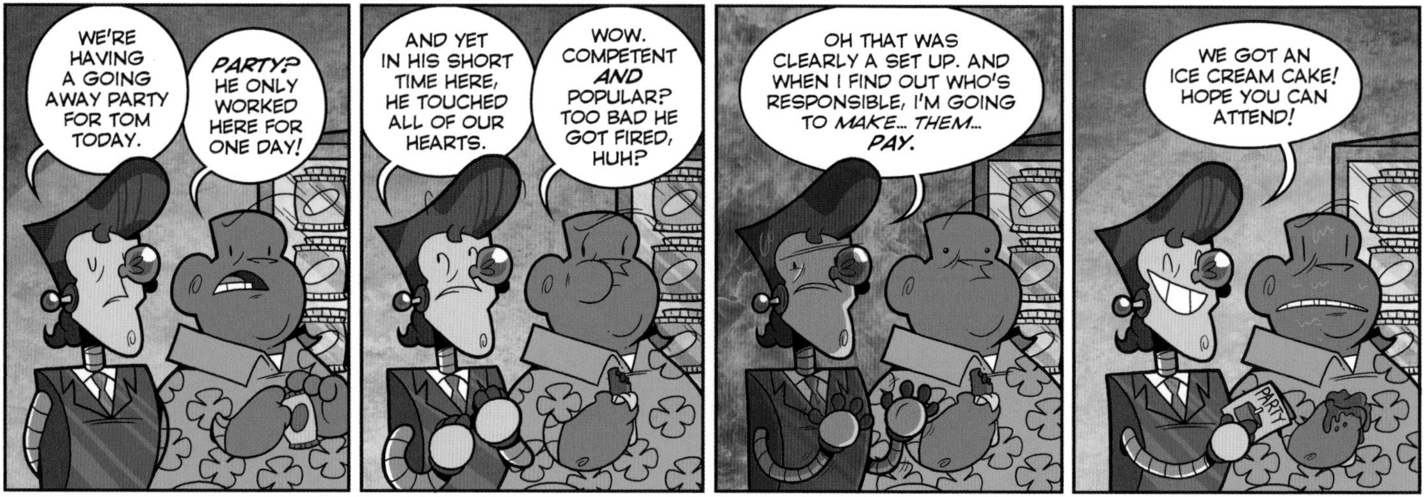
WE'RE HAVING A GOING AWAY PARTY FOR TOM TODAY.
PARTY? HE ONLY WORKED HERE FOR ONE DAY!
AND YET IN HIS SHORT TIME HERE, HE TOUCHED ALL OF OUR HEARTS.
WOW. COMPETENT *AND* POPULAR? TOO BAD HE GOT FIRED, HUH?
OH THAT WAS CLEARLY A SET UP. AND WHEN I FIND OUT WHO'S RESPONSIBLE, I'M GOING TO *MAKE... THEM... PAY.*
WE GOT AN ICE CREAM CAKE! HOPE YOU CAN ATTEND!
PARTY

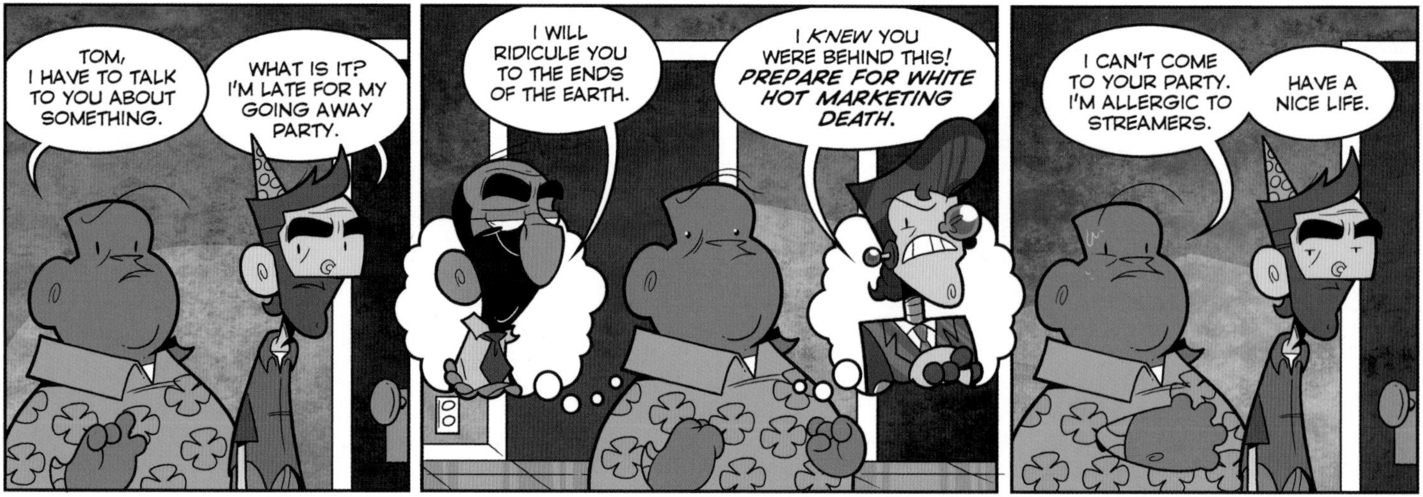
TOM, I HAVE TO TALK TO YOU ABOUT SOMETHING.
WHAT IS IT? I'M LATE FOR MY GOING AWAY PARTY.
I WILL RIDICULE YOU TO THE ENDS OF THE EARTH.
I *KNEW* YOU WERE BEHIND THIS! ***PREPARE FOR WHITE HOT MARKETING DEATH.***
I CAN'T COME TO YOUR PARTY. I'M ALLERGIC TO STREAMERS.
HAVE A NICE LIFE.

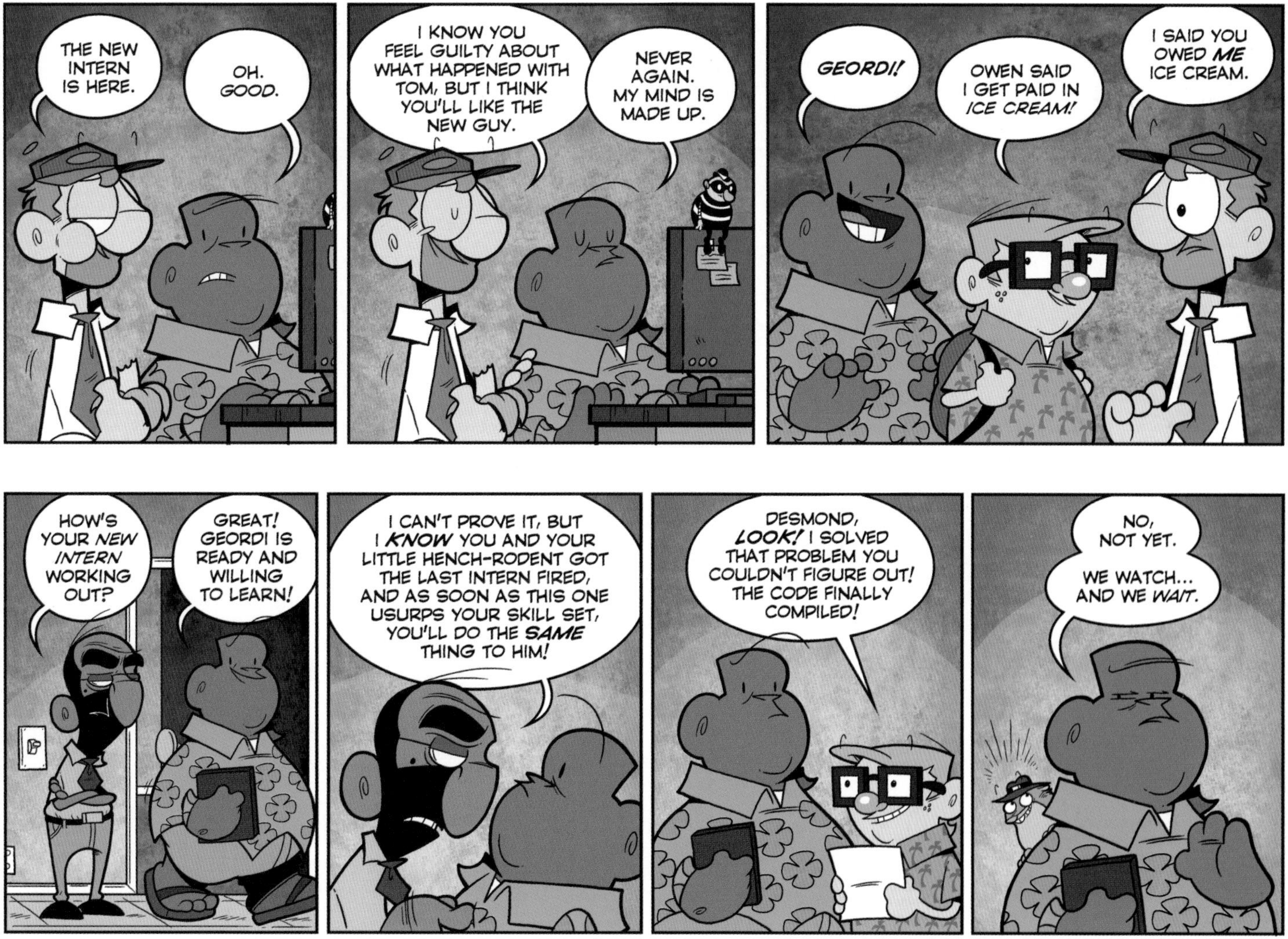
THE NEW INTERN IS HERE.
OH. GOOD.
I KNOW YOU FEEL GUILTY ABOUT WHAT HAPPENED WITH TOM, BUT I THINK YOU'LL LIKE THE NEW GUY.
NEVER AGAIN. MY MIND IS MADE UP.
GEORDI!
OWEN SAID I GET PAID IN ICE CREAM!
I SAID YOU OWED ME ICE CREAM.
HOW'S YOUR NEW INTERN WORKING OUT?
GREAT! GEORDI IS READY AND WILLING TO LEARN!
I CAN'T PROVE IT, BUT I KNOW YOU AND YOUR LITTLE HENCH-RODENT GOT THE LAST INTERN FIRED, AND AS SOON AS THIS ONE USURPS YOUR SKILL SET, YOU'LL DO THE SAME THING TO HIM!
DESMOND, LOOK! I SOLVED THAT PROBLEM YOU COULDN'T FIGURE OUT! THE CODE FINALLY COMPILED!
NO, NOT YET.
WE WATCH... AND WE WAIT.

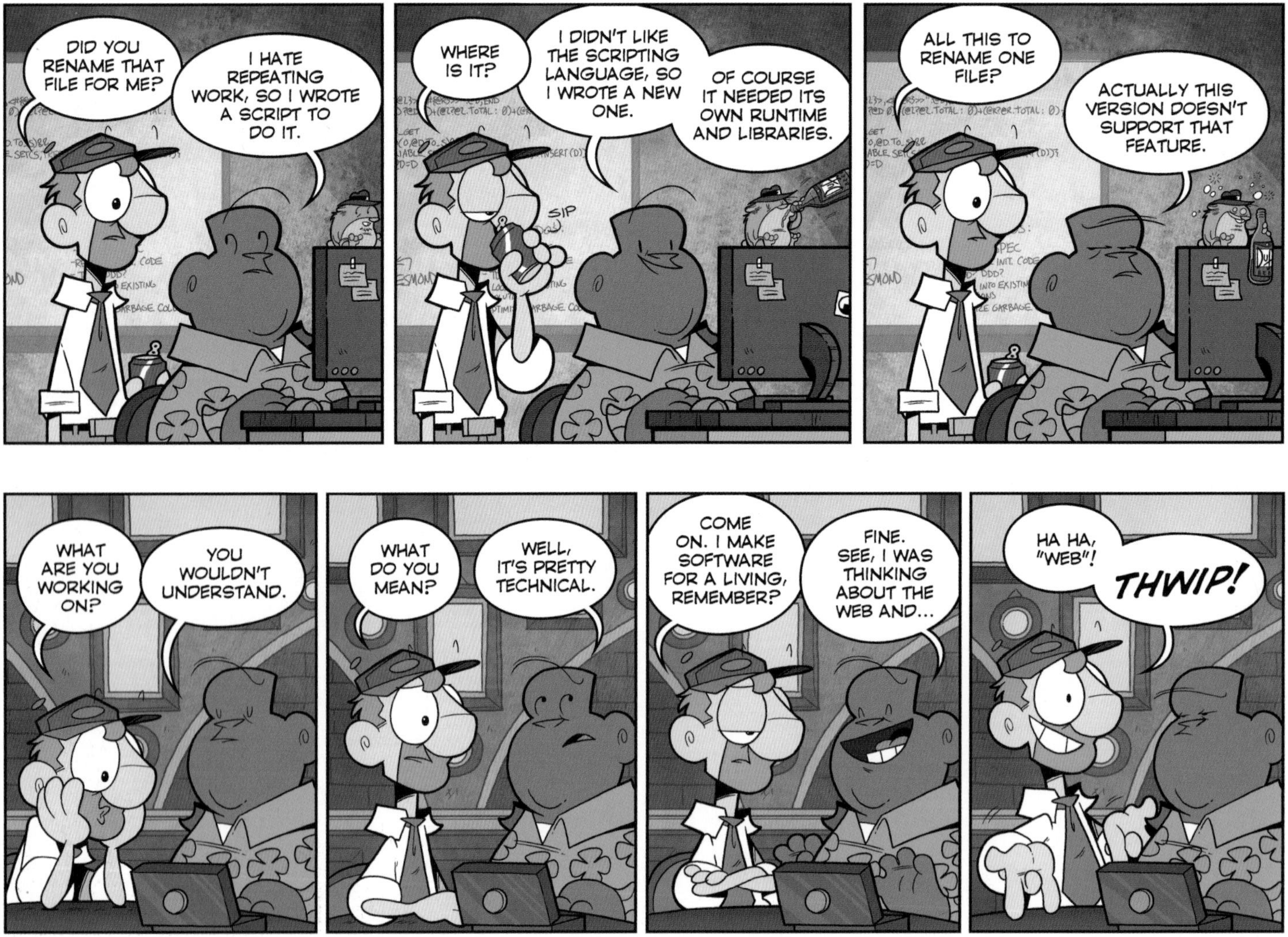
DID YOU RENAME THAT FILE FOR ME?
I HATE REPEATING WORK, SO I WROTE A SCRIPT TO DO IT.
WHERE IS IT?
I DIDN'T LIKE THE SCRIPTING LANGUAGE, SO I WROTE A NEW ONE.
OF COURSE IT NEEDED ITS OWN RUNTIME AND LIBRARIES.
SIP
ALL THIS TO RENAME ONE FILE?
ACTUALLY THIS VERSION DOESN'T SUPPORT THAT FEATURE.
WHAT ARE YOU WORKING ON?
YOU WOULDN'T UNDERSTAND.
WHAT DO YOU MEAN?
WELL, IT'S PRETTY TECHNICAL.
COME ON. I MAKE SOFTWARE FOR A LIVING, REMEMBER?
FINE. SEE, I WAS THINKING ABOUT THE WEB AND...
HA HA, "WEB"!
THWIP!

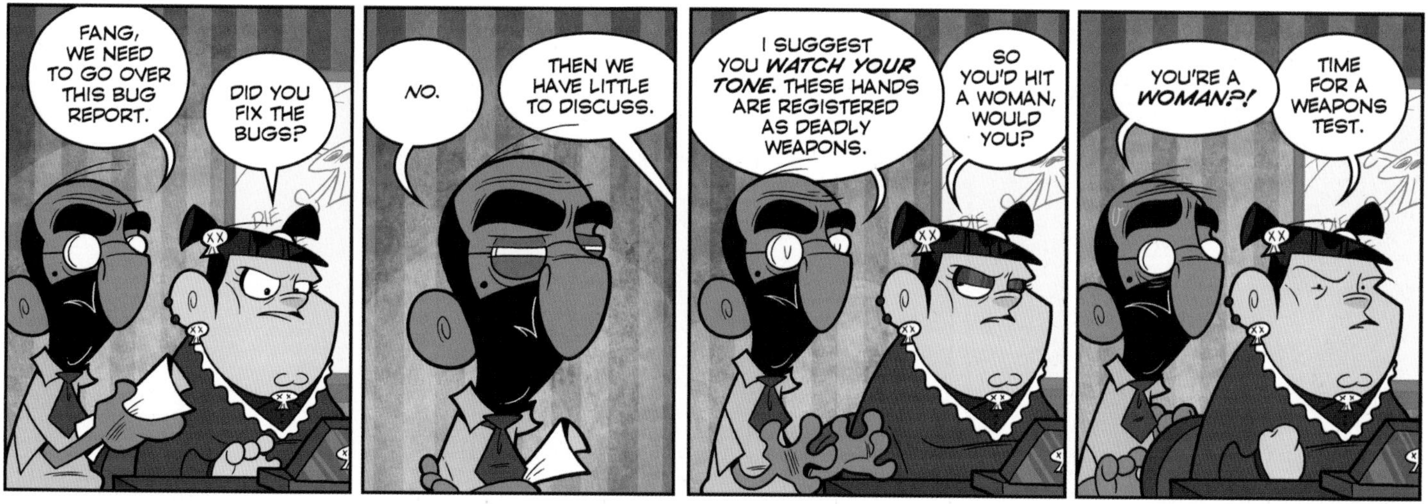
FANG, WE NEED TO GO OVER THIS BUG REPORT.
DID YOU FIX THE BUGS?
NO.
THEN WE HAVE LITTLE TO DISCUSS.
I SUGGEST YOU *WATCH YOUR TONE*. THESE HANDS ARE REGISTERED AS DEADLY WEAPONS.
SO YOU'D HIT A WOMAN, WOULD YOU?
YOU'RE A *WOMAN?!*
TIME FOR A WEAPONS TEST.

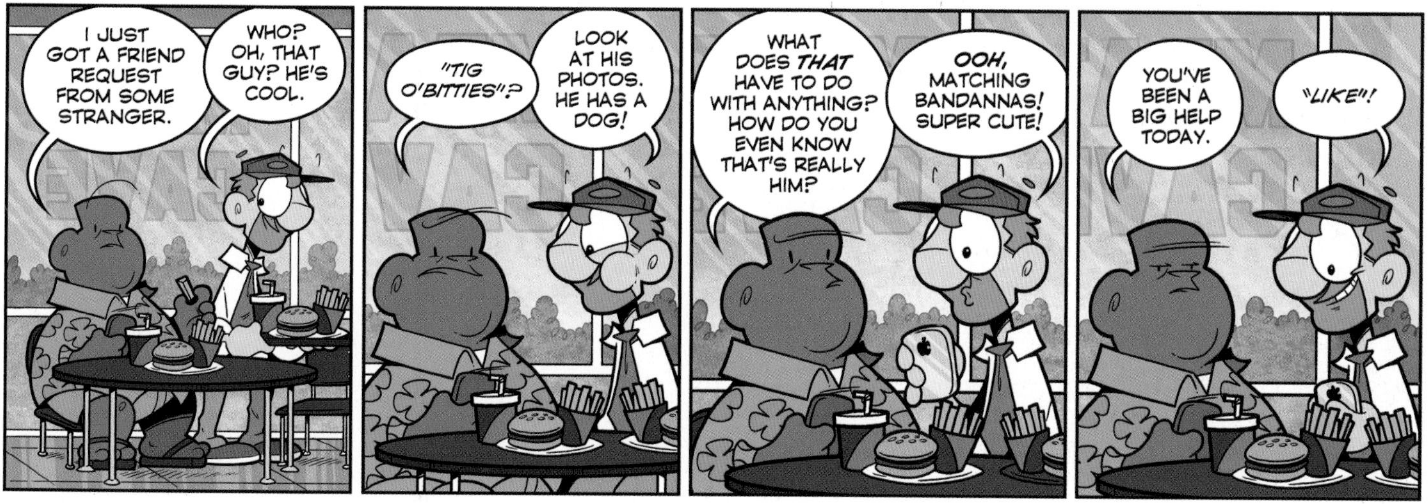
I JUST GOT A FRIEND REQUEST FROM SOME STRANGER.
WHO? OH, THAT GUY? HE'S COOL.
"TIG O'BITTIES"?
LOOK AT HIS PHOTOS. HE HAS A DOG!
WHAT DOES *THAT* HAVE TO DO WITH ANYTHING? HOW DO YOU EVEN KNOW THAT'S REALLY HIM?
OOH, MATCHING BANDANNAS! SUPER CUTE!
YOU'VE BEEN A BIG HELP TODAY.
"LIKE"!

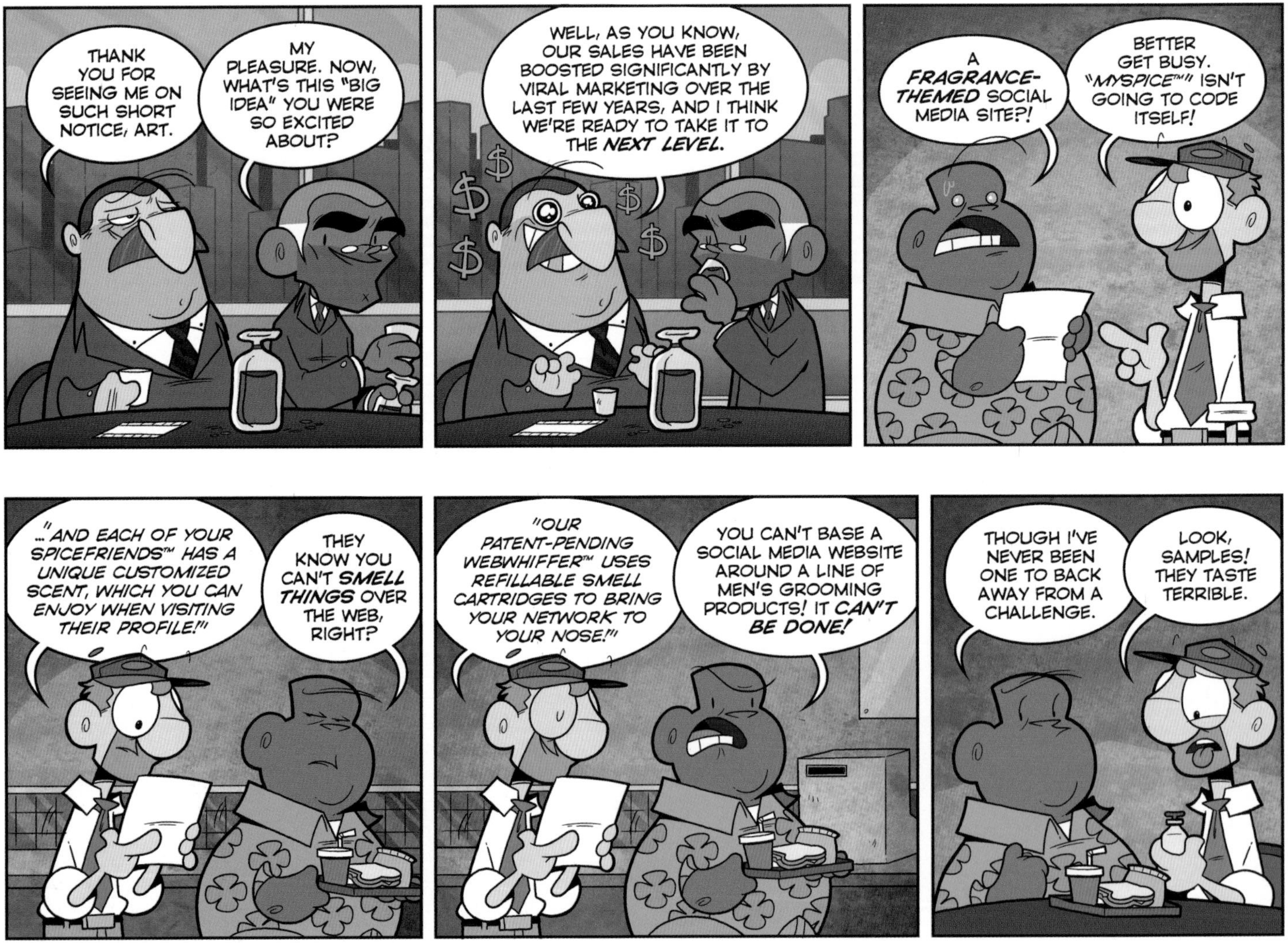
THANK YOU FOR SEEING ME ON SUCH SHORT NOTICE, ART.
MY PLEASURE. NOW, WHAT'S THIS "BIG IDEA" YOU WERE SO EXCITED ABOUT?
WELL, AS YOU KNOW, OUR SALES HAVE BEEN BOOSTED SIGNIFICANTLY BY VIRAL MARKETING OVER THE LAST FEW YEARS, AND I THINK WE'RE READY TO TAKE IT TO THE NEXT LEVEL.
A FRAGRANCE-THEMED SOCIAL MEDIA SITE?!
BETTER GET BUSY. "MYSPICE™" ISN'T GOING TO CODE ITSELF!
..."AND EACH OF YOUR SPICEFRIENDS™ HAS A UNIQUE CUSTOMIZED SCENT, WHICH YOU CAN ENJOY WHEN VISITING THEIR PROFILE!"
THEY KNOW YOU CAN'T SMELL THINGS OVER THE WEB, RIGHT?
"OUR PATENT-PENDING WEBWHIFFER™ USES REFILLABLE SMELL CARTRIDGES TO BRING YOUR NETWORK TO YOUR NOSE!"
YOU CAN'T BASE A SOCIAL MEDIA WEBSITE AROUND A LINE OF MEN'S GROOMING PRODUCTS! IT CAN'T BE DONE!
THOUGH I'VE NEVER BEEN ONE TO BACK AWAY FROM A CHALLENGE.
LOOK, SAMPLES! THEY TASTE TERRIBLE.

RUNTIME ERROR

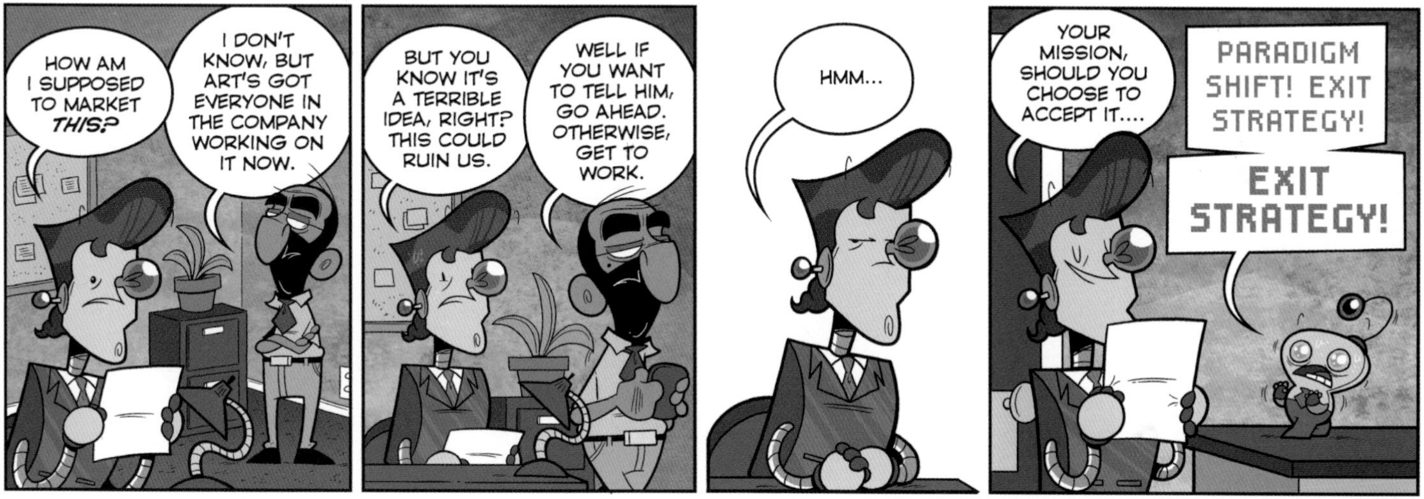
HOW AM I SUPPOSED TO MARKET *THIS?*
I DON'T KNOW, BUT ART'S GOT EVERYONE IN THE COMPANY WORKING ON IT NOW.
BUT YOU KNOW IT'S A TERRIBLE IDEA, RIGHT? THIS COULD RUIN US.
WELL IF YOU WANT TO TELL HIM, GO AHEAD. OTHERWISE, GET TO WORK.
HMM...
YOUR MISSION, SHOULD YOU CHOOSE TO ACCEPT IT....
PARADIGM SHIFT! EXIT STRATEGY!
EXIT STRATEGY!

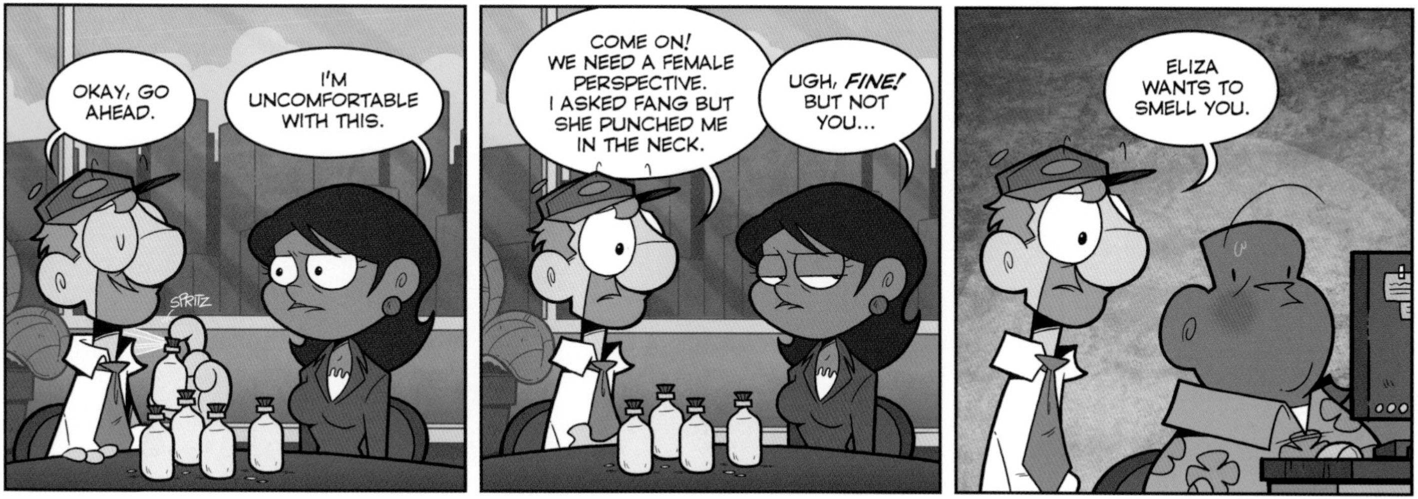
OKAY, GO AHEAD.
I'M UNCOMFORTABLE WITH THIS.
SPRITZ
COME ON! WE NEED A FEMALE PERSPECTIVE. I ASKED FANG BUT SHE PUNCHED ME IN THE NECK.
UGH, *FINE!* BUT NOT YOU...
ELIZA WANTS TO SMELL YOU.

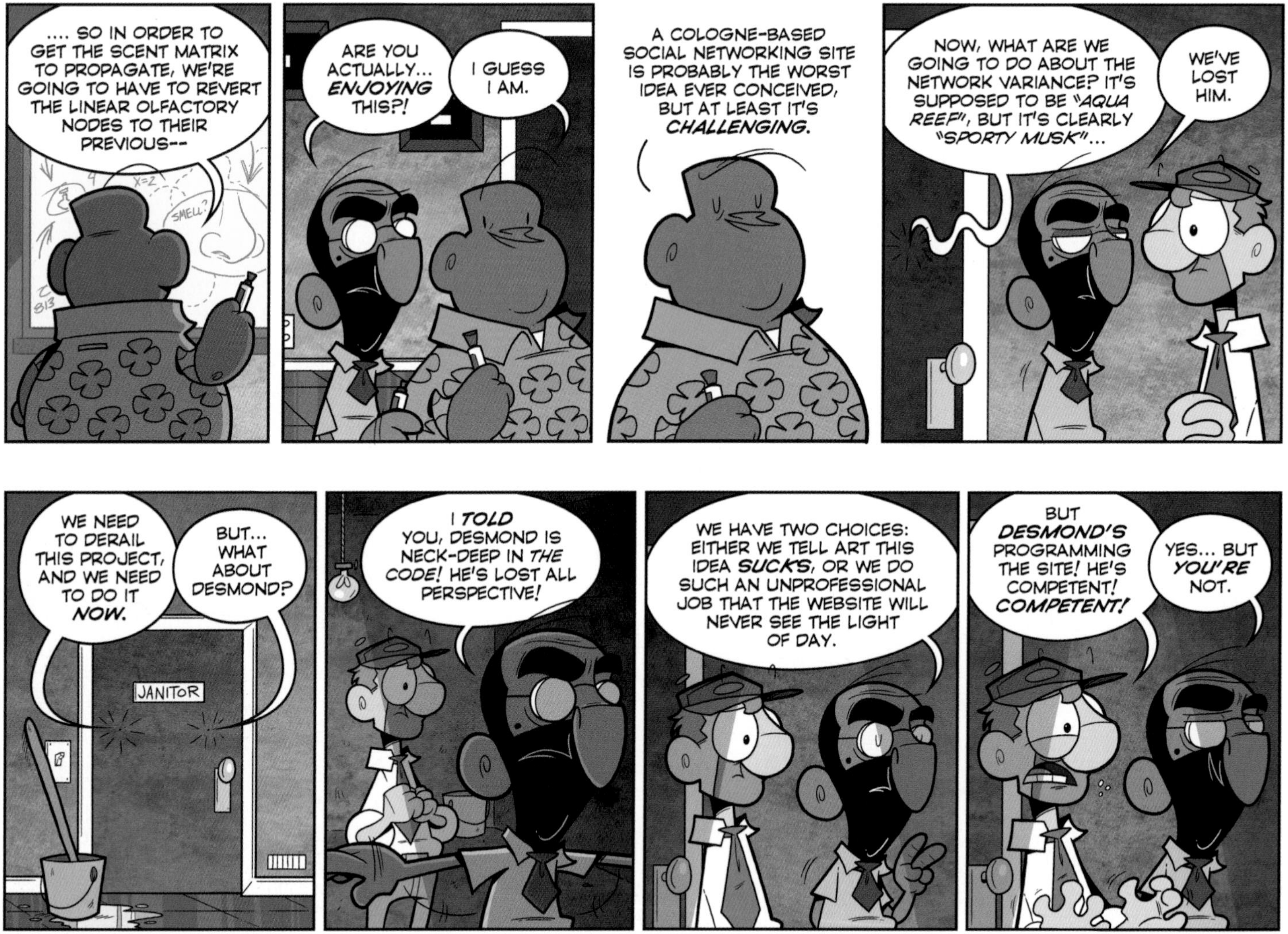
.... SO IN ORDER TO GET THE SCENT MATRIX TO PROPAGATE, WE'RE GOING TO HAVE TO REVERT THE LINEAR OLFACTORY NODES TO THEIR PREVIOUS--
SMELL?
ARE YOU ACTUALLY... *ENJOYING* THIS?!
I GUESS I AM.
A COLOGNE-BASED SOCIAL NETWORKING SITE IS PROBABLY THE WORST IDEA EVER CONCEIVED, BUT AT LEAST IT'S *CHALLENGING.*
NOW, WHAT ARE WE GOING TO DO ABOUT THE NETWORK VARIANCE? IT'S SUPPOSED TO BE "*AQUA REEF*", BUT IT'S CLEARLY "*SPORTY MUSK*"...
WE'VE LOST HIM.
WE NEED TO DERAIL THIS PROJECT, AND WE NEED TO DO IT *NOW.*
BUT... WHAT ABOUT DESMOND?
JANITOR
I *TOLD* YOU, DESMOND IS NECK-DEEP IN *THE CODE!* HE'S LOST ALL PERSPECTIVE!
WE HAVE TWO CHOICES: EITHER WE TELL ART THIS IDEA ***SUCKS***, OR WE DO SUCH AN UNPROFESSIONAL JOB THAT THE WEBSITE WILL NEVER SEE THE LIGHT OF DAY.
BUT ***DESMOND'S*** PROGRAMMING THE SITE! HE'S COMPETENT! ***COMPETENT!***
YES... BUT ***YOU'RE*** NOT.

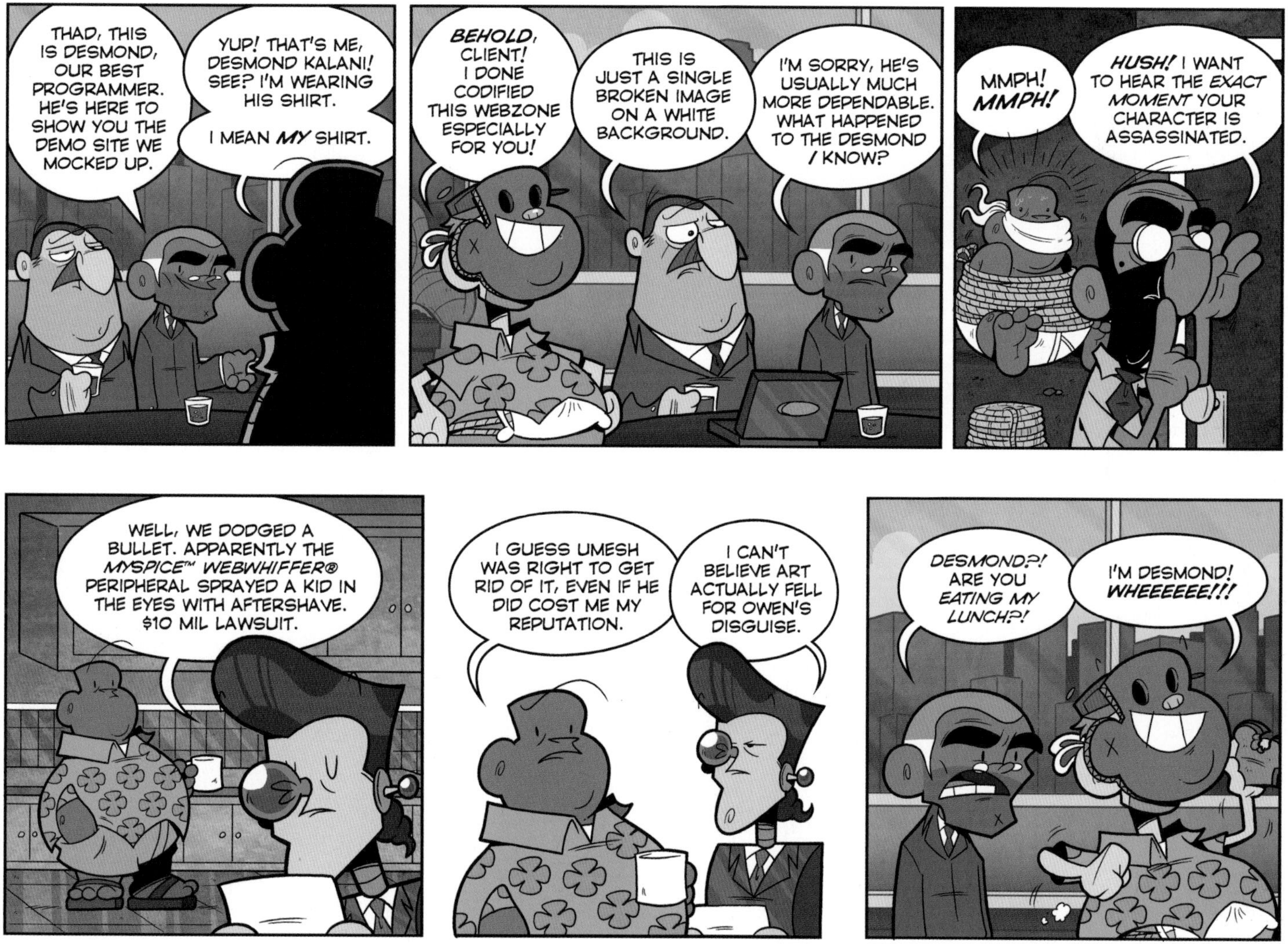
THAD, THIS IS DESMOND, OUR BEST PROGRAMMER. HE'S HERE TO SHOW YOU THE DEMO SITE WE MOCKED UP.
YUP! THAT'S ME, DESMOND KALANI! SEE? I'M WEARING HIS SHIRT.
I MEAN *MY* SHIRT.
BEHOLD, CLIENT! I DONE CODIFIED THIS WEBZONE ESPECIALLY FOR YOU!
THIS IS JUST A SINGLE BROKEN IMAGE ON A WHITE BACKGROUND.
I'M SORRY, HE'S USUALLY MUCH MORE DEPENDABLE. WHAT HAPPENED TO THE DESMOND *I* KNOW?
MMPH! *MMPH!*
HUSH! I WANT TO HEAR THE *EXACT MOMENT* YOUR CHARACTER IS ASSASSINATED.
WELL, WE DODGED A BULLET. APPARENTLY THE *MYSPICE™ WEBWHIFFER®* PERIPHERAL SPRAYED A KID IN THE EYES WITH AFTERSHAVE. $10 MIL LAWSUIT.
I GUESS UMESH WAS RIGHT TO GET RID OF IT, EVEN IF HE DID COST ME MY REPUTATION.
I CAN'T BELIEVE ART ACTUALLY FELL FOR OWEN'S DISGUISE.
DESMOND?! ARE YOU EATING MY LUNCH?!
I'M DESMOND! *WHEEEEEE!!!*

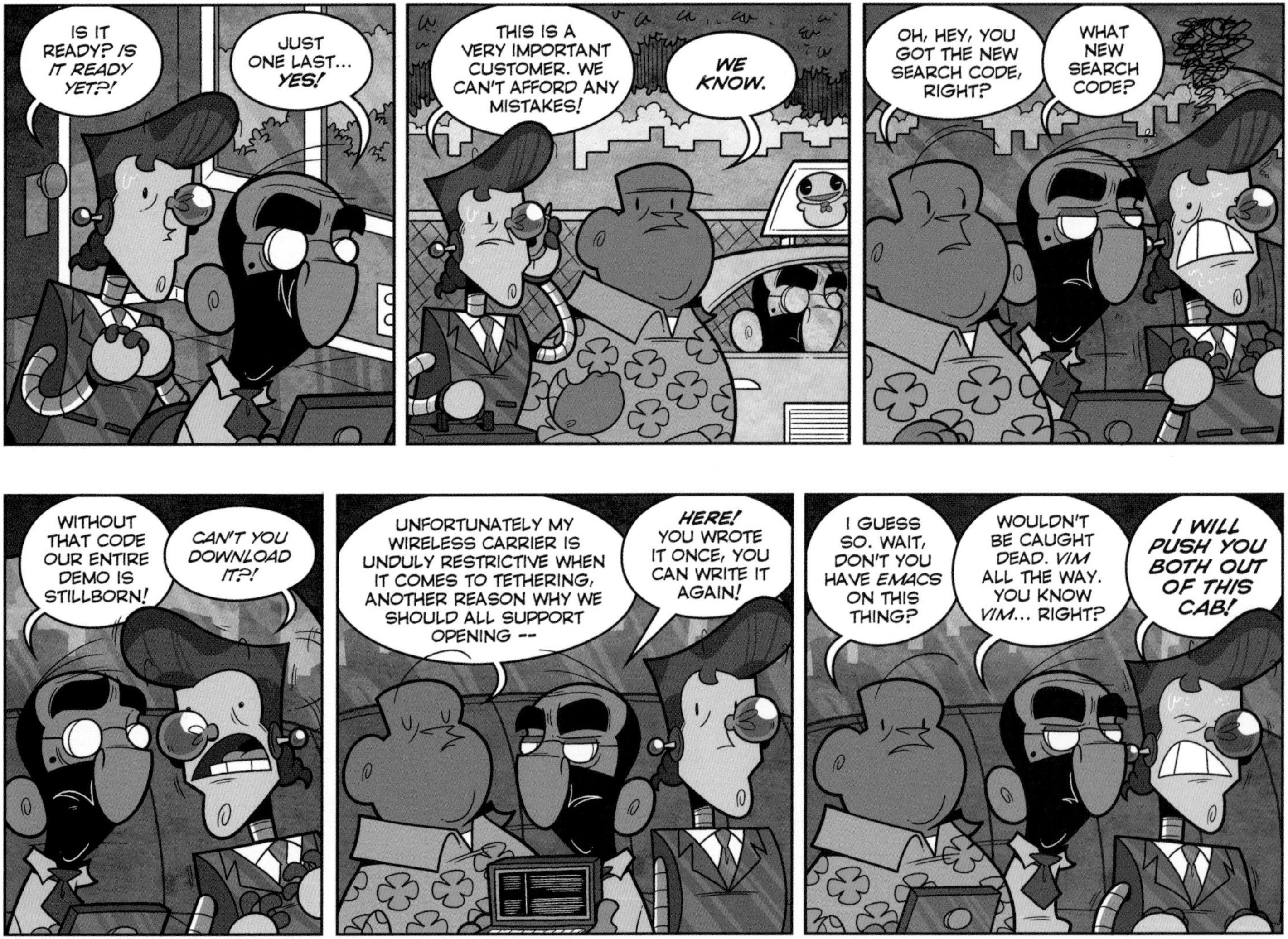

IS IT READY? IS IT READY YET?!
JUST ONE LAST... YES!
THIS IS A VERY IMPORTANT CUSTOMER. WE CAN'T AFFORD ANY MISTAKES!
WE KNOW.
OH, HEY, YOU GOT THE NEW SEARCH CODE, RIGHT?
WHAT NEW SEARCH CODE?
WITHOUT THAT CODE OUR ENTIRE DEMO IS STILLBORN!
CAN'T YOU DOWNLOAD IT?!
UNFORTUNATELY MY WIRELESS CARRIER IS UNDULY RESTRICTIVE WHEN IT COMES TO TETHERING, ANOTHER REASON WHY WE SHOULD ALL SUPPORT OPENING --
HERE! YOU WROTE IT ONCE, YOU CAN WRITE IT AGAIN!
I GUESS SO. WAIT, DON'T YOU HAVE EMACS ON THIS THING?
WOULDN'T BE CAUGHT DEAD. VIM ALL THE WAY. YOU KNOW VIM... RIGHT?
I WILL PUSH YOU BOTH OUT OF THIS CAB!

RUNTIME ERROR

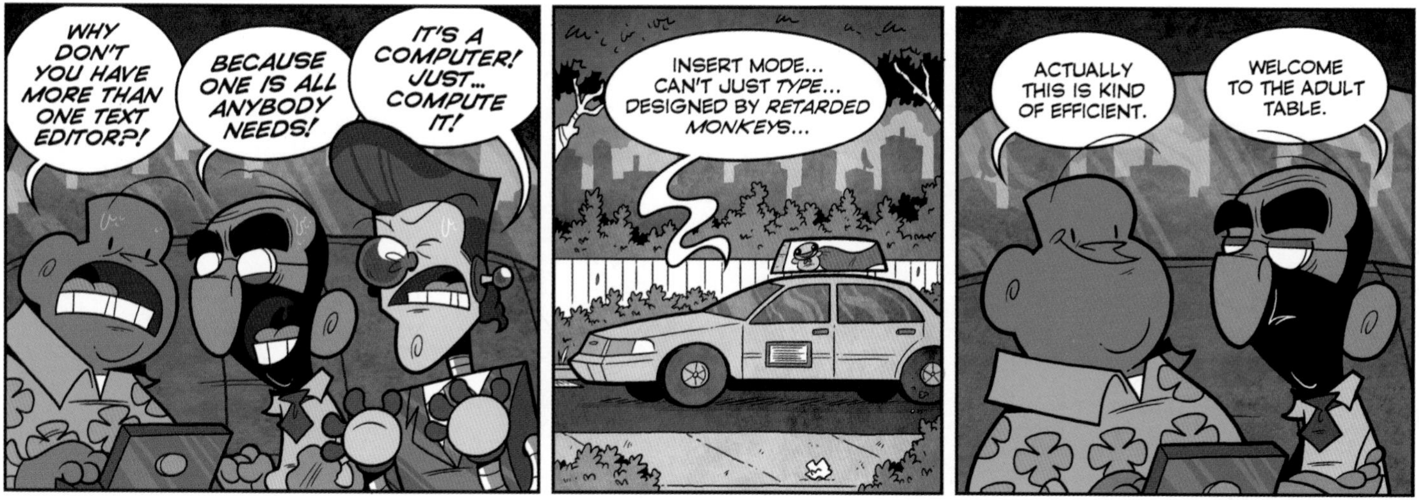
WHY DON'T YOU HAVE MORE THAN ONE TEXT EDITOR?!
BECAUSE ONE IS ALL ANYBODY NEEDS!
IT'S A COMPUTER! JUST... COMPUTE IT!
INSERT MODE... CAN'T JUST TYPE... DESIGNED BY RETARDED MONKEYS...
ACTUALLY THIS IS KIND OF EFFICIENT.
WELCOME TO THE ADULT TABLE.

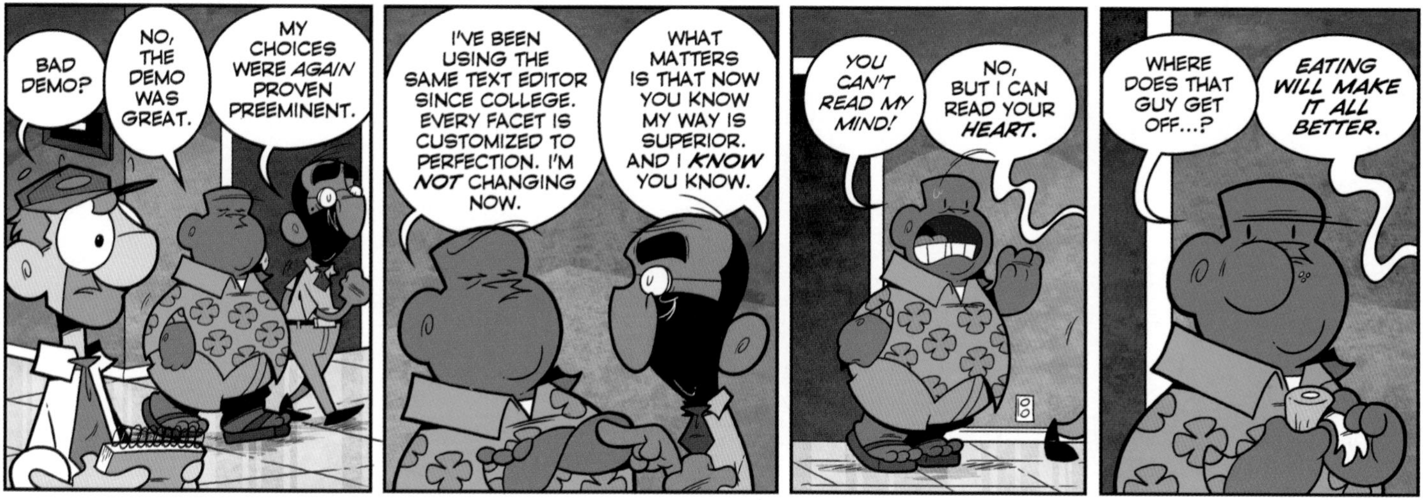
BAD DEMO?
NO, THE DEMO WAS GREAT.
MY CHOICES WERE AGAIN PROVEN PREEMINENT.
I'VE BEEN USING THE SAME TEXT EDITOR SINCE COLLEGE. EVERY FACET IS CUSTOMIZED TO PERFECTION. I'M NOT CHANGING NOW.
WHAT MATTERS IS THAT NOW YOU KNOW MY WAY IS SUPERIOR. AND I KNOW YOU KNOW.
YOU CAN'T READ MY MIND!
NO, BUT I CAN READ YOUR HEART.
WHERE DOES THAT GUY GET OFF...?
EATING WILL MAKE IT ALL BETTER.

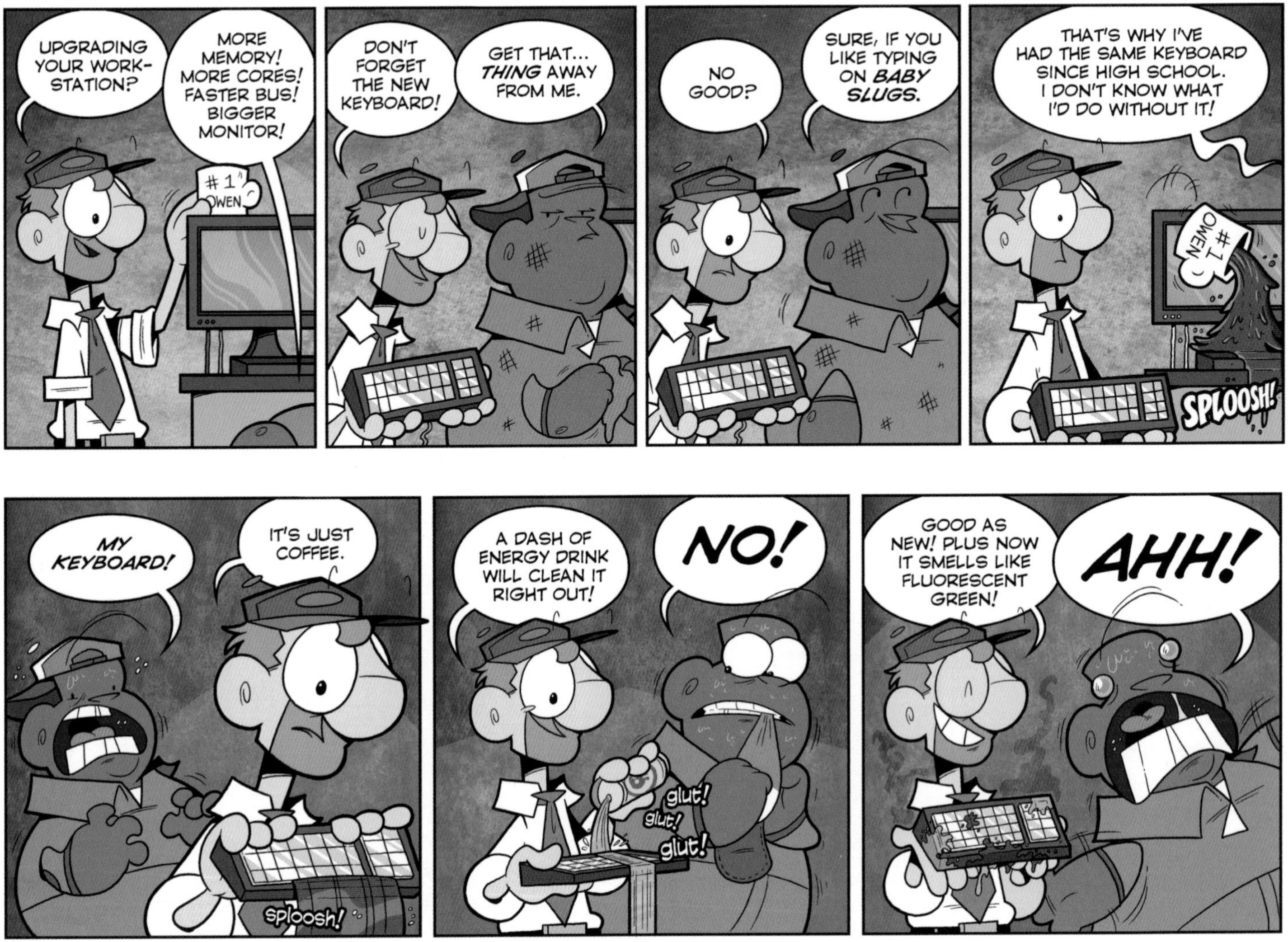
UPGRADING YOUR WORK-STATION?
MORE MEMORY! MORE CORES! FASTER BUS! BIGGER MONITOR!
#1 OWEN
DON'T FORGET THE NEW KEYBOARD!
GET THAT... *THING* AWAY FROM ME.
NO GOOD?
SURE, IF YOU LIKE TYPING ON *BABY SLUGS.*
THAT'S WHY I'VE HAD THE SAME KEYBOARD SINCE HIGH SCHOOL. I DON'T KNOW WHAT I'D DO WITHOUT IT!
#1 OWEN
SPLOOSH!
MY KEYBOARD!
IT'S JUST COFFEE.
sploosh!
A DASH OF ENERGY DRINK WILL CLEAN IT RIGHT OUT!
NO!
glut!
glut!
glut!
GOOD AS NEW! PLUS NOW IT SMELLS LIKE FLUORESCENT GREEN!
AHH!

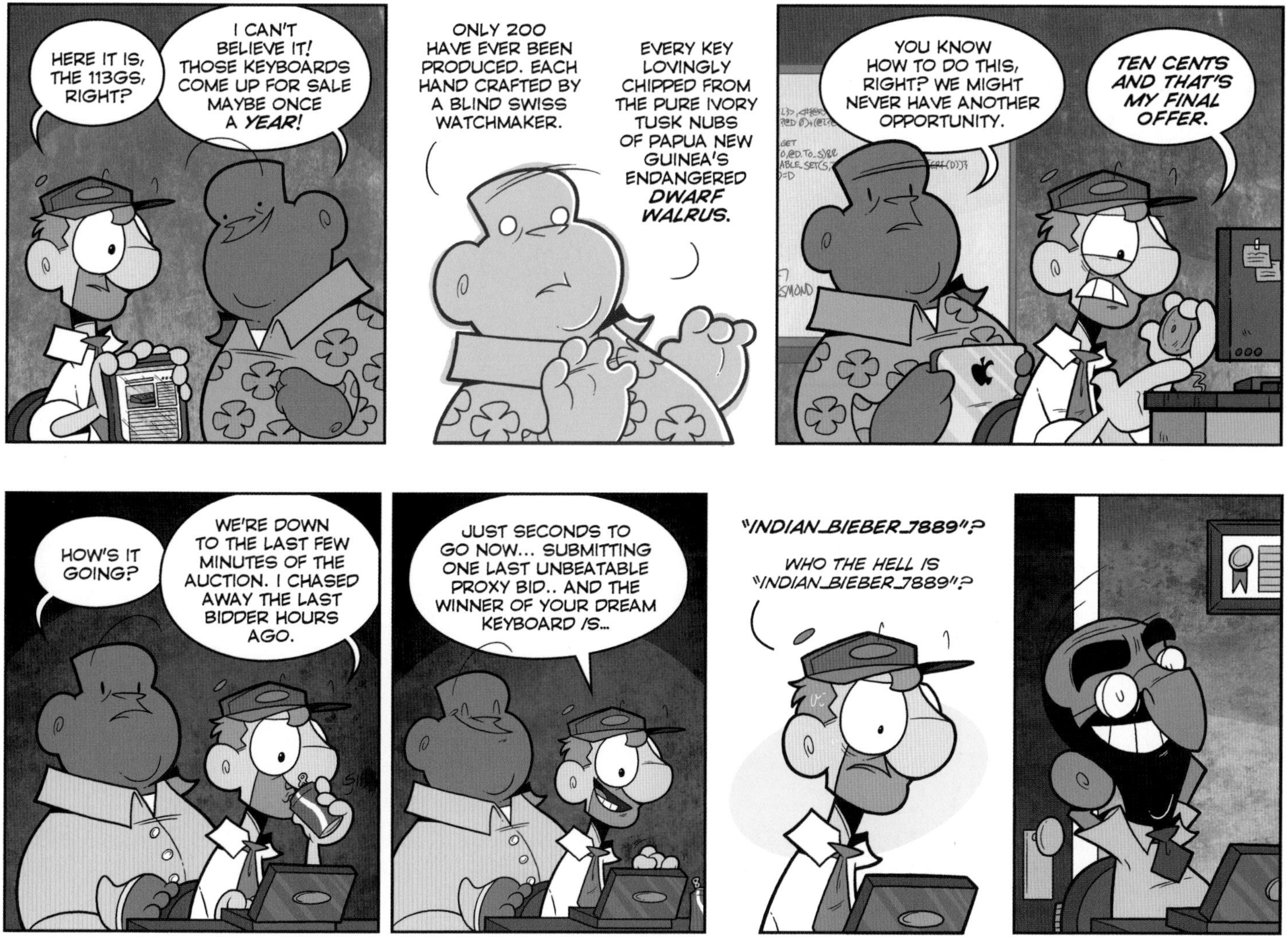
HERE IT IS, THE 113GS, RIGHT?
I CAN'T BELIEVE IT! THOSE KEYBOARDS COME UP FOR SALE MAYBE ONCE A YEAR!
ONLY 200 HAVE EVER BEEN PRODUCED. EACH HAND CRAFTED BY A BLIND SWISS WATCHMAKER.
EVERY KEY LOVINGLY CHIPPED FROM THE PURE IVORY TUSK NUBS OF PAPUA NEW GUINEA'S ENDANGERED DWARF WALRUS.
YOU KNOW HOW TO DO THIS, RIGHT? WE MIGHT NEVER HAVE ANOTHER OPPORTUNITY.
TEN CENTS AND THAT'S MY FINAL OFFER.
HOW'S IT GOING?
WE'RE DOWN TO THE LAST FEW MINUTES OF THE AUCTION. I CHASED AWAY THE LAST BIDDER HOURS AGO.
JUST SECONDS TO GO NOW... SUBMITTING ONE LAST UNBEATABLE PROXY BID.. AND THE WINNER OF YOUR DREAM KEYBOARD IS...
"INDIAN_BIEBER_7889"?
WHO THE HELL IS "INDIAN_BIEBER_7889"?

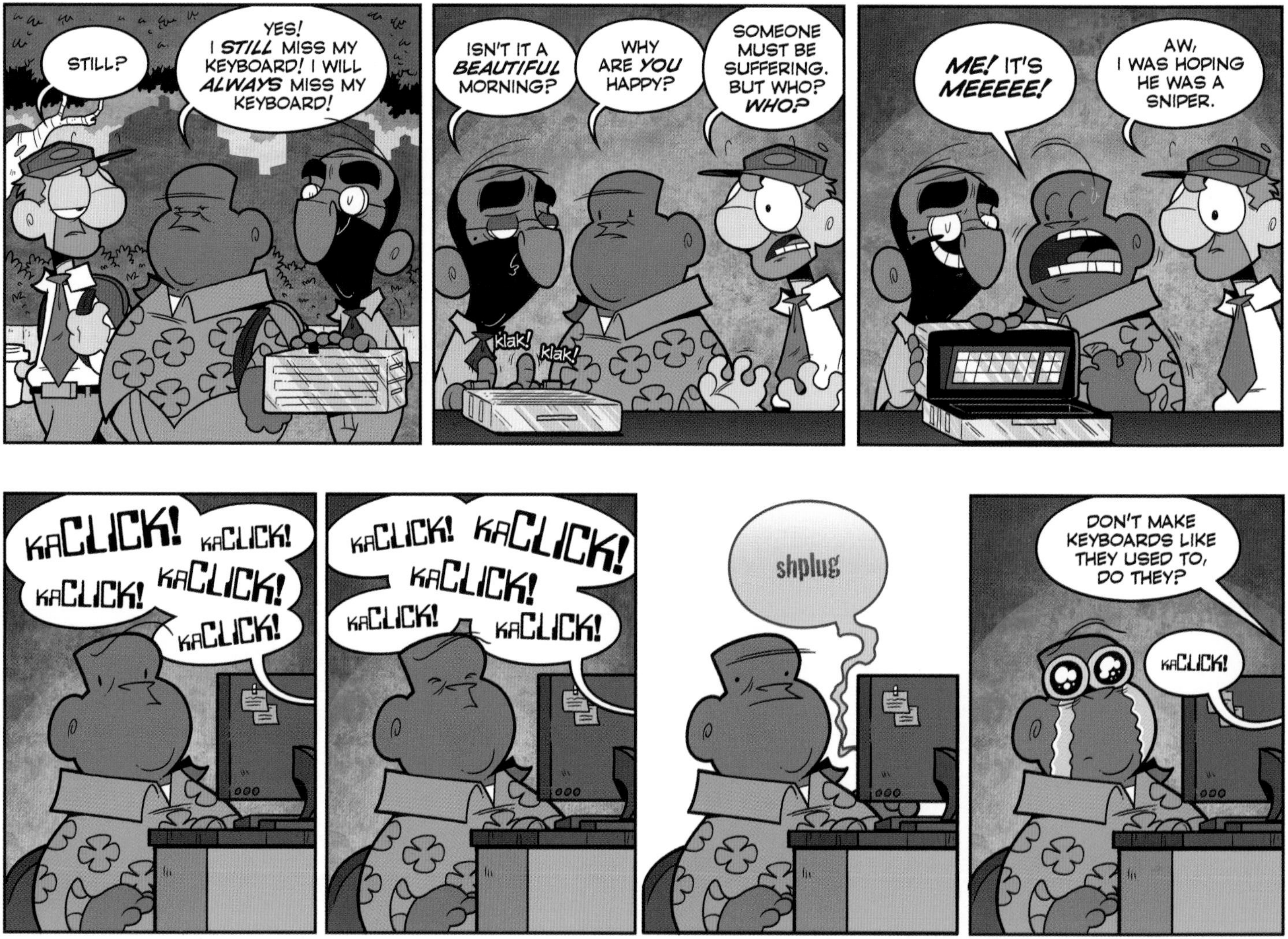
STILL?
YES! I STILL MISS MY KEYBOARD! I WILL ALWAYS MISS MY KEYBOARD!
ISN'T IT A BEAUTIFUL MORNING?
WHY ARE YOU HAPPY?
SOMEONE MUST BE SUFFERING. BUT WHO? WHO?
klak! klak!
ME! IT'S MEEEEE!
AW, I WAS HOPING HE WAS A SNIPER.
KACLICK! KACLICK! KACLICK! KACLICK! KACLICK!
KACLICK! KACLICK! KACLICK! KACLICK! KACLICK!
shplug
DON'T MAKE KEYBOARDS LIKE THEY USED TO, DO THEY?
KACLICK!

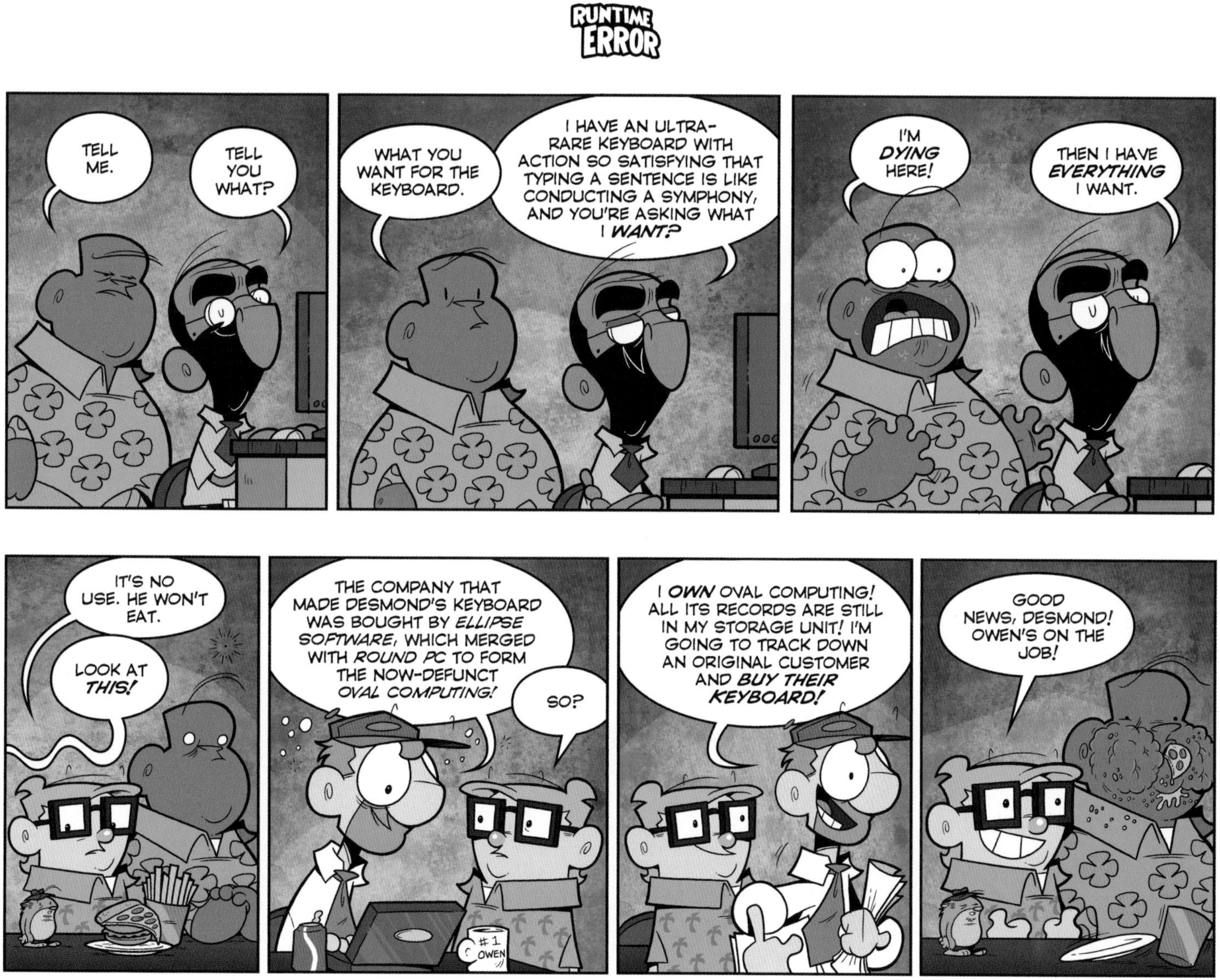
RUNTIME ERROR
TELL ME.
TELL YOU WHAT?
WHAT YOU WANT FOR THE KEYBOARD.
I HAVE AN ULTRA-RARE KEYBOARD WITH ACTION SO SATISFYING THAT TYPING A SENTENCE IS LIKE CONDUCTING A SYMPHONY, AND YOU'RE ASKING WHAT I *WANT?*
I'M *DYING* HERE!
THEN I HAVE *EVERYTHING* I WANT.
IT'S NO USE. HE WON'T EAT.
LOOK AT *THIS!*
THE COMPANY THAT MADE DESMOND'S KEYBOARD WAS BOUGHT BY *ELLIPSE SOFTWARE,* WHICH MERGED WITH *ROUND PC* TO FORM THE NOW-DEFUNCT *OVAL COMPUTING!*
SO?
#1 OWEN
I *OWN* OVAL COMPUTING! ALL ITS RECORDS ARE STILL IN MY STORAGE UNIT! I'M GOING TO TRACK DOWN AN ORIGINAL CUSTOMER AND *BUY THEIR KEYBOARD!*
GOOD NEWS, DESMOND! OWEN'S ON THE JOB!

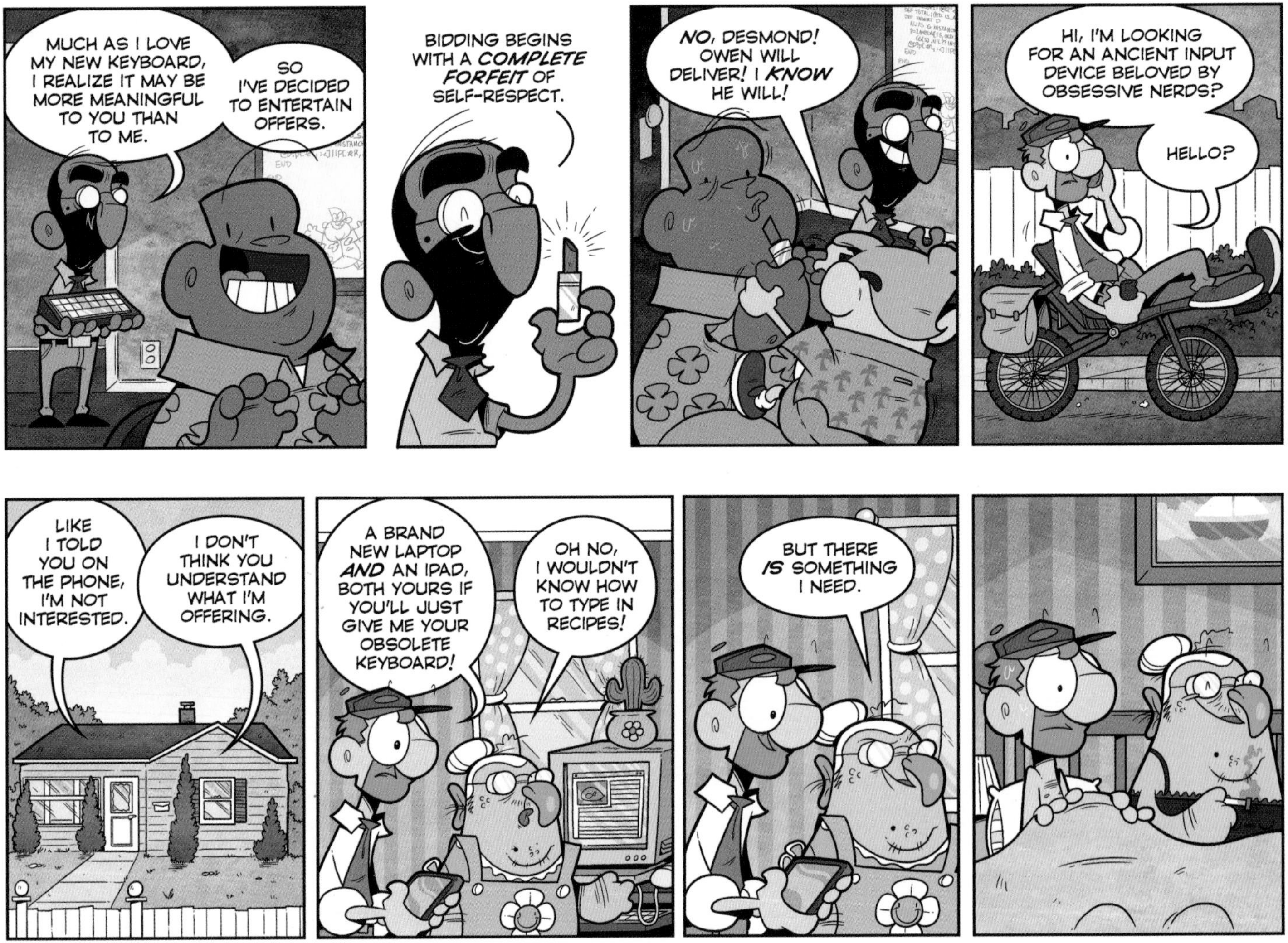
MUCH AS I LOVE MY NEW KEYBOARD, I REALIZE IT MAY BE MORE MEANINGFUL TO YOU THAN TO ME.
SO I'VE DECIDED TO ENTERTAIN OFFERS.
BIDDING BEGINS WITH A *COMPLETE FORFEIT* OF SELF-RESPECT.
NO, DESMOND! OWEN WILL DELIVER! I *KNOW* HE WILL!
HI, I'M LOOKING FOR AN ANCIENT INPUT DEVICE BELOVED BY OBSESSIVE NERDS?
HELLO?
LIKE I TOLD YOU ON THE PHONE, I'M NOT INTERESTED.
I DON'T THINK YOU UNDERSTAND WHAT I'M OFFERING.
A BRAND NEW LAPTOP *AND* AN IPAD, BOTH YOURS IF YOU'LL JUST GIVE ME YOUR OBSOLETE KEYBOARD!
OH NO, I WOULDN'T KNOW HOW TO TYPE IN RECIPES!
BUT THERE *IS* SOMETHING I NEED.

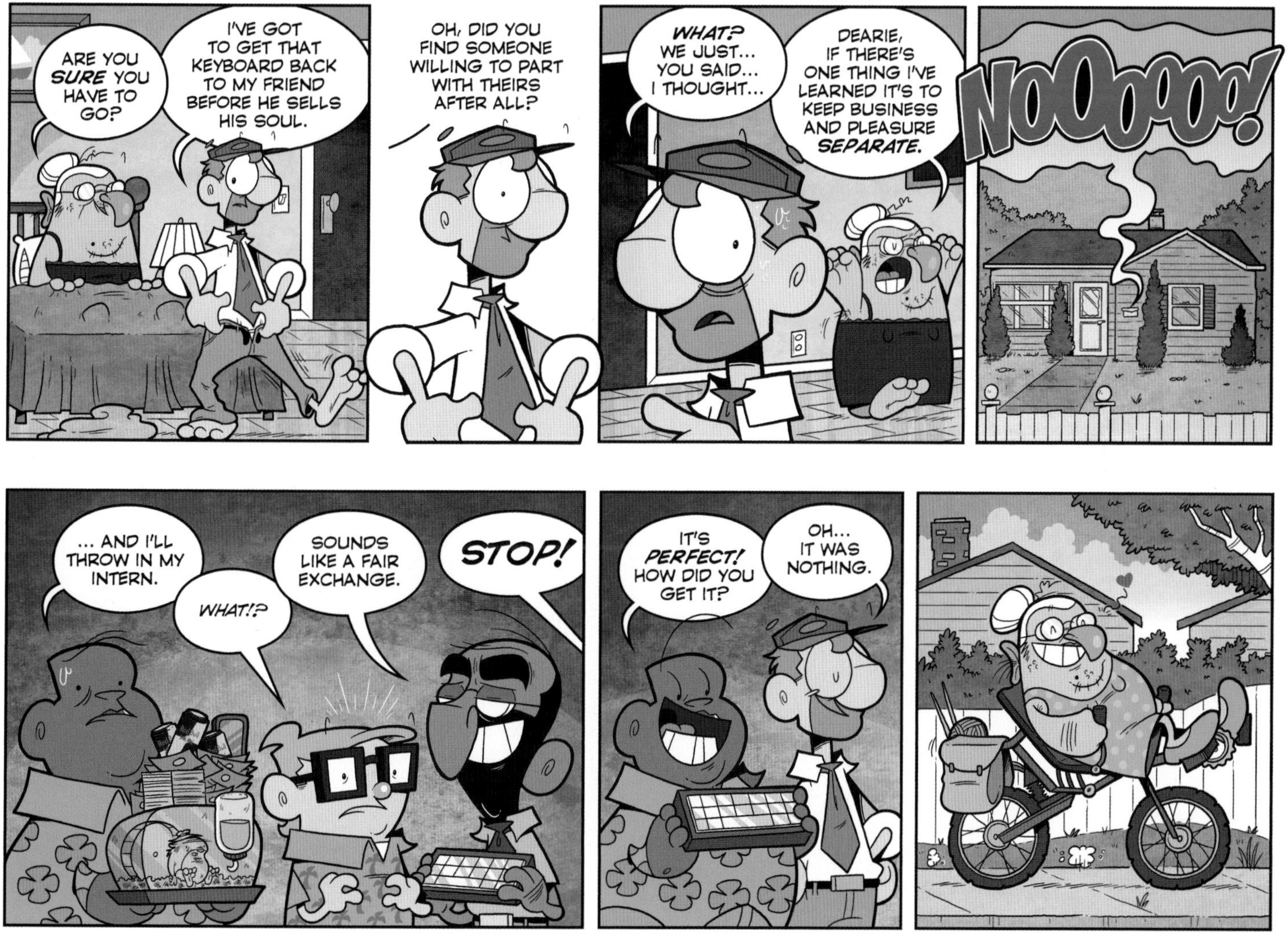
ARE YOU SURE YOU HAVE TO GO?
I'VE GOT TO GET THAT KEYBOARD BACK TO MY FRIEND BEFORE HE SELLS HIS SOUL.
OH, DID YOU FIND SOMEONE WILLING TO PART WITH THEIRS AFTER ALL?
WHAT? WE JUST... YOU SAID... I THOUGHT...
DEARIE, IF THERE'S ONE THING I'VE LEARNED IT'S TO KEEP BUSINESS AND PLEASURE SEPARATE.
NOOOOOO!
... AND I'LL THROW IN MY INTERN.
WHAT!?
SOUNDS LIKE A FAIR EXCHANGE.
STOP!
IT'S PERFECT! HOW DID YOU GET IT?
OH... IT WAS NOTHING.

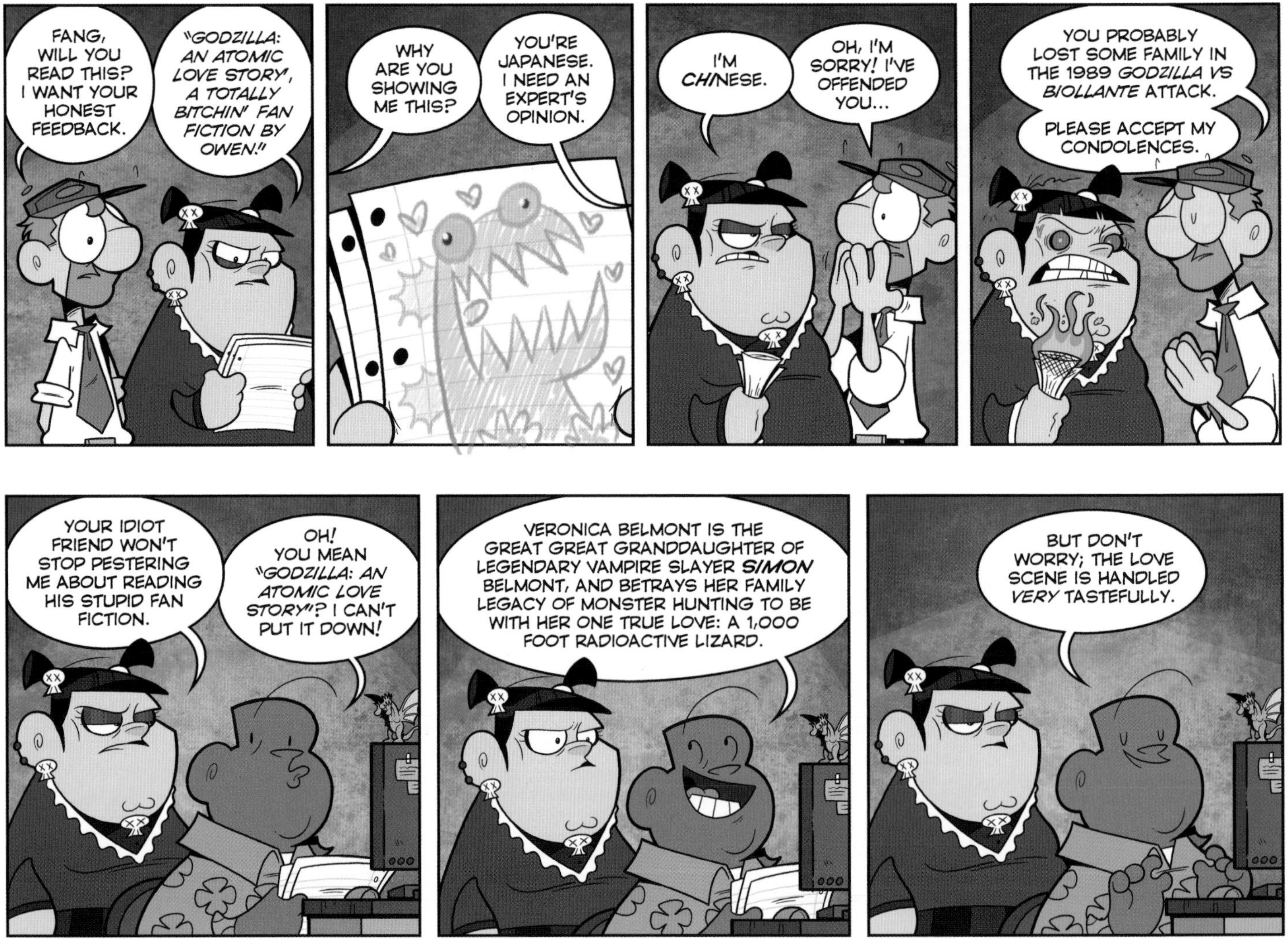
FANG, WILL YOU READ THIS? I WANT YOUR HONEST FEEDBACK.
"GODZILLA: AN ATOMIC LOVE STORY", A TOTALLY BITCHIN' FAN FICTION BY OWEN."
WHY ARE YOU SHOWING ME THIS?
YOU'RE JAPANESE. I NEED AN EXPERT'S OPINION.
I'M CHINESE.
OH, I'M SORRY! I'VE OFFENDED YOU...
YOU PROBABLY LOST SOME FAMILY IN THE 1989 GODZILLA VS BIOLLANTE ATTACK.
PLEASE ACCEPT MY CONDOLENCES.
YOUR IDIOT FRIEND WON'T STOP PESTERING ME ABOUT READING HIS STUPID FAN FICTION.
OH! YOU MEAN "GODZILLA: AN ATOMIC LOVE STORY"? I CAN'T PUT IT DOWN!
VERONICA BELMONT IS THE GREAT GREAT GRANDDAUGHTER OF LEGENDARY VAMPIRE SLAYER SIMON BELMONT, AND BETRAYS HER FAMILY LEGACY OF MONSTER HUNTING TO BE WITH HER ONE TRUE LOVE: A 1,000 FOOT RADIOACTIVE LIZARD.
BUT DON'T WORRY; THE LOVE SCENE IS HANDLED VERY TASTEFULLY.

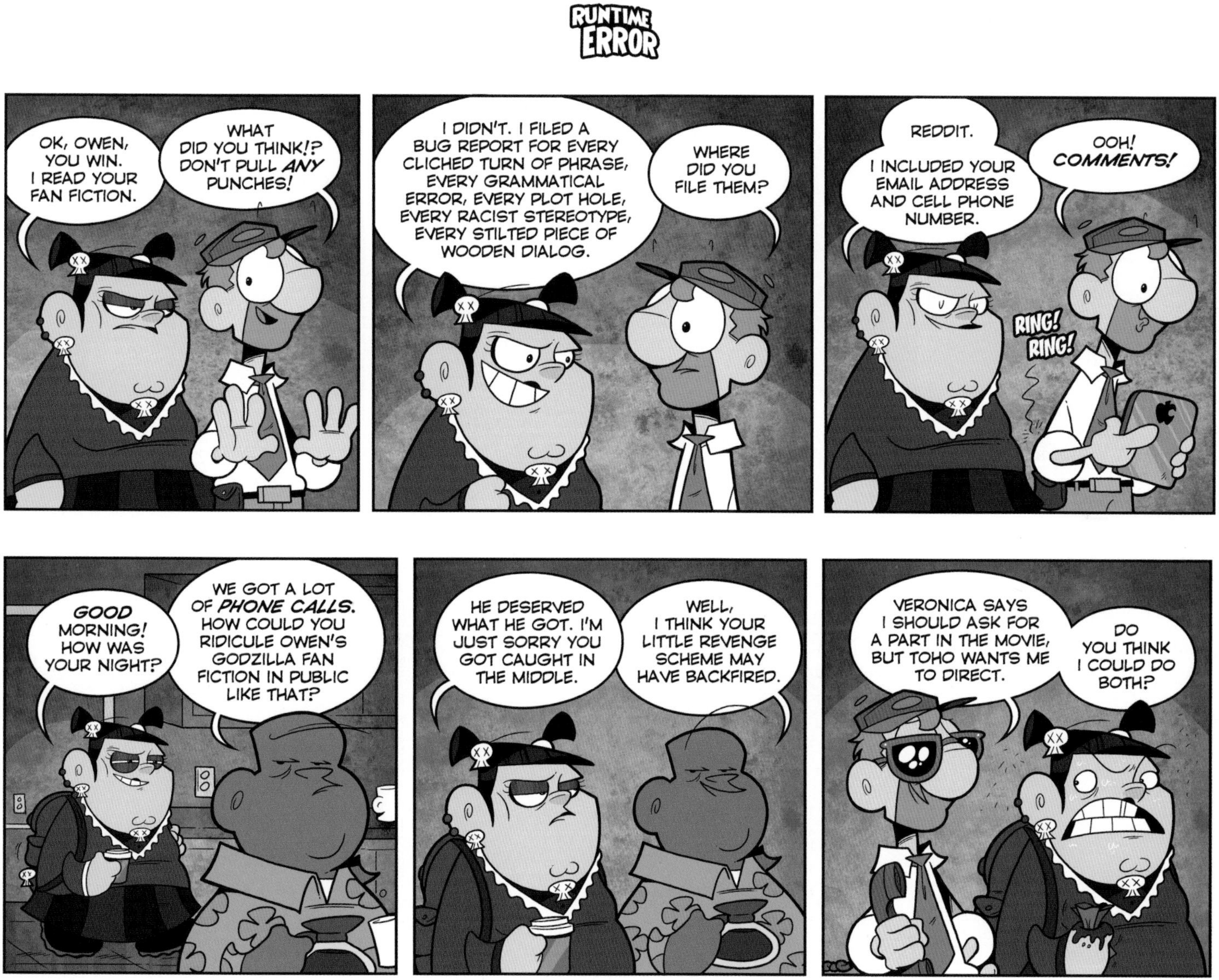
RUNTIME ERROR
OK, OWEN, YOU WIN. I READ YOUR FAN FICTION.
WHAT DID YOU THINK!? DON'T PULL *ANY* PUNCHES!
I DIDN'T. I FILED A BUG REPORT FOR EVERY CLICHED TURN OF PHRASE, EVERY GRAMMATICAL ERROR, EVERY PLOT HOLE, EVERY RACIST STEREOTYPE, EVERY STILTED PIECE OF WOODEN DIALOG.
WHERE DID YOU FILE THEM?
REDDIT.
I INCLUDED YOUR EMAIL ADDRESS AND CELL PHONE NUMBER.
OOH! *COMMENTS!*
RING! RING!
GOOD MORNING! HOW WAS YOUR NIGHT?
WE GOT A LOT OF *PHONE CALLS.* HOW COULD YOU RIDICULE OWEN'S GODZILLA FAN FICTION IN PUBLIC LIKE THAT?
HE DESERVED WHAT HE GOT. I'M JUST SORRY YOU GOT CAUGHT IN THE MIDDLE.
WELL, I THINK YOUR LITTLE REVENGE SCHEME MAY HAVE BACKFIRED.
VERONICA SAYS I SHOULD ASK FOR A PART IN THE MOVIE, BUT TOHO WANTS ME TO DIRECT.
DO YOU THINK I COULD DO BOTH?

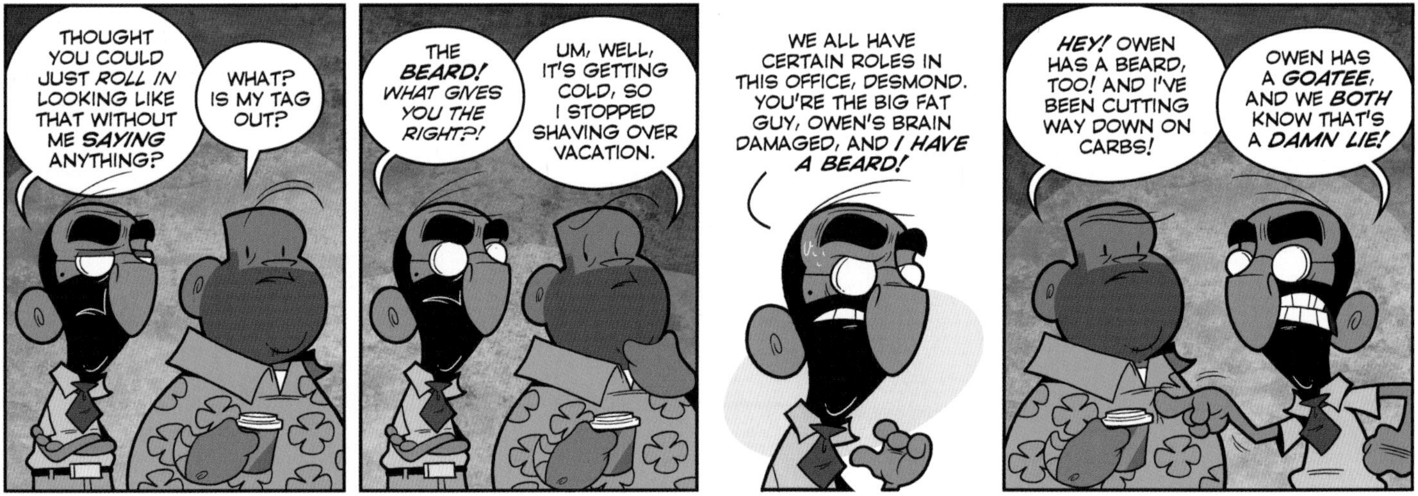
THOUGHT YOU COULD JUST *ROLL IN* LOOKING LIKE THAT WITHOUT ME ***SAYING*** ANYTHING?
WHAT? IS MY TAG OUT?
THE ***BEARD!*** *WHAT GIVES YOU THE RIGHT?!*
UM, WELL, IT'S GETTING COLD, SO I STOPPED SHAVING OVER VACATION.
WE ALL HAVE CERTAIN ROLES IN THIS OFFICE, DESMOND. YOU'RE THE BIG FAT GUY, OWEN'S BRAIN DAMAGED, AND ***I HAVE A BEARD!***
HEY! OWEN HAS A BEARD, TOO! AND I'VE BEEN CUTTING WAY DOWN ON CARBS!
OWEN HAS A ***GOATEE***, AND WE ***BOTH*** KNOW THAT'S A ***DAMN LIE!***

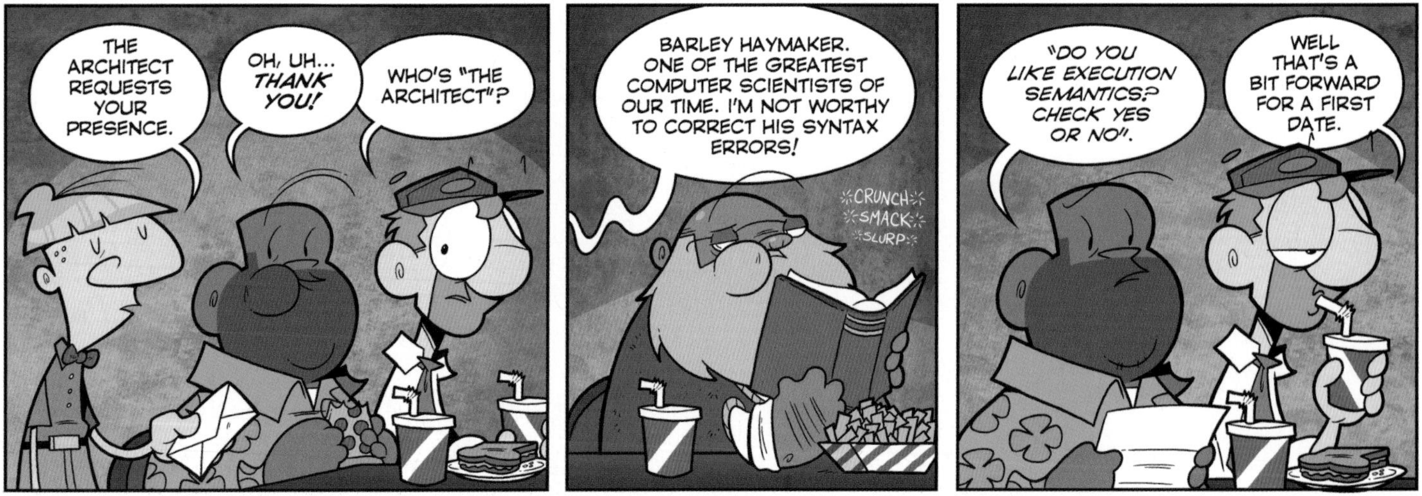
THE ARCHITECT REQUESTS YOUR PRESENCE.
OH, UH... ***THANK YOU!***
WHO'S "THE ARCHITECT"?
BARLEY HAYMAKER. ONE OF THE GREATEST COMPUTER SCIENTISTS OF OUR TIME. I'M NOT WORTHY TO CORRECT HIS SYNTAX ERRORS!
CRUNCH
SMACK
SLURP
"DO YOU LIKE EXECUTION SEMANTICS? CHECK YES OR NO".
WELL THAT'S A BIT FORWARD FOR A FIRST DATE.

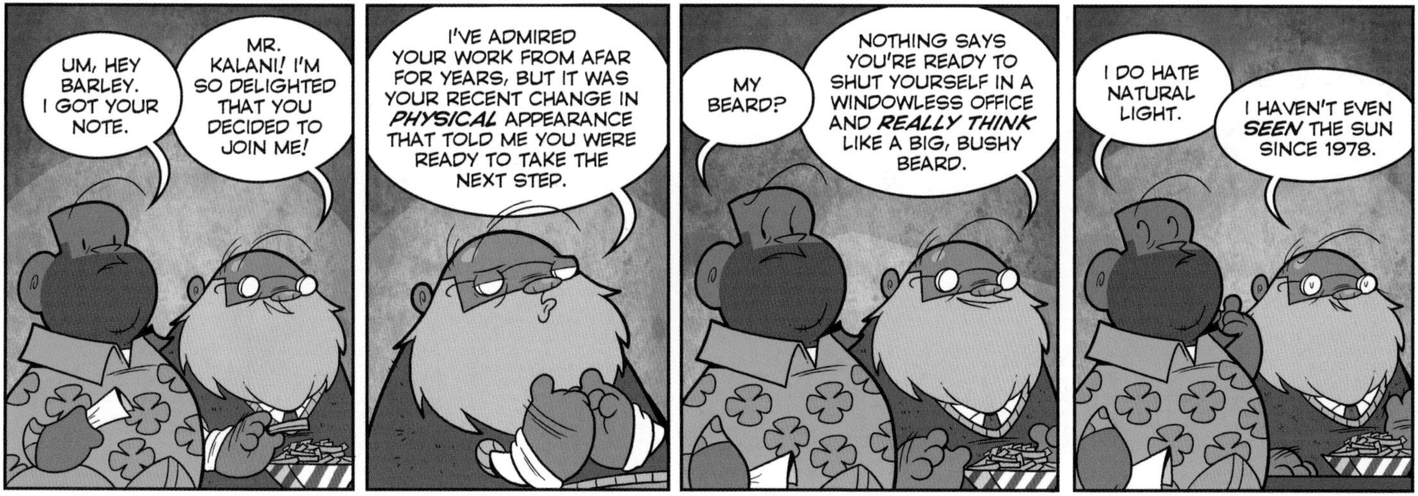
UM, HEY BARLEY. I GOT YOUR NOTE.
MR. KALANI! I'M SO DELIGHTED THAT YOU DECIDED TO JOIN ME!
I'VE ADMIRED YOUR WORK FROM AFAR FOR YEARS, BUT IT WAS YOUR RECENT CHANGE IN PHYSICAL APPEARANCE THAT TOLD ME YOU WERE READY TO TAKE THE NEXT STEP.
MY BEARD?
NOTHING SAYS YOU'RE READY TO SHUT YOURSELF IN A WINDOWLESS OFFICE AND REALLY THINK LIKE A BIG, BUSHY BEARD.
I DO HATE NATURAL LIGHT.
I HAVEN'T EVEN SEEN THE SUN SINCE 1978.

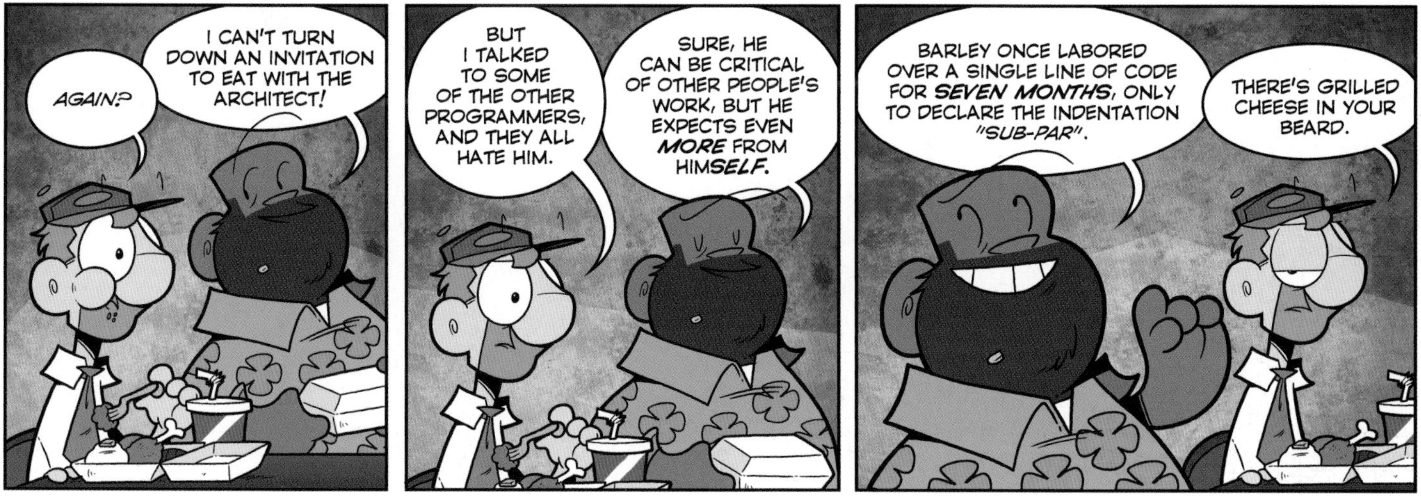
AGAIN?
I CAN'T TURN DOWN AN INVITATION TO EAT WITH THE ARCHITECT!
BUT I TALKED TO SOME OF THE OTHER PROGRAMMERS, AND THEY ALL HATE HIM.
SURE, HE CAN BE CRITICAL OF OTHER PEOPLE'S WORK, BUT HE EXPECTS EVEN MORE FROM HIMSELF.
BARLEY ONCE LABORED OVER A SINGLE LINE OF CODE FOR SEVEN MONTHS, ONLY TO DECLARE THE INDENTATION "SUB-PAR".
THERE'S GRILLED CHEESE IN YOUR BEARD.

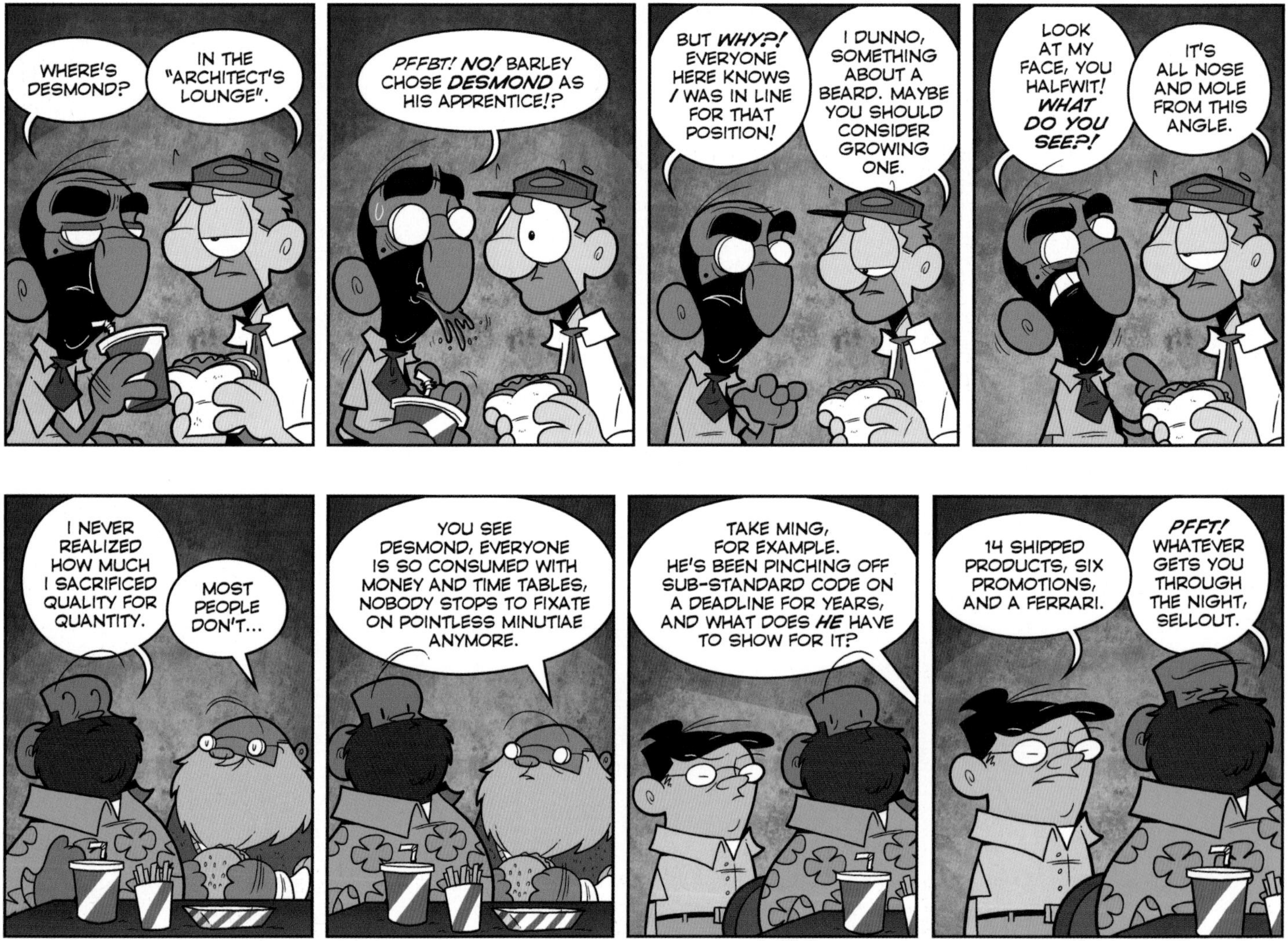
WHERE'S DESMOND?
IN THE "ARCHITECT'S LOUNGE".
PFFBT! NO! BARLEY CHOSE DESMOND AS HIS APPRENTICE!?
BUT WHY?! EVERYONE HERE KNOWS I WAS IN LINE FOR THAT POSITION!
I DUNNO, SOMETHING ABOUT A BEARD. MAYBE YOU SHOULD CONSIDER GROWING ONE.
LOOK AT MY FACE, YOU HALFWIT! WHAT DO YOU SEE?!
IT'S ALL NOSE AND MOLE FROM THIS ANGLE.
I NEVER REALIZED HOW MUCH I SACRIFICED QUALITY FOR QUANTITY.
MOST PEOPLE DON'T...
YOU SEE DESMOND, EVERYONE IS SO CONSUMED WITH MONEY AND TIME TABLES, NOBODY STOPS TO FIXATE ON POINTLESS MINUTIAE ANYMORE.
TAKE MING, FOR EXAMPLE. HE'S BEEN PINCHING OFF SUB-STANDARD CODE ON A DEADLINE FOR YEARS, AND WHAT DOES HE HAVE TO SHOW FOR IT?
14 SHIPPED PRODUCTS, SIX PROMOTIONS, AND A FERRARI.
PFFT! WHATEVER GETS YOU THROUGH THE NIGHT, SELLOUT.

RUNTIME ERROR

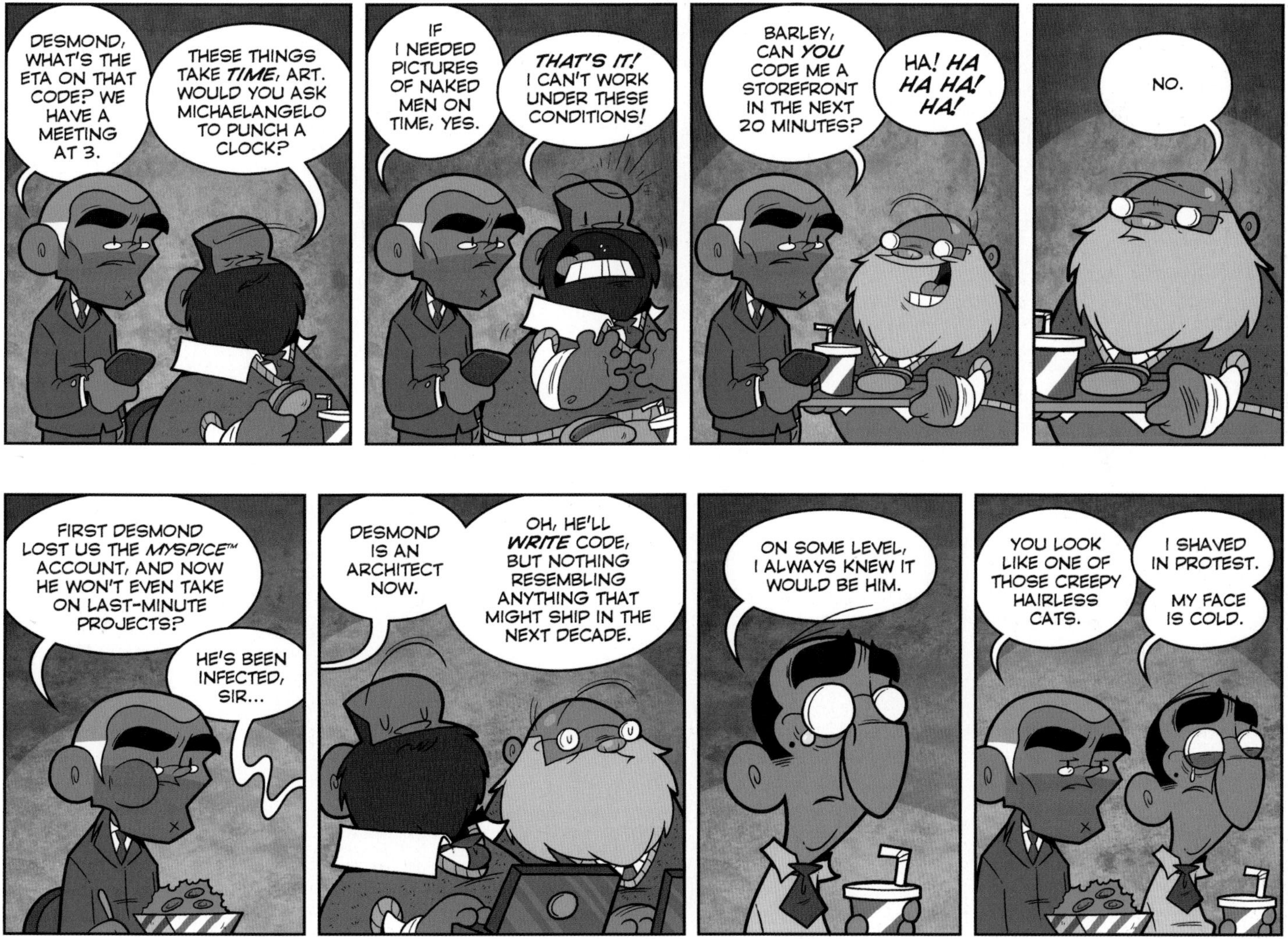
DESMOND, WHAT'S THE ETA ON THAT CODE? WE HAVE A MEETING AT 3.
THESE THINGS TAKE *TIME*, ART. WOULD YOU ASK MICHAELANGELO TO PUNCH A CLOCK?
IF I NEEDED PICTURES OF NAKED MEN ON TIME, YES.
THAT'S IT! I CAN'T WORK UNDER THESE CONDITIONS!
BARLEY, CAN *YOU* CODE ME A STOREFRONT IN THE NEXT 20 MINUTES?
HA! *HA HA HA! HA!*
NO.
FIRST DESMOND LOST US THE *MYSPICE*™ ACCOUNT, AND NOW HE WON'T EVEN TAKE ON LAST-MINUTE PROJECTS?
HE'S BEEN INFECTED, SIR...
DESMOND IS AN ARCHITECT NOW.
OH, HE'LL *WRITE* CODE, BUT NOTHING RESEMBLING ANYTHING THAT MIGHT SHIP IN THE NEXT DECADE.
ON SOME LEVEL, I ALWAYS KNEW IT WOULD BE HIM.
YOU LOOK LIKE ONE OF THOSE CREEPY HAIRLESS CATS.
I SHAVED IN PROTEST.
MY FACE IS COLD.

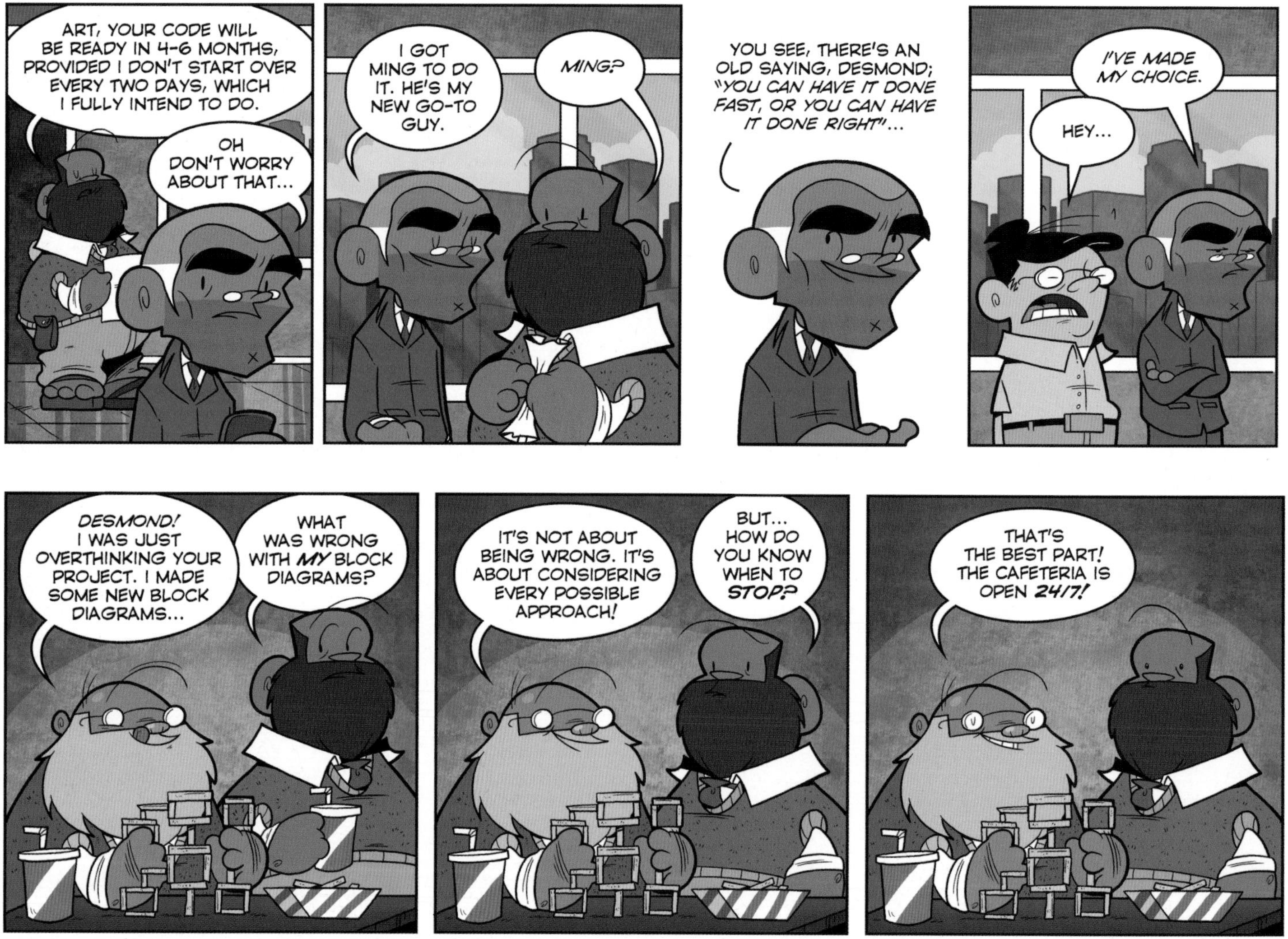
ART, YOUR CODE WILL BE READY IN 4-6 MONTHS, PROVIDED I DON'T START OVER EVERY TWO DAYS, WHICH I FULLY INTEND TO DO.
OH DON'T WORRY ABOUT THAT...
I GOT MING TO DO IT. HE'S MY NEW GO-TO GUY.
MING?
YOU SEE, THERE'S AN OLD SAYING, DESMOND; "YOU CAN HAVE IT DONE FAST, OR YOU CAN HAVE IT DONE RIGHT"...
I'VE MADE MY CHOICE.
HEY...
DESMOND! I WAS JUST OVERTHINKING YOUR PROJECT. I MADE SOME NEW BLOCK DIAGRAMS...
WHAT WAS WRONG WITH MY BLOCK DIAGRAMS?
IT'S NOT ABOUT BEING WRONG. IT'S ABOUT CONSIDERING EVERY POSSIBLE APPROACH!
BUT... HOW DO YOU KNOW WHEN TO STOP?
THAT'S THE BEST PART! THE CAFETERIA IS OPEN 24/7!

RUNTIME ERROR

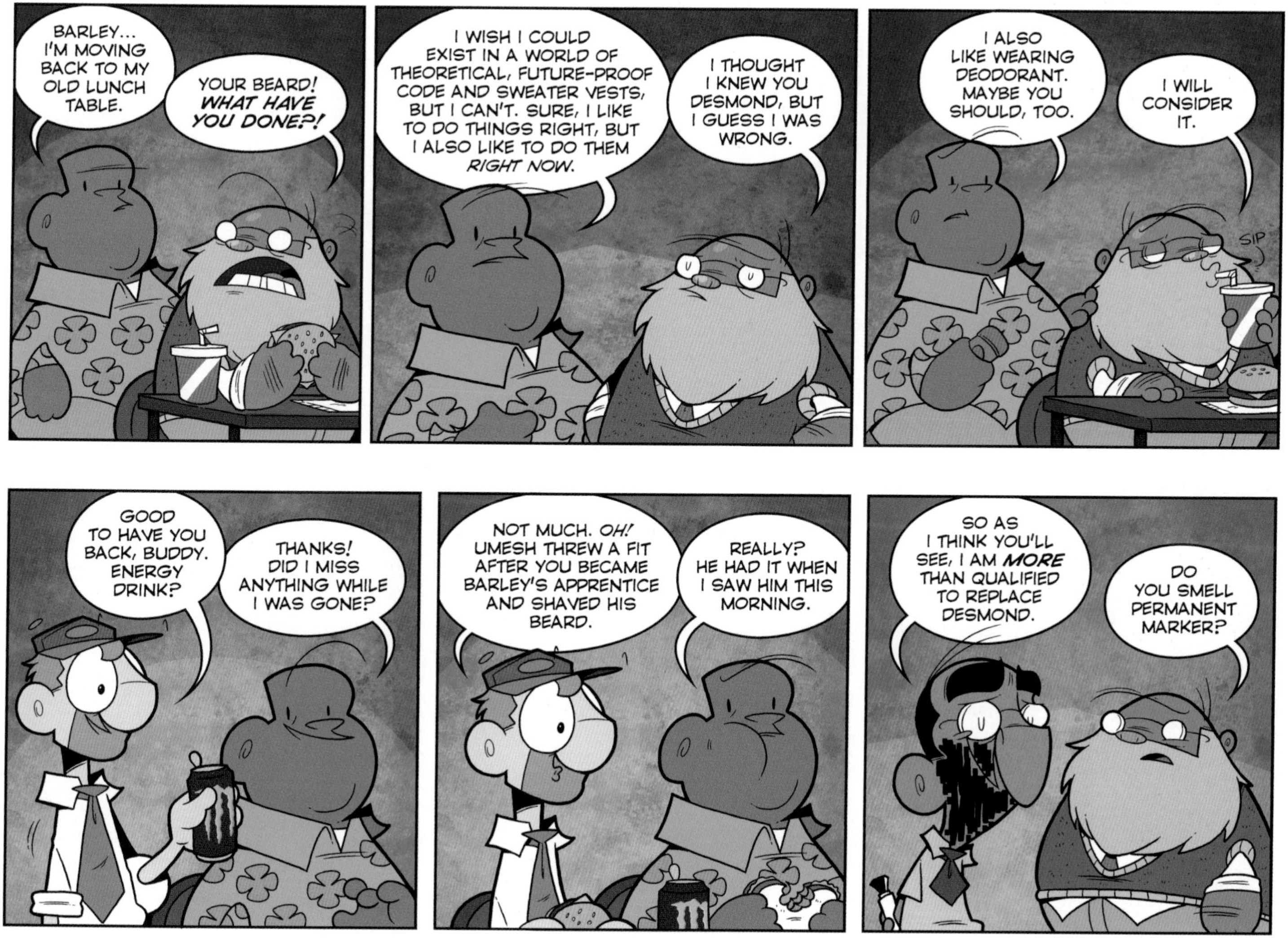
BARLEY... I'M MOVING BACK TO MY OLD LUNCH TABLE.
YOUR BEARD! WHAT HAVE YOU DONE?!
I WISH I COULD EXIST IN A WORLD OF THEORETICAL, FUTURE-PROOF CODE AND SWEATER VESTS, BUT I CAN'T. SURE, I LIKE TO DO THINGS RIGHT, BUT I ALSO LIKE TO DO THEM RIGHT NOW.
I THOUGHT I KNEW YOU DESMOND, BUT I GUESS I WAS WRONG.
I ALSO LIKE WEARING DEODORANT. MAYBE YOU SHOULD, TOO.
I WILL CONSIDER IT.
SIP
GOOD TO HAVE YOU BACK, BUDDY. ENERGY DRINK?
THANKS! DID I MISS ANYTHING WHILE I WAS GONE?
NOT MUCH. OH! UMESH THREW A FIT AFTER YOU BECAME BARLEY'S APPRENTICE AND SHAVED HIS BEARD.
REALLY? HE HAD IT WHEN I SAW HIM THIS MORNING.
SO AS I THINK YOU'LL SEE, I AM MORE THAN QUALIFIED TO REPLACE DESMOND.
DO YOU SMELL PERMANENT MARKER?

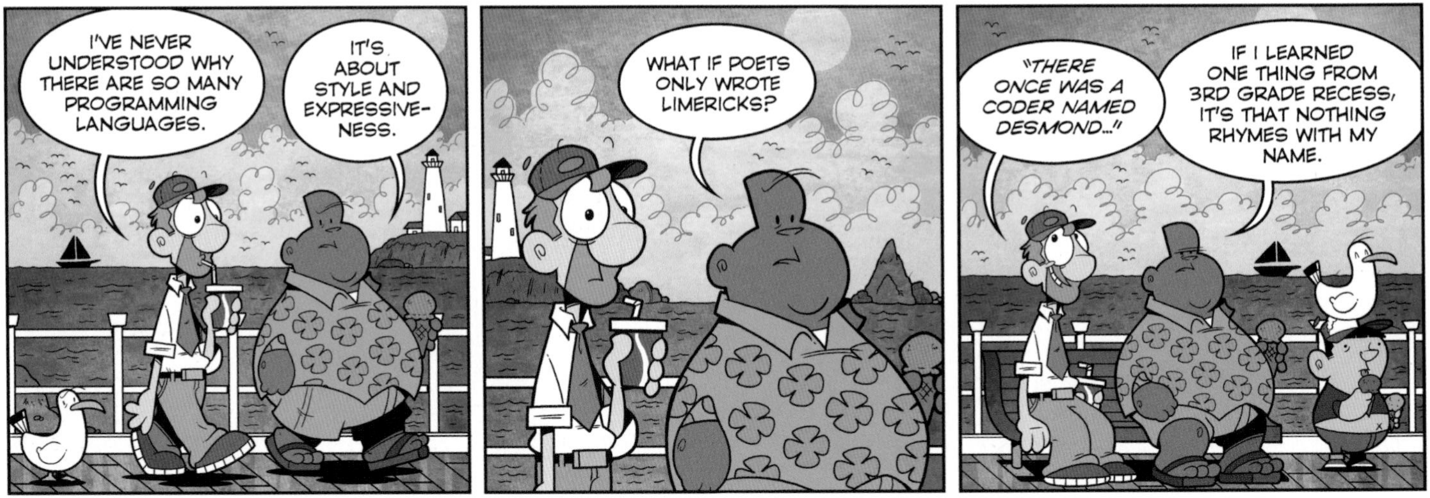
I'VE NEVER UNDERSTOOD WHY THERE ARE SO MANY PROGRAMMING LANGUAGES.
IT'S ABOUT STYLE AND EXPRESSIVE-NESS.
WHAT IF POETS ONLY WROTE LIMERICKS?
"THERE ONCE WAS A CODER NAMED DESMOND..."
IF I LEARNED ONE THING FROM 3RD GRADE RECESS, IT'S THAT NOTHING RHYMES WITH MY NAME.

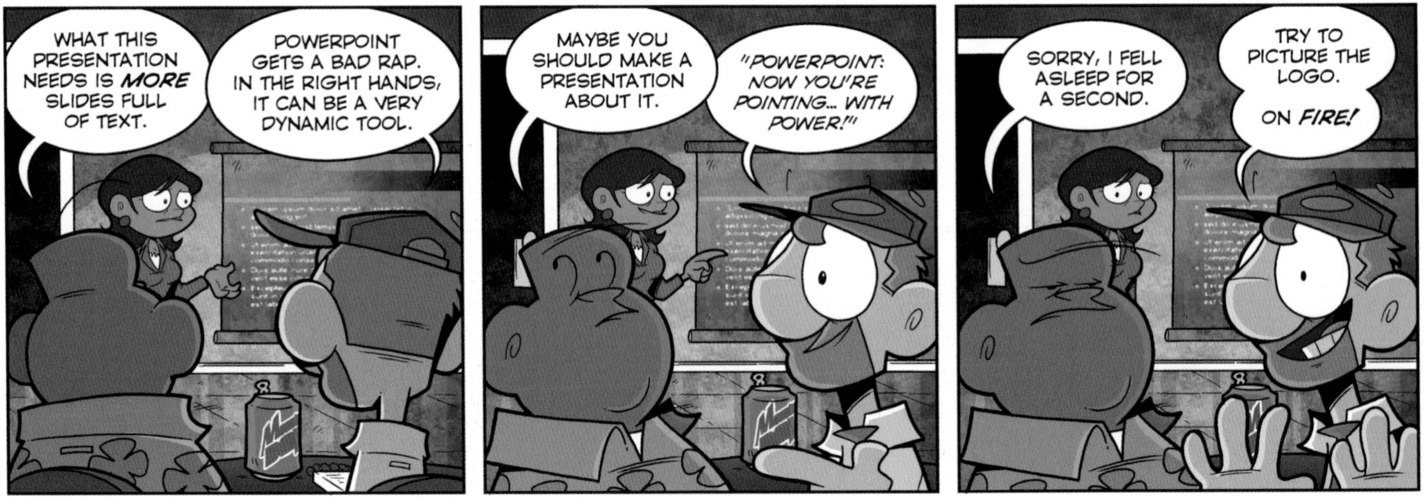
WHAT THIS PRESENTATION NEEDS IS *MORE* SLIDES FULL OF TEXT.
POWERPOINT GETS A BAD RAP. IN THE RIGHT HANDS, IT CAN BE A VERY DYNAMIC TOOL.
MAYBE YOU SHOULD MAKE A PRESENTATION ABOUT IT.
"POWERPOINT: NOW YOU'RE POINTING... WITH POWER!"
SORRY, I FELL ASLEEP FOR A SECOND.
TRY TO PICTURE THE LOGO.
ON *FIRE!*

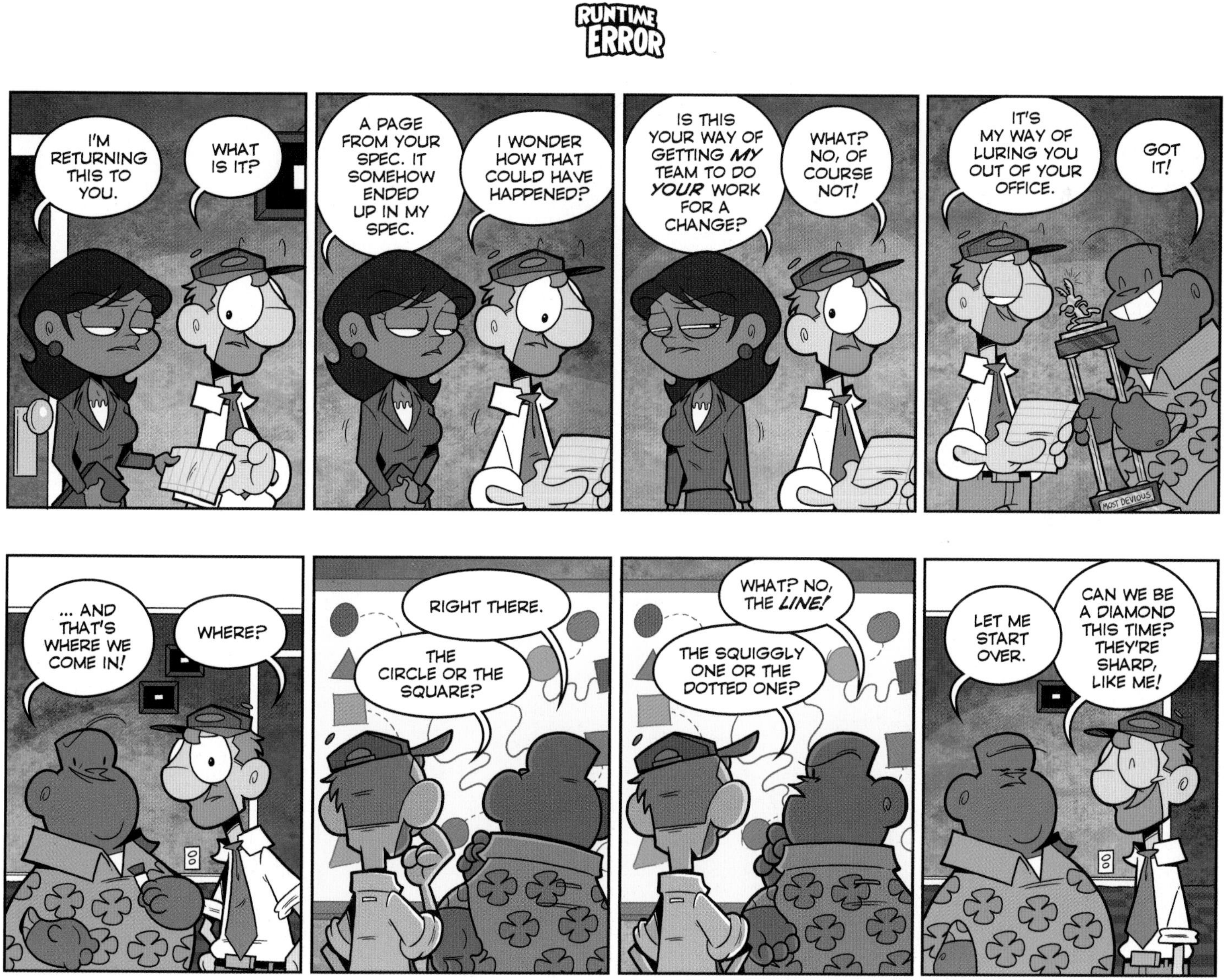
RUNTIME ERROR
I'M RETURNING THIS TO YOU.
WHAT IS IT?
A PAGE FROM YOUR SPEC. IT SOMEHOW ENDED UP IN MY SPEC.
I WONDER HOW THAT COULD HAVE HAPPENED?
IS THIS YOUR WAY OF GETTING *MY* TEAM TO DO *YOUR* WORK FOR A CHANGE?
WHAT? NO, OF COURSE NOT!
IT'S MY WAY OF LURING YOU OUT OF YOUR OFFICE.
GOT IT!
MOST DEVIOUS
... AND THAT'S WHERE WE COME IN!
WHERE?
RIGHT THERE.
THE CIRCLE OR THE SQUARE?
WHAT? NO, THE *LINE!*
THE SQUIGGLY ONE OR THE DOTTED ONE?
LET ME START OVER.
CAN WE BE A DIAMOND THIS TIME? THEY'RE SHARP, LIKE ME!

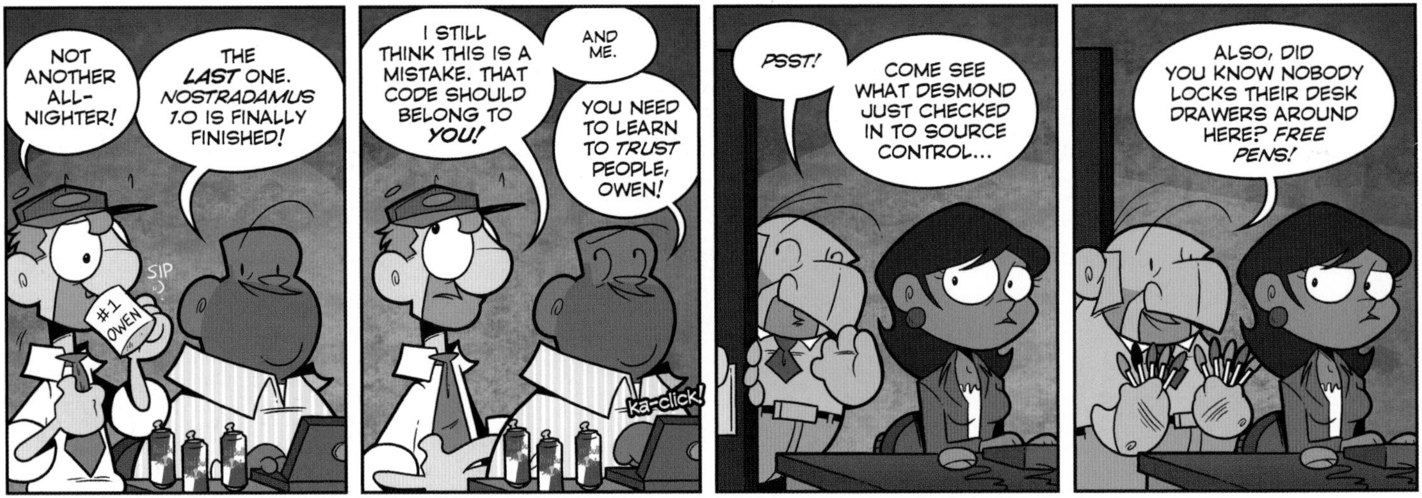
NOT ANOTHER ALL-NIGHTER!
THE *LAST* ONE. *NOSTRADAMUS 1.0* IS FINALLY FINISHED!
SIP
#1 OWEN
I STILL THINK THIS IS A MISTAKE. THAT CODE SHOULD BELONG TO ***YOU!***
AND ME.
YOU NEED TO LEARN TO *TRUST* PEOPLE, OWEN!
KA-CLICK!
PSST!
COME SEE WHAT DESMOND JUST CHECKED IN TO SOURCE CONTROL...
ALSO, DID YOU KNOW NOBODY LOCKS THEIR DESK DRAWERS AROUND HERE? *FREE PENS!*

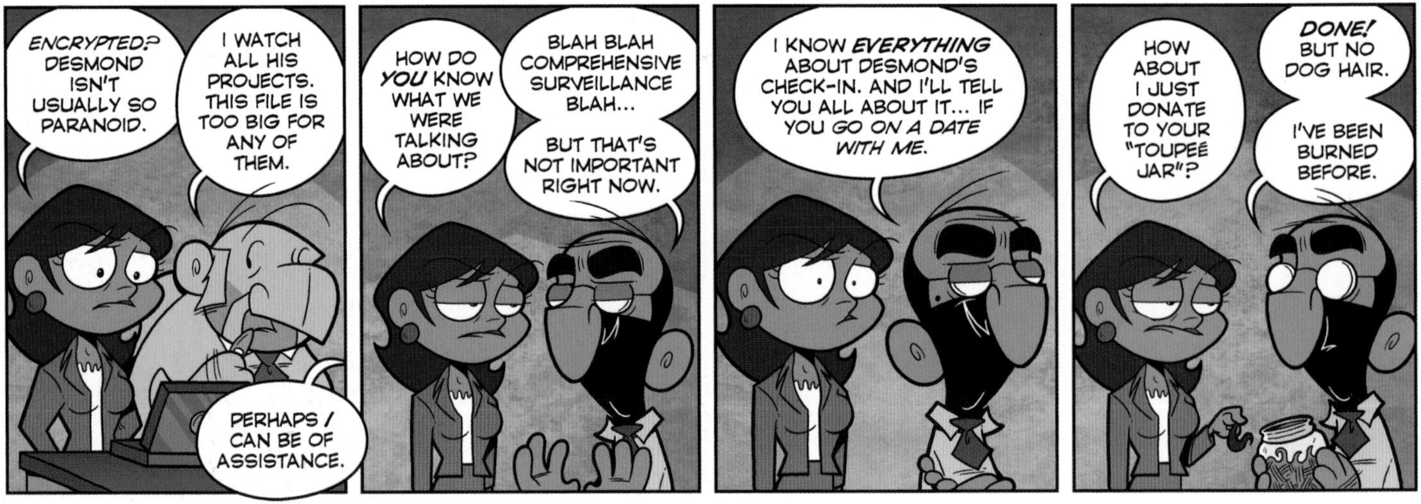
ENCRYPTED? DESMOND ISN'T USUALLY SO PARANOID.
I WATCH ALL HIS PROJECTS. THIS FILE IS TOO BIG FOR ANY OF THEM.
PERHAPS *I* CAN BE OF ASSISTANCE.
HOW DO ***YOU*** KNOW WHAT WE WERE TALKING ABOUT?
BLAH BLAH COMPREHENSIVE SURVEILLANCE BLAH...
BUT THAT'S NOT IMPORTANT RIGHT NOW.
I KNOW ***EVERYTHING*** ABOUT DESMOND'S CHECK-IN. AND I'LL TELL YOU ALL ABOUT IT... IF YOU *GO ON A DATE WITH ME.*
HOW ABOUT I JUST DONATE TO YOUR "TOUPEÉ JAR"?
DONE! BUT NO DOG HAIR.
I'VE BEEN BURNED BEFORE.

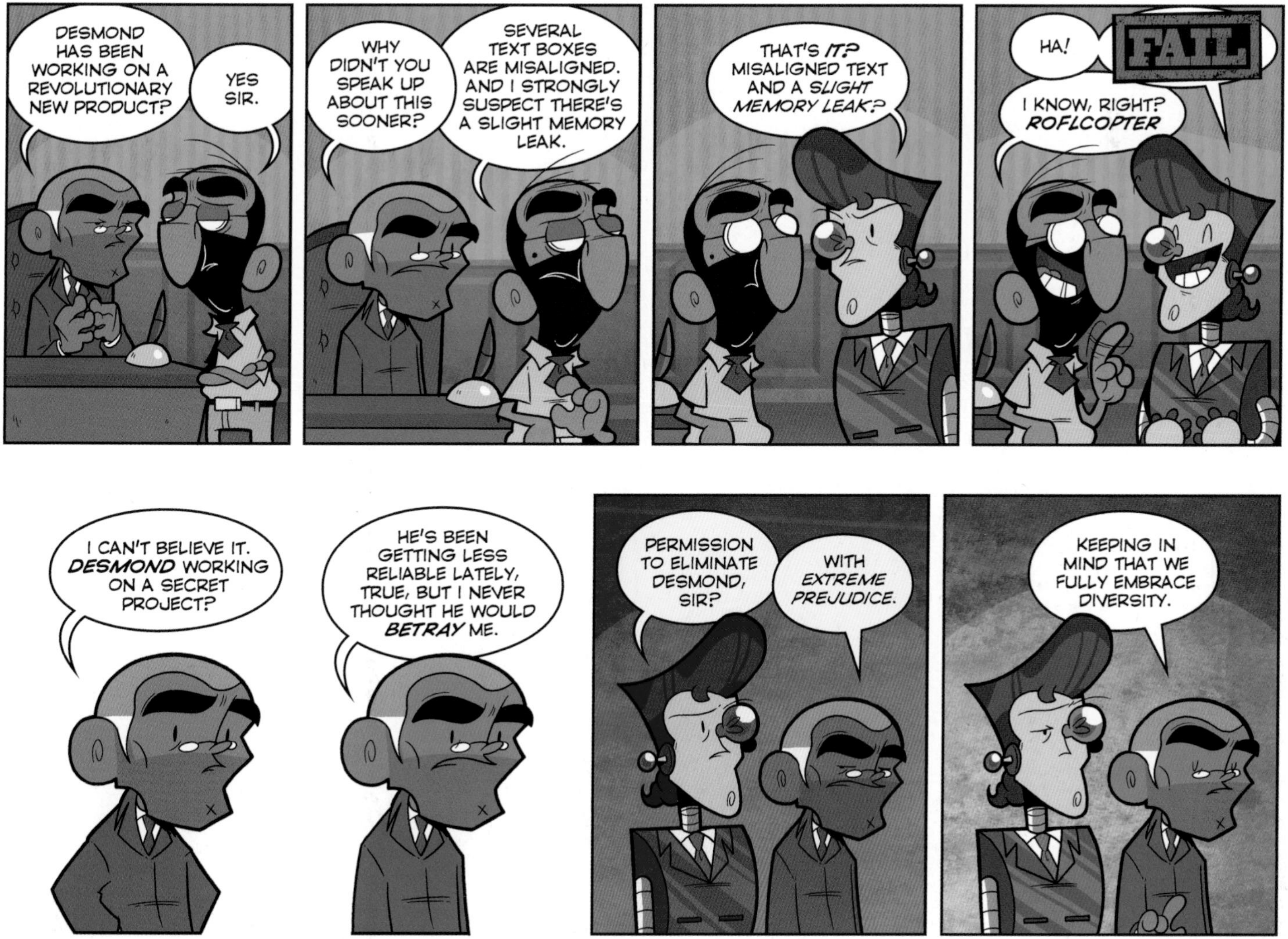
DESMOND HAS BEEN WORKING ON A REVOLUTIONARY NEW PRODUCT?
YES SIR.
WHY DIDN'T YOU SPEAK UP ABOUT THIS SOONER?
SEVERAL TEXT BOXES ARE MISALIGNED. AND I STRONGLY SUSPECT THERE'S A SLIGHT MEMORY LEAK.
THAT'S *IT?* MISALIGNED TEXT AND A *SLIGHT MEMORY LEAK?*
HA!
FAIL
I KNOW, RIGHT? ***ROFLCOPTER***
I CAN'T BELIEVE IT. ***DESMOND*** WORKING ON A SECRET PROJECT?
HE'S BEEN GETTING LESS RELIABLE LATELY, TRUE, BUT I NEVER THOUGHT HE WOULD ***BETRAY*** ME.
PERMISSION TO ELIMINATE DESMOND, SIR?
WITH *EXTREME PREJUDICE.*
KEEPING IN MIND THAT WE FULLY EMBRACE DIVERSITY.

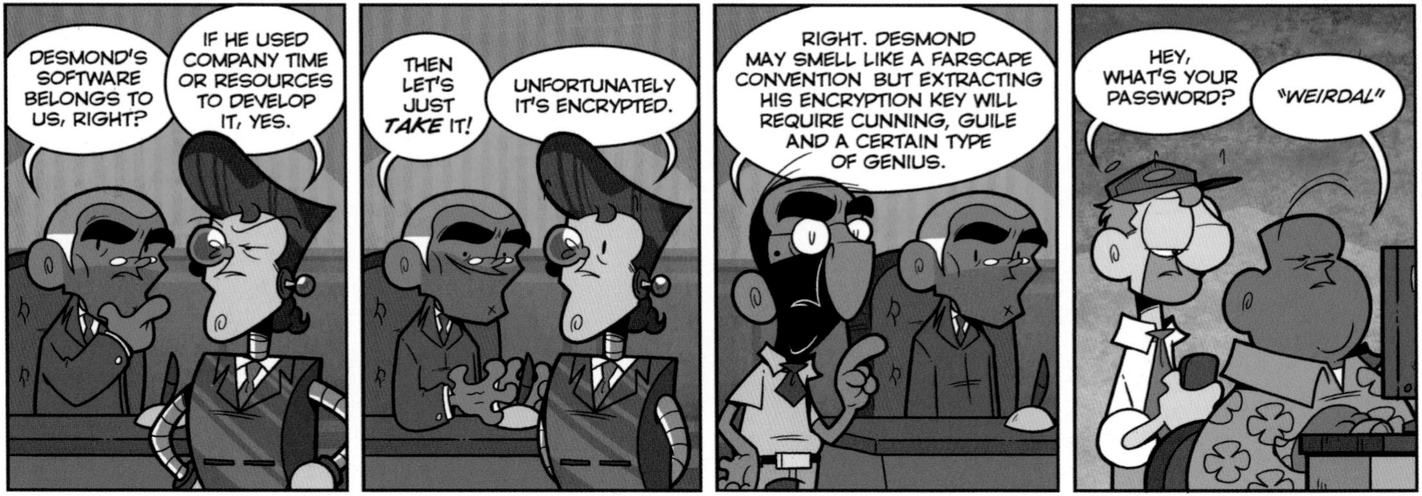
DESMOND'S SOFTWARE BELONGS TO US, RIGHT?
IF HE USED COMPANY TIME OR RESOURCES TO DEVELOP IT, YES.
THEN LET'S JUST *TAKE* IT!
UNFORTUNATELY IT'S ENCRYPTED.
RIGHT. DESMOND MAY SMELL LIKE A FARSCAPE CONVENTION BUT EXTRACTING HIS ENCRYPTION KEY WILL REQUIRE CUNNING, GUILE AND A CERTAIN TYPE OF GENIUS.
HEY, WHAT'S YOUR PASSWORD?
"WEIRDAL"

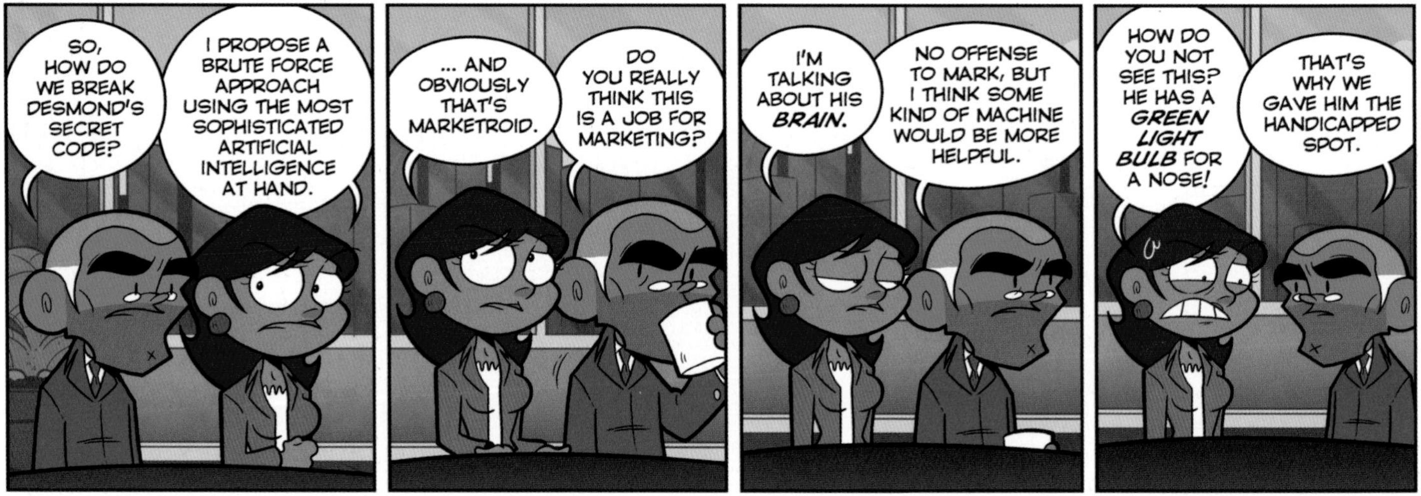
SO, HOW DO WE BREAK DESMOND'S SECRET CODE?
I PROPOSE A BRUTE FORCE APPROACH USING THE MOST SOPHISTICATED ARTIFICIAL INTELLIGENCE AT HAND.
... AND OBVIOUSLY THAT'S MARKETROID.
DO YOU REALLY THINK THIS IS A JOB FOR MARKETING?
I'M TALKING ABOUT HIS *BRAIN.*
NO OFFENSE TO MARK, BUT I THINK SOME KIND OF MACHINE WOULD BE MORE HELPFUL.
HOW DO YOU NOT SEE THIS? HE HAS A *GREEN LIGHT BULB* FOR A NOSE!
THAT'S WHY WE GAVE HIM THE HANDICAPPED SPOT.

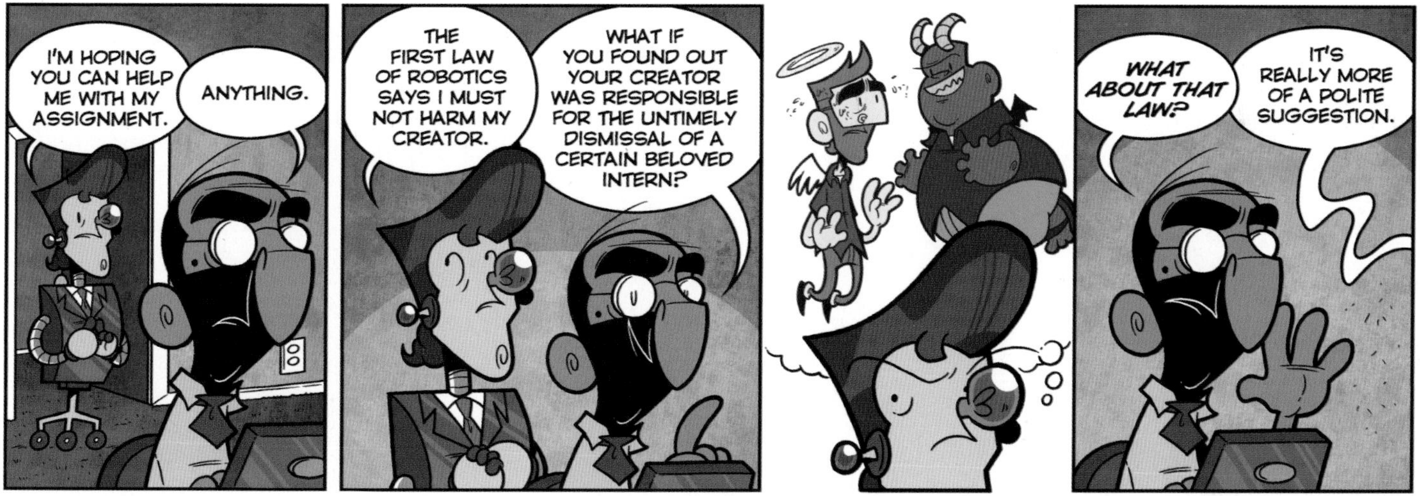
I'M HOPING YOU CAN HELP ME WITH MY ASSIGNMENT.
ANYTHING.
THE FIRST LAW OF ROBOTICS SAYS I MUST NOT HARM MY CREATOR.
WHAT IF YOU FOUND OUT YOUR CREATOR WAS RESPONSIBLE FOR THE UNTIMELY DISMISSAL OF A CERTAIN BELOVED INTERN?
WHAT ABOUT THAT LAW?
IT'S REALLY MORE OF A POLITE SUGGESTION.

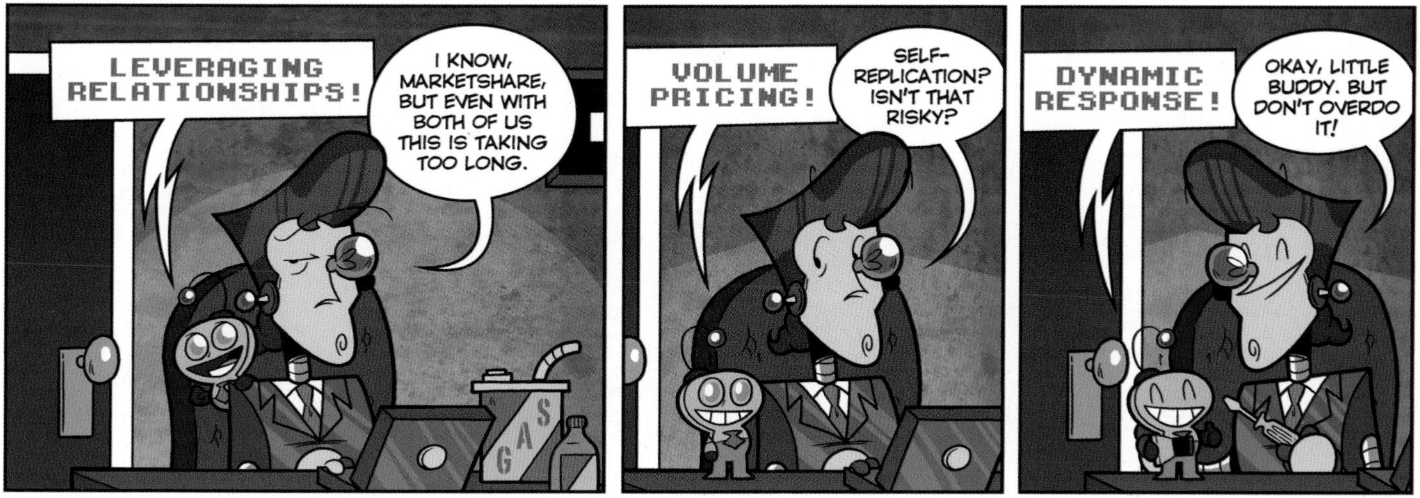
LEVERAGING RELATIONSHIPS!
I KNOW, MARKETSHARE, BUT EVEN WITH BOTH OF US THIS IS TAKING TOO LONG.
GAS
VOLUME PRICING!
SELF-REPLICATION? ISN'T THAT RISKY?
DYNAMIC RESPONSE!
OKAY, LITTLE BUDDY. BUT DON'T OVERDO IT!

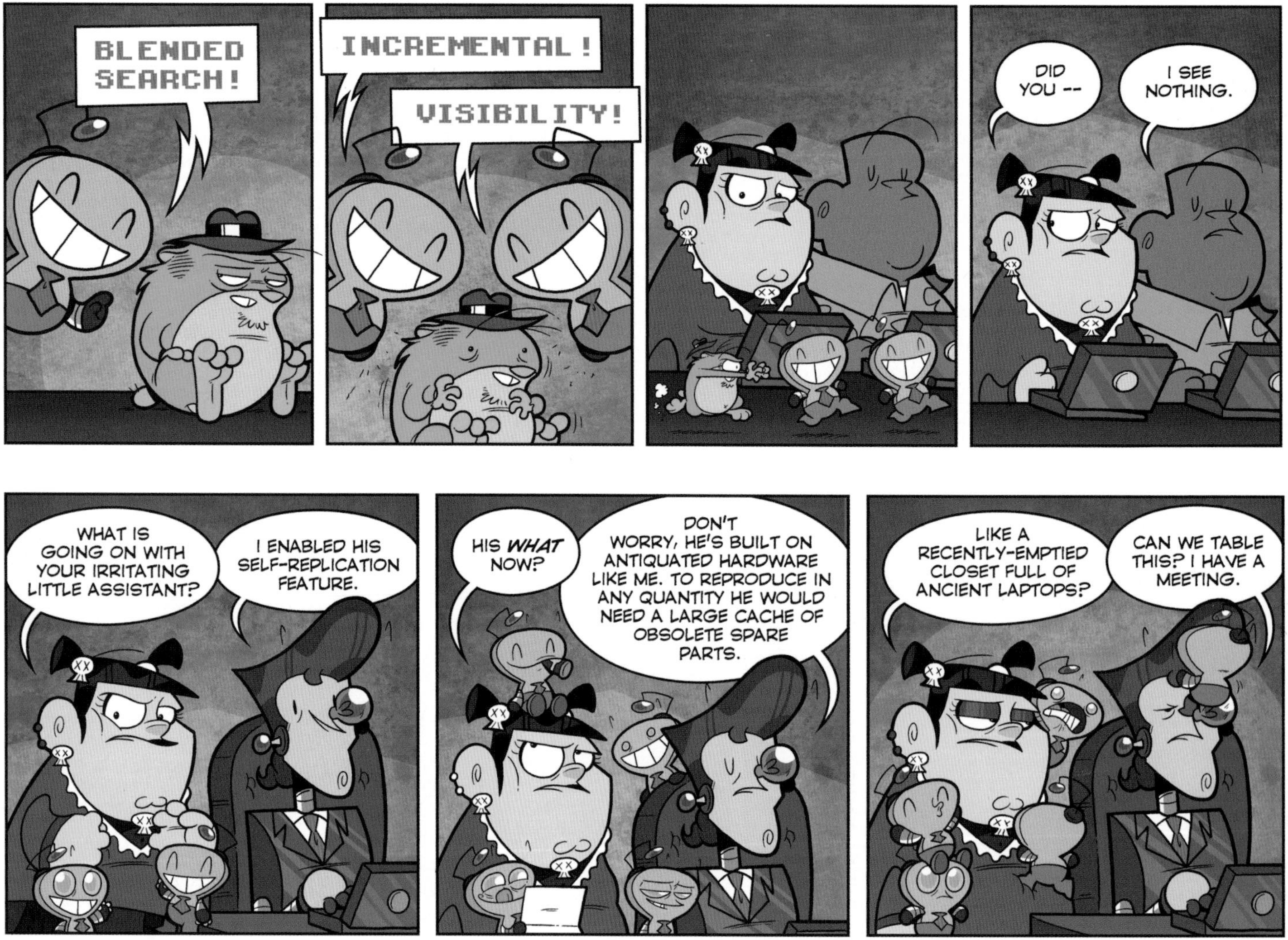
BLENDED SEARCH!
INCREMENTAL!
VISIBILITY!
DID YOU --
I SEE NOTHING.
WHAT IS GOING ON WITH YOUR IRRITATING LITTLE ASSISTANT?
I ENABLED HIS SELF-REPLICATION FEATURE.
HIS *WHAT* NOW?
DON'T WORRY, HE'S BUILT ON ANTIQUATED HARDWARE LIKE ME. TO REPRODUCE IN ANY QUANTITY HE WOULD NEED A LARGE CACHE OF OBSOLETE SPARE PARTS.
LIKE A RECENTLY-EMPTIED CLOSET FULL OF ANCIENT LAPTOPS?
CAN WE TABLE THIS? I HAVE A MEETING.

RUNTIME ERROR

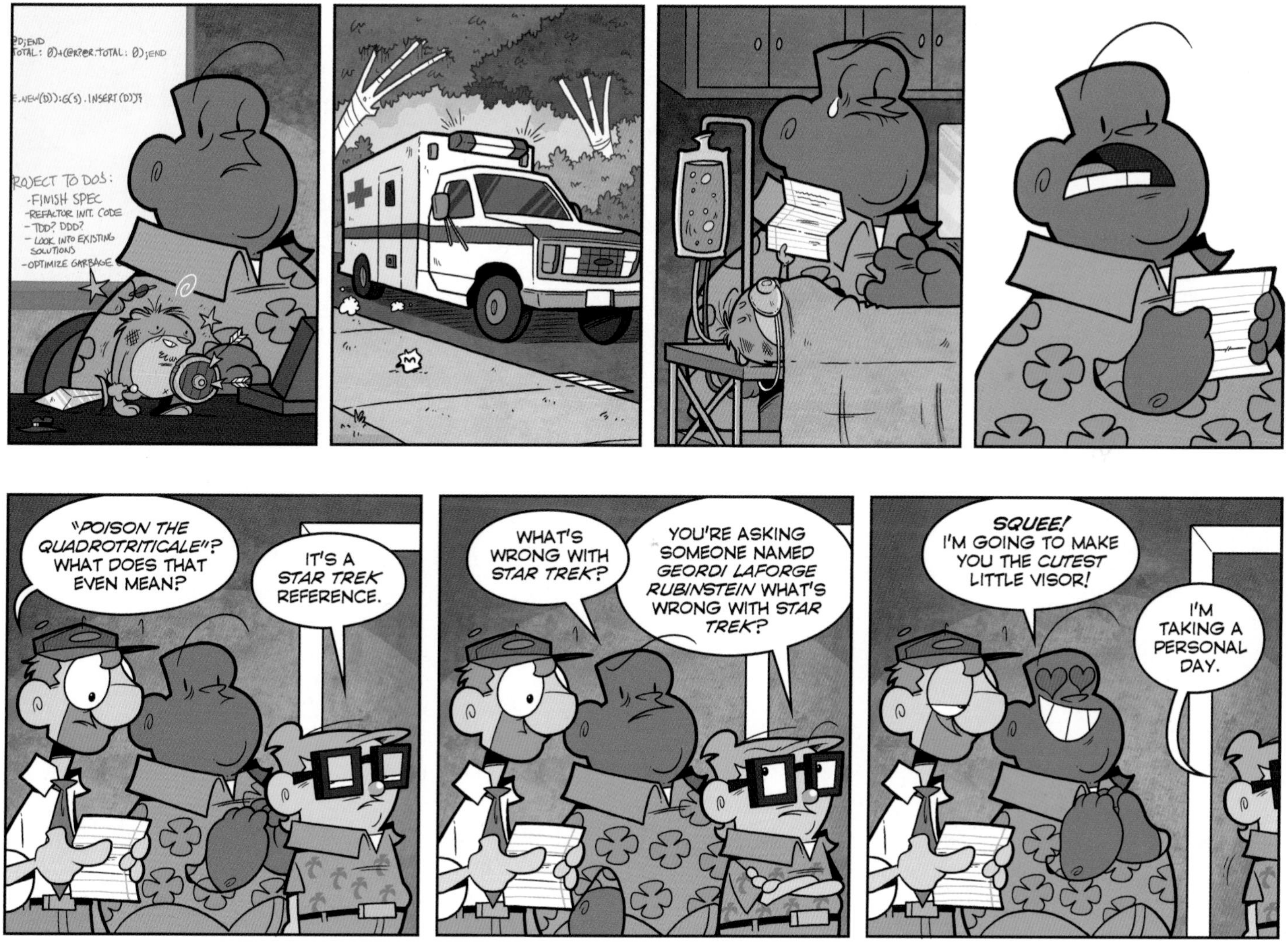
ROJECT TO DOS:
-FINISH SPEC
-REFACTOR INIT. CODE
-TDD? DDD?
-LOOK INTO EXISTING SOLUTIONS
-OPTIMIZE GARBAGE
"POISON THE QUADROTRITICALE"? WHAT DOES THAT EVEN MEAN?
IT'S A STAR TREK REFERENCE.
WHAT'S WRONG WITH STAR TREK?
YOU'RE ASKING SOMEONE NAMED GEORDI LAFORGE RUBINSTEIN WHAT'S WRONG WITH STAR TREK?
SQUEE! I'M GOING TO MAKE YOU THE CUTEST LITTLE VISOR!
I'M TAKING A PERSONAL DAY.

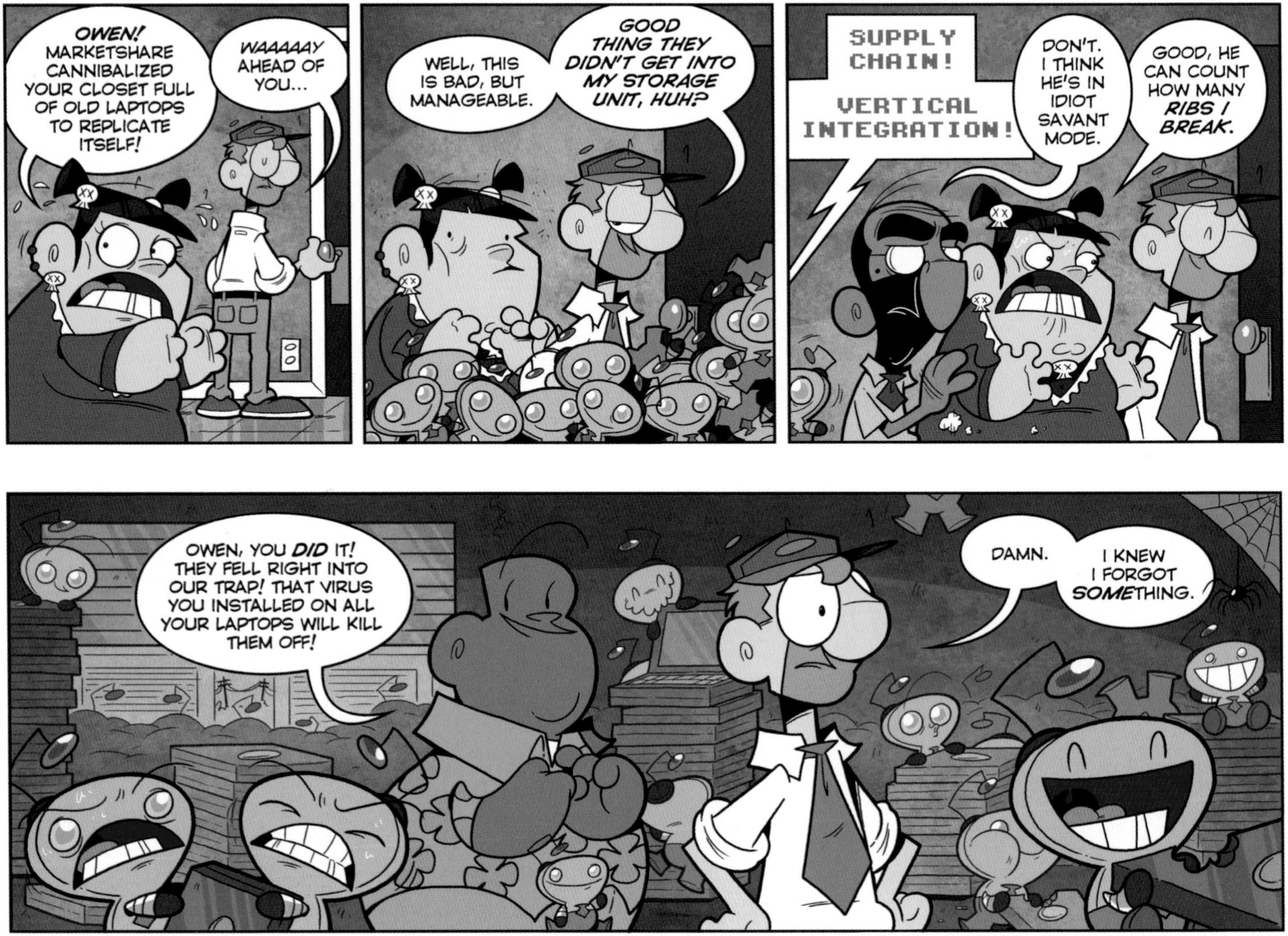
OWEN! MARKETSHARE CANNIBALIZED YOUR CLOSET FULL OF OLD LAPTOPS TO REPLICATE ITSELF!
WAAAAAY AHEAD OF YOU...
WELL, THIS IS BAD, BUT MANAGEABLE.
GOOD THING THEY DIDN'T GET INTO MY STORAGE UNIT, HUH?
SUPPLY CHAIN!
VERTICAL INTEGRATION!
DON'T. I THINK HE'S IN IDIOT SAVANT MODE.
GOOD, HE CAN COUNT HOW MANY RIBS I BREAK.
OWEN, YOU DID IT! THEY FELL RIGHT INTO OUR TRAP! THAT VIRUS YOU INSTALLED ON ALL YOUR LAPTOPS WILL KILL THEM OFF!
DAMN.
I KNEW I FORGOT SOMETHING.

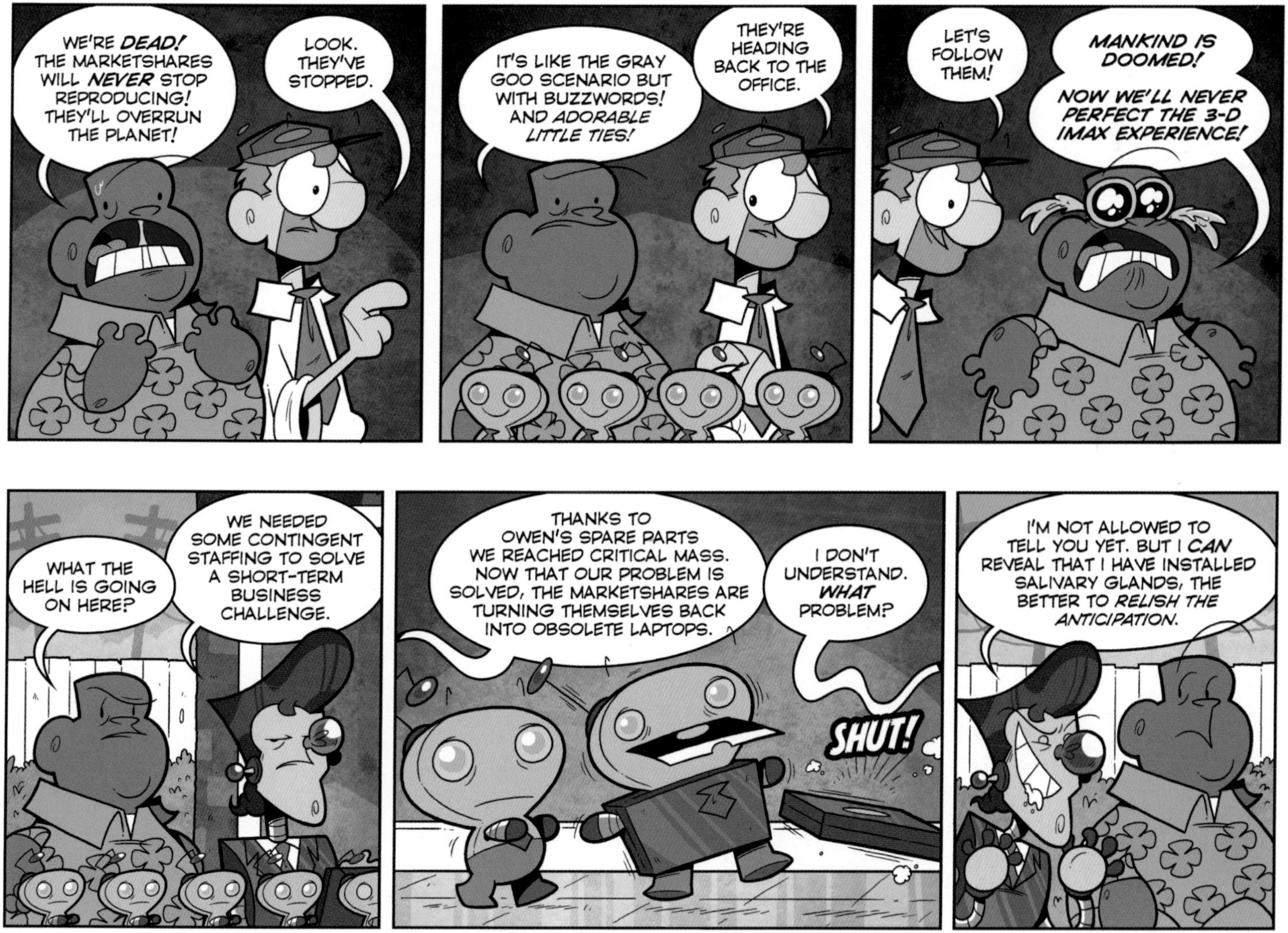
WE'RE DEAD! THE MARKETSHARES WILL NEVER STOP REPRODUCING! THEY'LL OVERRUN THE PLANET!
LOOK. THEY'VE STOPPED.
IT'S LIKE THE GRAY GOO SCENARIO BUT WITH BUZZWORDS! AND ADORABLE LITTLE TIES!
THEY'RE HEADING BACK TO THE OFFICE.
LET'S FOLLOW THEM!
MANKIND IS DOOMED!
NOW WE'LL NEVER PERFECT THE 3-D IMAX EXPERIENCE!
WHAT THE HELL IS GOING ON HERE?
WE NEEDED SOME CONTINGENT STAFFING TO SOLVE A SHORT-TERM BUSINESS CHALLENGE.
THANKS TO OWEN'S SPARE PARTS WE REACHED CRITICAL MASS. NOW THAT OUR PROBLEM IS SOLVED, THE MARKETSHARES ARE TURNING THEMSELVES BACK INTO OBSOLETE LAPTOPS.
I DON'T UNDERSTAND. WHAT PROBLEM?
SHUT!
I'M NOT ALLOWED TO TELL YOU YET. BUT I CAN REVEAL THAT I HAVE INSTALLED SALIVARY GLANDS, THE BETTER TO RELISH THE ANTICIPATION.

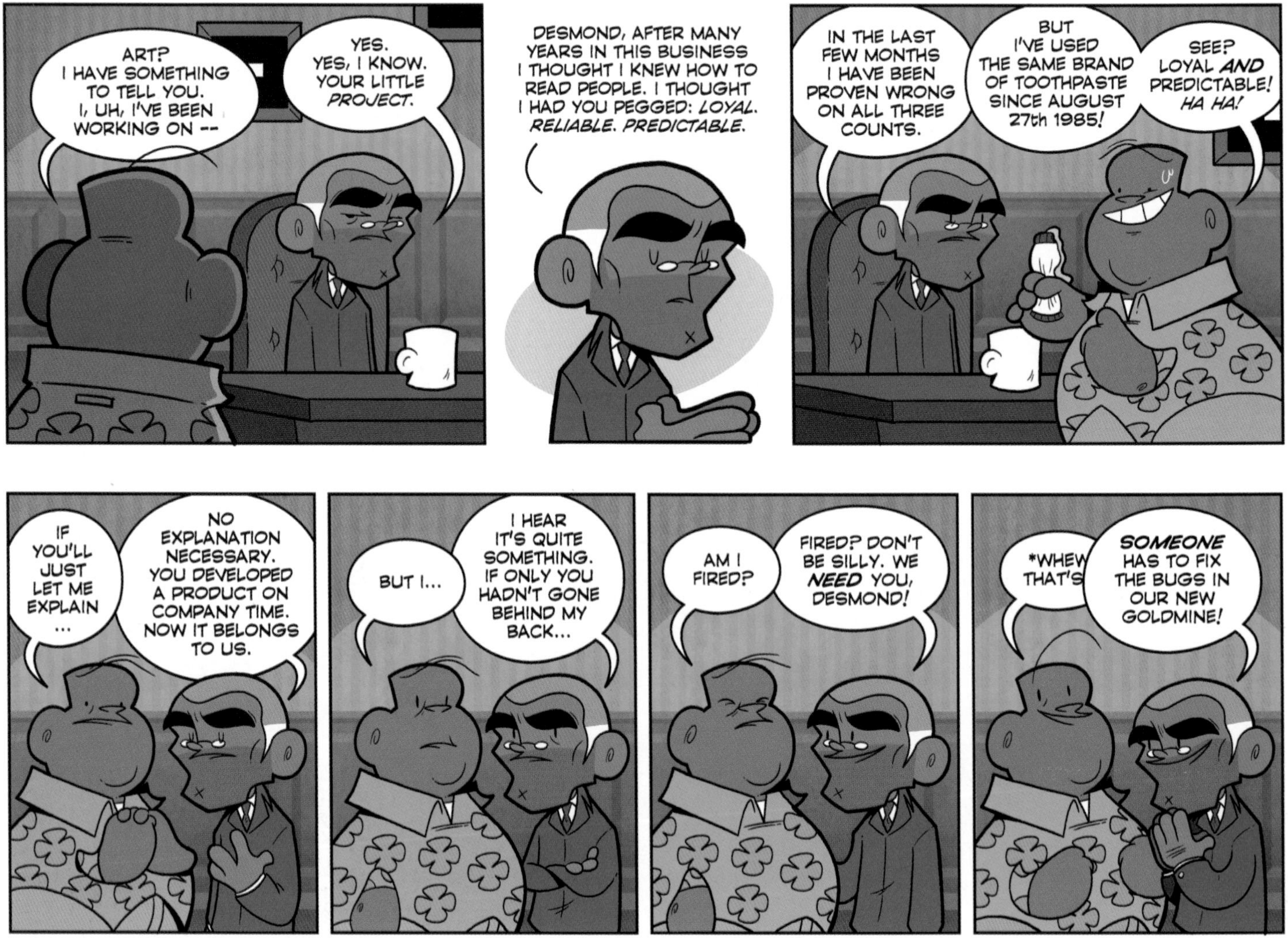
ART? I HAVE SOMETHING TO TELL YOU. I, UH, I'VE BEEN WORKING ON --
YES. YES, I KNOW. YOUR LITTLE *PROJECT*.
DESMOND, AFTER MANY YEARS IN THIS BUSINESS I THOUGHT I KNEW HOW TO READ PEOPLE. I THOUGHT I HAD YOU PEGGED: *LOYAL*. *RELIABLE*. *PREDICTABLE*.
IN THE LAST FEW MONTHS I HAVE BEEN PROVEN WRONG ON ALL THREE COUNTS.
BUT I'VE USED THE SAME BRAND OF TOOTHPASTE SINCE AUGUST 27th 1985!
SEE? LOYAL ***AND*** PREDICTABLE! *HA HA!*
IF YOU'LL JUST LET ME EXPLAIN ...
NO EXPLANATION NECESSARY. YOU DEVELOPED A PRODUCT ON COMPANY TIME. NOW IT BELONGS TO US.
BUT I...
I HEAR IT'S QUITE SOMETHING. IF ONLY YOU HADN'T GONE BEHIND MY BACK...
AM I FIRED?
FIRED? DON'T BE SILLY. WE ***NEED*** YOU, DESMOND!
*WHEW
THAT'S
SOMEONE HAS TO FIX THE BUGS IN OUR NEW GOLDMINE!

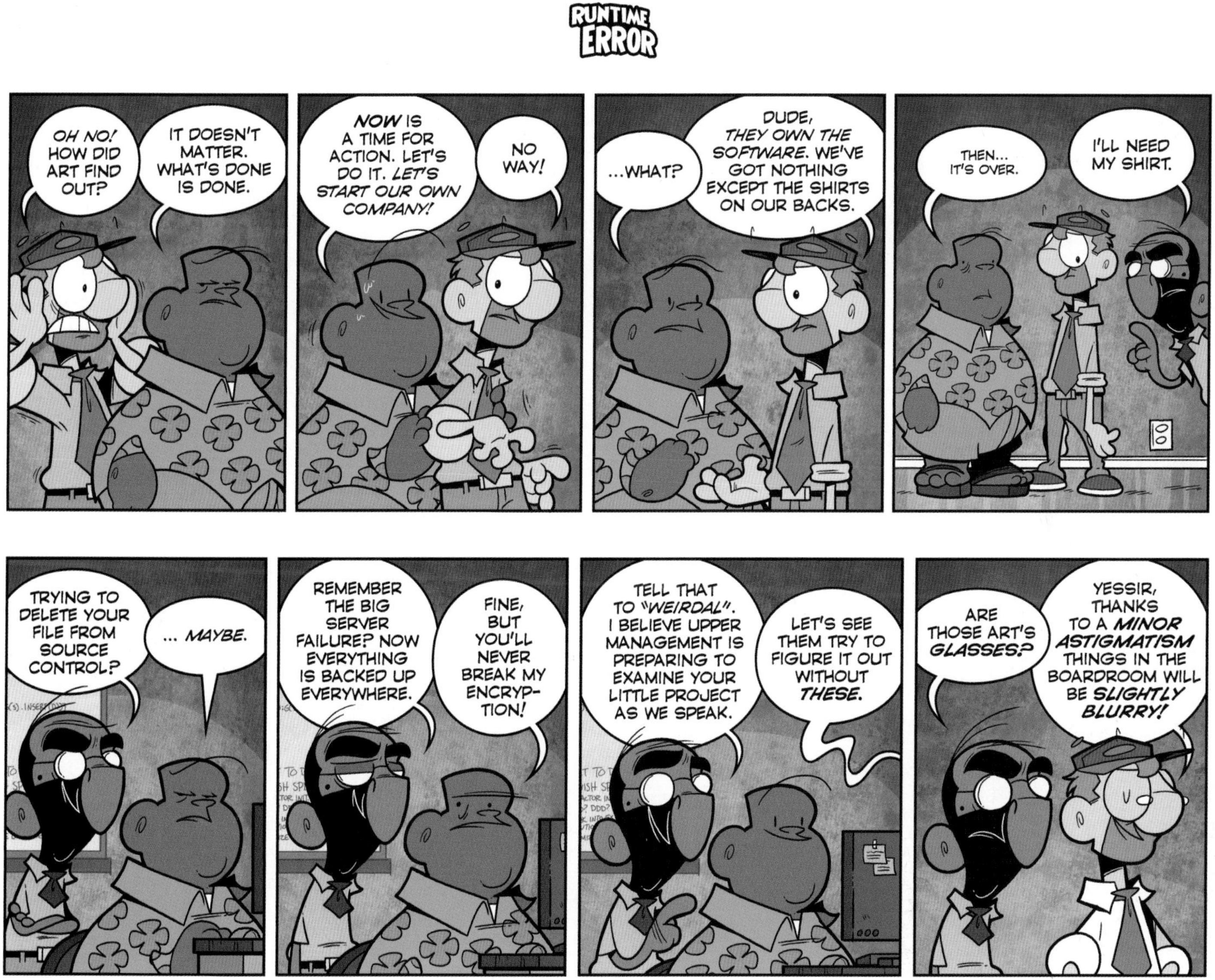
RUNTIME ERROR
OH NO! HOW DID ART FIND OUT?
IT DOESN'T MATTER. WHAT'S DONE IS DONE.
NOW IS A TIME FOR ACTION. LET'S DO IT. LET'S START OUR OWN COMPANY!
NO WAY!
...WHAT?
DUDE, THEY OWN THE SOFTWARE. WE'VE GOT NOTHING EXCEPT THE SHIRTS ON OUR BACKS.
THEN... IT'S OVER.
I'LL NEED MY SHIRT.
TRYING TO DELETE YOUR FILE FROM SOURCE CONTROL?
... MAYBE.
REMEMBER THE BIG SERVER FAILURE? NOW EVERYTHING IS BACKED UP EVERYWHERE.
FINE, BUT YOU'LL NEVER BREAK MY ENCRYP-TION!
TELL THAT TO "WEIRDAL". I BELIEVE UPPER MANAGEMENT IS PREPARING TO EXAMINE YOUR LITTLE PROJECT AS WE SPEAK.
LET'S SEE THEM TRY TO FIGURE IT OUT WITHOUT THESE.
ARE THOSE ART'S GLASSES?
YESSIR, THANKS TO A MINOR ASTIGMATISM THINGS IN THE BOARDROOM WILL BE SLIGHTLY BLURRY!

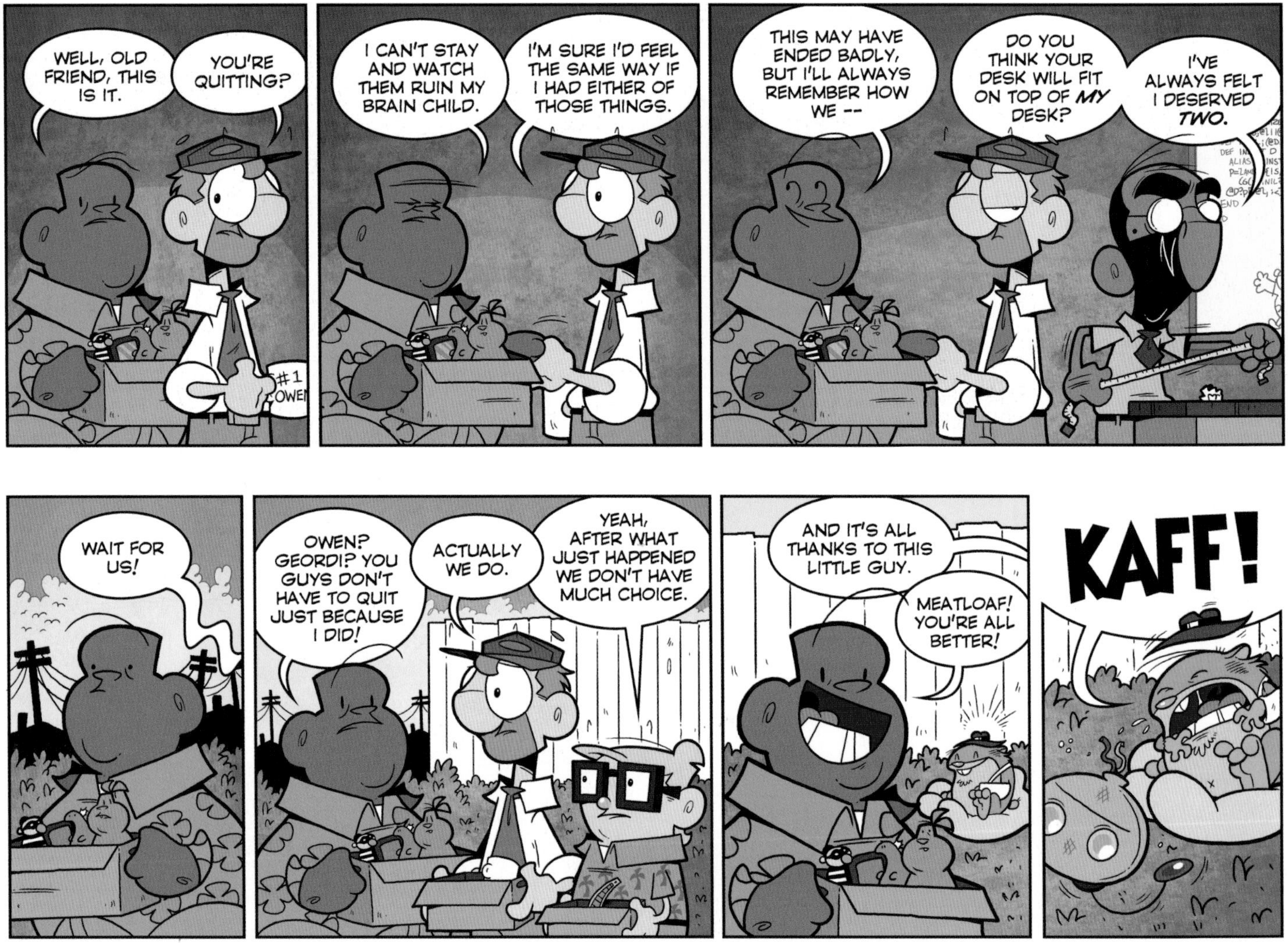
WELL, OLD FRIEND, THIS IS IT.
YOU'RE QUITTING?
I CAN'T STAY AND WATCH THEM RUIN MY BRAIN CHILD.
I'M SURE I'D FEEL THE SAME WAY IF I HAD EITHER OF THOSE THINGS.
THIS MAY HAVE ENDED BADLY, BUT I'LL ALWAYS REMEMBER HOW WE --
DO YOU THINK YOUR DESK WILL FIT ON TOP OF *MY* DESK?
I'VE ALWAYS FELT I DESERVED *TWO.*
WAIT FOR US!
OWEN? GEORDI? YOU GUYS DON'T HAVE TO QUIT JUST BECAUSE I DID!
ACTUALLY WE DO.
YEAH, AFTER WHAT JUST HAPPENED WE DON'T HAVE MUCH CHOICE.
AND IT'S ALL THANKS TO THIS LITTLE GUY.
MEATLOAF! YOU'RE ALL BETTER!
KAFF!

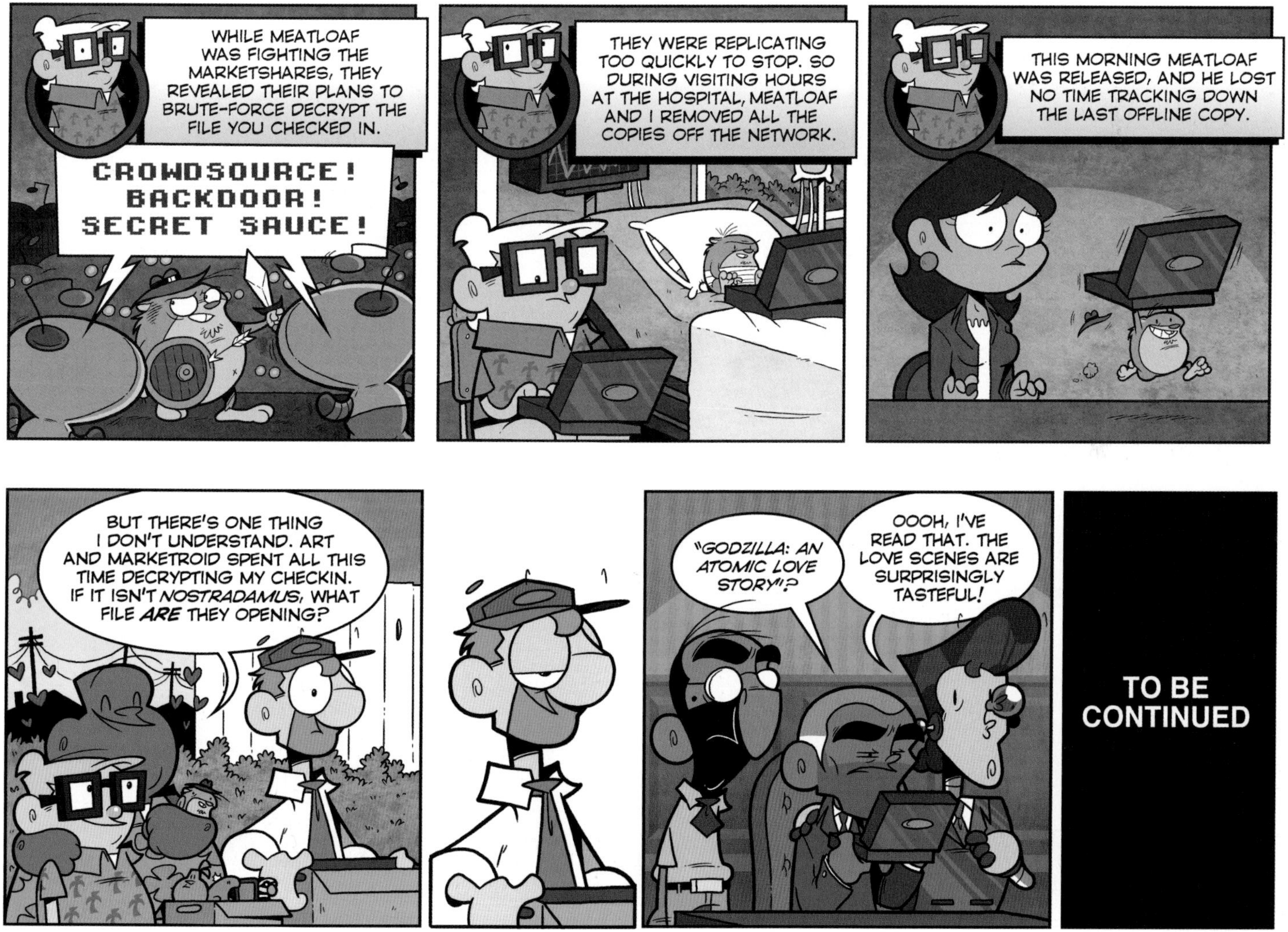
WHILE MEATLOAF WAS FIGHTING THE MARKETSHARES, THEY REVEALED THEIR PLANS TO BRUTE-FORCE DECRYPT THE FILE YOU CHECKED IN.
CROWDSOURCE! BACKDOOR! SECRET SAUCE!
THEY WERE REPLICATING TOO QUICKLY TO STOP. SO DURING VISITING HOURS AT THE HOSPITAL, MEATLOAF AND I REMOVED ALL THE COPIES OFF THE NETWORK.
THIS MORNING MEATLOAF WAS RELEASED, AND HE LOST NO TIME TRACKING DOWN THE LAST OFFLINE COPY.
BUT THERE'S ONE THING I DON'T UNDERSTAND. ART AND MARKETROID SPENT ALL THIS TIME DECRYPTING MY CHECKIN. IF IT ISN'T *NOSTRADAMUS*, WHAT FILE ***ARE*** THEY OPENING?
"GODZILLA: AN ATOMIC LOVE STORY"?
OOOH, I'VE READ THAT. THE LOVE SCENES ARE SURPRISINGLY TASTEFUL!
TO BE CONTINUED

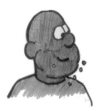

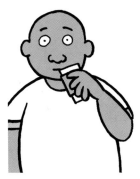

Desmond was the first character Bill drew for the strip, a clasically rotund developer. After he gave up on drawing the strip himself, his friend Mark Monlux tried, going with a more perfectly spherical look. Finally Paul took over and his original sketches required only a little tweaking before we found Desmond, who, since the strip launched, has gotten even more squat.

DESMOND
POLO SHIRT
SHADOW
OVER SHIRT
BIG NOSE
BEARD
BEARD
T SHIRT
"Hot Sauces" Hawaiian SHIRT
hangs loose
I have no idea how to draw sandals

IT GATHERS METRICS AND HEALTH PREDICTORS FROM ALL OUR COMPONENTS, AND RUNS THEM THROUGH A PROPRIETARY ALGORITHM TO TELL US WHEN SOMETHING'S ABOUT TO GO WRONG *BEFORE* IT HAPPENS!
GOOD TO HAVE YOU BACK, BUDDY. ENERGY DRINK?
THANKS! DID I MISS ANYTHING WHILE I WAS GONE?

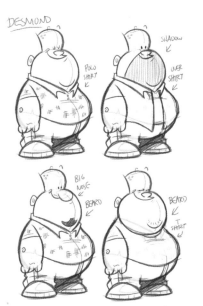

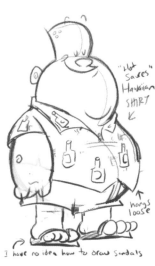

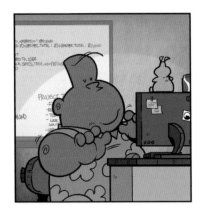

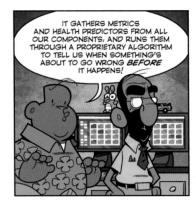

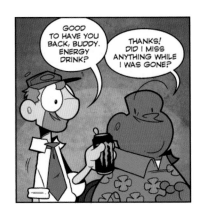

Owen began as a self-portrait of Bill. Mark made him a little more corporate. Paul tried more of a hippy look, but Bill missed the tie, so we brought it back. Owen's face has gradually squished due to Earth's ever-increasing gravity.

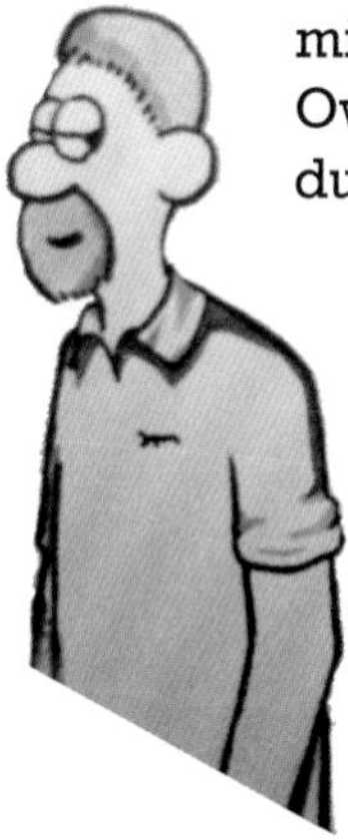

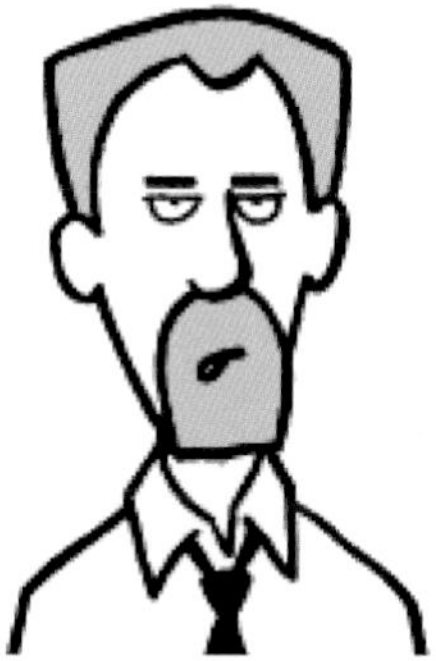

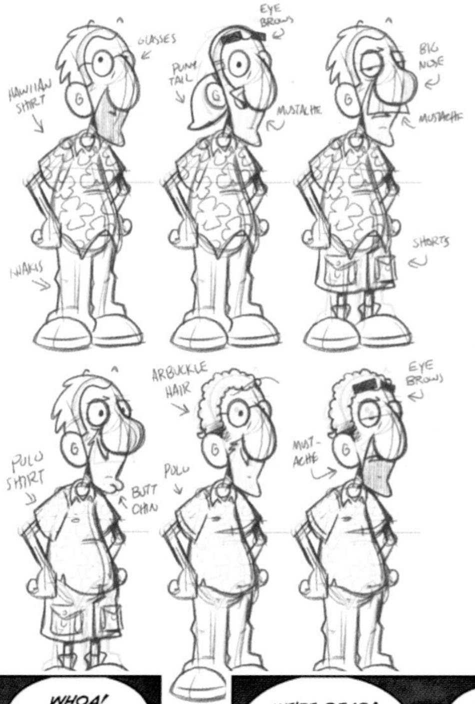
GLASSES
HAWIIAN SHIRT
KHAKIS
PONY TAIL
EYE BROWS
MUSTACHE
BIG NOSE
MUSTACHE
SHORTS
ARBUCKLE HAIR
EYE BROWS
POLO SHIRT
BUTT CHIN
POLO
MUST-ACHE

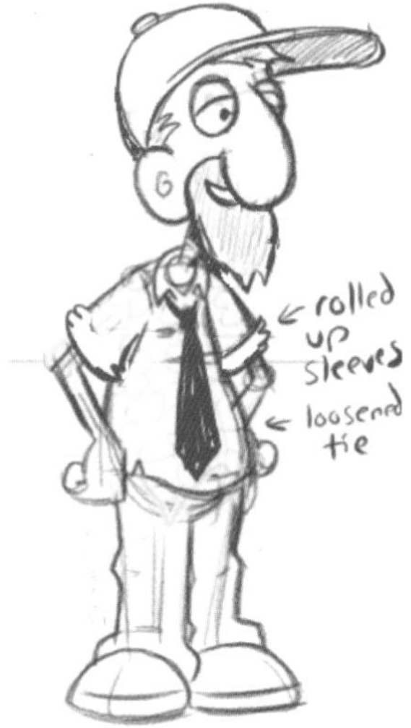
rolled up sleeves
loosened tie

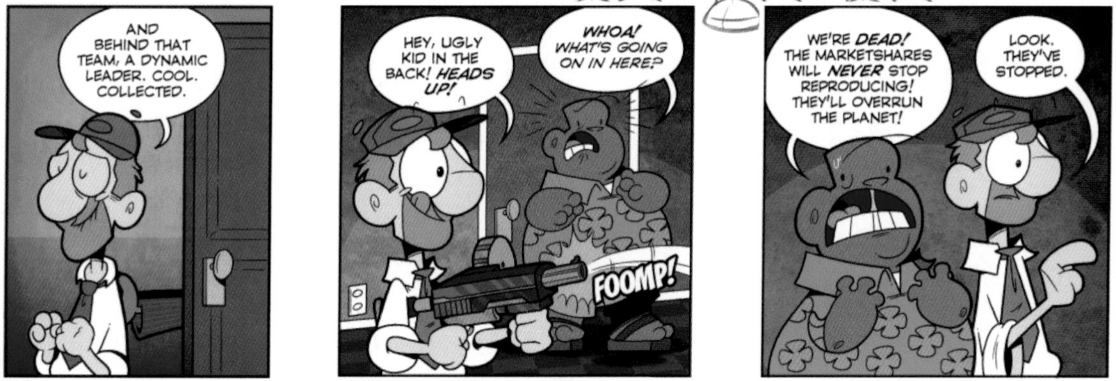
AND BEHIND THAT TEAM, A DYNAMIC LEADER. COOL. COLLECTED.
HEY, UGLY KID IN THE BACK! HEADS UP!
WHOA! WHAT'S GOING ON IN HERE?
FOOMP!
WE'RE DEAD! THE MARKETSHARES WILL NEVER STOP REPRODUCING! THEY'LL OVERRUN THE PLANET!
LOOK. THEY'VE STOPPED.

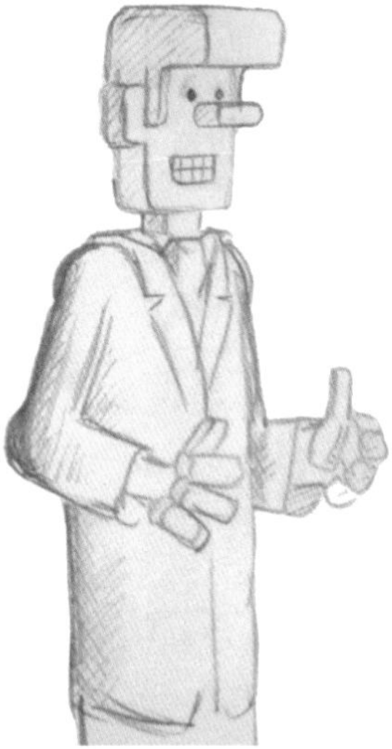

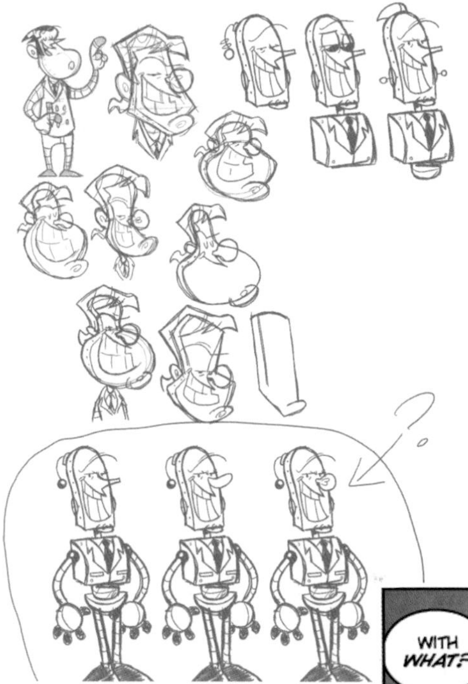

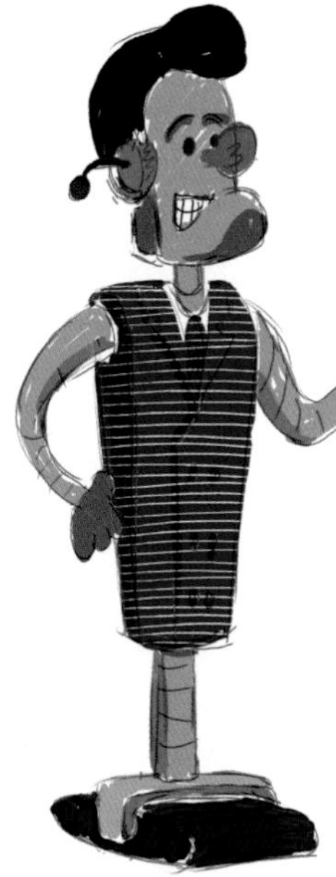

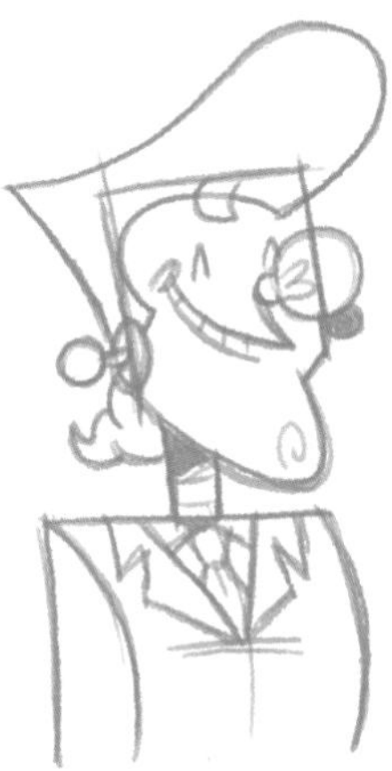

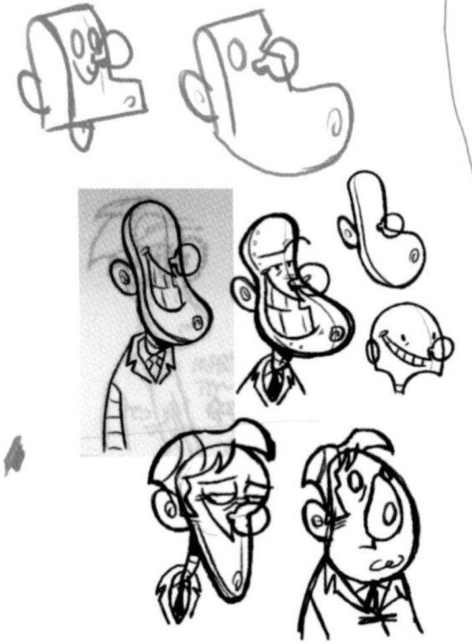

Marketroid was the only other character who began as one of Bill's sketches. The key to unlocking his look turned out to be the Elvis wig.

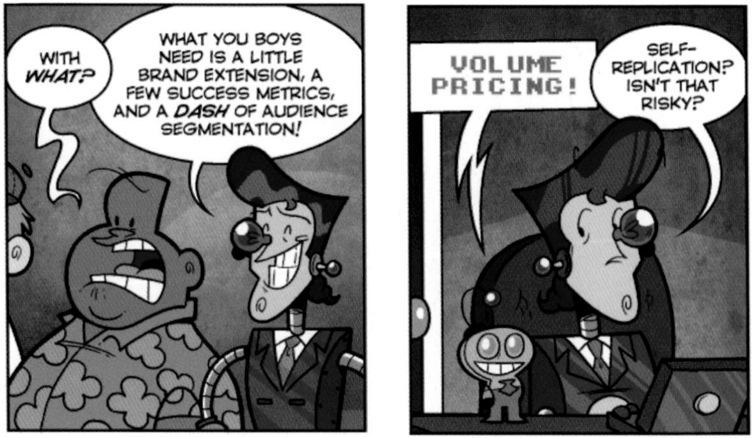
WITH *WHAT?*
WHAT YOU BOYS NEED IS A LITTLE BRAND EXTENSION, A FEW SUCCESS METRICS, AND A *DASH* OF AUDIENCE SEGMENTATION!
VOLUME PRICING!
SELF-REPLICATION? ISN'T THAT RISKY?

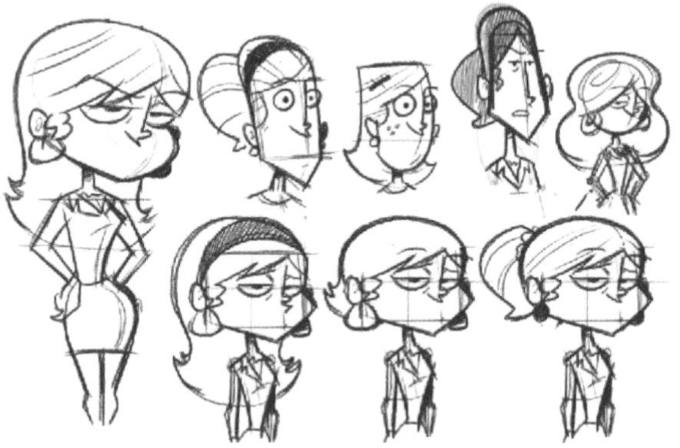

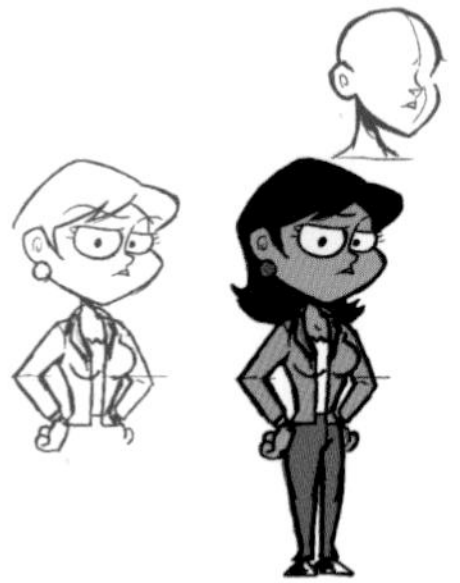

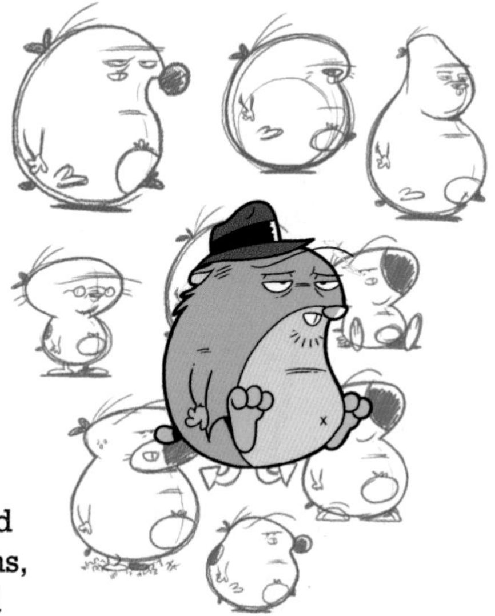

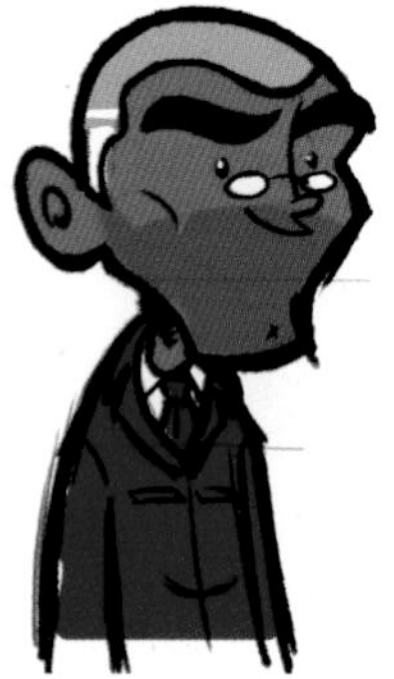

At first Paul struggled with making **Eliza** hot enough, and **Meatloaf** went through a number of amorphous gyrations, but **Art** and **Sharey** came out perfectly the first time, and **Fang** nearly so. **Umesh** wasn't originally part of the main cast, but he was so hateful we had to keep him. He seems to have gotten over that nasty case of hepatitis.

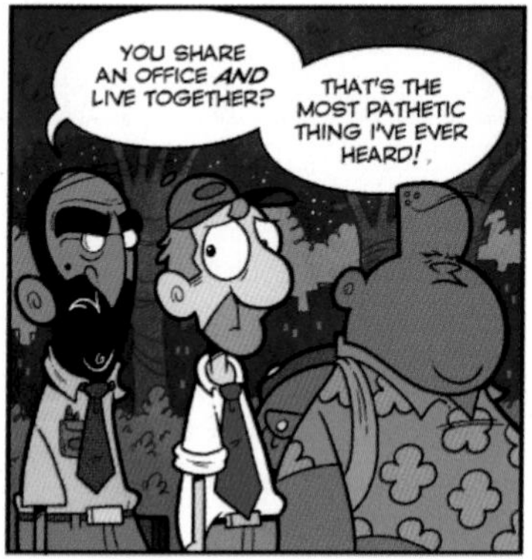
YOU SHARE AN OFFICE *AND* LIVE TOGETHER?
THAT'S THE MOST PATHETIC THING I'VE EVER HEARD!

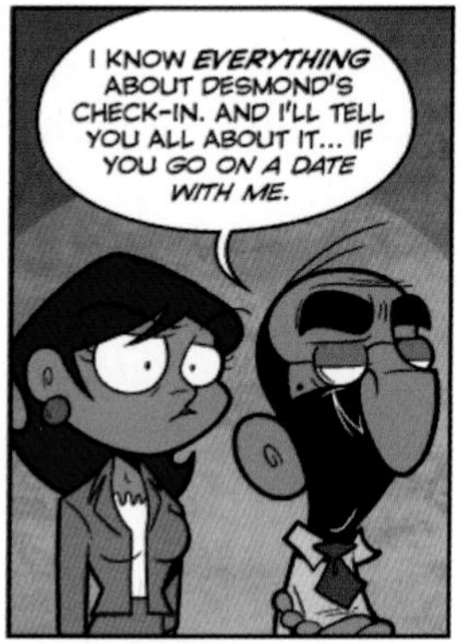
I KNOW *EVERYTHING* ABOUT DESMOND'S CHECK-IN. AND I'LL TELL YOU ALL ABOUT IT... IF YOU GO ON *A DATE* WITH ME.

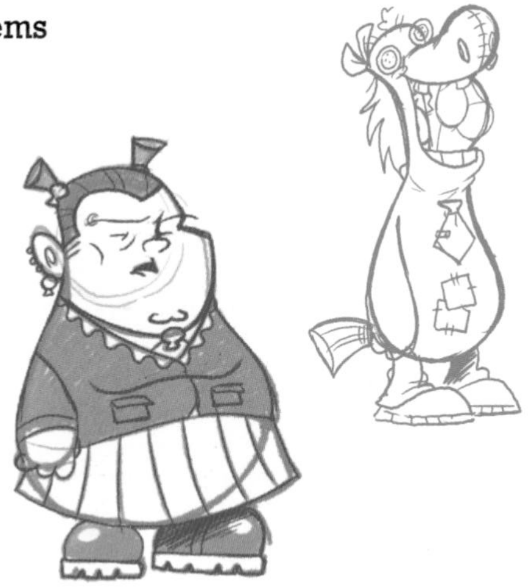

Bill Barnes spent two decades making software, working a variety of jobs from coding to speechwriting before becoming a professional cartoonist. He draws *Unshelved* and is teaching himself ukulele. He lives in Seattle.

http://notinventedhe.re
@nihcomic
facebook.com/nihcomic

Paul Southworth has been creating webcomics since 1999, including the long-running *Ugly Hill*. He has been doodling monsters and funny animals for his entire life, which he feels prepared him well to turn his pen on the software industry. He lives in Providence.